JUSTICE FOR ALL

Dick Thompson Morgan

DECEMBER 6, 1853 – JULY 4, 1920

ALSO BY MICHAEL J. HIGHTOWER

HISTORY AND BIOGRAPHY

Frontier Families: The Records and Johnstons in American History
(Oklahoma City, 2010)

Banking in Oklahoma before Statehood
(Norman, Oklahoma, 2013)

Banking in Oklahoma, 1907–2000
(Norman, Oklahoma, 2014)

Loyal to Oklahoma: The BancFirst Story
(Oklahoma City and Charlottesville, Virginia, 2015)

1889: The Boomer Movement, the Land Run, and Early Oklahoma City
(Norman, Oklahoma, 2018)

At War with Corruption: A Biography of Bill Price, U.S. Attorney for the Western District of Oklahoma
(Oklahoma City and Charlottesville, Virginia, 2021)

Brother Bankers: Frank P. and Hugh M. Johnson, Founders of the First National Bank and Trust Company of Oklahoma City
(Oklahoma City and Charlottesville, Virginia, 2023)

SOCIOLOGY

Inventing Tradition: Cowboy Sports in a Postmodern Age
(Saarbrücken, Germany, 2008)

FICTION

The Pattersons: A Novel
(Oklahoma City and Charlottesville, Virginia, 2012)

JUSTICE FOR ALL

Dick T. Morgan, Frontier Lawyer and Common Man's Congressman

Michael J. Hightower

With a foreword by Dr. Bob L. Blackburn

2
Cities
Press

This book is published with the support of Dick T. Morgan's great-grandsons, David and Kenyon Morgan, and Inasmuch Foundation of Oklahoma City, with administrative support from the Friends of the Oklahoma History Center.

Published by 2 Cities Press

Distributed by the University of Oklahoma Press
2800 Venture Drive, Norman, OK 73069
To order, contact Longleaf Services, Inc., (800) 848-6224 ext. 1

Cover, text, and book design by Carl Brune

Copyediting by Stephanie Marshall Ward

Cover images courtesy of David and Kenyon Morgan

Printed in Canada

ISBN 978-0-9847056-8-9

Library of Congress Control Number: 2024945946

Table of Contents

VII FOREWORD

IX PREFACE

CHAPTER ONE
1 *Indiana My Birth Place*

CHAPTER TWO
21 *Hoosier Politics*

CHAPTER THREE
41 *A Favored Spot on the AT&SF Line*

CHAPTER FOUR
63 *A Big Boom*

CHAPTER FIVE
85 *Building a Reputation*

CHAPTER SIX
113 *"Justice Is Our Battle Cry!"*

CHAPTER SEVEN
139 *Indiana with a Panhandle*

CHAPTER EIGHT
169 *The Right Kind of State*

CHAPTER NINE
197 *Mr. Morgan Goes to Washington*

CHAPTER TEN
219 *The Million-Dollar Congressman*

CHAPTER ELEVEN
249 *From (Alleged) Standpatter to Progressive*

CHAPTER TWELVE
275 *Duty of the Hour*

EPILOGUE
305 *With Malice toward None; with Charity for All*

323 NOTES

359 BIBLIOGRAPHY

371 INDEX

FOREWORD

WITH THIS BOOK, it is time to add another name to the founding fathers of Oklahoma who made a difference for their fellow citizens, their state, and their country. Dick T. Morgan, the forgotten champion of the common man, deserves a place of honor in our shared history.

Michael Hightower, with the active support and insight of Morgan's two great-grandsons, David and Kenyon Morgan, has created a masterful biography that goes far beyond the chronology of "what happened" in the life of one man to include the why and how he achieved so much, and just as importantly, what his achievements meant for the future of his adopted state. For curious students of history who want to trace the many threads woven through the fabric of Oklahoma's frontier beginnings, this book will add much to their understanding.

Hightower skillfully breaks the story into two acts: one about Dick T. Morgan the attorney, who helped ease the transition of Oklahoma from public to private property, and the other about Dick T. Morgan the dedicated reformer, who served six terms in Congress fighting for the common man. Running through each act is Morgan's strength of character, which rests on his self-described trinity of church, education, and family. This is a story of a good man who strove to help others through service.

Raised and educated in Indiana, Morgan was a staunch Lincoln Republican who believed in fair treatment for all in the true spirit of democracy. Throughout his life he condemned racism, fought for fair treatment under the law, and championed the virtues of the frontier experience. Armed with these core values, he settled first in Guthrie during the land run of 1889, moved to Perry for the Cherokee Outlet land run of 1893, and joined one last land opening in El Reno before the lottery of 1901. While serving his clients in land disputes, he wrote a book about land law that became the standard legal reference work before statehood.

In 1908, after moving to Woodward to serve as register of the U.S. Land Office, Morgan was elected a congressman from the new state of Oklahoma. He quickly earned a reputation as a confirmed agrarian reformer who could navigate the balancing act between William Jennings Bryan's populism and Theodore Roosevelt's progressivism. During his six terms in Congress, he shared credit for creating the Federal Trade Commission and the Federal Farm Loan program and laid the foundation for future passage of the FDIC, to protect bank depositors, and the GI Bill, to provide benefits for veterans. When Dick T. Morgan died in office, Oklahoma acting governor Martin Trapp honored him with full ceremonies in the state capitol.

Dick T. Morgan was a man of the frontier who never flinched in his duty to his community, his state, and his country. He was a man of faith who believed everyone should treat others with love and respect. And he was a man who believed in the rule of law that treated everyone fairly, regardless of social status or race. Through the remarkable story of his life, we get the sense that he was the kind of man we all want as a leader, whether at the dawn of statehood or the dawn of a new century. This book should be mandatory reading for anyone who claims to be a leader.

I want to thank Michael for writing this book with special praise for David and Kenyon Morgan, who sensed that it is a story that all of us should know. Dick T. Morgan now will have a place of honor in our shared history.

— DR. BOB L. BLACKBURN

PREFACE

THE POLISH PHILOSOPHER STANISŁAW BRZOZOWSKI, a much younger contemporary of the subject of this biography—whose concept of socially engaged intellectuals and artists might or might not have trickled into Oklahoma—recorded in his diary that "what is not biographical, does not exist at all."[1]

If that's true, what are we to make of biographies that never get written? How might those biographies inform our historical perspectives?

David Morgan probably wasn't thinking about Stanisław Brzozowski when he called me at my home in Charlottesville, Virginia, to see if I might be interested in writing a biography of his great-grandfather Dick Thompson Morgan. But he was thinking about how fickle history can be in shaping our historical consciousness. As I was about to learn, through the phone conversations, emails, and eventually face-to-face meetings that led to this book, David's great-grandfather ranks among the leaders whose stories are woven into Oklahoma's foundation narrative. Yet nobody had ever written Dick Morgan's biography, and you have to dig deeply into archival collections and scholarly literature to find much of anything about him.

It wasn't long after David called me and started flooding my inbox with articles and letters and photos, many of them plucked from the Morgan family's archives, that I came to this conclusion: if anyone warrants a biography, it is surely Dick Thompson Morgan.

David's great-grandfather was born and grew up on a farm in Prairie Creek Township in western Indiana, where his character was molded to the contours of his family, church, and school. His family's farm was situated at a crossroads of North and South, and what he recalled as a tranquil upbringing was upended as soldiers made their way south to the killing fields of the Civil War. Repulsed by the Southern Cause and drawn to politics, Morgan acquired a fierce loyalty to the Republican Party—that is, the party of Lincoln—which fueled his election to the Indiana General Assembly and put the fire in his belly to advocate for progressive causes that would transform the nation between 1880 and 1920.

Morgan served a single term in the Indiana General Assembly (1881–82) then lost his bid for reelection. After several years spent practicing law, editing a newspaper, and struggling to find a path forward in politics, he did what so many in his generation did when their dreams were thwarted back east—he went west. First he headed to Garden City, Kansas, to work for the Atchison, Topeka, and Santa Fe Railroad (AT&SF). Then he went to the newly formed town of Guthrie, Indian Territory, to participate in the Run of April 22, 1889, establish a dual career in law and real estate, and promote church building. From that storied day until the declaration of Oklahoma statehood on November 16, 1907, Morgan parlayed his superior intellect into becoming an expert in homestead law and public land policy. Gifted with a flair for writing and speechmaking, he revived his political aspirations, which had been stymied in Indiana. At the same time, he became the go-to person for homesteaders and townsite claimants who shared his determination to bring law and order to the rapidly developing territory.

A career in public service, which had been cut short in Indiana, now beckoned with endless possibilities in Oklahoma Territory, and after an unsuccessful bid to become the first territorial governor, he quickly worked his way into the Republican Party's inner circle. Morgan complemented his political activities with service to the Christian Church (Disciples of Christ), an avocation that encouraged the expansion of congregations and Sunday schools across Oklahoma. There is plenty of evidence to suggest that his religious convictions were just as vital as his Republican creed in framing his career in politics.

Inevitably, Morgan's prominence in territorial politics attracted the attention of higher-ups in the Republican Party. In 1904, President Theodore Roosevelt appointed him as register of the U.S. Land Office in Woodward, in northwest Oklahoma Territory, a position that put a seat in Congress within his reach. A year after Oklahoma and Indian territories were admitted to the Union as a single state, Morgan was elected to Congress. He was seated in 1909 and, even though he represented a heavily Democratic state, voters in northwest Oklahoma returned him to the U.S. House of Representatives in five subsequent elections. Representing the progressive wing of the Republican Party, he championed policies and sponsored bills that created some of the nation's most enduring laws and institutions.

Like two founders of another era, Thomas Jefferson and John Adams, Morgan died on America's birthday. He died on July 4, 1920, at a far younger age (sixty-six) than his illustrious predecessors. Such was Morgan's stature that Oklahoma acting governor Martin C. Trapp asked his widow, Orietta (also known as Ora, and often Ode in letters from her husband), for permission to allow his body to lie in state. He was likely the first person to be honored in this way in the state's new capitol building.

"His passing," wrote the acting governor to the grieving widow, "we all deeply regret and as a mark of respect to his memory, may I ask the honor and privilege, on behalf of the people of Oklahoma, of having his body lie in state in the State Capitol during such time as you may designate. A multitude of friends, I am sure, would appreciate the opportunity of paying their last tribute of reverence and respect to your illustrious husband and distinguished public servant."[2]

Orietta agreed, and between two and four o'clock in the afternoon of Thursday, July 8, 1920, those multitudes flocked to the capitol for a final glimpse of the fallen congressman. Standing at attention were soldiers representing the second infantry of the Oklahoma National Guard. Flags that Oklahomans had carried into battle during the recently concluded hostilities in Europe festooned the rotunda. At the head of the casket, roses and lilies sent by Morgan's former colleagues in the U.S. House of Representatives aimed to brighten the spirits of an otherwise somber assembly.[3] Four congressmen were among the sixty honorary pallbearers.

"Brother Morgan was a Christian legislator, a wise counselor, thoroughly reliable and held in great esteem by all who knew him," ran his obituary in the *Christian Evangelist*. "God give us more men like Dick T. Morgan."[4]

Back in his district, everyone had known that they could count on

Dick Morgan for more than wise legislation. When funding for the First Christian Church of Woodward's new building came up short, Morgan had stepped up as the answer to parishioners' prayers, and although he spent most of his time in Washington and had been called upon to help build churches across Oklahoma, he had not hesitated to contribute enough money to finish the job. Most knew Morgan as a congressman. But in his adopted hometown and throughout his district, he had been "a main stay, elder, Sunday School superintendent, leader in public worship, depended upon in all things."[5]

And yet, how many of us know about Dick T. Morgan?

David Morgan didn't offer profound statements during the first of our many phone conversations, texts, and email exchanges, and he had no need to lecture me about the value of biographies. On that score, we were on the same page. Since retiring as general counsel of MidFirst Bank in Oklahoma City in 2016, David had been on a quest to learn as much as he could about his ancestor, and I was in the business of writing histories and biographies. What David did was to convince me that his great-grandfather deserved (as his more famous contemporary, President Teddy Roosevelt, might have said) a bully pulpit, not just because he happened to be a Morgan ancestor, but because of his importance to his territory, state, and nation.

There's another reason to rescue Dick T. Morgan from obscurity. As a representative of the Republican Party's progressive wing, Morgan epitomizes progressivism between 1880 and 1920, a period that dovetails with his career in public service. Even as I was clicking my inbox every day with a mixture of trepidation and excitement, I began to contemplate a narrative in which Morgan's story would contextualize Oklahoma's contribution to the progressive movement and progressivism's transformative effect on post-frontier America.

Now that my interest was piqued, I continued to field phone calls and texts and click on emails, most with documents and photos attached, all with David's insights into his great-grandfather's career. During one of my regular trips from Charlottesville to Oklahoma City, David, his brother Kenyon, and I sealed the deal over hamburgers and a hotdog (mine) at the Shack, a ten-minute stroll from David's house along the ninth hole at the Oklahoma City Golf and Country Club. As golfers putted to my right and teed off to my left and hometown acquaintances streamed through the door, David and Kenyon offered me a deal I couldn't refuse: relying on their research, archival collections at the Carl Albert Congressional Research and Studies Center in Norman, the Oklahoma History Center in Oklahoma City, the University of Virginia libraries, and whatever print and online sources I could find, I would write a biography that would broaden our perspectives on the territorial and early statehood periods by following the trail of this extraordinary, and largely unknown, Oklahoman.

I was eight months into this project when David, Kenyon, and I visited three of the communities in Oklahoma where Dick T. Morgan and his family lived from their arrival in Indian Territory in 1889 to his death in 1920. David and I made a fourth and final trip to Woodward, sadly without Kenyon, as he was on a family trip to Legoland in California.

First on our itinerary was Guthrie, Morgan's first residence in the territory, where he arrived by train with the first wave of settlers on April 22, 1889. Over the next three and a half years, he leveraged his expertise in public land law to become one of the busiest attorneys in Oklahoma Territory, as he was recognized far and wide for his legal acumen and political ambitions. When the Cherokee Outlet was opened to non-Indian settlement in September 1893, Morgan put down roots in Perry (third on our itinerary), where a U.S. Land Office was located, and stayed there for nearly eight years. Between our visits to Guthrie and Perry, we traveled to Morgan's third residence, El Reno, whose location on the ninety-eighth meridian put it at the red-hot center of two land openings: the run of 1889 into the Unassigned Lands that blossomed into the six counties of central Oklahoma, and the run of 1892 into the Cheyenne and Arapaho Reservation. Our final trip, this one without Kenyon, was to Morgan's fourth residence in Woodward, where he served three and a half years as President Roosevelt's appointee as register of the U.S. Land Office before winning election to Congress in 1908. Although Woodward would be his official residence for the rest of his life, his duties in Congress and frequent visits to family in Oklahoma City did not leave him with much time to spend in his adopted hometown.

I called those trips walkabouts, because that's what we did—we walked down streets and alleys, loitered in front of and inside and behind buildings, clambered up and down stairs to dusty storage rooms, toured churches and museums, hobnobbed with locals, took photos, and feasted in iconic diners where cholesterol has yet to gain a shady reputation. That was not the case in Woodward, where Mikel Robinson, executive director of the Plains Indians and Pioneers Museum, joined David and me for lunch at Al's Steakhouse, a lovely eatery furnished with white tablecloths, an impressive wine list, and a menu with a few healthy options. Nor was there much walking about in Woodward. With a cold north wind blowing, David and I spent most of our time in the museum, where Mikel guided us through the exhibits, and former executive director Robin Hohweiler regaled us with tales of early-day Woodward. After that, we did most of our sightseeing from David's SUV.

As a retired architect, Kenyon was in his element on our first three walkabouts, complementing David's running commentary on their great-grandfather's doings with speculation on the age of buildings and the likelihood of long-forgotten additions and demolitions and even conflagrations. Among his many insights, one stood out and helped me frame this narrative: to understand people and what truly matters to them, we need to know something about their physical environment. With his extraordinary eye for detail, Kenyon was convinced that the First Christian Church of El Reno, founded during Dick's flurry of church building, deserves placement on the National Register of Historic Places. Maybe this book will spur some action. Buildings cannot speak, but Kenyon certainly could, and I came away from our first three walkabouts with a profound respect for the intricacies of Oklahoma architecture in the territorial period.

Several other walkabouts deserve mention, and they happened long before the Morgan brothers brought me on board to write this biography. In 2011, Kenyon traveled to Washington, D.C., to find the hotels where Dick and Orietta lived. Knowing from their correspondence that they lived "in a grand hotel," and after researching architectural records in the Library of Congress, Kenyon located the former site of the Congress Hall Hotel on New Jersey Avenue between Independence and E Street S.E. It was built in the same style as the U.S. Capitol, and it was demolished in 1929 to make room for the Longworth House Building, which opened in 1933.

"Its location was superb for Dick, as it was a short walk to the Capitol and Library of Congress," said Kenyon. "They lived there during Dick's last three years in Congress. For the previous nine years, they lived in the Dewey Hotel, likewise demolished and, like the Congress Hall Hotel, relegated to memories and archival records of the lost Washington."

Kenyon now had a mental map of the built environment, and it allowed him to imagine the nation's capital through his great-grandfather's eyes during his six terms as northwest Oklahoma's representative to Congress. "I walked the path which Dick, then sixty-six years old, and Orietta most likely took to Union Train Station to begin what would be their final trip to Oklahoma in June 1920," continued Kenyon.

> Traversing the east facade of the Capitol and the Library of Congress, I imagined how Dick must have felt. He was at the peak of his powers, yet the pinnacle seemed just ahead. It looked like Republicans would win both houses of Congress and the White House in the upcoming election. Most likely, he would have chaired the House Judiciary Committee in the Sixty-Seventh Congress. I went deep in thought to imagine what might have been. What a life he lived! And oh, what might have been!

Kenyon had something else destined to become a centerpiece of the Morgan family's memorabilia, and it became a source of contemplation during his Washington walkabout: the satchel that Dick carried to and from work and, more than likely, on his final trip to Oklahoma. Among the documents that Kenyon discovered in that satchel were a carbon copy of a letter that Dick had written to his siblings on June 18, 1920, and a note that he and Orietta were on their way to Oklahoma, with detours to Canada and Indiana.

"His destination was Oklahoma City," said Kenyon, "but he died on the way."[6]

The next walkabout came about a year before David retired from MidFirst Bank, when he and his wife, Ellen, traveled to Indiana to follow Dick's trail from the family farm near Prairie Creek and Union Christian College (UCC), in Merom, to Terre Haute, where he launched and won his first political campaign to represent his district in the Indiana General Assembly. Kenyon had made a similar trip several years earlier. Those trips planted a seed in David's and Kenyon's minds that their great-grandfather's story might be of interest to more than just family. That seed took root when they decided that people with a bent toward history and biography might like to learn about post-frontier America, during what the irascible Mark Twain famously dubbed "the Gilded Age," through the eyes of their ancestor. Maybe Dick's journey from humble beginnings on the family farm to the zenith of power and influence in Congress—as Kenyon put it, with a flair for the dramatic, "from guts to glory" —could become a portal into that transitional period in American history and illustrate the development of a statesman who fought on the right side of history.

More pieces fell into place when David and Ellen traveled to three more towns: Bonesteel and Yankton, South Dakota, to learn about Dick's participation in the opening of the Rosebud Reservation to non-Indian settlement in 1904; and Garden City, Kansas, where he worked for the AT&SF Railway from 1885 to 1889 and honed his skills as a land lawyer.

Although David knew he was on to something important, it took three more experiences to convince him that his great-grandfather's story needed to be published. First, David and Ellen's son D. J. gave him a rather unusual Father's Day gift: five hefty binders of newspaper articles about Dick T. Morgan published in the *Daily Oklahoman* between 1890 and 1920. Reading those articles prompted David to follow his brother's advice and visit the Carl Albert Congressional Research and Studies Center in Norman, where Dick and Orietta's copious collection of papers, memorabilia, and photographs had been archived for more than six decades. Finally, more intrigued than ever to stumble across a biographer's field of dreams, he started to forage in long-forgotten boxes stored in his and Kenyon's homes. They were jam-packed with newspaper articles, books Dick had written, speeches he had delivered in Congress, and sepia-tinted photos from his dozen years in Washington.

"I started to feel like Dick and Orietta were talking to me from the past," said David. "Most was personal, and that was very interesting. But then I realized that my great-grandfather's career in law and politics, and avocation in church building, spanned a pivotal era in history. And the more I learned, the more he came across as a kind and caring person—not to mention an overachiever! —brimming with ideas about how to help others." [7]

So why had he earned little more than a footnote in the historical record?

Here's a confession. When David proposed walkabouts to his great-grandparents' adopted hometowns in Oklahoma, I was skeptical. As a biographer, I rely on documents, websites, and sometimes oral history interviews to tell the story of a person's life. Other than enjoying the company of men who had become good friends over the course of this project, what would I gain from meandering the streets and visiting courthouses and office buildings in small-town Oklahoma? Wouldn't I be better off in front of my computer screen, where newspaper articles, scholarly journals, books, and websites—and, of course, David's emails—were teaching me all I needed to know about Dick Thompson Morgan?

I was wrong. By the time we went on our walkabouts, I was two-thirds of the way to completing a draft of this biography, and I was sure I had enough research material to carry me all the way through an epilogue. But then I climbed out of David's SUV in Guthrie, blinking in the harsh sunlight and dripping sweat on that hot September day, and my perception shifted. There and, later that week, in El Reno and Perry, and later still in Woodward, I relied on my companions' observations and my own imagination to picture the people and events I had been writing about, and to think deeply about the issues that framed Dick T. Morgan's career.

In this book, I touch on what I gleaned from those walkabouts, the ones that predated my participation, newspaper articles that

David has written about his great-grandfather, and David's notes and recollections from the dozens of presentations (including a joint effort with his daughter, Kristin Morgan Fares) that he has given throughout Oklahoma to supplement what I was learning from my research.[8] I also relied on sources that whizbang technology is rendering obsolete and utterly unintelligible to younger generations: handwritten (i.e., the vanishing art of cursive) letters between Dick, Orietta, and their son, Porter. As David Morgan explained about his treasure trove of family correspondence, "Those letters, to me, set up the family relationship, and where they were, geographically. I think those letters are important for the story, not only about their relationship, but also historically."[9]

Hopefully, walking in Morgan's footsteps, and plowing through letters that occasionally defied transcription, has resulted in the story of a flesh-and-blood character who fought to bring fairness to a lopsided economy and dignity to people whose stories will never be told.

My other hope is that readers will come away from *Justice for All* with a fresh perspective on Oklahoma history. As Kenyon put it in an interview at his brother's house, Oklahomans have been weaned on iconic images of land runs and the scramble that came after the dust settled—of homesteaders racing across the prairie on foam-flecked horses to carve out their slices of the American Dream, and of entrepreneurs risking it all to transform ramshackle townsites into mighty cities and muscle their way into America's networks of business and finance.

"But the reality..."

Kenyon paused to collect his thoughts as we observed golfers strolling down the fairway a few yards distant.

He continued:

> Here you have a great mix of people at all levels of sophistication coming into the Oklahoma country, and along comes Dick Morgan on the day of the run. He writes and sells his books, offers free maps to homesteaders, sets up law offices, advertises his services, and builds churches. Through persistence, he goes to Congress, and spends the last twelve years of his life crafting legislation to help farmers and ranchers in his district. You've got a story here that's tied into the

whole idea of America! His career shows what the closing of the frontier really meant, and how it was really done.[10]

Then, it was David's turn: "Kenyon, I think what you're saying is, he was looking at it in a very intellectual way. When he saw a problem, he would go to the Congressional Library and research it. He wanted to know these issues really well. When everybody else was talking, he was in the library! He does the research, writes the bills and speeches, and goes to the floor in Congress to make things happen."

In David's telling, his great-grandfather saw himself as a spokesman for issues that were important not only to Oklahomans, but also consumers, farmers, and soldiers across the nation. What is more, Morgan was deliberate in choosing the people he wanted to represent. As David said, Dick chose "people who made the country, not the bankers in the East. They were the people who were out doing the work, struggling day to day."[11]

At some point in our conversation, Kenyon touched on what is surely the most familiar narrative of westward expansion: Frederick Jackson Turner's frontier thesis. Writing in 1893, the young historian from Wisconsin revolutionized American historiography by positing the frontier as the crucible of American character development. "Up to our own day," wrote Turner, "American history has been in a large degree the history of the colonization of the Great West. The existence of an area of free land, its continuous recession, and the advance of American settlement westward explain American development."[12]

But so do people such as Dick T. Morgan.

Morgan made his mark as Oklahoma was shedding its frontier persona and connecting with modern networks of finance, commerce, and industry. That period, stretching from the 1880s to the early 1900s, resonates today for its glaring inequities, mainly because they bear a striking resemblance to our own age of, well, glaring inequities. Morgan's multifaceted career in business, politics, and church building illuminates the formation of organizations and institutions aimed at mitigating the most egregious abuses that inspired Twain to depict his era as a gilded age of mighty fortunes juxtaposed with grinding poverty. Through Morgan's experience and leadership, we catch a glimpse of political maneuvering that not only transformed the nation, but also clarifies Oklahoma's role in furthering the progressive agenda.

Like other progressives whose legacies are better known, Morgan fought to level an uneven playing field. That message came through loud and clear in my communications and travels with David and Kenyon. Their and, later, our journeys of discovery contributed in countless ways to this book, and collaborating with them made it fun to write. In adopting what might seem like an unorthodox approach to biography, I took a cue from one of the greatest storytellers of our time, David McCullough, who once quipped, "No harm's done to history by making it something someone would want to read."[13]

You be the judge. One thing's for sure: if I have failed to measure up to that high bar of historical and biographical know-how, I will surely hear about it.

Writing this book would have been a very different experience, and might not have happened at all, without the help of people who contributed to David's, Kenyon's, and my research: Mike McCormick, a historian in Terre Haute who guided David and Ellen in their pilgrimages to Indiana; Cheryl DeJager, a former accountant with Ditch Witch in Perry who answered all our questions about Noble County history; Richard and Lynda Fogg with the Fogg Law Firm in El Reno, one of Oklahoma's oldest law firms, where Dick T. Morgan practiced his trade for eight years; and Mikel Robinson and Robin Hohweiler at the Plains Indians and Pioneers Museum in Woodward. These folks made walkabouts in their communities far more informative, and more fun, than they would have been without them.

Thanks also go to Dr. Bob L. Blackburn, former executive director of the Oklahoma Historical Society (OHS), for encouraging David and Kenyon to get this book written and teeing it up with his foreword; Trait Thompson, Dan Provo, Jeff Briley, Sarah Dumas, and Samonia Byford at the OHS for their administrative assistance; JA Pryse, Michael Crespin, Nathan Gerth, Cindy Rosenthal, and their colleagues at the Carl Albert Congressional Research and Studies Center in Norman, Oklahoma, for making Morgan's papers instantly accessible, both in person and online; library and archival staff and photo archivists Jon May, Jim Meeks, and Jason Hadley at the OHS, Amy Vedra at the Indiana Historical Society, and Kate McGinn at the Indiana State Public Library for responding so quickly to my research and photo requests; Kelly Wollman, editor and owner of the *Bonesteel Enterprise*, Doug Spitzenberger, recognized for his knowledge of South Dakota history, Kelly Hertz, editor of the *Yankton Daily Press & Dakotan*, and Crystal Nelson and Megan Hansen at the Mead Cultural Education Center in Yankton, all of whom provided historical context for the Morgan family's adventures in South Dakota in the summer of 1904; and Beth Youngdale, David and Kenyon's cousin, who recently retired from teaching writing at the University of Texas Law School, and Richard Bard, Kenyon and David's high school friend and longtime journalist with the *Miami* (Florida) *Herald*, for their careful editing of my drafts. Credit also goes (once again!) to Richard Bard and Robin Hohweiler who, along with Clark Musser, served as content readers, the last line of defense against historical inaccuracies and authorial blunders.

Of course, no list of contributors would be complete without thanks to Ellen Records Morgan and Judy Walston Hightower for their frequent insights, technical expertise, and nonstop good cheer.

Finally, my thanks go to David and Kenyon for trusting me to tell their great-grandfather's story. Given their extensive research and guidance from start to finish, if I have failed to get it right through errors of omission or commission, it's nobody's fault but mine.

MICHAEL J. HIGHTOWER
OKLAHOMA CITY AND CHARLOTTESVILLE, 2025

CHAPTER ONE

Indiana My Birth Place

The three forces which constitute
the strength of a free Government are
the church, the school, and the home.

DICK T. MORGAN
INDIANA MY BIRTH PLACE

IN THE LATE FALL OF 1908, Dick T. Morgan traveled from his home in Woodward, Oklahoma, to Washington, D.C., to attend to his duties as a newly elected member of the Sixty-First Congress. He left plenty of time to visit his mother, Frances Ann, who lived on the family farm, about a mile from Prairie Creek (a.k.a. Middletown) in Vigo County, Indiana, and fifteen miles south of the county seat in Terre Haute. "Mother was in many respects a remarkable woman," wrote Morgan in an unfinished and unpublished autobiography. "I knew that she, above all others, would rejoice over my election."

After what was surely a joyful reunion, Frances made her first and probably only request to her influential son: could he leverage his congressional clout to have her mail delivered to her door instead of the Prairie Creek post office a quarter mile down the road? Dick responded in the affirmative, and when he reached Washington, he made straight for the Post Office Department to conduct his first item of official business. "The mail route was slightly modified," wrote Morgan, "without discommoding others, and mother's mail was soon being delivered at her door."[1]

No sooner had news of Morgan's successful intervention on his mother's behalf hit the back roads of Vigo County than his mailbox was deluged with requests for home mail delivery. As a representative from Oklahoma, there was not much he could do to help Frances's neighbors in Indiana, so he referred their requests to their representative, the Honorable Ralph W. Moss. Like his colleague from Oklahoma, Moss had just won his first election to Congress, and he was no doubt happy to ease his constituents' burdens. Morgan and Moss served together until 1917, when Moss's string of election victories came to an end. He retired to his farm near Ashboro, where he succumbed to injuries sustained from a rampaging bull.[2]

Morgan's election to Congress in 1908 from the brand-new state of Oklahoma was the first of many, and his cross-country treks became routine. So did his detours to the family farm. Routine notwithstanding, one imagines another joyful reunion when he arrived at his mother's house on November 17, 1911. Frances, now approaching ninety years of age, was no doubt bursting with pride over a son who had represented his native Vigo County in the Indiana General Assembly, relocated to Indian Territory to guide Oklahoma from territorial status to statehood, and succeeded in two campaigns to represent his adopted state in Congress. Dick, too, had reasons to be proud of a mother who had instilled in him many of the qualities that led him to the red-hot center of political influence, and who personified the heart and soul of Indiana. As his schoolboy acquaintance and, many years later, Oklahoma magazine editor C. J. Phillips wrote, when Dick was a freshman congressman, faith in God and humanity gave Indiana a moral standing "that is not surpassed by any commonwealth in the world."[3]

Morgan was still with his mother on November 20. Sometime during the previous three days, maybe several times, Frances had sat her son down and told him the family story. Then he did something we rarely do and often live to regret. He wrote it down. His account of Frances's story survives today in the Morgan Family Collection under the unassuming title "Prairie Creek, Vigo County, Indiana, November 20, 1911."[4]

This is Frances Morgan's story.

"I think grandfather [David] Thompson was born in Virginia but possibly in Ohio," began Frances. She might have paused before deciding that such details would likely be of little consequence to her son. Her grandfather's family was from Virginia, and that was enough.

David Thompson lived most of his life and died in Sullivan County, Indiana, where he accumulated land and operated a ferry near the town of Merom, on the Wabash River.

In the summer of 2015, David Morgan and his wife, Ellen, traveled to Indiana to confer with newspaperman and local historian Mike McCormick, author of several articles about Dick Morgan, in Terre Haute before heading south to discover ancestral sites in Sullivan and Vigo counties. It turned out that Thompson did indeed operate a ferry in Merom. It was known, rather unimaginatively, as Thompson's Ferry. As David put it, "Ellen and I think we found the actual location, just a few blocks down from where the family owned some city blocks in Merom."[5]

Somewhere along the porous boundary between fact and fiction, Frances got wind that her grandmother, Rachel Thompson, might have been a sister, or maybe a niece, of Benjamin Franklin.

David Thompson was the second to marry Frances's mother, Barbara Lutz. Barbara's maiden name, together with her linguistic preference, point to her German ancestry and probably her birthplace. She and her first husband, John Ray, lived near Cincinnati, where they brought nine children into the world. In circumstances lost to history, John froze to death. Fortune smiled more favorably on John's brother James who served in both houses of the Indiana General Assembly and served two terms as governor (1825–31). James Ray was Indiana's fourth governor, and he was the last nonpartisan candidate to rise to the state's highest office.[6]

Frances was born to David and Barbara Thompson on March 15, 1822, in Riley Township, Vigo County, Indiana. David died when Frances was a toddler. She was just shy of her twentieth birthday when, on January 20, 1842, a pioneer Baptist preacher, Asa Frakes, joined her in holy matrimony to Valentine Morgan. Born on January 30, 1817, in Bourbon County, Kentucky, Valentine moved to Indiana with his father at the age of thirteen. Frances was fairly sure that Valentine's mother, Lucretia Crawford, was a born-and-bred Virginian.[7]

A milestone in Frances's life, and a precursor to her son's commitment to spreading the Gospel in Oklahoma Territory, came in September 1851 when she united with the Christian Church (later, the Christian Church of the Disciples of Christ) in her tiny village of Prairie Creek. Since its beginnings, shortly after the American Revolution, the Christian Church had branded itself as a blend of New Testament Christianity and American idealism. With an unwavering faith in scripture, congregants self-identified as "A New Testament People." Among their core beliefs were the simplicity of their creed ("No Creed but Christ"), obedience to Christ's commands, and reverence for the Bible as the only source of faith and practice. Most importantly, congregants centered their faith in Jesus Christ. When a new church building was completed in 1854, Valentine was named as one of the first three trustees.

Frances joined the church under the preaching of Elder Joseph Wolf, who later presided over her baptism. "That has been over sixty years ago," said Frances. "I was one of the charter members of that church."[8]

On December 6, 1853, Frances gave birth to her seventh child, Dick Thompson Morgan, probably in the same house where, for three days, she kept him spellbound with her deep dive into family history. Frances, whom Dick recalled as "a woman of exceptional mental and physical strength," died on November 13, 1913, at the age of ninety-one, two years practically to the day after Dick had the good sense to record his mother's stories for the benefit of posterity. She was buried in a cemetery near the family farm where she had lived since her marriage to Valentine. With an insistence on numerical precision that had become his trademark, Morgan quantified her fifty-four descendants: eight children, twenty grandchildren, twenty-three great grandchildren, and three great-great grandchildren. As Dick's oldest brother, C. H., commented at a family meeting at the time of her passing, "We had a good father and the best mother that ever lived." Dick agreed, and in the obituary he penned for the *Christian Evangelist*, he described her as "a woman of high ideals" who "did all in her power to have her children go out into the world imbued with the highest standards of manhood, womanhood, and citizenship." Dick's political success deepened his love and affection for her and enabled him "to appreciate more keenly the debt of gratitude I owed to her."[9]

Living at a crossroads of North and South, the Morgans were caught up in escalating tensions between unionists and secessionists. Even though Indiana's southern counties tended to identify with the Confederacy more than the rest of the state, Valentine and Frances were staunch members of the short-lived Whig Party that was formed in 1834 by opponents of President Andrew Jackson and the radical (small d) democrats who fell in behind him. The party's moniker derived from the English anti-monarchist party and reflected conservatives' portrayal of Jackson as "King Andrew."[10] In its American iteration, the Whig Party stood firmly against slavery, for perpetuation of the Union at all costs, and for free-market capitalism. It was one of two major political parties from the late 1830s

The Morgan family home in Prairie Creek, Indiana, n.d.
COURTESY OF THE MORGAN FAMILY COLLECTION

through the early 1850s. When it fizzled on the eve of the Civil War, the Morgans joined most of their fellow Whigs in casting their lot with the Republican Party.

Such was the Morgans' commitment to Whig and, later, Republican principles that they named their son after Richard Wigginton Thompson (no relation to Frances's family), a Virginia native who relocated to Indiana to become the most prominent Whig in Terre Haute. Known for his campaign oratory, Thompson served in both houses of the Indiana General Assembly before he was elected to the U.S. Congress in 1841 and 1847. During the Civil War, he was active in raising, training, and forwarding troops. Indiana governor Oliver P. Morton rewarded Thompson for his commitment to the Union by appointing him commander of the aptly christened Camp Thompson near Terre Haute and provost marshal of the Terre Haute district.[11] As David Morgan explained, "I don't know if the Morgan family knew Richard W. Thompson personally or were just fans because of his Whig roots. The origin of his name was very important to Dick, so much so that he described it in detail in his unpublished autobiography: 'My real name was Dick, not Richard. I was named after Richard W. Thompson of Terre Haute. While his name was Richard, he was almost universally called Col. Dick Thompson. My father intentionally gave me his nickname, and it is so recorded in the family record.'"[12]

Dick was almost seven years old when Abraham Lincoln was elected president. His earliest memories of the looming conflict and, after the shelling of Fort Sumter, open hostilities were of visiting Camp Thompson with his older brother and watching soldiers conduct drills in preparation for battle. Vigo County's loyalties were unevenly divided between unionists, who were in the majority, and Confederate sympathizers, known colloquially as copperheads or, alternatively, butternuts, which were emblematic of their gray uniforms. To manifest their Confederate predilections, men came to Prairie Creek adorned with charms fashioned from butternut shells. Unionists responded by ripping the offensive emblems from their clothing; the inevitable result was skirmishes that began as fist fights and occasionally escalated into shootouts. Fights often broke out at school, where a brazen *hurrah* for

Confederate president Jeff Davis could only be answered with blood. As unionists were generally in the majority, butternuts were on the receiving end of severe floggings.

Watching the soldiers drill made a deep impression on Dick. He was about eight years old when he put his allegiance to the Union into action by learning to play the tenor drum. His efforts were rewarded when he was invited to join his community's fife and drum corps to help "beat up" for volunteers. Some of his most vivid memories from those bellicose days were of Union rallies attended by thousands. As the war ground on, communities established home guard companies as a defense against enemy depredations. "I was very proud to march at the head of our Home Guard Company, beating the tenor drum," recalled Dick. "That was the nearest I came to being a soldier." Imbued with a spirit of patriotism, Dick felt the first stirrings of what it might be like to serve his fellow citizens, if not as a soldier, then perhaps as a public servant. One thing is for certain: casting his lot with the party of Lincoln ignited a passion that would one day blossom into a career in progressive politics.[13]

The exigencies of war notwithstanding, Valentine's and Frances's lives revolved around raising their nine children, three girls and six boys, and running one of the largest and most prosperous farms in southern Vigo County. When they were not in school, the boys were at work on the farm. "I never knew the time when there was not something pressing to be done," wrote Dick. "It was a pleasant farm home." Yet the Morgans' lives were not all work and no play. Diversions from dawn-to-dusk chores came in the form of spelling contests, singing classes, get-togethers with neighbors, picnics, and swimming in Prairie Creek, a tributary of the Wabash River on the Indiana side. To earn extra money, the boys often slipped off after dark to hunt for raccoons and possums; during daylight hours, they saddled up and went after foxes with foxhounds, their barking and baying echoing across the countryside, in hot pursuit. They supplemented the money they earned for pelts (and spent, sometimes without reporting it to their parents) by clearing brush, chopping wood, and hauling it to a nearby mill for a dollar a load. As Dick noted with a touch of pride, "In this way, I earned my first dollar."[14]

To add to his earnings from hunting and brush clearing and wood chopping, Dick went into business as a singing instructor. Inspiration came from two sources: his parents, who owned a piano and instilled in their children an appreciation for music; and an instrumental music teacher who set up shop in Prairie Creek. As Dick explained, "The first money of any importance I earned was in teaching singing-school. When I was about sixteen years old, an instrumental music teacher came to Prairie Creek and gave instruction on the organ and piano. In a short time, there were a number of farmers who purchased organs or pianos. My father was among the number."

Churchgoers (that is, pretty much everyone) could also enjoy music at Prairie Creek's two churches, one Baptist and the other Christian (later, Disciples of Christ). As Dick wrote with a flair for understatement, "It was decidedly a religious community." To ensure that children would be raised in the radiance of the Holy Spirit and protected from sin, both churches forbade dancing at social gatherings. Young people who dared to challenge convention were, in Dick's recollection, "hardly in good standing in the best society." As members of the Christian Church, Valentine and Frances were mortified when Dick was caught dancing. The young rebel's flouting of social norms quickly earned him the opprobrium of his community. Worse yet, his own family branded him as the proverbial black sheep.

After sowing his wild oats, Dick came to his senses and followed his parents' example to unite with the Christian Church. "The religious impressions received in those days have in a very large measure dominated my career in life," wrote Dick many years later. Those impressions, together with his experiences on the family farm, left him with lasting memories of an idyllic agricultural community.

Another formative influence was the education Dick received both at home and in Prairie Creek. His and his siblings' elementary education took place in a log-house school, sparsely appointed with homemade furniture, which was located on their family farm. At some point, Dick graduated to a frame building in Prairie Creek that served as the community's first real school. Teachers came and went, with few qualifications and a penchant for corporal punishment. Dick's first teacher, Robert Allen, had a fondness for the rod, and he used it unsparingly. "I did not escape entirely," wrote Dick. "Generally, I deserved more punishment than I received." In one instance, Valentine and Frances were infuriated when their son was punished unjustly, and they forbade him and his brothers and sisters to return to school. Vindication came when the elderly, bald-headed Robert Allen, whom Dick described as a throwback to Indiana's pioneer days, was dismissed and "gave way to a better class of teachers." Eventually, Prairie Creek was blessed with a brand-new schoolhouse and, presumably, teachers with a more enlightened attitude toward maintaining discipline. Some graduates went on to college, and a few returned to Prairie Creek to teach.

Dick's sister Lucretia was one of those graduates who attended college in nearby Merom. She returned to Prairie Creek to open "a select school" in a church near the public school. "It was an innovation, and [it] was not well received," wrote Dick about his sister's decision to tilt the playing field in favor of elite education. "Those who attended it were looked upon as aristocrats. The school was referred to in derision as 'Morgan College.'"[15]

In 1870, a two-story brick building with three schoolrooms was built to become Prairie Creek High School. Dick entered the new high school at the age of fifteen, and he wasted no time in joining the debate team. "This was the foundation of my career as a lawyer and public official," wrote Dick about his early foray into public speaking. Following his graduation in 1872, he became one of Prairie Creek's fortunate sons and daughters to attend college.[16]

In later years, Morgan would express his guiding principles in a mantra he borrowed from James A. Garfield, an older contemporary and member of the Disciples of Christ Church: "The three forces which constitute the strength of a free Government are the church, the school, and the home."[17]

As dyed-in-the-wool unionists, the Morgans spoke highly of Indiana's wartime governor, and President Lincoln's faithful ally, Oliver P. Morton. Today, his towering bronze statue, flanked by two Union soldiers, stands on the steps of the Indiana Statehouse, in the heart of downtown Indianapolis. A bronze plaque testifying to Morton's stature among his fellow Hoosiers reads in part: "In all ways and at all times the friend of the Union soldier. The friend of the country. The upholder of Abraham Lincoln. The defender of the flag and the Union of the States. Patriot. Statesman. Lover of Liberty. Heroic in heart. Inflexible in purpose and ever to be known in history as The Great War Governor."[18]

Even though he was a child when war broke out, Dick shared his parents' admiration for Indiana's great war governor, and he alluded to him later in life when he reflected on the people who had influenced his own career in public service. "I had great admiration for Morton," wrote Dick in his autobiography. "He is universally recognized as one of the greatest men Indiana has ever produced."[19]

Morton was also recognized as one of Indiana's greatest orators. His election as governor was still in the future when, in July 1860, he delivered a campaign speech on a swing through Sullivan County that left no doubt about his commitment to the Republican Party. "Mr.

The Morgan family, circa 1868. Dick is sitting third from left.
COURTESY OF THE MORGAN FAMILY COLLECTION

Morton's opening speech was masterly—clear, logical, conclusive," wrote a reporter for the *Wabash Express*. "He presented the great doctrines of the Republican Party with so much force, with so much intellectual power, and with so much eloquence, that all, the most illy informed must have fully understood them. He exposed the fallacies of the Democratic party with such irresistible arguments, that the most blinded Democratic partisan dupe, could not help but feel uneasy for the fate of the party to which he belonged."[20]

As though Morton's partisan listeners needed reminding, the Republican Party remained committed to its policy of preventing the spread of slavery into the territories. In excoriating the South's rallying cry of popular sovereignty as inconsistent and unmanly, Morton reserved special scorn for the Supreme Court's decision in *Dred Scott v. Sanford* (1857). At issue was the fate of Dred Scott, a slave in Missouri who, along with his wife, Harriett, sued for freedom for themselves and their two daughters. The Scotts believed that their freedom was warranted because Dred had lived in Illinois and the Wisconsin Territory for four years, where slavery was illegal, before he and his family returned with their enslaver to Missouri, which was a slave state. In a landmark case that brought the North and South ever closer to war, the U.S. Supreme Court decided 7–2 against Scott, finding that neither he nor anyone else of African ancestry could claim citizenship, so they had no right to bring suit in federal court. As the court put it, ruling in his favor would be to "improperly deprive Scott's owner of his legal property."[21]

After describing Morton's diatribe against popular sovereignty and its corollary in the Dred Scott decision, the *Wabash Express* continued: "He avoided or evaded nothing, but met all of the great issues of the day, with a manly willingness that was refreshing to his friends, and perplexing to his political foes." Unlike politicians who merely mimicked what their followers wanted to hear, Morton never indulged in base epithets or obfuscation. On the contrary, he met every proposition and question head-on with clarity and conviction. In representing his party's platform, Morton "bore his banner aloft in the withering discomfiture of his opponents, and the delighted admiration of his friends."[22]

As governor, Morton built a legacy based not only on the political battles he waged, but also on his willingness to tackle the often thankless and always exhausting work of a wartime executive. During his tenure in the statehouse, Morton transformed Indiana's tradition of electing strong legislatures and weak governors into a system that favored strong executives with expanded authority and the ability to set and drive the agenda—a powerful example for a young man like Dick Morgan with a yen for public speaking and an affinity for politics. Although Morton never wavered in his commitment to the Republican Party, he provided a model for nonpartisanship by appointing Democrats as well as Republicans to office.

By the time Morton assumed office in January 1861, secession from the Union was gaining traction across the South. The new governor viewed this as treason, pure and simple, and he leveraged an 1852 militia law to enlist more soldiers in the Union army than any state except New York, thereby delaying a mandatory draft in Indiana. Morton was adept at forming public-private partnerships to procure trains, food, medicine, and uniforms and to manage other wartime logistics, a model that foreshadowed the way future Indiana governors would approach economic development. He sometimes spent his own money, and leveraged his own credit, to supply troops with arms and equipment. Personal visits to camps went a long way toward energizing his troops and convincing them that bureaucratic red tape was meant to be cut.

At war's end, Morton looked forward to completing his term as governor, helping to restore the peace, and maybe making a run for national office. But exhaustion had taken its toll, and in October 1865, he suffered a stroke that left him paralyzed from the waist down. He recovered sufficiently to win the Indiana General Assembly's appointment to the U.S. Senate, where he assumed the mantle of a radical Republican and viewed the conflicts attending Reconstruction as a continuation of the recently concluded hostilities. In war and the uneasy peace that followed, he stood for ordered liberty under the law, racial equality, and preservation of the Union.[23]

Another politician who left a lasting mark on Dick Morgan and, indeed, Indiana politics in general was Daniel W. Voorhees, who replaced Morton in the U.S. Senate following Morton's death in 1877 and remained there for the next twenty years. Known throughout Indiana as "the tall Sycamore of the Wabash," Voorhees engaged in a series of debates with Thomas H. Nelson during the Civil War. They compared favorably, and perhaps were second only in importance, to the Lincoln-Douglas debates that attracted listeners by the thousands in neighboring Illinois in the run-up to the election of 1860. Nelson would hire Dick after his graduation from law school to work in his law office, and he became one of the young man's most valued mentors.

The Voorhees-Nelson debates captivated Indiana voters and branded Voorhees as the number one orator in the Democratic Party.[24] Even though Dick opposed much of what Voorhees stood for, he was drawn to his passionate oratory on the stump, defense of the U.S. Constitution, and faithful service to his constituents. Long after he launched his career in public service, Morgan would recall those debates as a source of inspiration: "When I was a boy, I remember reading an account of the debates between Abraham Lincoln and Stephen A. Douglas and later on I heard debates between a very distinguished citizen of Indiana, Daniel W. Voorhees and Tom Nelson and there in my early manhood, early boyhood, I thought those men were the greatest men I had ever seen and then and there I thought perhaps some day I might get out before the public, when I grew to be a man, and discuss public questions."[25]

Dick Morgan sailed through Prairie Creek High School in two years and graduated with distinction in 1872.[26] By then, Vigo County's economy was in a tailspin; as Dick noted in his autobiography, the time "was unfavorable to agriculture." Plummeting prices for farm products and a steep decline in land values after the Civil War left many farmers hopelessly in debt. "Father was a leader in his community, and an up-to-date farmer for his time," wrote his son. "He was well posted upon public affairs." But neither Valentine's social standing nor his political acumen was enough to free him from a bind that was squeezing farmers nationwide. Eventually, after Valentine died in 1880, half of their farm had to be sold to settle his estate. Frances retained the deed to the remaining two hundred acres, and she remained there until she died in 1913.[27]

Even before his father's death, Dick was at a crossroads, unsure of what the future held as he watched his parents struggle during the 1870s to save their farm. Should he stay home after his graduation from high school and help his family navigate the postwar depression, or should he construct a new life beyond the confines of his tight-knit community? Given his political awareness and affinity for public speaking, his decision to continue his education was practically foreordained, and he made it with his parents' blessing and Valentine's bankroll to pay his tuition. In the late summer of 1872, Dick journeyed sixteen miles south to Merom and enrolled in Union Christian College.

The community of Merom dates back to a chilly day in February 1817 when a committee appointed by the Indiana state legislature gathered at a scenic sandstone bluff two hundred feet above the Wabash River to select a location for the Sullivan County seat. The new townsite was named "Merom," the biblical designation for "high place."

For the next three decades, Merom reigned as the most important trading center between Vincennes and Terre Haute. Fleets of flatboats carried farm produce from Merom down the Wabash, Ohio, and Mississippi rivers to Memphis and New Orleans. Shipments bound for Illinois depended on entrepreneurs such as Dick's grandfather David Thompson to ferry them across the Wabash. Merom's glory days entered their twilight in January 1843, when the town of Sullivan usurped its position as county seat. With completion of the Evansville & Terre Haute Railroad in 1854, the riverboat trade was doomed, and Merom faced a slide to obscurity as just another tiny outpost in western Indiana.

But then, about the time Dick Morgan was born in late 1853, the Reverend Evans W. Humphrey and several Sullivan County community leaders arrived at Merom's abandoned county courthouse and decided that the two-story building would suffice for a school. They named it Merom Bluff Academy, and thanks to Reverend Humphrey's proselytizing throughout the Midwest, it prospered. On

November 4, 1858, organizers passed a resolution to rebrand Merom Bluff Academy as Union Christian College. Although other towns vied to relocate the school, Merom cinched the deal with a $35,000 grant to fund its operations. Thomas Kearns, president of the executive committee, made the announcement on June 8, 1859: "In [*sic*] behalf of the Locating Committee, and as its President, upon our mutual understanding, and in full confidence of your good will and wishes, and in consideration of your most liberal donation, I now, in the name of God, locate Union Christian College at Merom, in Sullivan County, in the State of Indiana."

Later that summer, sixteen newly elected trustees chose Kearns as president. Fears that construction would come to a halt after the shelling of Fort Sumter, in the spring of 1861, were unfounded, and on Christmas Day 1862, a dedication ceremony was held for the first of many buildings that sprouted on the twenty-seven-acre campus. Although less visible, another sign of progress came in the form of gender equality. As David Morgan explained about his great-grandfather's alma mater, "I have heard that Union Christian College was one of the few places in the country that allowed women to take any course offered to men."[28]

Dick considered Union Christian College to be "a high-grade institution," and he remained there until he graduated in 1876, at the age of twenty-two. Although his focus was on mathematics, Dick sang in the school choir and, following his parents' advice, broadened his curriculum by taking a few courses in music to complete his bachelor's degree. He spent his summers as a singing teacher back in Prairie Creek (for which he earned the considerable sum of fifty dollars) and, presumably, helping out on the family farm. Somewhere between studying and singing and farming, he began a courtship with Orietta Heath, the daughter of A. R. and Mary (née Maxwell) Heath. Reverend Heath, a minister of the Christian Church, was a founding father of Union Christian College and served the school for many years as secretary and treasurer.

During his college days, Dick became acquainted with students and professors at Ascension Academy, a school in nearby Sullivan, Indiana, that enjoyed a good-natured rivalry with Union Christian

College. One of the professors, John T. Hays, was the father of Will H. Hays, who would one day be elected chairman of the Republican National Committee and serve in President Warren G. Harding's cabinet as postmaster general. Dick could not have foreseen that, many years hence, he and Will would become friends in Washington, D.C. As Dick noted in his autobiography, whenever he crossed paths with his friend in the nation's capital, he could not help but reflect on "the solid virtues of the splendid family from which he came."[29]

Following his graduation from college, Dick accepted a job as a teacher back in his hometown. Two months into his small-town teaching career, he was called back to Union Christian College to become a professor of mathematics, a position he retained for the rest of the school year. His next opportunity came when school officials in Hagerstown, a community about sixty miles east of Indianapolis and a hundred and fifty miles east of Prairie Creek, offered him a position as school superintendent. During his two years at Hagerstown, Dick managed a faculty of six teachers and oversaw construction of a school building "of which the Hagerstown people [were] justly proud." Dick also joined other dignitaries in delivering a speech at its dedication.[30]

A benefit of working in Hagerstown was that his hundred-dollar-a-month salary gave him the bankroll he needed to marry his college sweetheart, Orietta Heath, who had graduated from Union Christian College in 1877 with a bachelor's degree in mathematics. They were married on May 30, 1878.[31] Upon the newlyweds' return to Hagerstown, school officials were confident that Orietta's influence would make Dick a better superintendent: "Dick T. Morgan returns to take charge of the Hagerstown schools with a new wife, and the prospects of his permanent success are thereby much increased."[32]

Dick T. Morgan as a student at Union Christian College, circa 1875.
COURTESY OF THE MORGAN FAMILY COLLECTION

Ten miles down the road from Hagerstown was Cambridge City, the home of former governor Oliver P. Morton. "I was teaching school at Hagerstown at the time of his death," wrote Morgan. "Tens of thousands of people from all parts of the state went to take a last look at his lifeless form." Morgan promptly dismissed classes and traveled to Indianapolis to pay his respects "for one whom I had been taught from almost childhood to admire and honor."[33]

Following his tenure as school superintendent in Hagerstown, Morgan returned to Prairie Creek to become principal of his former high school. He arrived just in time to help prepare for closing exercises on May 30, 1879. Under the moniker "Free Schools, the Palladium of our Free Institutions," the program kicked off at 8:00 p.m. with a prayer by Rev. W. A. Ingram, a performance by the school choir, and two solos, one of which was Morgan's "Grand Father's Clock." Two other Morgans, presumably Dick's siblings, performed a comic duet titled "Reuben and Rachel." The grand finale was a theatrical performance billed as "a grand Temperance Drama in Three Acts" and titled "The Fruits of the Wine Cup," a not-so-subtle allusion to the perils of strong drink. No one was surprised to see several members of the Morgan family on stage: Dick as Hamilton, H. L. as Speculation, and Flora as Kate Hamilton. The closing number featured a trio, including Dick and Flora, singing "King Alcohol" to an audience admonished since birth to confront demon rum with the force of righteous conviction. All money above expenses raised in support of the closing exercises was earmarked for the Middletown Temperance Society.[34]

It seems likely that Morgan had returned to his alma mater not as a defining career move, but as an interim position that would put money in his pocket and enable him to spend some quality time with his family in a community he cherished.[35] Knowing that teaching high school was not his life's calling, he returned to Union Christian College to earn a master's degree and spent several months reading the law. After a brief stint in the law office of I. N. Pieree, he enrolled at Central Law School in Indianapolis, which later became part of the Indiana School of Law. Among his classmates were Merrill Moores, later Indianapolis's "able and distinguished" representative in Congress; William L. Taylor, who was later elected attorney general of Indiana; and Byron K. Elliott, who became a judge and authored several books. At the end of the term, Morgan was selected from among the forty graduates to give the valedictory address. It was printed in full the next day in the *Indianapolis Sentinel.*

Although the Hagerstown school system had been sorry to see Morgan go, he left with the community's best wishes. "The many friends of Prof. D. T. Morgan, former superintendent of our public school, will be glad to hear that he graduated with distinction at the Central Law College, Indianapolis," ran a story in the local newspaper. "Prof. Morgan must have been making the best of his time and talent since he left this place, a year ago, as he graduated with Class Honors, and his oratory was held in such high esteem, by his instructors and fellow students, that he was given the honor of delivering the valedictory, in [*sic*] behalf of the school. We understand that he will, in a short time, locate at Terre Haute, and apply himself to his profession." The Hagerstown community continued to track Morgan's career. As late as 1907, a local newspaper commemorated him as the first superintendent after the new school building was erected and opened in 1877. "Everybody liked Dick," ran the laudatory remembrance, "especially his pupils and he conducted an excellent school."[36]

Clearly, Morgan's star was on the rise in Indiana's legal community, and after his graduation from law school, he applied himself to his profession by accepting Thomas H. Nelson's offer to join his law firm in Terre Haute. Nelson, who had risen to prominence in his debates with Daniel Voorhees during the Civil War, had gone on to serve as ambassador to Chile and Mexico during the Lincoln and Grant administrations.[37]

Once Dick and Orietta were settled in Terre Haute, life-changing events happened in quick succession. On Columbus Day, October 12, 1880, Orietta gave birth to a son. That same day, at the age of twenty-six, Dick was elected to the Indiana state legislature to become its second youngest representative. As Dick put it, simply and without fanfare, "The Republicans carried the county, and I was elected."[38]

Up to and including the election of 1880, Indiana was an October state, meaning that voters went to the polls to elect state officers nearly a month before national balloting in November. Consequently, poll

Orietta Morgan, circa 1910.
COURTESY OF THE MORGAN FAMILY COLLECTION

watchers scrutinized Indiana's elections to discern political currents that might influence voters in the rest of the country. On larger political stages, poll watchers were surely interested to see voters choose two other Republicans for high office: Dick Morgan's friend Albert Gallatin Porter, a skilled debater and captivating orator who was elected and served as Indiana's governor from 1881 to 1885; and James Abram Garfield, who was elected president of the United States, and whose term in the White House was cut short by an assassin's bullet four months into his first year in office.[39]

"It appears that Dick's and Orietta's son was going to be named Garfield Heath Morgan or Porter Garfield Morgan, but that was changed to Porter Heath Morgan," explained David Morgan about his grandfather's naming. Dick and Orietta went so far as to announce the birth of Garfield Heath Morgan, their "election day" son. "I don't know why the name was changed," continued David. "I've guessed it might have been that Garfield was still just a Republican candidate in a close race. As much as Morgan admired and respected Garfield, he and Orietta might not have wanted to take a chance that their son would be named after a losing candidate!" Their final decision likely hinged on a simple assessment: naming their son after Dick's friend governor-elect Albert G. Porter was altogether fitting for an up-and-coming politician's son in Indiana. They added Orietta's maiden name in deference to her lineage, her father's ministry in the Christian Church, and his service to Union Christian College.[40]

Now that his son was properly named, Morgan turned his attention to the family he needed to support and the people of Vigo County, who had elected him as their representative in Indianapolis. "It was a new experience for me," he wrote about his election. "It was the first time that important political power was placed in my hands. I took my duties seriously."[41]

Over the ensuing four decades, Morgan would learn how to wield that power. But he already knew how to take his duties seriously.

CHAPTER TWO

Hoosier Politics

The Constitution was the work of the people,
and they were recognized as the true source
of all political power.

DICK T. MORGAN
CAMPAIGN SPEECH, JULY 12, 1882

ONE OF THE FIFTY-SECOND GENERAL ASSEMBLY's first orders of business was to invite the newly elected governor to deliver his inaugural speech. Eschewing the platitudes that one might expect in such a gathering, Governor Porter called on Indiana's legislators to put wartime animosities behind them and acknowledge, once and for all, that Blacks were entitled to the rights of citizenship. Many had fought, and many had died, to secure those rights. "Their right now to vote is guaranteed by the Constitution, and it is as complete as the right of those who formerly held rule over them," declared Porter. "If, in education, or whatever else is desirable, they do not come up to the standard of those who once ruled them, it is not their fault. The fault is with those who now strive to deprive them of this inestimable franchise." The time had come for former Confederates "to right the great wrong inflicted by slavery by conceding with generous alacrity to those who were oppressed, and to their descendants, every Constitutional right with which the Nation has invested them."

As he wound toward his conclusion, Porter vented his number one beef with the legislature: in planning the cornerstone of the new capitol building then under construction, nobody had thought to include the names of Indiana's sons who had fallen in service to the Union. One imagines Dick Morgan nodding in agreement as his friend and son's namesake chided the legislature for its failure to commemorate the dead and honor their sacrifice. Like Indiana's great war governor,

Oliver Morton, Albert Porter stood foursquare behind the party of Lincoln and the soldiers who had died for its principles, a lesson that was not lost on the freshman representative from Vigo County.[1]

With speeches delivered and formalities concluded, legislators got down to the business of choosing a successor to Joseph E. McDonald, the Democratic incumbent in the U.S. Senate. At the time, state legislators were responsible for appointing U.S. senators, and Republicans were bent on sending Benjamin Harrison, an Indianapolis attorney and former brevet brigadier general in the Union Army, to Washington. Harrison had emerged as a major figure in the GOP since his unsuccessful campaign for governor in 1876. As Republicans were in the majority, Harrison was nominated by acclamation.

When it came time to choose two representatives to deliver nominating speeches, Morgan was stunned to find himself in the spotlight. "Wholly unsolicited on my part, and entirely unexpected, I was invited to make one of the speeches." In his brief but poignant remarks to the Indiana House of Representatives, Morgan identified Harrison as the right man for the job, as there had not been an Indiana Republican in the U.S. Senate since Morton's death. In recalling his pilgrimage from Hagerstown to Indianapolis to pay his final respects to Indiana's great war governor, Morgan left no doubt about the kind of politician he sought to emulate:

> Some years ago, I saw the corridors of this temple of justice filled with aching hearts. They came here to behold for the last time the

Albert G. Porter, Porter Morgan's namesake, served as Indiana's governor from 1881 to 1885. COURTESY OF THE PRINTS & PHOTOGRAPHS DIVISION, LIBRARY OF CONGRESS, WASHINGTON, D.C.

> cold remains of a lamented citizen; a man whose strong heart, and heroic deeds had endeared him to the people. That man was Oliver P. Morton. From that time until this the Republican party has had no representative in the United States Senate: but on last October, the sun of Republicanism arose with resplendent glory. I believe that we on this side of the House rejoice on this occasion. Benjamin Harrison came to this city twenty-six years ago, and commenced the practice of law. He was not rich, but he had a strong, active mind, and as he was content to be useful, his honest heart brought its reward.[2]

Morgan's speech, printed in its entirety in the unmistakably Republican-leaning *Indianapolis Journal*, branded him as a rising star with a flair for speechmaking: "Dick T. Morgan, yesterday in seconding the nomination of General Harrison, made a most favorable impression upon the House and has the promise of becoming a most effective speaker. He is one of the youngest members of the House and his address had none of the faults which often characterize the efforts of our young debaters." The *Indianapolis Leader* chimed in with its own assessment of the freshman representative: "Among those who seconded the nomination of General Harrison, was Hon. Dick T. Morgan, of Vigo, one of the youngest members of the House. The gentleman's speech was pithy and eloquent, and delivered in a manner which stamps Mr. M. as one of the coming men from the Wabash." In one of history's convergences, Harrison's selection as a senator became a stepping stone to his election as president in 1888, a position that entitled him, on March 23, 1889, to issue a proclamation opening central Indian Territory (a.k.a. the Unassigned Lands and, alternatively, the Oklahoma country) to non-Indian settlement, an event that came crashing into history as Harrison's Horse Race.[3]

With Harrison's appointment to the U.S. Senate secured, the General Assembly turned its attention to amending the Indiana constitution. Adopted in 1851, the constitution was woefully inadequate to address the myriad ways Indiana had changed since pre–Civil War days. But neither the new Republican governor and young Porter Morgan's namesake, Albert G. Porter, nor the Republican-controlled legislature agreed that amendments were necessary. Nevertheless, during a special session in March 1881, four amendments to the constitution were proposed, two of which aligned with Dick Morgan's evolving philosophy of governance: one prohibited the sale and manufacture of liquors in Indiana; the other granted suffrage to women. The first proposal became a hot-button issue that enraged the Indiana Liquor League, a group of brewers and distillers who made it their mission to unseat the Republicans who supported the amendment in the upcoming 1882 elections. The second, although destined for defeat by a narrow margin, inspired people prescient enough, including Dick Morgan, to realize that denying women the right to vote was a clear violation of their rights under the U.S. Constitution.[4] Less than three months into his political career, Morgan was already distinguishing himself as a Republican more interested in social justice than a narrow adherence to his party's dictates.

"Forty-three ayes out of *eighty-nine votes* is a showing well calculated to inspire confidence, courage and zeal," ran an upbeat article in the *Indiana State Sentinel.*

> It emphasizes the fact that the star of woman suffrage is rising grandly to the zenith. It shows that Indiana, a State which boasts of its schools, its churches, its Christianity and its civilization, is not to be the eternal abode of error. It is the chosen battleground of truth, whose devotees are panoplied for the fight... 'Up and at them' is their battle cry. They have exhaustless resources of right, light and truth. The Sentinel congratulates the women of Indiana upon the vote in the House of Representatives. Forty-three ayes to forty-six nayes presages victory at an early day.[5]

During his tenure in the Indiana House of Representatives, Morgan supported bills that would soon be branded as progressive. He continued to advocate for women's suffrage and, to the consternation of the state's brewers and distillers, supported the temperance movement, which was sweeping the nation. As a former teacher and school superintendent, he was a natural pick to chair the Education Committee. He demonstrated his commitment to extending constitutional rights to all Americans by opposing a particularly odious clause in the Indiana constitution that banned Black residency. This might have been the first time, but certainly not the last, that Morgan spoke out on behalf of African Americans, whose emancipation from slavery was scant protection from the virulent racism that cast its pall across Gilded Age America.[6]

In his support for Indiana's Black citizens, Morgan drew inspiration from his role model, James A. Garfield, whose inauguration as president coincided with Morgan's service in the Indiana General Assembly. In his inaugural speech on March 4, 1881, Garfield railed against those who would deny Blacks the rights and protections afforded by the U.S. Constitution. Like Morgan, Garfield believed that fully enfranchised Blacks would add immeasurably to the common good. "The elevation of the negro race from slavery to the full rights of citizenship is the most important political change we have known since the adoption of the Constitution of 1787," declared Garfield.

> NO thoughtful man can fail to appreciate its beneficent effect upon our institutions and people. It has freed us from the perpetual danger of war and dissolution. It has added immensely to the moral and industrial forces of our people. It has liberated the master as well as the slave from a relation which wronged and enfeebled both. It has surrendered to their own guardianship the manhood of more than 5,000,000 people, and has opened to each one of them a career of freedom and usefulness. It has given new inspiration to the power of self-help in both races by making labor more honorable to the one and more necessary to the other. The influence of this force will grow greater and bear richer fruit with the coming years.
>
> No doubt this great change has caused serious disturbance to our Southern communities. This is to be deplored, though it was perhaps unavoidable. But those who resisted the change should remember that under our institutions there was no middle ground for the negro race between slavery and equal citizenship. There can be no permanent disfranchised peasantry in the United States. Freedom can never yield its fullness of blessings so long as the law or its administration places the smallest obstacle in the pathway of any virtuous citizen.[7]

After the Indiana General Assembly adjourned in 1881, Morgan formed a partnership with N. G. Buff, one of the most prominent attorneys in Terre Haute. That partnership would last until January 1884.[8] Aiming for another term in the legislature, Morgan supported positions that were typically associated with Democrats. Nevertheless, in the run-up to the 1882 elections, he ran afoul of the heavily Democratic Indiana Liquor League, which was determined to unseat Republicans with a distaste for intoxicating spirits. On the national stage, Morgan was deemed guilty by association with Republicans who had allegedly committed voter fraud and swayed the 1880 elections that sent Garfield and his running mate, Chester A. Arthur, to the White House.[9]

In his effort to keep his seat, Morgan delivered a campaign speech, on July 12, 1882, that set the tone for the rest of his career in politics. "I like this 1882 speech, because it is the earliest speech that I have of his," said David Morgan. "The principles that he set forth in 1882 seemed to be ingrained for the next four decades. He believed in a strong national government that would do good things for its citizens and a good citizenry that would work hard and faithfully and have trust in the national government." David went on to speculate about his great-grandfather's electability in the toxic politics of the early twenty-first century: "It would be interesting where he would land in today's world. He probably wouldn't be able to be elected dogcatcher."[10]

Dick Morgan, then only twenty-eight years old, began his 1882 speech with a paean to the Founding Fathers, who had pledged their lives, their fortunes, and their sacred honor to opposing tyranny. Their gambit paid off, and the first nation to arise from republican principles was about to become a beacon to the world. But when the guns fell silent after the Battle of Yorktown in October 1781, the founders faced an even greater task than defeating the mightiest empire on Earth: they had to carry through on their pledge to create a Republic "based on the sacred will of the people." Disappointed with the short-lived Articles of Confederation and inspired by a love for freedom, they set about writing a constitution based on the principles set forth in the Declaration of Independence aimed at preserving and perpetuating the priceless bonds of liberty and independence. "The Constitution was the work of the people," declared Morgan, "and they were recognized as the true source of all political power. Self-Government was to have a fair trial, recognized as the true principle."

European opinion leaders had predicted that the former colonies' experiment in self-government would fail. But they were wrong, and to understand why, Morgan urged his listeners to review the nation's founding documents, particularly Washington's Farewell Address, the writings of Thomas Jefferson and James Madison, and John Adams's speeches– "men whose strong arms, clear heads, and patriotic hearts did so much for the cause of humanity." By reading those documents and reflecting on the wisdom of the men who wrote them, Morgan's fellow Indianans might renew their faith in the free, happy, prosperous, and united nation that was their birthright.

And then, there was this:

> That the people should be happy in the enjoyment of all the glorious and sacred privileges of free citizenship–That the people should be united–united in the support of all our free institutions–united in their hatred to oppression and in their love for liberty, united in their unswerving attachment to the Constitution, united in their determination to maintain order, and enforce the laws, united in that glorious sentiment, voiced by the immortal Webster– "Liberty and Union, Now and forever, one and inseparable!!"

Following his stirring call to patriotism, Morgan admonished his listeners to think seriously about the upcoming November elections and the deficiencies embedded in the Democratic platform. Quoting scripture, Morgan castigated the Democrats' interpretation of state sovereignty: thirty-eight sources of authority instead of one, a constitution more suited to a loose confederation than a basis for unity, and states as "distinct, separate, and independent nations" that loaned their decision-making ability to the federal government only when circumstances warranted a temporary transfer of power. As usual, Morgan could not resist voicing his abhorrence of state laws that permitted the manufacture and sale of intoxicating spirits. In thwarting the people's wishes and condoning the debasement of culture, the Democratic platform was nothing less than a pretense and a sham– "a Judas Iscariot to real, genuine democracy, which it betrays, abuses, crowns with thorns, and sacrifices." And the Democratic Party? With the force of righteous conviction, Morgan thundered toward his conclusion: it was nothing less than a "modern Belshazzar of parties that sits drunken with harlots, insulting the decencies and moralities of that age, and speaking great lies and blaspheming the name of the Most High God."

Morgan then returned his attention to his party, whose platform stood foursquare for the principles handed down by the Founding Fathers. "Why, democracy means the power of the people," declared Morgan. "A democratic government is one where the power of the government is simply the power of the people. It is the organ of popular will, and it seeks to follow that will under all circumstances."[11]

Morgan's oratory notwithstanding, Republicans were unable to stem the Democratic tide that swept across Indiana in the fall of 1882. The Party's state ticket won by a margin of nearly eleven thousand votes, and Indiana's congressional delegation switched to a nine-to-four Democratic advantage.[12]

The new year dawned to find Indiana's General Assembly dominated by Democrats.

And Dick Morgan was out of a job.

But not entirely. In addition to his legal work, Morgan acquired the *Saturday Courier*, a widely circulated and typically partisan weekly newspaper that supported the Republican Party. Soon thereafter he founded the equally partisan *Terre Haute Daily Courier*. Both newspapers wielded considerable influence during the campaign of 1884. For assistance, he turned to his brother-in-law Evan W. Heath. In 1884, he sold a half interest in the newspaper to John Donaldson, whose firm aimed, rather ambiguously, "to improve the paper in many respects."[13] In all likelihood, Morgan was reducing his commitment to the newspaper in an effort to shed responsibilities, and perhaps raise money, in preparation for his next big move: another run for state office, this time in the Indiana Senate.

To signal his ongoing interest in politics, Morgan attended a meeting of the Republican State Central Committee in April 1884 and was chosen as one of two assistant secretaries.[14] Two months later, at a convention of the Young Men's Republican Clubs of Indiana, Morgan was elected to the executive committee as a representative from Terre Haute.[15] At the Eighth District Republican Nominating Convention on July 10, assembled to nominate candidates for Congress, Morgan was elected as permanent chairman. After thanking the convention for the honor of being selected as its presiding officer, he expressed confidence in the party's nominees, including James T. Johnston, a former soldier in the Union Army who had been nominated for Congress on the first ballot. To second Johnston's nomination, R. H. Catlin of Vigo County declared that "there could be no truer or braver man than James T. Johnston. He is a friend of the laborer and the soldiers, and a whole-souled enemy of the Democratic party."[16] Johnston went on to win election to the U.S. House of Representatives in 1884 and again in 1886.

Morgan's turn for nomination—not to the U.S. Congress, but to the Indiana Senate—came on July 19, 1884, when Vigo County Republicans put his name on the ticket.[17]

While Morgan was hobnobbing with other Republicans and campaigning for the Senate, a nearby neighbor from Terre Haute, whose name would later resonate on the radical fringe of American politics, was making a run for the Indiana House of Representatives. His name was Eugene Debs, a Democrat who had served as city clerk of Terre Haute from 1879 to 1883. A decade later, Debs would become a household name when he organized a boycott by members of the newly formed American Railway Union (ARU), one of the nation's first industrial unions. Many of Debs's recruits into the ARU had participated in a wildcat strike, over pay cuts, against the Pullman Palace Car Company in the summer of 1894, and they were fully prepared to heed Debs's call for rebellion.

The Pullman Strike affected most railroad lines west of Detroit and drew support from more than 250,000 workers in twenty-seven states. As a leader of the ARU, Debs was convicted on federal charges of defying a court injunction against the strike and served six months in prison. Debs took advantage of his down time by reading up on socialist theory. Bent on leveling a playing field skewed by trusts and monopolies, he cast his lot with the international Socialist movement to become America's most prominent activist on behalf of workers' rights. Debs is perhaps best known for his five campaigns as a Socialist candidate for the U.S. presidency, one of which he organized from behind bars. In 1916, he made an unsuccessful bid to represent Indiana in Congress.

Although Debs never earned more than 6 percent of the vote in any presidential campaign, his success in attracting workers who felt victimized by an unregulated economy would not be lost on Dick Morgan as he developed his own ideas about social justice. From his first plunge into state politics, in the early 1880s, to his service in Congress, beginning in 1909, Morgan understood better than most, and certainly better than most Republicans, the need for regulations to curb the worst excesses of a laissez-faire economy and mitigate threats posed by an angry electorate.[18]

"I have not discovered any direct relationship between Debs and Dick T., but I assume they had to know each other," said David Morgan. "They were close to the same age, lived in the same general area of Terre Haute, and were both active in politics, albeit different parties." When Election Day arrived in November 1884, Morgan lost his Senate campaign to Democrat Philip Schloss, a popular Terre Haute clothing manufacturer. Debs won his race for the lower house and went on to represent Indiana's seventeenth district from 1885 to 1887.[19]

Sidelined from politics, Morgan had plenty of time to reflect on Indiana's transition from a primarily rural and agricultural society to an urban and industrial commonwealth, a process that was roaring to life by the early 1880s and enlarging the chasm between the haves and have-nots that came to characterize the Gilded Age. Not surprisingly in an era of rapid change, postwar Indiana careened into a period of bitter political divisions. Party affiliation was akin to religious denomination, and the passing of the Civil War and Reconstruction brought no respite from partisanship. Those same toxic politics summoned legions of candidates, many of whom had commanded Union armies, to run for office. Between 1880 and 1896, Indiana was second only to New York in the number of its citizens placed on national party tickets. Although several of Indiana's favorites vied for the presidency, only one, Ohio-born Republican Benjamin Harrison, was successful. Otherwise, in the race for the White House, Hoosiers had to settle for their state's brand as "the mother of vice presidents."[20]

Arguably, there was an upside to Indiana's divided politics and the consistent voting patterns they produced: neither party was able to achieve a long-term advantage between 1880 and 1900. Indiana remained a strong two-party state where minor parties never gained much traction and election victories tended to be so narrow that the two parties remained locked in an uneasy balance.[21] Years later, Morgan would reflect on the balance between Republicans and Democrats in Indiana in the run-up to statehood in Oklahoma, where Oklahoma Territory's two-party equilibrium—a sign of good governance in a well-functioning state—stood in stark contrast to southern Democrats' dominance in Indian Territory and posed challenges to uniting the territories into a single state.

In Indiana, a state where partisan loyalties depended on sectional and socioeconomic factors, Democrats were known to favor soft money and hard liquor. Their power base was in the southern counties, where small farmers coaxing a living from poor soil were receptive when reformers and agitators came calling. Republicans favored temperance and fiscal conservatism, and they were far more numerous in central and northern Indiana, a region of fertile soil and rapid industrialization. As northern and central counties were outstripping their southern neighbors in both wealth and population, Indiana was becoming more Republican toward century's end.

Although national issues such as protective tariffs garnered their fair share of attention, parties tended to fight most vigorously over local questions and personal rivalries. And whatever the issue of the day, Hoosiers had to contend with the social and economic dislocations that came with industrialization. To complicate matters even more, wartime bitterness was never far from the surface. Waving the "bloody shirt," an oratorical flourish from Civil War days aimed at rekindling wartime passions and hardships and guaranteed to provoke animosities whenever it was resurrected, began to dissipate from rhetoric only after Oliver P. Morton's death in 1877. When the Indiana Senate appointed Democrat Daniel Voorhees to the U.S. Senate, those animosities came howling back to remind partisans on both sides of the aisle that some controversies are immune to the passage of time.[22]

Other than lingering issues from the Civil War and Reconstruction, nothing riled Indiana's electorate more than the apportionment of voting districts, a process of drawing district lines to favor whichever party had the most clout. Reapportionment, an inelegant yet descriptive slice of political argot, has always been fraught with disagreements over whose votes really count, and why. Curiously, historians have shied away from reapportionment, perhaps in deference to more alluring and exciting topics. This neglect seems particularly odd when, in the late nineteenth century, reapportionment dominated politics, disrupted legislatures and courts, enraged voters, and provoked constitutional crises. It was, simply put, the elephant in the room that linked a trifecta of voter behavior, political power, and public policy. As one historian of nineteenth-century apportionment has written, "Far more than mapping of districts by self-interested legislators, apportionment was an issue, at base, of political legitimacy, where Americans wrestled with beliefs about equity and democracy."[23]

According to laws in effect since ratification of the U.S. Constitution, congressional representation was a function of each state's population as determined by the federal census taken every ten years—except in Indiana, where the state constitution mandated a census every six years. State legislatures were tasked with the thorny job of establishing voting districts. But the U.S. Constitution was mute as to how—or even whether—the states should do it, leaving Republicans and Democrats, and the occasional third party, at each other's throats when it came to mapping districts. Hence the term "gerrymandering," another inelegant moniker used to describe the process of manipulating district lines. It dates to 1812, when Massachusetts governor Elbridge Gerry famously approved his state's serpentine electoral boundaries. As the competitive two-party system evolved from the 1830s onward, disputes over gerrymandering intensified to shape party formation and organization and influence campaigns and elections.[24]

In the Midwest, where population was growing and shifting in tandem with industrialization, the competition between parties was particularly fierce, and Indiana was widely seen as a reflection of the nation's balance of power. The ground rules for reapportionment originated in the Northwest Ordinance of 1787, which prescribed that voting districts, ideally comprised of compact and contiguous territory, "contain as near as practicable an equal number of inhabitants." That same ordinance, predating ratification of the U.S. Constitution by a single year, established protocols for state formation, and further required legislatures to redistrict periodically in response to population shifts. Those deceptively simple rules left it up to partisan legislatures to battle over boundaries that would conform to party and ideological allegiances. People (that is, mostly white males at least twenty-one years of age) who wanted their votes to be just as valuable as everyone else's—a cornerstone of America's experiment in representative democracy—often saw those fundamental rights of citizenship dashed on the shoals of politics. And minorities suffered virtual disenfranchisement—not the denial of their actual votes, but the destruction of their "effective suffrage"—that is, their practical right to vote.[25]

To further complicate matters, party allegiances depended not only on political ideologies but, perhaps even more, on ethnicity, religion, race, and the peculiarities of local communities. Savvy operators knew this and attempted to assure their party's power by manipulating district lines to alter the geographic distribution of partisan voters, thereby maximizing their party's influence at the polls at the expense of other parties. Gerrymanders, flagrantly designed to misrepresent voters' sentiment, were common in the late nineteenth century. Bizarre boundary lines summoned analogies to shoestrings, sausage links, and horseshoes; others conformed to so-called communities of interest whose inhabitants shared socioeconomic and cultural values. Indiana's voting districts took the prize for visual imagery in their resemblance to forked lightning.[26]

Republicans' dominance in the Midwest in the 1870s and 1880s left most apportionments in their hands. Democratic congressmen calculated in 1890 that one-third of their partisans' votes were "suppressed by fraudulent gerrymandering laws." However, given the opportunity, Democrats did not hesitate to craft gerrymanders in their favor. In uber-partisan Indiana, Republicans engineered a gerrymander in 1873, but in 1879, it was Democrats' turn to get creative. Whereas some politicians competed to promote their own interests, others strove to make districts favorable to their localities, regardless of who was running for office. Their goal was to protect or improve their community's prospects not merely in controlling nominations and elections, but also in ensuring patronage, raising public funds, and furthering economic development.[27]

Dick Morgan was no doubt pondering his future in politics following his defeat in the 1884 elections when the Indiana General Assembly, now dominated by Democrats, crafted what became known as the Gerrymander of 1885. What the Democratic majority did in terms of redistricting was indeed exceptional, but mainly because, this time, it represented a reversal of partisan apportionments that had usually (but not always) favored Republicans. Bolstered by their success at the polls, Democrats gathered at the state capitol for the 1885 legislative session on a mission to use reapportionment to accomplish two goals: first, strengthen their party's control of Indiana's congressional and legislative delegations; and second, improve their chances of unseating Senator Benjamin Harrison and replacing him with a Democrat.

Other than ramping up their invective in the Indiana General Assembly and in newspapers loyal to the GOP, Republicans had few practical options to avoid disaster. Some of their more impractical options included fomenting mass protests in their districts and resigning en masse from the legislature. Concluded one glum Republican legislator: "We are at rope's end" and "must submit to disfranchisement by legislative enactment instead of tissue ballots and the shotgun."

Rattled by the turn of events back home, Harrison, only partially in jest, proposed a no-nonsense title for the pending measure: "A Bill to Prohibit the Election of a Republican United States Senator from Indiana." He denounced the bill as nothing less than a "revolutionary" attempt to "suppress the Republican vote of our state" and characterized it as the Democrats' attempt to align with the old Confederacy.

Heeding Harrison's call to arms, Republicans fought the Democratic gerrymander by every means possible, from public relations campaigns and mass mailings to speeches at every opportunity. As a result, the Gerrymander of 1885 became a national issue, and it figured prominently in Harrison's failure to earn reappointment to the Senate, albeit by a narrow margin. At the same time, Harrison's principled opposition to gerrymandering made him one of the most attractive politicians in the GOP, and his calendar filled up with speaking engagements and high-level meetings. Kansas senator Preston Plumb was more prescient than he knew when he predicted that Harrison's "magnificent" campaign against gerrymander politics had placed him "in the line of Presidential promotion." Vindication would come three years after the Gerrymander of 1885 when Harrison won election to the presidency.[28]

As usual, newspapers squared off in a war of words to see whose fiery oratory might carry the day. One fiercely partisan editor denounced the Democrats' brazen ploy as "the most outrageous gerrymandering scheme that was ever proposed." Republicans' most loyal mouthpiece in Indiana, the *Indianapolis Journal*, expressed its distaste for Democratic shenanigans in no uncertain terms: "The bill is simply in the nature of an infamous political robbery. On a joint ballot the Democratic majority in the Legislature is now forty-eight. The bill proposes a gerrymander for the legislative districts, regardless of all considerations of fairness, which contemplates an increase of the majority to seventy." If enacted—which it was—the bill "would deprive nearly twenty percent of the citizens of the State the representation to which they are entitled."[29]

The *Indianapolis Journal* kept up its rant the following day: "The infamous robbery of political rights from a majority of the people of the State should not be permitted, if the exhaustion of every possible means short of revolution will prevent it." The *Journal* credited "honorable and fair-minded Democrats" for avoiding membership in "the unscrupulous majority" then answered its own rhetorical question with a not-too-veiled summons to insurrection:

> What obligation, therefore, is there upon the Republican members to quietly acquiesce? If red-shirted night riders were at work before election, and guns and clubs were in the hands of Democrats on the day of election to suppress the Republican vote in Indiana, there is

> no man anywhere, not a coward by nature and a poltroon by conduct, who would doubt or question the propriety of bloodshed if necessary to meet such a crime against political equality.

"This is not child's play," concluded the *Journal*. "It is a bold and insolent attempt to introduce the Mississippi plan into Indiana" and thereby make Indiana "the tail of the solid South." The *Journal* urged Republicans to be unrelenting in their demand for what was right and just. Republicans' reward for firmness would surely come from voters willing to fight the good fight "in any means, less than revolution, to vindicate their political rights and equality."[30]

Slightly cooler heads, and something akin to sober analysis, prevailed in Washington, D.C., where the *National Republican* reminded its partisans (as though they needed reminding) that Indiana had not secured a presidential cabinet seat in the recent election and that Democrats in Indianapolis were making it all but impossible for Republicans, absent a significant increase in their numbers in the General Assembly, "to secure any material results."[31] The paper went on to castigate Indiana legislators for wasting so much time in gerrymandering that they failed to pass appropriation bills, forcing the governor to call an extra session.[32] For the Washington, D.C., *Evening Critic*, the real problem caused by unrelenting agitation was not only threats to congressional seats, but also the likely loss of judicial appointments to Democrats: "The impression prevails that the most direct benefit will issue to the party gerrymandering will be the securing of a number of judges. If a Republican judge is gerrymandered out of office, the place will be filled by the Governor, and then some Republican circuits will for the greater portion of the term of four years be presided over by Democrats."[33]

Somewhere between Republican hyperbole and political punditry was a fact that Indiana's candidates had to face in assessing their prospects for election: Democrats were in power, and likely would be for years to come. In hindsight, it seems clear that the Gerrymander of 1885 helped Democrats maintain a majority position in the Indiana General Assembly, and thereby exert outsized influence in congressional and judicial appointments, for an unprecedented ten years.[34]

Major life decisions often require both a push and a pull. In Morgan's case, he tells us what the push was to leave his ancestral home in 1885 and move his family to a place called Garden City in southwestern Kansas. In his own words, from an 1888 interview, he says that he was defeated in an election to the Indiana State Senate in 1884 and decided to move west the next year. But that was not the entire story. He had also failed in his bid for a seat in the Indiana House of Representatives in 1882, and finally, the Gerrymander of 1885 had effectively ended his political career in Indiana. As David Morgan put it, "Apparently, Dick T. saw the handwriting on the wall and prepared to move his family to Kansas. Or," continued David, "it may have been as simple as a good job offer to do legal work for the AT&SF with the possibility of a political future in a Republican state."[35]

Morgan signaled his life-changing intentions at the same time Democrats in the Indiana General Assembly were putting the final touches on their historic gerrymander. On February 17, 1885, the *Indianapolis Journal* reported that A. H. Dooley was negotiating a purchase of Morgan's *Terre Haute Evening Courier.*[36] Less than two weeks later, Morgan sold his interests in the paper not to Mr. Dooley, but to George M. Allen, proprietor of the *Terre Haute Express*. Mr. Allen planned to continue publishing the paper as an afternoon daily with no change in its Republican leanings.[37] On March 10, the *Indianapolis Journal* published its obituary for Morgan's newspaper: "The *Terre Haute Courier* is no more, as it will hereafter be known as the evening issue of the *Terre Haute Daily Express*."[38]

If politics provided the push for Morgan to leave Indiana, what was the pull, and why southwestern Kansas? Morgan's choice was not entirely random. His younger brother Fred had been teaching at the Quapaw Agency in northern Indian Territory, just south of the Kansas border, since 1884. Whatever news he sent back to his family in Indiana must have nudged Dick and Orietta toward a belief that America's future lay on the Great Plains. After considering several upstart communities, they settled on Garden City, Kansas, where Dick was employed as a lobbyist and attorney for the AT&SF Railroad.

Given Dick's profound spirituality, he likely thought the town's lyrical name signaled the possibility of a fresh start. Maybe that's where he and Orietta could carve out their share of the American Dream.[39] What is more, moving to Garden City would put the Morgans near Indian Territory, where wannabe homesteaders, dubbed "boomers" in the press, were challenging the federal government's prohibition of non-Indian settlement in bold invasions that were captivating the nation's attention and spawning bitter rivalries over control of the area's resources.

With several years' legal experience in Thomas H. Nelson's and N. G. Buff's offices in Terre Haute, ownership of two newspapers, and a two-year stint in the Indiana General Assembly on his résumé, Morgan had plenty to offer the railroad as it expanded its services along the fast-fading line of frontier settlement. "Most important for his future career in politics was his experience as a legislator," said David Morgan. "Learning from his friend and mentor, Governor Porter, and grappling with issues ranging from congressional redistricting to postwar polarities gave him the legal and political skills that would enable him to build a new life in Kansas."[40] In addition, growing up on a family farm and watching helplessly as half of the property was sold to settle his father's estate had taught him about the perils of farming. Southwestern Kansas was swarming with homesteaders whose livelihoods were threatened at every turn by unregulated corporations, inadequate financing, and public land laws that failed to meet their needs. Some of those homesteaders surely needed a good lawyer.

As an added incentive to uproot his family and relocate to Kansas, Morgan must have known that, in addition to his brother, there were plenty of Hoosiers in the area. By 1890, Kansas was home to an estimated 98,000 immigrants from Indiana. Many of them were farmers from the poorer counties of southern Indiana, and some no doubt hailed from Morgan's homeland in Vigo County.[41] And who knows? In southern Kansas, where anger toward politicians in cahoots with Big Money was reaching the boiling point, there might be a way for Morgan, described in the *Indianapolis Leader* as "one of the coming men from the Wabash" with a knack for public speaking, to rekindle his political career.

One wonders whether, as the Morgans packed their bags for the adventure of a lifetime, Dick took time to reflect on *New York Tribune* founder and editor Horace Greeley's iconic advice to the young and unemployed: "Go West, young man, and grow up with the country."[42]

FINE
CABINET PHOTOS
FROM
MAIN ST.,
GARDEN CITY,
KAS.

CHAPTER THREE

A Favored Spot on the AT&SF Line

Go West, young man,
and grow up with the country.

HORACE GREELEY
New York Tribune

DICK, ORIETTA, AND PORTER, five years old and surely bursting with curiosity, stepped off the train in Garden City in the fall of 1885 to encounter an alien landscape. Gone were Vigo County's rolling croplands and forests teeming with game; enticing swimming holes along the banks of the Wabash River; churches, schools, and colleges pulsing with career opportunities and avenues for social bonding; and the up-and-coming industrial centers north and east of Terre Haute, a cosmopolitan city of thirty thousand brimming with job prospects and modern amenities. In their place was a treeless expanse stretching to the horizon and a tiny cluster of buildings where the Morgans were supposed to build new lives.

Perhaps, as he and Orietta and Porter gathered their luggage and the train chugged off to parts unknown, Dick took a moment to reflect on the explorations that had brought the southern Great Plains into recorded history. First, there was the twenty-nine-year-old Francisco Vázquez de Coronado who, in 1540, earned everlasting fame as the first European to lead an expedition into America's heartland, then known simply as Terra Nueva. Leading his small band of conquistadores northeastward across Mexico and into what later became the Texas and Oklahoma panhandles and western Kansas, Coronado was on a mission to conquer, pacify, and Christianize native populations. Borrowing techniques honed to perfection during the Inquisition, he would compel his captives to point the way to the mysterious city of

---

Dick, Orietta, and Porter Morgan in Garden City, Kansas, circa 1885.
COURTESY OF THE MORGAN FAMILY COLLECTION

Cibola, where legendary caches of gold, silver, and precious fabrics beckoned as the fulfillment of New World promise. What he found were modest villages whose inhabitants had no inkling of cities piled high with treasures. The conquistadores vented their frustration in a campaign of terror that set the tone for relations between Europeans and Terre Nueva's indigenous inhabitants.

Next came Don Juan de Oñate y Salazar, another ambitious Spaniard who hoped to find whatever had eluded his predecessor a half century earlier. Although his exact route across the Texas Panhandle remains contested, he almost certainly skirted past the Antelope Hills in present-day northwestern Oklahoma before encountering, somewhere in southwestern Kansas, the Great Settlement—mile after mile of primitive dwellings, and not a nugget of gold to be found. Like Coronado, Oñate found the Great Plains to be the Great Disappointment. And like Coronado, he and his conquistadores directed their displeasure into a violent blitzkrieg that etched another bleak milestone into European and Native American relations.[1]

Expeditions from the east were longer in coming. Most famous was the Lewis and Clark Journey of Discovery, a grueling hike across the vast territory of Louisiana, purchased in 1803 from France for a pittance, that gave the tiny group of explorers their first glimpse of the northern plains, the Rocky Mountains, and the Pacific Ocean. Exploring the southern plains had to wait fifteen years for Major Stephen S. Long's 1819 expedition to traverse the eastern slope of the Rocky Mountains. What he wrote to his higher-ups in Washington was far less sanguine than his counterparts' report from the Northwest. In Long's downbeat assessment, the region between the Missouri River and the Rockies "is almost wholly unfit for cultivation, and of course uninhabitable by a people depending on agriculture for their subsistence."[2]

Long's description confirmed what a few intrepid travelers from the East already knew. Except for traders who traversed the Santa Fe Trail from western Missouri through Kansas and on to the Spanish settlements of Nuevo Mexico, migrants tended to scurry across the Great Plains as fast as they could on their way to the more hospitable climes of California and Oregon. What Major Long branded as the

Great American Desert was best left to the vast herds of bison and the Native Americans who had been subsisting on them for millennia.

Yet big changes were in the wind. By the 1840s, Manifest Destiny was taking root in Americans' imaginations, and pioneers who had hesitated at the edge of the eastern woodlands began to trickle onto the Great Plains. As the frontier line of settlement pushed westward, lawmakers found themselves under increasing pressure to figure out what to do with all that uncharted real estate. In the early years of the Republic, federal laws forbade settlements in the public domain—that is, land that had not yet been settled by non-Indians—and pioneers found themselves under threat of expulsion for putting down roots without legal sanction. But as farms and settlements dotted the nation's midsection, Congress loosened its restrictions and began debating ways to facilitate the transfer of land from the public domain to private ownership. Congress's motivations were twofold: first, in keeping with the nation's core ideology, lawmakers wanted to extend America's bounty to ordinary citizens; and second, in terms of fiscal responsibility, they perceived the nation's resources as an unlimited source of revenue to fund the federal treasury.

Deliberations in Congress over what to do with the public domain resulted in three land laws that opened the floodgates to westward migration and, as the nineteenth century barreled toward its closing decade, became central to Dick T. Morgan's varied career in law, business, and progressive politics. The first of those laws was the Preemption Act of 1841, which allowed settlers to establish homes on both surveyed and unsurveyed land. Small landowners of not more than 320 acres in any state or territory were entitled to purchase a quarter section (160 acres) for as little as $1.25 per acre. To thwart speculators, buyers were required to use and improve the land rather than resell it.

The second and most consequential of the three land laws, destined to inform Morgan's career as a land attorney in Oklahoma Territory, was the Homestead Act of 1862. Its most ardent promoter in Congress was Galusha A. Grow, a Republican representative from Pennsylvania whose moniker, "father of the homestead law," reflected his passionate belief in giving free homes to free men. Like Morgan, Grow was raised on a family farm and learned at an early age what chores were all about; unlike Morgan, his father died when he was a child, leaving him, his mother, and his five siblings to manage as best they could. Grow's encounter with homesteading came at an early age when his family ventured "up-country" to the wilds of northern Pennsylvania. The ten-year-old Grow was only dimly aware of the westering movement that was expanding the nation's boundaries across the continent. But he was certainly aware of, and transfixed by, the deep satisfaction that came with carving a home out of the wilderness. As his biographers wrote a decade after his death in 1907, "It was given to him to perceive the glamour of the new land and the inherent hardship of its conquest at that period when youth moves mountains by a wave of the hand, seeing its high vision with the clarity of reality."[3]

Grow was a teenager when he caught his first glimpse of slaves at work near Annapolis, Maryland. At the same time, odd jobs such as delivering lumber and driving cattle to market brought him into contact with land sharks and speculators who stymied honest-to-goodness settlers at every turn. Equipped with real-life experiences and, later, the benefits of a classical education at Amherst College, he became a determined foe of slavery and set his sights on a career in the law. His fellow students were more prescient than they knew when they predicted that, within five years, Grow would win a seat in Congress.[4]

After practicing law for several years in Pennsylvania, Grow campaigned as a Democrat and won a seat in Congress in 1851 to become its youngest member. He arrived in Washington as debates over the proper disposition of public lands were reaching fever pitch. Displaying his considerable oratorical skills, Grow became embroiled in those debates, and as the Union careened ever closer to dissolution, he stood up for laws that would encourage internal development, turn settlers into bona fide landowners at minimal cost, and end, once and for all, the scourge of slavery. In his maiden speech, under the title "Man's Right to the Soil," Grow exhorted Congress to do the right thing and hand over the public domain to settlers whose labors would accrue to the common good.[5] Under his leadership, the House passed homestead bills in 1852, 1854, 1859, and twice in 1860, all of which met with resistance from President James Buchanan and/or the planter-dominated Senate.[6] Such was Grow's disgust with the Democratic Party's obeisance to southern slaveholders that he switched his allegiance to the newly formed Republican Party, whose main mission was to prevent the extension of slavery into the western territories. His model of public land policy came from two principal contributors to the American experiment: Thomas Jefferson, who famously posited that "the earth belongs in usufruct to the living";[7] and John Locke, the seventeenth-century philosopher who believed that a person's right to property and his physical abilities were equal contributors to society, and that government was obliged to honor both with policies that encouraged private ownership of property.[8]

Like a later generation of legislators from rural states and territories that would include Dick T. Morgan, Grow prioritized agricultural interests. "It is agriculture which is of permanent and lasting interest," declared Grow. He believed that land should be granted to men who wanted to cultivate it, "free them from the extortions and exactions of capital of the country, which has been permitted to take from their hard-earned savings too large an amount."[9]

When Lincoln's election to the presidency in 1860 sent southern Democrats fleeing to their home states, Grow won an easy vote to become Speaker of the House, and passage of a homestead bill seemed finally within reach. Self-branded as a radical Republican with a deep affection for President Lincoln, Grow was now at the pinnacle of his career; as William Holman of Indiana commented, "No man who was ever Speaker more largely or more beneficially influenced the general course of our legislation."[10]

That influence came to fruition on May 20, 1862, when Lincoln signed the Homestead Act. After a dozen years of frustration, Grow's principles were now the law of the land, and they would guide the path of westward migration for generations to come.

Unlike the Preemption Act, the Homestead Act granted title to homesteads by continuous residence, improvements over a period of five years, and the payment of a nominal fee for an application. Applicants had to swear that they were heads of families or twenty-one years of age, had never borne arms against the United States or encouraged its enemies, and would reside on their land for their "exclusive use and benefit." Applicants were required to provide proof of citizenship or, if they were foreigners, prove that they intended to become citizens. Their homesteads were limited to 160 acres. At the end of a five-year residency requirement, homesteaders would receive a patent for their land as long as they had not abandoned it for more than six months. Anyone who had acquired title to a homestead in the regular way (except by commutation), or who owned 160 acres in any state or territory with no regard to the way they obtained it, was barred from homesteading on an Indian reservation or any other Indian lands.[11] Otherwise, the act was remarkably liberal in opening homestead applications to widows, deserted wives, married male minors, and guardians of minors, invalids, and younger siblings. As the law was gender neutral, more women had an opportunity to acquire property in their own names in the West than in other parts of the country.[12]

Joining Grow in his crusade was George W. Julian, a Republican from Morgan's home state of Indiana. To confirm his and his party's position on public land policy as reflected in the Homestead Act, Julian delivered a speech on March 6, 1868—six years after passage of the Homestead Act—under the no-nonsense title "Our Land Policy—Its Evils and their Remedy." In Julian's opinion, the U.S. government had a moral obligation to make land as productive as possible, and maximum productivity could be achieved only on small holdings tilled by their proprietors. Like Grow and other Jefferson disciples, whose number would one day include Dick Morgan, Julian envisioned a nation of small farmers whose progeny would carry the nation's promise to the Pacific Ocean. To support his argument, Julian quoted passages not from Jefferson, but from Europe's most renowned philosophers—John Locke, John Stuart Mill, and others who would have been familiar to his erudite listeners—who extolled the virtues of a free and independent peasantry. "They are the voice of reason and justice," intoned Julian, "affirming, in different forms of speech, the scriptural truth that the earth belongs 'to the children of men.'" For evidence that small farmers were the backbone of a sound economy, one needed to look no further than Europe, where landowners with tiny acreages routinely outproduced large proprietors and their tenants. One of Julian's authorities put it this way after a trip to France: "Give a man the sure possession of a bleak rock, and he will turn it into a garden; give him a nine years' lease of a garden, and he will convert it into a desert."[13]

Like the church elders in Dick Morgan's religiously grounded community, Julian hammered home his message with the force of biblical imagery. Just as frogs had once inflicted pestilence on Pharaoh's Egypt, public land laws were perverting the national character, poisoning social life, and encouraging people to congregate in overcrowded cities teeming with criminals and tenements. In closing, Julian invoked the Declaration of Independence to urge his fellow congressmen to reform public land laws and thereby "extend the borders of our civilization, increase our national wealth, curb the ravages of monopolists, satisfy the earth-hunger of the multitudes who are striving for homes on our soil, and thus practically reassert the right of people to life, liberty, and the pursuit of happiness."[14]

Horace Greeley was also a firm supporter of homestead laws. "To throw open all the lands of the republic free of charge, and bid each citizen to help himself to a quarter section, will open a new era in the history of labor," declared Greeley in the *New York Tribune* on May 14, 1862. Hailing the end of the old system, under which the best public lands had fallen into the clutches of speculators and monopolists, Greeley's tribute to the much-anticipated act reflected his ardent support for homesteading. It was published six days before Lincoln signed it and added to the chorus of jubilation over a truly epochal piece of legislation.

America's promise now rested on four cornerstones: free lands, free immigration, free enterprise, and free political institutions. Between the Civil War and World War I, those freedoms turned America into an economic powerhouse and set the stage for its rise to global leadership.[15]

The third and final of the three laws pertaining to public lands was the Timber Culture Act of 1873. Designed to supplement the Homestead Act, the Timber Culture Act allowed homesteaders to obtain another 160 acres if they planted trees on one-fourth of their land. This was seen as critical on the Great Plains, where, according to nineteenth-century science, afforestation would promote rainfall and thereby bend the climate and ecology to the contours of agriculture. A second and more long-range motivation was the need for timber on the frontier.[16]

Two other acts of Congress hastened economic development on the Great Plains. First was the Pacific Railway Act, passed on July 1, 1862. Since the nation's founding, internal improvements had been a hot topic in Congress. With the advent of railroads, visionaries hatched a plan to span the continent and, in the 1850s, commissioned topographical surveys to determine the best route. Knowing that private corporations would never take on such a daunting project without federal assistance, Congress passed the Pacific Railway Act to guarantee funding and provide land grants for rights-of-way. The act's most celebrated achievement came on May 10, 1869, when two railroad companies—the Union Pacific, building west from Omaha, and the Central Pacific, building east from Sacramento—joined and drove the final spike at Promontory, Utah. With the completion of what was arguably the most audacious engineering feat in American history, a journey that had taken several months was reduced to a week. Congress eventually authorized four transcontinental railroads and granted 174 million acres of public lands for rights-of-way.[17]

A day after passage of the Pacific Railway Act, Congress continued its economic development spree by passing the Morrill Act on July 2, 1862. Sponsored by Senator John Morrill of Vermont, the act authorized states to establish public colleges funded by the development or sale of associated federal land grants, largely by expropriating tribal lands. With their focus on agriculture and mechanical arts, the new land-grant institutions opened opportunities to farmers and laborers who had been excluded from higher education. Seeking those opportunities, prospective settlers who had hesitated at the edge of the Great Plains, or perhaps scurried across the nation's midsection en route to more hospitable climes further west, decided that the flatlands might not be so inhospitable after all.[18]

The Great Plains, heretofore shunned as a land unfit for white settlers, was open for business.

In 1859–three years before President Lincoln affixed his signature to three historic acts of Congress that would transform the nation–Topeka businessman Cyrus K. Holliday did his part to promote westward migration by founding one of America's iconic railroads: the Atchison, Topeka & Santa Fe Railway. In a letter to the *Atchison Globe*, Holliday was not bashful about his role in organizing a railway link between Topeka and Atchison: "I wrote the charter, every word, paragraph and section, near the close of the legislative session of 1859, at Lawrence, and had the whole thing complete except filling in the names of the incorporators." As territorial Kansas had yet to create general incorporation laws, Holliday depended on the legislature to authorize a charter for what was to be known as the Atchison and Topeka Railroad Company. Funding for such enterprises came in the form of state and federal land grants, and sometimes cash. Additional money derived from counties, cities, and townships that issued bonds in exchange for railroad stock, often with the company's guarantee that it would build a switch or depot in their vicinity.[19] At a meeting to organize the company, held at the Eldridge House in Lawrence on February 3, 1859, Holliday alluded to the importance of the road to central, southern, and southwestern Kansas, "and hoped that it would receive the assistance and encouragement from those interested to which it was entitled." Holliday, who chaired the meeting, was then elected the company's permanent president, and future Kansas senator Preston B. Plumb of Emporia was named secretary.[20]

Holliday and his board of directors had more to think about than building a railroad. Kansas was in the grip of a severe drought in the early 1860s that threatened to upend their entire operation. "A terribly destructive drouth hung over our newly cultured fields like a poisonous blight," ran a story in the *Emporia News* on September 23, 1870, "crushing every expectation even of moderate harvests, and presaging inevitable disaster." Still reeling from wartime disruptions, Kansans now had to contend with the wrath of Mother Nature, and the project languished. But Holliday and his colleagues never gave up, thereby reserving a place in Kansas's pantheon of frontier culture heroes. "[T]hey nursed the enterprise through a struggling precarious infancy," rhapsodized the *Emporia News*, "and at last had the supreme satisfaction of seeing it firmly established as among the most flourishing adventures of this prolific and progressive age. All honor to the resolute men who quailed not in the presence of manifold discouragements, and who, not despising the day of small things, builded [*sic*] better than they knew."[21]

Throughout the early 1870s, the railway pushed relentlessly across central and southwestern Kansas with the ultimate purpose of building a terminus in Santa Fe. As its tentacles spread south and west of the Arkansas River, farmers and businessmen salivated at the prospect of easy access to distant markets. Excitement heightened as Texas cattlemen arrived with their herds in southern Kansas in dire need of transportation to ship their rangy Longhorns to Kansas City and Chicago and points east. "We take it that the town lot fever will soon commence to rage in the vicinity of the Arkansas," concluded the *Emporia News* in September 1870.

> It has not been determined at what point the road will strike the river, but wherever that point may be, a large and prosperous town is certain to spring up. We understand that it will be the policy of the company to donate a site in the Texas interests, which are expected to develop the locality and to make the town the great depot and emporium of their colossal traffic. There will be many interested in ascertaining the locations of this favored spot.[22]

Garden City was one of the towns in southwestern Kansas interested in becoming a favored spot. The town was in Sequoyah County, renamed Finney County in 1883 for Kansas lieutenant governor David Wesley Finney. It was on the north bank of the Arkansas River some sixty miles northwest of Dodge City, sixty-five miles east of the Colorado border, and seventy miles north of No Man's Land (later, the Oklahoma Panhandle). It was founded in February 1878 by businessmen William D. and James R. Fulton, John A. Stevens, and Charles J. Jones.[23] Apparently undaunted by an unbroken horizon dotted with sagebrush, soap weeds, and the loose, sandy loam beneath their feet, the Fulton brothers imported materials to erect two frame houses. William's one-and-a-half-story dwelling, with two rooms on the ground and two rooms above, was optimistically designated as the Occidental Hotel. Construction halted until November 1878, when two more buildings were added to the Garden City skyline. With typical frontier boosterism, the *Dodge City Times* did its part to encourage development in its upstart neighbor to the northwest. "We have four substantial frame houses, containing from four to six rooms each, and three or four more under contract," ran an upbeat appraisal on November 9, 1878. And the real estate business was just getting started: "Messrs. Jones and Weeks, land agents and surveyors, are kept busy locating land seekers every day. They are live men and understand their business."[24]

A milestone in Garden City history came when the Fulton brothers convinced the AT&SF to build a switch station in their fledgling community, a development that lured homesteaders to the area and spurred the hamlet's first population boom.[25] The next big development, an irrigation system, helped keep Garden City on the map. In a region where the annual rainfall was about fourteen inches, residents put irrigation at the top of their agenda and, in the spring of 1880, dug enormous ditches to tap into the Arkansas River and its tributaries. The first ditch was eight feet wide and two feet deep and cut through thirty miles of prairie. "It is expected that the water from these ditches will irrigate at least 100,000 acres of rich soil," ran an article in the *Dodge City Times*. "If the anticipation excited by the results of irrigation at Garden City are half realized next year, attempts will doubtless be made hereafter in other portions of the state to render the farmer independent of this fickle climate." The gambit worked, leaving attendees at the Bismarck Fair in 1880 and the State Fair in Topeka in 1881 to marvel at Garden City's "fine display of vegetables."[26]

Wary of losing readers to an upstart competitor, the *Dodge City Times* was less sanguine about the town's plan, in December 1885, to publish the *Garden City Sentinel* as a daily newspaper. The inaugural issue of the *Sentinel* had been published on April 3, 1879, and three months later it had declared "there are forty buildings in town." A story in the *Times* cautioned: "Garden City is young and has grown prodigiously. In its youth and tenderness it wants to do just like old and mature towns that have grown wise and wealthy. Garden City ought to wait until it has outgrown its swaddling clothes, before it puts on garments of maturer years." None doubted that Garden City had "vim and energy" and that, within a few short years, it would swell with immigrants. Still, "the towns must depend for support from the ordinary growth of the country, and this must be slow in the natural order of things."[27]

Garden City was by no means an old and mature town when the Morgans arrived in 1885, but it had certainly come a long way since its scrappy beginnings in the 1870s. In addition to irrigation ditches snaking across Finney County's parched landscape and the switch station connecting it to the AT&SF, Garden City boasted a branch of the U.S. Land Office, where homesteaders, lawyers, and real estate agents filed and adjudicated their claims. Horse-drawn wagons, teams of oxen, and pedestrians jostled for room on crowded streets that billowed dust during the dry season and turned to mud when storms thundered across the plains. During the height of the boom that brought the Morgans all the way from Indiana, Garden City boasted nine lumberyards, thirteen drug stores, and two daily newspapers. Anyone who doubted Garden City's prosperity had only to visit the train station, where immigrants by the score arrived daily to participate in Finney County's soaring economy.[28]

Dick Morgan's first order of business was to hang out his shingle as an attorney. "Dick T. formed the law office of Morgan & Davis with Webster Davis, who also had a real estate office," explained David Morgan. "They maintained an office near the U.S. Land Office. When it was relocated a few blocks away, they moved their law office to be nearby and represented homesteaders." Working alongside the principal partners was Fred Morgan, Dick's brother, who had been teaching at the Quapaw Agency in northern Indian Territory and was now branding himself as a land attorney. In the spring of 1889, Dick added his brother's name to the firm to become Morgan & Morgan; no word on what happened to Davis.[29] Relying on the Preemption Act of 1841, the Homestead Act of 1862, and the Timber Act of 1873,

Morgan helped homesteaders with their claims and kept them flocking to Finney County.

"Garden City was a boomtown for homesteaders in the mid-1880s," continued David Morgan, "growing in population from 300 to 6,000 from 1883 over the next few years before peaking in 1886." Although David was not sure about his great-grandfather's position with the railroad, he deemed it most likely that he served as an outside attorney and maybe as a lobbyist. Perusing archival collections in Garden City, David Morgan realized the extent to which his ancestor advertised his business in the city directory and newspapers. When he was not engaged in business-building activities, Dick Morgan was busy at the Christian Church, which grew rapidly from thirty-five members in 1884 to six hundred in 1886.[30]

Beneath the exuberance that was fueling Garden City's growth and Dick Morgan's law and real estate businesses were troubling signs that the boom had peaked. Nowhere was the trouble more apparent than in the range cattle industry. Anticipating a wave of homesteaders (a.k.a. nesters, in cowboys' derisive lexicon) bent on turning the grasslands into farms, many ranchers had borrowed to the hilt at high interest rates to stock ranges that were plenty stocked already. In keeping with the inexorable law of supply and demand, beef prices plummeted, leaving ranchers with depleted bank accounts and vast herds of cattle to fend for themselves on the open prairie.[31] Cattlemen's troubles were compounded when Kansas, Colorado, Nebraska, and New Mexico Territory acceded to homesteaders' demands and quarantined themselves against Texas cattle, whose diseases, known alternately as Texas or Spanish fever, had the potential to wipe out entire herds. Hemmed in by barbed wire and strictly enforced quarantines, Texas cattlemen could no longer rely on overland trails through Indian Territory to the railheads in Kansas and points north. As the open range became ever less open, the future of the cattle industry appeared to lie in cheap beef raised on small farms, mainly in Texas, where former cattle barons would have to make do with smaller herds and restricted ranges.[32]

Signs that the range cattle industry had entered its twilight were evident at the second annual cattlemen's convention in St. Louis in November 1885. Attendance was significantly down from the heavily attended convention in 1884. Kansas sent only a few representatives, and the all-powerful Cherokee Strip Live Stock Association, representing ranchers in northern Indian Territory, was barely represented. Perhaps cattlemen who stayed home had the right idea. The *Barber County Index* put it in stark terms: "The range cattlemen of the Indian Territory and southwestern Kansas were wise in doing no big blowing this year."[33]

As usual, Mother Nature had the last word. "The winter of 1885-86 turned out to be one of the coldest on record in the history of the town," wrote David Morgan after his research in Garden City. Disaster struck on New Year's Eve of 1885, when the first blizzard of the season came howling across Kansas. In what was etched into Great Plains lore as "the big die-up," milk cows and horses perished in their stalls as temperatures plunged to levels unheard of since the earliest days of settlement. Snow drifts piled up to eighteen feet and made travel impossible. Cattle drifted into arroyos and barbed wire fences, where they either froze to death under a blanket of snow or suffocated in bovine heaps. As one ranch foreman recalled, "I never saw such a sight. There are big mounds of cattle, nothing visible but horns, for the snow had drifted over them and you are spared meantime the horrible sight of seeing piles of carcasses." Cattlemen reported losses during that dreadful winter at 65–75 percent.[34]

"The Morgans had been in Kansas only a few months when the blizzards came roaring through," continued David. "You wouldn't have blamed them if they had hightailed it back to Indiana!"[35]

While some immigrants to southwestern Kansas left, or at least thought about it, others began to gaze southward toward Indian Territory. Indian tribes were confined to reservations, and pressure was mounting on the federal government to open nearly two million acres in the middle of the territory to non-Indian settlement. Known alternately as the "Unassigned Lands" and "the Oklahoma country," the region that would one day blossom into the six counties of central Oklahoma was the last parcel of land in Indian Territory not assigned to one of the Indian tribes that had been removed to reservations.

Those monikers drifted into common usage in 1879, when mixed-blood Cherokee and railroad attorney Elias C. Boudinot published an article in the *Chicago Times* describing lands in central Indian Territory that the federal government could—and, in his opinion, should—open to non-Indian settlement. The Unassigned Lands' boundaries, established through negotiations dating back to the Reconstruction Treaties of 1866, were with the Cherokee Outlet to the north, the Chickasaw Nation to the south, the Cheyenne and Arapaho Reservation to the west, and a hodgepodge of reservations to the east inhabited by the Potawatomi, Shawnee, Sac and Fox, Pawnee, and Iowa tribes.

Of all the Unassigned Lands' neighbors, none had a more convoluted history than the Cherokee Outlet, a seven-million-acre swath of grassland stretching from the Arkansas River in the east to No Man's Land in the west. Prior to the Civil War, the Cherokee Nation in northeastern Indian Territory was granted hunting rights to that vast domain, an arrangement that was not challenged until prospective homesteaders set their sights on its hardy grasses and fertile valleys. Then came the Reconstruction Treaties of 1866, which punished the Cherokees for their allegiance to the Confederacy by stripping away those rights. The eastern third of the Cherokee Outlet was redefined as surplus and set aside to accommodate smaller tribes that were losing their homelands to the relentless tide of westward migration. The rest was prized as some of the finest grazing land that the Great Plains had to offer, and it quickly became a theater of Gilded Age contention between railroad magnates, cattlemen, and homesteaders, all of whom had their own ideas about economic development.[36]

Geographically, the Unassigned Lands were crossed by five rivers: the Canadian, the North Canadian, the Cimarron, the Deep Fork, and the Little. The river valleys provided rich bottomland, while the uplands offered thinner topsoil ideal for grazing. Although there was plenty of timber along the rivers, the uplands varied from the nearly impenetrable undergrowth of the rolling Cross Timbers on the east to the flat plains and grasslands on the west. It was this transition zone from timber to prairie that convinced AT&SF engineers to lay north–south tracks through the Unassigned Lands in 1886.

The federal government's refusal to open the Unassigned Lands to non-Indian settlement on the pretext that the region was reserved for Native Americans and Blacks from the former Confederacy was the catalyst for the boomer movement, a protest campaign waged by prospective homesteaders in the southern plains and supportive politicians in Washington, D.C. From 1879 through 1888, the crusade coalesced around two charismatic leaders: David L. Payne, who died suddenly before his dream could be realized; and William Couch, who seized the mantle of leadership following Payne's death. Their highly publicized expeditions (dubbed incursions by their opponents) into Indian Territory became fodder for newspapers nationwide. These expeditions invariably led to arrests and cavalry escorts back to southern Kansas, northern Texas, or wherever the so-called boomers had started their journeys. By the late 1880s, public lands disputes in Indian Territory, and the boomer movement they spawned, had become a western arena of Gilded Age politics where powerful interests (the much-maligned trusts and monopolies) thwarted wannabe settlers at every turn.[37]

The vitriol between boomers and anti-boomers reached a crescendo in the late 1880s, and nowhere more so than in southwestern Kansas, where a trickle of southbound migration threatened to become a flood, leaving ghost towns and abandoned homesteads in its wake. In displays of partisanship that typified late nineteenth-century journalism, newspapers squared off in rhetorical fights to the finish. Some extolled the benefits of non-Indian settlement to the south, while others disparaged Indian Territory as a land utterly unfit for cultivation, let alone for prospective settlers' way of life.

As a businessman in Garden City whose glory days were fading, the former publisher of the *Terre Haute Daily Courier*, and an aspiring politician looking to reignite his career, Dick Morgan came down with a severe case of Oklahoma fever. One imagines him reading newspaper articles out loud to Orietta and maybe Porter, the pages flickering under the glare of a gas lamp, with mounting intensity, wondering how he might be of service to dispossessed farmers. He believed their only crime was to demand their rights under public lands laws and as

U.S. citizens whose constitutional rights were being trampled. And whatever the exact nature of his work for the AT&SF in Garden City, Morgan surely knew that a railroad attorney would have no shortage of opportunities in a territory set to explode.

By the spring of 1888, an unmistakable pall was settling over southwestern Kansas. "Over this short time period, almost all of the land in the county was claimed and the area started declining in activity in 1887-1888," explained David Morgan after two research trips to Garden City. The boomer movement went into overdrive after June 1887, when the AT&SF completed its line from Arkansas City, a frequent staging area for boomer raids—aimed at establishing permanent settlements in Indian Territory—about two hundred and sixty miles east of Garden City, through the Unassigned Lands to Walnut Creek (later, Purcell) at the northern boundary of the Chickasaw Nation. Businessmen more interested in railroads and town lots than homesteads were particularly interested in the two principal depots on the AT&SF line that would likely become thriving commercial centers.[38] They were Deer Creek (later, and hereafter, referred to as Guthrie) and Oklahoma Station (later, and hereafter, referred to as Oklahoma City).[39] David Morgan continued: "The Oklahoma movement was so drastic to Garden City, that on one day in 1889, over 300 members of the Christian Church gave notice that they were leaving for Oklahoma."[40]

But not everyone was susceptible to Oklahoma fever. In western Missouri, the *Butler Weekly Times* warned its readers of dire consequences for those foolish enough to buy into all the hype: "If it should prove true that the boasted Oklahoma country is not adapted to agricultural pursuits, and hence of no value as homes, the amount of suffering among those who have gone there will be terrible," ran one of several downbeat articles. "That there will be serious trouble is apprehended all over the country."[41] Kansas's troubles notwithstanding, the *Barber County Index*, one of many newspapers in the southwestern part of the state that discouraged immigration to the Oklahoma country, advised Kansans in January 1889 to stay put, particularly with spring coming on: "Oklahoma will not be opened this season in time for a crop; but Barber county is always open. Its rich and productive soil is even now waiting to be tickled by the industrious farmer. Now is the time to come and get a farm."[42]

While boomers were playing cat-and-mouse games with U.S. cavalry patrols and skirting around (and often through) Indian reservations, their spokesmen in Washington, D.C., were entering the endgame. On February 27, 1889, longtime boomer partisan and Illinois representative William M. Springer added a rider (section 13) to the annual Indian appropriation bill that authorized the president to proclaim the Unassigned Lands open to non-Indian settlement. Known as the Springer Amendment, the rider authorized settlement under the provisions of the Homestead Act of 1862, but with a warning to scofflaws: anyone who had put down roots in defiance of federal laws (dubbed "sooners" in the evolving frontier lexicon) was denied squatter's rights. They were to be expelled, and 1,887,796 acres heretofore off limits to homesteaders were to be opened in a land run. President Grover Cleveland signed the Indian Appropriation Act, as amended, on March 2, 1889, his second to last day in office.

"Three cheers for the champions of the Oklahoma bill, three cheers for the *Wichita Eagle* and a tiger for Caldwell!" was how Wichita's leading newspaper announced passage of the Indian Appropriation Act and its celebrated rider. Festivities in Caldwell and towns across southern Kansas began at daybreak and continued far into the night. Commerce ground to a halt as businessmen and farmers flocked into the streets to shake hands and congratulate one another on a successful campaign. Posters and banners quickly festooned the business districts.[43]

Two days after the president affixed his signature to the Indian Appropriation Act, America's peaceful transfer of power ended the Cleveland administration. His successor, former Republican U.S. senator Benjamin Harrison of Indiana, was immediately under pressure to declare a time and date for the opening. He followed through on March 23 with a proclamation setting the date for April 22. The president's proclamation contained a warning of dire consequences for entry prior to noon on the appointed day.[44]

Three weeks after President Cleveland signed the Indian Appropriation Act, Dick Morgan was in Washington, D.C., for high-level meetings pertaining to the opening. But his thoughts were never far from his family. Writing to his son on March 21, from the Ebbitt House at the corner of 14th and F Streets, Morgan regretted being away for so long. His concerns were twofold: first, Porter's recent sickness, which might have kept him out of school for a few days; and second, the health of the boy's horse, Charlie, whose fitness must have been in doubt. "Have you taken any rides?" asked Morgan as snow was falling and promptly melting to render the streets in Washington a slushy mess. "When I get home, it will soon be warm enough so that you and Mama and I can take lots of nice rides." He urged Porter to look after his mother and promised to return to Garden City soon. "Be a good boy," wrote Morgan in closing, "help mama all you can. I have been expecting letters from you, and should like to hear from you. Your papa, Dick T. Morgan."[45]

In a subsequent letter to Orietta and Porter, penned on U.S. Senate stationery at three o'clock in the morning and dated March 28, 1889, Morgan got down to business. His primary goal in traveling to Washington had been to meet with President Harrison, whose senatorial nomination he had endorsed in his speech before the Indiana General Assembly in January 1881. Morgan had high hopes for a presidential appointment in Indian Territory, if not as governor, then perhaps as attorney general, U.S. Attorney, or Supreme Court justice.

But the meeting was not to be.

"I went to White House this morning at 10 and waited until 12 but did not see Harrison," wrote a discouraged and probably sleep-deprived Dick Morgan. "Could not get a chance his time was occupied by others." Aiming to head back to Garden City the next day, Morgan wished his wife and son well and closed with his customary words of affection.[46] Had Morgan managed to visit the Oval Office, we can be sure that he would have congratulated his fellow Hoosier on his successful run for the presidency and thanked him for standing up for homesteaders in issuing his proclamation. We can be doubly sure that the two men would have reminisced about the good old days in Indiana.

It seems that a delay in Morgan's departure from Washington left time for him to receive a letter from Orietta—just what he needed to lift his spirits. "Your very welcome letter came to hand this morning," wrote Morgan in response. "I was very glad indeed to hear from you. I will start home tomorrow, and will probably reach home Tuesday p.m. I hope this will find you well, and that I will get home safe to you. I enjoyed your letter more than you can appreciate."[47]

Morgan's bid for high office was a non-starter and left him deeply disappointed by the presidential snub. He had better luck in scheduling meetings with Kansas senator Preston B. Plumb to discuss, among other things, the AT&SF. Whatever the substance of their discussion, Morgan was no doubt aware of the clout that Senator Plumb wielded with the railroad. Whereas Morgan had been representing the railroad since 1885, Plumb claimed a much deeper connection, as he had been named secretary of the fledgling railroad company at its organizational meeting in February 1859. Clearly, Morgan and Plumb had plenty to talk about as opening day approached.

Then it was back to Garden City to plan his expedition, now officially sanctioned, to the Unassigned Lands. Eager though he was to join the exodus, he must have felt a twinge of remorse over leaving a community where he had wielded considerable influence and made lots of friends. Gifted with what one newspaper deemed "a natural disposition to engage in political affairs," Morgan had immersed himself in Republican Party politics and earned sufficient respect as a lawyer and businessman to put him in the running for district judge in Kansas's twenty-sixth judicial district. None doubted that he would be missed. As noted in the newspaper's retrospective of Morgan's four years in Garden City, he was "a true friend, a liberal but unflinching partisan, who enjoys the unbounded respect of his most prominent political opponents, a tireless man of business and a Christian gentleman, he is by all numbered among the best of our citizens, enjoying the confidence and respect of all classes."[48]

Morgan had already given notice to his church that he was leaving. "Reluctant though he was to leave his church, Dick T. left Garden City on a high note," said David Morgan. "His law practice was thriving, his political aspirations were showing promise, and he doesn't seem to have been discouraged by setbacks. He had every reason to be optimistic about moving to the Oklahoma country."[49]

Morgan bade goodbye to his wife and son and was on his way to Arkansas City, or maybe had arrived there, by Monday, April 15, when the *Garden City Weekly Sentinel* published the First Christian Church's farewell message to its faithful congregant:

> Whereas, our dear brother and elder, Dick T. Morgan, is about to depart from our midst for another field of action. Therefore be it
>
> RESOLVED: That we as members of the First Christian Church of Garden City, Kansas, in congregation assembled, do hereby express to him our heartfelt gratitude for the faithful service he has rendered as our Elder.
>
> That we tender to him our sincere regrets at his departure, realizing that we are losing a faithful advocate of the cause of Christ.[50]

Morgan bought his ticket, likely at a discount. Then, in a melee that made headlines from coast to coast, he boarded a southbound train in Arkansas City on Monday, April 22, for a ride to another field of action in a place called Guthrie.

U.S. Land Office in Guthrie, Indian Territory, April 22, 1889.

COURTESY OF THE OKLAHOMA TERRITORIAL MUSEUM, GUTHRIE, OKLAHOMA

CHAPTER FOUR

A Big Boom

Never before, in the history of this country,
was there such an excitement,
such a universal desire to secure homes,
as was witnessed at the opening of Oklahoma.

MARION TUTTLE ROCK
Illustrated History of Oklahoma, 1890

IF DICK MORGAN PENNED AN ACCOUNT of his trip to Guthrie on April 22, 1889, it has not yet come to light. All we know is that he was one of about ten thousand people, more than two hundred of whom were lawyers, who turned a train depot and a few ramshackle buildings on the AT&SF line into a tent city over the course of an afternoon. Here's how David Morgan summed up his great-grandfather's trip from Garden City to his new field of action: "Dick arrived in Guthrie on April 22, 1889. He was 35 years old. He had left his family–wife and eight-year-old son–in Garden City, Kansas, where they had lived for 3½ years. He came to Guthrie on the train." That very day, he opened a law office, presumably in a tent.[1]

In the absence of Dick Morgan's story of his trip to Guthrie, we turn to Hamilton Wicks, a reporter for *Cosmopolitan* magazine who traveled from the East Coast to capture the scoop of a lifetime. Like everyone else infected with Oklahoma fever on that crisp spring day in southern Kansas, Wicks elbowed his way through a packed platform toward one of several trains, their engines hissing and steaming, with thick black smoke belching from their chimneys, only to find every car packed beyond capacity. "From the peace and reserve of a mere traveler I was at once hurled into the conflict for personal supremacy with a seething mass of 'boomers,'" wrote Wicks. "It was as though I had suddenly been interjected into a confused Fourth-of-July celebration, where the procession had resolved itself into a mob."[2]

For Wicks, it was time to get creative, so he bribed a brakeman to secure a seat in a caboose. His reportorial radar went on high alert when he sat down to find himself in the company of some real power brokers: Colonel D. B. Dyer, a future mayor of Guthrie; Judge John Guthrie ("large, pompous, and genial"), Guthrie's namesake; C. R. McLain who, within the next few hours, would become a co-founder with J. M. Ragsdale of the Commercial National Bank of Guthrie; and Jim Geary, a former scout with a reputation as a cool-headed marksman. If Morgan read Wicks's article in *Cosmopolitan*'s September 1889 issue, he probably agreed with the reporter's assessment of history in the making: "Civilization and barbarism seem here to come into immediate contact; industry and shiftlessness here stand face to face; order and lawlessness seem to glare at each other across the border."[3]

As the train chugged across the Kansas border and into the Cherokee Outlet, Wicks watched in awe as caravans wound their way toward the starting line at the Outlet's southern boundary. A typical party consisted of a prairie schooner crammed with farming implements, dogs, and chicken coops. At the reins was a man sporting a shaggy beard shouting commands to his mules or scrawny horses. Seated next to him was a disheveled woman whose children, no better off than their mother and clad in rags, sat behind their parents or peered out the rear of the wagon, wide-eyed and surely frightened as the wagon lurched onward. In what must have been a jarring juxtaposition, real estate agents and lawyers in carriages drawn by sleek, high-stepping horses jostled for position. Men and women on horseback, unencumbered by baggage or extra passengers, maneuvered for position at the starting line at the northern boundary of the Unassigned Lands.

Those with nothing but their feet to carry them forward kept up as best they could, smiling and waving like revelers on parade. "Everyone imagined that Eldorado was just ahead," wrote Wicks, "and I dare say the possibility of failure or disappointment did not enter into the consideration of a single individual on that cool and delightful April day."

Traffic slowed to a crawl at stream crossings and stopped altogether at the southern edge of the Cherokee Outlet some twenty-one miles north of the railroad depot at Guthrie. Boomer camps and livestock fanned out to the horizon, and soldiers struggled to keep the crowd from surging forward before the appointed hour. Before them lay 3,500 square miles: the Unassigned Lands, which expectant settlers knew as the Promised Land. Although the Unassigned Lands contained only 5 percent of what would become, eighteen years hence, the state of Oklahoma, its fertile soil and abundant resources exerted a powerful pull on the nation's last generation of pioneers.

The merriment that Wicks had observed was gone, replaced by an unyielding determination etched into every expectant face: "All was excitement and expectation. Every nerve was on tension and every muscle strained. The great event for which these brawny noblemen of the West have been waiting for years was on the point of transpiring."[4]

Then, at the stroke of noon, shots were fired and bugles were sounded, and three centuries of westward expansion ended in a roar that etched itself into American history as the Run of '89. A scant year and a half later, that storied event was commemorated in a book. *Illustrated History of Oklahoma*, written and dictated by participants, opens a window into the eighty-niner experience on Monday, April 22, 1889: "Never before, in the history of this country, was there such an excitement, such a universal desire to secure homes, as was witnessed at the opening of Oklahoma," wrote its author, Marion Tuttle Rock. Although images of eighty-niners on horses and driving wagons and buggies frame our understanding of this and subsequent land runs, those who rode into the Unassigned Lands in the relative comfort of a train had their own stories to tell. Morgan did not record that experience, but Rock did:

> The long railway trains, too, with ear-piercing shrieks from their engine whistles, joined in the race. From the windows of every coach came shouts of cheer and the waving of flags and handkerchiefs to those that were racing to the south on either side of the fast-flying trains. The ranks of the racers are diminishing on every side; they are seen to leap from their horses; a happy shout, a waving of their hat, the setting of a flag or stake. They have taken a homestead. Oklahoma was the home of the white man.[5]

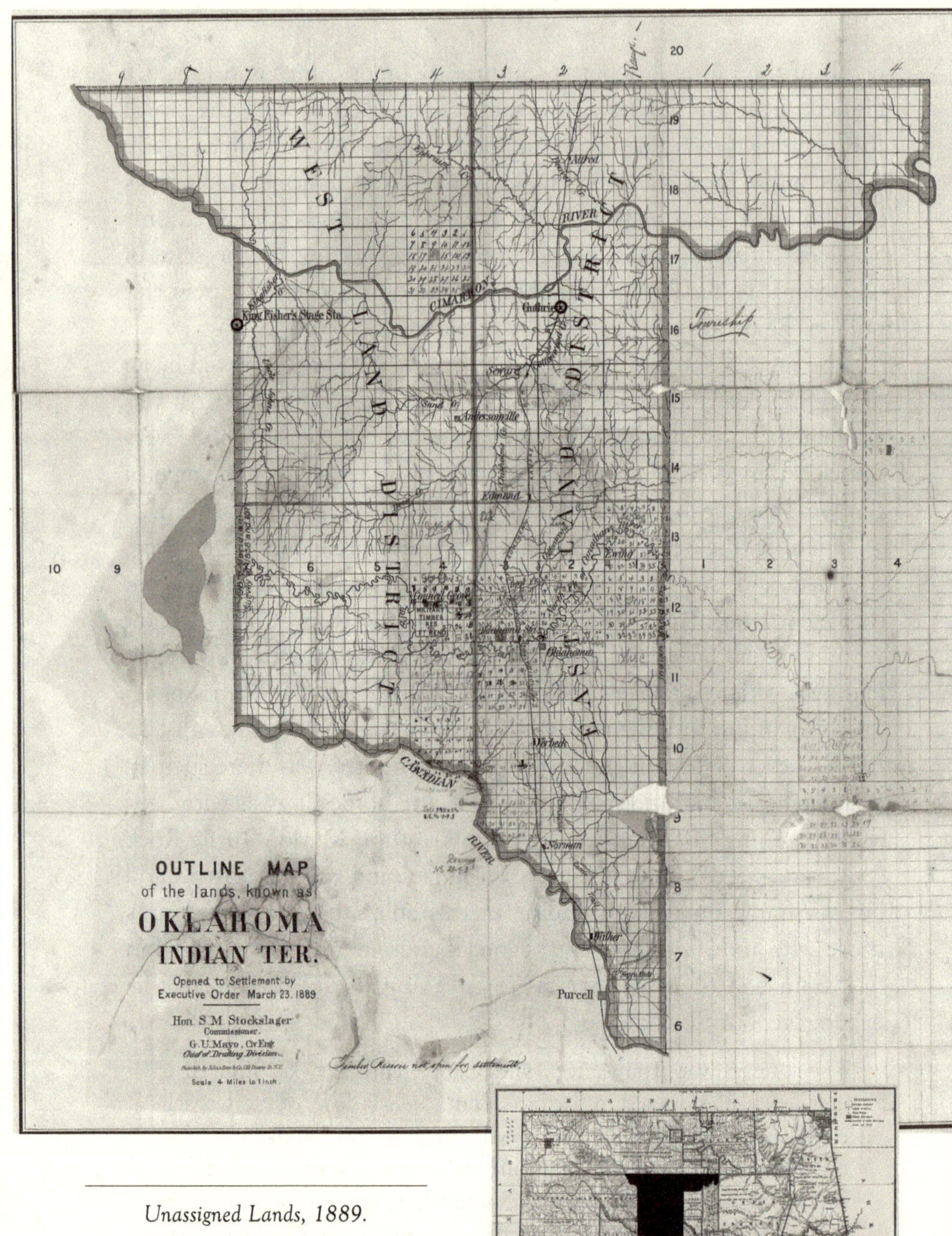

Unassigned Lands, 1889.

COURTESY OF THE OKLAHOMA HISTORICAL SOCIETY, OKLAHOMA CITY

A few blurry sepia-tinted photographs, taken through a veil of dust that seems to waft from the images, tell a story subject to multiple interpretations. Was the Run of '89 the final act in America's heroic expansion from sea to shining sea? Or was it a naked invasion into land once promised to Native Americans for as long as the grasses grew and the waters ran?

It seems safe to assume that contestants in Harrison's Horse Race weren't thinking about their place in history. They had more urgent things on their minds.

No sooner had the dust cleared than Dick Morgan hung out his shingle as a lawyer in a town that, unlike Rome, had been built in an afternoon during a big boom that was unprecedented in American, and probably world, history. To accommodate the population, which had exploded from a few railroad employees the morning of the run to ten thousand by nightfall, enterprising newcomers had laid out streets, staked off town lots, and made their first tentative steps toward formation of a municipal government.

Not for the first time and certainly not for the last, Morgan's decision on where to hang that shingle was all about location, location, location. "Morgan opened a law office directly across the street from the U.S. Land Office," explained David Morgan. "If you walked out the door of the U.S. Land Office, and went directly across the street, you would walk into his front door. He always located near the U.S. Land Office."

Knowing something about Dick T.'s modus operandi, I was not surprised when David began our walkabout in Guthrie at the block where his great-grandfather practiced law. Sure enough, directly across the street from his former office was signage indicating where the U.S. Land Office once drew a seemingly endless stream of homesteaders. That U.S. Land Office, a false-front frame building measuring eighteen by thirty feet, stood on a hill east of the depot. One imagines throngs of dust-caked settlers threading their way through a sea of tents to find the tiny structure and register their claims. The *Kansas City Gazette* captured the scene on April 23: "The crowd around the land office is too great to be numbered. Those who did not get in to file their claims that night slept where they were in the line to be on hand this morning." And all around those prospective settlers, saloons and gambling dens and houses of ill repute were popping up to brand the area as Hell's Half Acre, a designation that was replicated in Oklahoma City and other upstart towns throughout the territory.[6]

Jostling for advantage in those first frenzied days of settlement, Morgan had neither time nor inclination to write about his accommodations and day-to-day activities. We need to look elsewhere for a glimpse of what transpired in a U.S. Land Office and the types of services homesteaders and town lot claimants expected from their attorneys.

Fortunately, just such a record survives in the April 1909 edition of *Sturm's Oklahoma Magazine*. Published monthly in Oklahoma City from October 1906 until 1911 and boasting a circulation of ten thousand, this general-interest magazine covered everything from Native American history and harrowing reminiscences from early-day settlers to stylish homes and women's fashions, and it provided local authors with a forum to showcase both fiction and nonfiction.[7] One of those authors was James L. Brown, an attorney who arrived at Oklahoma City in April 1889 to provide the same services that Dick Morgan was offering in Guthrie.

At the outset, Brown reflected on Oklahoma's lawless beginnings and what attorneys and land registers were up against. Although U.S. Land Offices were open for business in Guthrie (self-designated in its newspapers as the Queen City of the Cimarron) and Kingfisher, about thirty miles west of Guthrie, on the day of the run, there were no courts and no practical means of collecting debts, imposing liens, recovering stolen property, and enforcing civil rights. The only possibility for redress for civil wrongs in the Unassigned Lands' burgeoning towns and cities came from ad hoc provisional governments, whose popularly elected representatives operated without legal authority. The equally ad hoc courts and the judgments they produced were ultimately "bare-faced nullities, and all judgements rendered by them void and incapable of being legally enforced."

On the day of the run and for many months afterward, there were far more homestead and town lot claimants than there were quarter sections and town lots to go around. Claimants, also known as entrymen, spent their days milling around the land office, hoping for a chance to file their claims or entries. Land office registers dealt with claimants on a first-come, first-served basis; in cases where there were several claimants, the one who got in front of the register first was usually awarded a homestead entry.

A dispute, commonly known as a contest, was basically a lawsuit, and it began with a trial in the local land office. Someone on the losing end of a homestead entry was required to file an affidavit that typically included at least one of four charges against an opposing entryman: (1) he had crossed the proclamation line before noon on April 22 (more on that later); (2) the first entryman had staked his claim before his adversary had made his homestead entry (commonly called a prior settlement case); (3) the first entryman had staked his claim for speculative purposes and was therefore subject to disqualification; or (4) the winning entryman had exhausted his homestead rights by making a prior claim. Congress eventually passed legislation to disqualify any entryman who already owned more than a quarter section of land and had transferred it to his wife or children in order to make a second entry.

The person bringing the lawsuit had to swear to the accuracy of his affidavit and find a disinterested person to corroborate his testimony. Once the affidavit was filed, a trial could begin. Contests were subject to appeal with the commissioner of the General Land Office in Washington, D.C. If an appeal did not settle the contest, an entryman could make another appeal to the secretary of the interior, and his decision was final.

Of all the insults that flew between contesting entrymen, none drew more ire than the ultimate insult of the day: *sooner*. But being accused of *soonerism* (an inelegant moniker, to be sure) was not automatic grounds for disqualification, as sooners and anti-sooners stood an equal chance of winning their claims. Those accused of soonerism often referred to the famously ambiguous wording in President Harrison's proclamation that provided a fig leaf to prospective settlers who entered the Unassigned Lands early, decided where they wanted to stake their claims, and returned to the starting line in plenty of time to make the run with the certainty of knowing where they were going.

"All the foregoing led to contention and disputes to such an extent that it was simply confusion confounded," wrote Brown as he wound toward his conclusion, "and opened wide the doors for men to swear at each other in the land office with a vengeance. Large numbers of men bound themselves together in groups to swear each other through; innocent men were sworn into the penitentiary or sworn out of their lands or lots." When the U.S. District Court in Wichita was designated to try cases in central Indian Territory, there was a mighty rush of criminal prosecutions, nearly all of which were based on perjury. On the upside, when the Cherokee Outlet was opened for settlement in September 1893, the meaning, force, and effect of the words "enter upon and occupy" were clarified to prevent early entries, and claimants were spared the litigation that snarled the legal system in the Unassigned Lands and, later, Oklahoma Territory, for generations.[8]

Dick Morgan caught a glimpse of his contentious future when three men were murdered just east of town. Word spread quickly that vigilantes were in hot pursuit. Meanwhile, a call went out for newly arrived immigrants to elect an arbitration committee to settle disputes, which were already reaching fever pitch. Six men, including Morgan, were promptly elected to what was dubbed, tongue-in-cheek, the Supreme Court of Oklahoma.[9] Barring future discoveries, whatever disputes they settled in those first few hours of chaos have been lost to history.

Morgan's reputation for level-headedness in mitigating conflicts had preceded his arrival in Guthrie. That reputation was confirmed when, shortly after his election to the arbitration committee, he encountered a gambler who had jumped (i.e., stolen) someone's lot. Omar K. Benedict, an onlooker who later became the *Tulsa Daily World*'s correspondent in Washington, D.C., captured the altercation between the gambler and the lot claimant, and Morgan's role in easing tensions, in an October 1917 homage to Morgan, a man whom he honored with the appellation "Oklahoma's Giant":

> The gambler led a bunch of hoodlums and bodily picked the poor man up and carried him off his lot, tore down his fence and when he started back for his lot he was met with a six-shooter in the hands of a desperate man. A call had been made for the soldiers. A mob formed. Dick T. Morgan climbed upon a stool and began talking with the crowd until the soldiers could arrive.

Watching an all-too-common conflict escalate, Benedict was struck by Morgan's "long, raven-black hair" and his equally dark goatee– "as fine a looking man as could be molded." Benedict was further impressed by Morgan's "soothing words of justice" whose effect was to calm everyone down until soldiers arrived. Once order was restored, Morgan led a group of onlookers to gather the gambler's possessions and throw him off the property. Cheers erupted when the aggrieved landowner was carried back to his lot. From that day forward, Morgan was recognized "as the leading lawyer in the territory," and his practice took off. A saloonkeeper chimed in with his own tribute to the teetotaling Morgan's character: "He doesn't mix much with our crowd, but he is sincere, and a conscientiously good man."[10]

DICK T. MORGAN,
Guthrie.

Morgan wasted no time in addressing the spiritual needs of his community. Across the street from his residential lot was the one staked by the Church Extension Board of the Christian Church. Within a week of the opening, Morgan tacked up a notice asking his fellow congregants from Garden City, some three hundred in number, to meet him at his lot on the morning of Sunday, May 5. "Two hundred Garden City people responded to the invitation," wrote David Morgan, "and they went across the street to the church lot and organized the First Christian Church of Guthrie."[11]

Morgan's church work was part of a building frenzy that has few parallels in American history. Guthrie was originally organized into

Dick T. Morgan in Guthrie, Oklahoma Territory, circa 1890. COURTESY OF MARION TUTTLE ROCK, ILLUSTRATED HISTORY OF OKLAHOMA (TOPEKA, KANS.: O. B. HAMILTON & SON, 1890), 265–66

four towns, and they coalesced to constitute the largest settlement in the Unassigned Lands. Two enterprises towered above all the rest: the AT&SF Railroad, with its connections to power brokers in Washington, D.C.; and the U.S. Land Office, whose political employees held Guthrie's future in their hands. Within a month of the opening, four thousand homes were under construction, a lighting system was in operation, and a contract was signed to begin construction of an urban railway system. Commercial development included five banks, fifteen hotels, and three music halls. Activity was just as frenzied at Oklahoma City. As Oklahoma City founder Angelo C. Scott put it, in the inaugural issue of the *Oklahoma Times* on May 9, "The record of these days is best told by the hammer and the saw."[12] Nevertheless, Guthrie's opinion leaders were convinced that fortune was on their side. With annoying conceit, aimed as much at Oklahoma City as their own readers, newspapers blared claims that Guthrie was "the future Capital and Metropolis of Oklahoma." Such was their confidence in Guthrie's destiny as a seat of government that, two days after the opening, they set aside a ten-acre plot and designated it as "Capitol Hill." The stage was set for a high-stakes battle between Guthrie and Oklahoma City that would dominate territorial politics for the next two and a half decades.[13]

While he was establishing a Christian Church, Morgan was also forming a law partnership with J. B. Kenner, a former colleague in the Indiana legislature.[14] Not surprisingly, the firm specialized in land disputes. Despite a steady stream of clients and fierce competition with other lawyers, Morgan was always thinking about his family, and he was counting the days until Porter finished his school term in Garden City so they could join him in Guthrie, assuming the raucous village would be settled enough to accommodate women and children. He often walked to the train station in hopes that Orietta and Porter would be waiting for him. When they were not, he would return home, disappointed and lonely. Writing on Kenner & Morgan letterhead to his wife and son on the last day of May, Morgan worried that Orietta might be short on cash: "I wondered the other day if you would not be out of money soon as you were making preparations to come down here. I enclose you $10.00 and you can doubtless get anything you want on credit—so you can hold back on your cash—if you are liable to run short." Morgan made tentative plans to return to Garden City within the next couple of weeks. In the meantime, he would wait anxiously for return correspondence. "I am always in hurry," wrote Morgan in closing. "Tell Porter I will expect his letter every day till I get it."[15]

Morgan was back at his desk on the night of Sunday, June 2, to report that he had risen early that morning, taken a bath, enjoyed a late breakfast, and gone to the Opera House Tent for a church service, only to find that he had arrived too late for Sunday school. Nevertheless, he enjoyed Reverend J. M. Monroe's sermon before returning to his office in the early afternoon. There, he met with George Tanner, a friend and perhaps client who lived with his wife ("quite young," and "a very pleasant woman") and next door to his father-in-law. Morgan enjoyed a midday meal in the Tanners' modest home (a "lean-to" board house with one room and a kitchen) consisting of roast beef, potatoes, butter, coffee, strawberries, and a cake and pie of unknown ingredients. After dinner and renewed discussion with his friend, Morgan walked across the Cottonwood River to West Guthrie to inspect two lots where he was helping establish a mission church. "Services were to be held at 4 o'clock," reported Morgan with his customary precision, "but few were there." On the way back to his office, he stopped off at the stable where his horse, Charlie, seemed to be getting along well despite an injured thigh.

After stopping at his office for what must have been a solitary meal, he visited lots in East Guthrie where he and his fellow congregants expected to build their principal church. Following a seven o'clock service featuring another sermon by Reverend Monroe (who arrived late!), Morgan went back to his office to compose his letter. He closed, as usual, by promising to visit Orietta and Porter soon and asking what they were up to back in Garden City: "Need now tell me what has my wife and boy been doing? I have thought of you many times to-day. I dreamed seeing you the other night. I hope you have had a pleasant day."

As a sort of postscript, he turned to business and urged Orietta not to be annoyed by a sheriff's visit that had something to do with a loan. "Sorry you were annoyed by that Sheriff," wrote Morgan, "but you need not give the matter any attention. We will not be hurt—if we want to pay off the interest. I will see to it when I come home."[16]

Sometime in May 1889, Morgan found time to join other leaders in Guthrie and its neighbors in the northern Unassigned Lands in summoning people to attend a convention, set to convene on July 17, to establish a provisional government. Four counties were proposed to facilitate the workings of territorial governance: Weaver County, with the county seat at Guthrie; Couch County, with the county seat at Oklahoma City; Springer County, with the county seat at Cooper; and Perkins County, with the county seat at Sells. The organizers further proposed that delegates to the convention elect an executive committee, a county judge, three commissioners for each county, and a congressional delegate. The provisional government was to remain in charge until Congress saw fit to pass legislation for territorial governance.

To put it mildly, settlers south of Guthrie (mainly Oklahoma City) were unimpressed. Convinced that Guthrie's gambit to brand itself as the capital of the territory was nothing more than an old-fashioned power grab, the acting mayors of several provisional towns summoned a counter-convention. They were to meet on July 15 in Frisco, a tiny outpost about fifteen miles northwest of Oklahoma City ("just a wide place in the road," according to Angelo Scott) on the north side of the Canadian River. Mayors and other officials answered the summons and took turns denouncing Guthrie's brazen ploy. As speakers attempted to outdo one another in condemning their northern neighbor's effrontery, Sidney Clarke rose to the podium. Clarke was a former congressman from Kansas, the boomer movement's most prominent spokesman, and, later, one of Oklahoma City's founding fathers. He read the convention's resolutions. He closed with a thundering testament to frontier democracy and a rebuke to Guthrie's plot to elevate its interests above all others and win congressional favor: "Believing, therefore, that the attempt to establish a so-called provisional government would be detrimental to the best interests of the people of Oklahoma, we not only declare our hostility to it, but we also give notice that we refuse to recognize any such government by every honorable means in our power."[17]

Guthrie's conventioneers gathered on July 17 with a consensus to ignore the goings-on in Frisco. As their perfunctory sessions drew to a close, their main accomplishment was agreeing to reconvene on August 20 so that committees would have time to prepare their reports. Perhaps feeling more emboldened, delegates reassembled on the appointed day at City Hall in East Guthrie, a prefab structure shipped from a grocery firm in Chicago with some assembly required. The stars and stripes rippled in the breeze to symbolize the freedom of speech that was on full display inside the bland edifice.

To cover the territorial convention for readers in Indiana, the *Indianapolis News* dispatched J. Will Piercy to report on what he deemed, perhaps hyperbolically, "one of the most unique and entertaining assemblages of the kind ever held on the American continent." Piercy's article was published, on September 7, 1889, under a heading that left no doubt as to why Hoosiers should pay attention to the power play in faraway Indian Territory: "An Indianan Booming in Oklahoma Territory. Other Hoosiers to the Front in the 'Woolly' West–The Wonderful Proceedings of the Constitutional Convention."[18]

The chaos of the Unassigned Lands' opening and the early days of non-Indian settlement had been front-page news nationwide for months, so Piercy's readers were not shocked to read about the region's absence of law and order and the violence that went with it. What might have piqued their interest was the spirit of equality that delegates, representing nearly every state in the Union, exhibited as they paraded into City Hall. Some, such as a boomer from "Mizzouree," clad in a checkered shirt and slouch hat, and a Texan sporting a sombrero and Colt revolver, clearly came from humble backgrounds. Others, most notably lawyers, were hoping to build their reputations and, maybe, have a shot at winning a seat in Congress.

Delegates were called to order, and invocations of divine guidance quickly gave way to what Piercy described as a cacophony of oratory: "Everybody was inflamed with an intense desire to be heard. There were chances that a good speech would lead to prominence and to–office. Such an opportunity therefore could not be passed by." No sooner did one delegate rise to address points of order than another seized the floor. "Ambitious members drove at every question with awful recklessness and sat down but to rise again," wrote Piercy. "Their seats apparently had springs." Accusations flew that everyone—except, of course, whoever had the floor—was "laboring under misapprehensions" about whatever topic had been raised. The nattily dressed chairman, "clearly chosen for his appearance rather than familiarity with parliamentary rules," was verbally battered "like a straw in a storm" and utterly incapable of maintaining order.

Piercy gave far more credit to another delegate whose roots, not surprisingly, were in Indiana: Horace Speed, an attorney who had worked in Benjamin Harrison's law firm in Indianapolis before moving to Winfield, Kansas, and then to Guthrie, where he set up a law practice.[19]

"On two occasions the convention came near breaking up in a row, and it was only through the diplomacy of a former Indianapolitan, Horace Speed, that the outcome was averted." Such was Speed's popularity that many people and organizations, including the influential *Guthrie Daily News*, were booming him for territorial governor. As Piercy noted, with a nod to scripture, Speed "was the Moses that led the convention out of the intricate maze of legal and parliamentary questions."[20]

Another Hoosier in attendance was W. J. Ladd, chairman of the committee on stock and stock raising and a self-described "cattleman from the Wabash." With a touch of self-deprecation, he deferred to Indianans Daniel W. Voorhees and Dick Thompson—Dick T. Morgan's namesake—as far more rousing orators than he. Sporting a pompadour hairstyle and a wild-eyed mien, Ladd "bubbled over with good humor," claiming that he had been too busy chasing Texas steers out of his cornfield with a shotgun to prepare a proper report for his committee. His request for an extension to finish his committee report was duly granted. Other expatriate Indianans included D. M. Stocksinger of New Albany, who had been elected as mayor of East Guthrie; and Dick T. Morgan of Terre Haute, who "had many well-founded ideas of much value to the convention."[21]

Topics ran the gamut from constitutional law, banking, and finance to a topic that must have swept Morgan into the fray: women's suffrage. Someone shouted that the word "male" should be stricken from the franchise provision of the U.S. Constitution. Somehow, when it seemed the din could not get any louder, W. J. Ladd gained the floor. "Oh woman!" he bellowed, "beautiful, angelic creature! I would build you a monument to the skies. I would wreath about your lovely form a vine of gold and silver to the blue vaulted starry heavens, yea, yes! I..."

The rest of Ladd's paean to womanhood was lost in a burst of merriment, and Ladd surrendered the floor to Reverend Monroe of the Christian Church of Guthrie, which he and Morgan had co-founded less than two weeks after the opening. "But the refractory delegates refused to show [Monroe] the respect due the clergy," continued Piercy. When Reverend Monroe interpreted a comment from Mayor Stocksinger as an assault on the Women's Christian Temperance Union, "he lost his clerical dignity" and unleashed a torrent of unclerical insults. Bedlam reigned as a delegate named Terrell seized the gavel and "pounded the table to splinters." When that failed to restore order, he commanded the sergeant-at-arms to toss three delegates (unnamed in Piercy's account) out the door.

"It was an unfortunate move," declared Piercy with a flair for understatement. "A fight ensued in the doorway. Pistols were drawn and bloodshed was imminent. The reporters crawled under a table and the crowd, now panic-stricken, went pell-mell out the windows and all possible exits."

Eventually, cooler heads prevailed, and delegates reconvened that evening. Efforts to focus on drafting a constitution went by the wayside when women's suffrage came up. Recriminations flew; one delegate compared that vexing issue to the Missouri Compromise to illustrate what happens when vital issues are ignored or postponed. A big boomer from Texas challenged the "petticoat men" in the crowd to step outside and duke it out. A fistfight was averted when delegates voted to submit the question of women's suffrage to a popular vote and resume their deliberations on a constitution.[22]

Against all odds, the delegates drafted a constitution and scheduled it for a vote on October 22, six months to the day after the opening of the Unassigned Lands. Although military officers assured delegates that soldiers backed by the full force of the federal government would be on hand to quell disturbances, none doubted that trouble was imminent. One thing was certain: delegates could count on resistance from Oklahoma City and its confederates.

On September 10, a self-proclaimed territorial central committee assembled at Frisco to encourage participation in Guthrie's election for the express purpose of voting down the constitution. Far better to wait for Congress to do its job than bow to the dictates of power brokers in Guthrie. The meeting in Frisco adjourned on a high note, as a congressional delegation was expected to arrive in the Unassigned Lands a few days later to assess settlers' needs. Perhaps seeing with their own eyes what six months of anarchy had wrought would accomplish what an endless stream of telegrams and letters to Washington, D.C., had not: convince Congress to stop its dithering and establish territorial governance in the Unassigned Lands.[23]

With hopes fading for a successful vote on the constitution, Guthrie's dignitaries prepared to roll out the red carpet for the congressional delegation, whose mission was to assess the Unassigned Lands' eligibility for territorial status. Optimism ran high that the congressmen, slated to arrive in Guthrie on the AT&SF in mid-September, would return to Washington with a favorable impression of what settlers had accomplished since the opening. Dipping into his mythological repertoire, a reporter for the *Oklahoma City Daily Times* likened the congressmen to Aladdin and his magic lamp in their ability to raise cities from the desolate plains and lighten the hearts of grateful citizens.[24]

Dick Morgan was surely there to greet them when they stepped off the train. Included in the delegation were William M. Springer of Illinois, whose popularity had soared since he had slipped his famed rider into the Indian appropriation bill in the final hours of the Cleveland administration. It also included Charles H. Mansur of Missouri, Samuel R. Peters and Bishop W. Perkins of Kansas, Charles S. Baker of New York, and John M. Allen of Mississippi. After the requisite speechmaking and gladhanding and a tour of the "Queen

City of the Cimarron," the congressmen were feted at a reception in the ballroom of the aptly named Hotel Springer.

For a few hours on that memorable evening, ladies and gentlemen clad in fashionable attire might as well have been dancing the night away beneath a New York or San Francisco skyline. It is safe to assume that Dick and Orietta Morgan were among the revelers, if not swaying to the orchestra and sipping fine wine, then surely reminiscing about equally grand soirees in Terre Haute and Indianapolis. Duly impressed, the congressmen sped off toward Oklahoma City the next morning trailing promises that the legislation so sorely needed, and so long delayed, was right around the corner.[25]

As it turned out, right around the corner meant another seven months of contentious provisional governance and, in the absence of civil authority, military rule. In the meantime, Guthrie's leading citizens poured their energies into building a viable community, all the while keeping a close eye on their prospects for public office.

In April 1890, Dick Morgan was back in Washington, D.C., where he was helping influence legislation for territorial governance. His hopes to revive his political career took a severe hit when fellow Hoosier President Benjamin Harrison declined to appoint him as territorial governor. Although Morgan's youth (thirty-six years old) and lack of military experience likely counted against him, the *Blackwell Times-Record* published an account of his meeting with the president that seems to settle the matter.

"Were you present at the opening?" asked President Harrison.

"I was," replied Morgan.

"Then it will not be policy to appoint you as the first governor."

Crestfallen at having come "within an ace" of being appointed the territory's first governor, Morgan left the president's office. It seemed that the president preferred to appoint an outsider to the top job rather than entrust it to a man, no matter how qualified, who had been in the thick of frontier lawlessness since the opening.[26]

A glimpse into Morgan's routine in Washington survives in a letter to Orietta and Porter dated April 13, 1890. Writing on a

Sunday evening, Morgan reported that he had arisen at eight o'clock and enjoyed a ten-cent breakfast of coffee and a ham sandwich. He then attended Sunday school and a worship service at a Christian Church, where he declined an invitation to speak. "They invited me to speak—but I was modest—and excused myself." Contrary to his custom since arriving in the nation's capital, he skipped Sabbath School that afternoon. After a twenty-five-cent dinner consisting of boiled eggs, bread and butter, an apple, an orange, and water, he conversed with an acquaintance before retiring to his room to catch up on his correspondence.

Although Morgan was clearly disappointed that the president had turned down his bid for governor, he had assurances that he remained eligible for other appointments. "My friends here tell me Harrison will do something for me, and that I should not go away," he wrote to Orietta and Porter. "This may be little comfort to you and yet my dear wife you must look at this thing in a business way and I know you will." In a particularly poignant closing, he reminded his wife that his heart was always with her, regardless of the number of miles that separated them and what setbacks he might suffer:

> For myself, I can get along any way—but I desire above all other things on earth to provide well for my dear Ode and Porter—to be able to give you an easier time—and more enjoyment of life, and what I can do for this I shall do. While I am away from you I think much of you, and about how good you are and what a treasure a man has who has a good, true loving wife and how great a pleasure it should be for a man to do all in his power to repay this goodness, love and faithfulness. So I resolve to try harder in the future to please my good wife—whether I succeed or not in securing the appointments I seek.[27]

Less than three weeks after Morgan penned his heartfelt letter to his wife and son, President Harrison brought Oklahoma Territory into existence by signing the Organic Act of May 2, 1890. The legislation had been anticipated for weeks, but it came too late for the people who had organized Guthrie's anniversary bash to commemorate the Run of '89. Their celebration on April 22, complete with a floral arrangement presented by the loveliest corps of flower girls they could muster, came off as planned, but it would have been more festive if the president and Congress had seen fit to lift the Unassigned Lands out of limbo. In hopes that territorial status would be granted in time for the anniversary, a messenger had been dispatched on horseback to the Santa Fe Depot to receive the news and relay it to the partiers. But the message never came, leaving the good people of Guthrie to enjoy their celebration and wonder when, if ever, they could finally claim territorial status.[28]

The Organic Act spelled out the protocols for territorial governance as a prerequisite to statehood, and they followed the model of state formation dating back to the Confederation Congress in 1784 and 1785 and the Northwest Ordinance of 1787. Those protocols predated the U.S. Constitution, and they guaranteed that the federal government's expansion into the Unassigned Lands would be democratic in character.[29] After thirteen months of self-government and, when all else failed, military interventions, residents could finally enjoy the rights, privileges, and responsibilities afforded by U.S. laws. The Unassigned Lands' dalliance with frontier democracy and its corollary in provisional governments was coming to an end.

News that President Harrison and Congress had done their duty reached Guthrie about seven o'clock in the evening of May 2. Within an hour, the town was ablaze with bonfires. Pistol shots rang out across the prairie as partiers paraded through town, firing their weapons and cheering their hearts out. As noted in the Washington, D.C., *Evening Star*, "Dispatches from other points in the new territory state that the news was received with great rejoicing."[30]

Under the auspices of the Organic Act, President Harrison announced his slate of territorial officials. To serve as territorial governor, he chose George W. Steele, a four-term congressman from Indiana who had retired from public service (temporarily, as it turned out) the previous March. As noted in the *Indianapolis Journal*, Steele was "familiarly known in army circles, is popular and has the natural ability and experience to make a most excellent governor." Fifty-one years old at the time of his appointment, Steele had served in the Eighth Indiana Infantry and had been appointed as first lieutenant of the U.S.

Infantry. His military service took him to the battles of Chattanooga and Missionary Ridge, and he rode alongside Major General William T. Sherman in his scorched-earth blitzkrieg from Savannah to Atlanta.

Steele was discharged with the rank of lieutenant colonel in July 1865. After a brief and disappointing flirtation with the grocery business in Kansas City, he enlisted once again in the Army, this time to serve frontier settlements in wars against the Indians. After his second discharge, he ran successfully for the U.S. House of Representatives from his home state of Indiana and remained in office from 1881 to 1889.[31]

Steele's service on the southwestern frontier gave him a preview of his future in Oklahoma Territory, where experience in Indian affairs and public land controversies would rank high on anyone's résumé. Although Steele had not been considered as a candidate for governor, he accepted Harrison's appointment with support from civilian as well as military officials.[32] Others on Harrison's roster of territorial appointments, deemed by the *Indianapolis Journal* to be "men of most excellent character and a high grade of ability," included Robert Martin of El Reno as secretary; Warren Lurty of West Virginia as U.S. marshal; Edward B. Green of Illinois as chief justice of the supreme court; and Abraham J. Seay of Missouri and John F. Clark of Wisconsin as associate justices. The three judges did double duty as district judges. Horace Speed, recently considered a shoo-in for territorial governor, was named as U.S. district attorney. Republicans in Oklahoma Territory were less enthusiastic than the *Indianapolis Journal* about the appointments, as they believed there were plenty of worthy candidates in the territory and derided outsiders from the States as carpetbaggers.[33]

Like so many presidential appointees and government officials, most men selected for service in Oklahoma Territory had served in the Union Army during the Civil War. Military experience was not necessarily a requirement, but it certainly enhanced a candidate's chances for a federal post, as every president but one, from Grant to McKinley, had been a soldier. The only exception was Grover Cleveland, who had hired a substitute to do his fighting during the Civil War. Steele, Martin, and all three members of Oklahoma

Territory's supreme court shared a common pedigree as soldiers.[34]

To accommodate territorial growth, the Organic Act provided that all reservations in western Indian Territory would automatically come into Oklahoma Territory under the terms of settlement. Indian Territory to the east remained a hodgepodge of federal and tribal authority until 1907, when it joined Oklahoma Territory to become the state of Oklahoma. Far to the southwest, Old Greer County was technically included within Oklahoma Territory's boundaries but was specifically exempted from homestead law or further settlement until the Red River boundary dispute with Texas could be settled. Future controversy was assured when the territorial capital was located temporarily in Guthrie. Six county seats in counties designated by number were established at Guthrie (County 1), Oklahoma City (County 2), Norman (County 3), El Reno (County 4), Kingfisher (County 5), and Stillwater (County 6).[35]

The same act of Congress that opened the Unassigned Lands to non-Indian settlers authorized the president to appoint commissioners to negotiate with western tribes to open their surplus lands for settlement. Known as the Jerome Commission for its chairman, former Michigan governor David H. Jerome, the group included Warren G. Sayre of Indiana and Alfred M. Wilson of Arkansas. Over a period of five years, the commission negotiated with tribal leaders to allot acreage to each man, woman, and child on official tribal rolls. The federal government did its part by purchasing the tribes' surplus land–that is, land left over after allotments had been assigned–and opening it to homesteading through land runs and lotteries. In the ensuing years, tribal land in central and western Indian Territory dwindled and, in some cases, disappeared altogether under an inexorable tide of homesteading and urbanization.[36]

In addition to the six counties carved out of the Unassigned Lands, there was a strip of land far to the northwest whose residents took (and continue to take!) a perverse pride in the fact that nobody wanted it. Known generally as No Man's Land and officially as the "Neutral Strip" or "Public Land Strip," the swath of prairie came into Oklahoma Territory as part of the Organic Act. Originally designated as County 7, with its county seat at Beaver, No Man's Land's borders took shape as the United States defined its boundaries. Unintentionally, the U.S. government allowed that area to fall outside the jurisdiction of any territory, state, Indian reservation, or protectorate. Eventually, what came to be known as the Oklahoma Panhandle was divided into three counties, from west to east: Cimarron, with its county seat at Boise City; Texas, with its county seat at Guymon; and Beaver, with its county seat at Beaver.

Predictably, law and order were hard to come by in No Man's Land. Cattlemen let their herds graze where they pleased, and outlaws plied their trade with impunity, leaving old pioneers (those who settled in No Man's Land before 1890) to quip that the land was owned by "no man, only God." Ownership had become more confusing than ever when Kansas newspapers in the 1880s blared the news that No Man's Land was open to homesteading. Between 1885 and 1888, the population swelled from fewer than 2,000 to as many as 14,000. But in the absence of a U.S. Land Office in which to file homestead claims and a discouraging mix of droughts and dust and blizzards to dishearten all but the hardiest settlers, the population dwindled to fewer than 3,000 by 1890.[37] Its inhospitable climate and dearth of people notwithstanding, No Man's Land was swept into Oklahoma Territory with the stroke of a pen, leaving its citizens with a considerable commute to visit their fellow Oklahomans to the southeast—or, as they like to call them, "downstaters."

In August 1890, voters throughout Oklahoma Territory were invited to participate in a name-that-county contest. They responded with Kingfisher, Logan, Payne, Canadian, Oklahoma, and Cleveland Counties in the former Unassigned Lands and Beaver County in No Man's Land.[38]

For the time being, Oklahoma Territory's formation was complete. And, as Dick Morgan had discovered, the opportunities it afforded a young man with ambition and a yen for public service were practically endless.

CHAPTER FIVE

Building a Reputation

> The above firm will give careful attention to all business placed in their care, and give special attention to business before the United States Land Office.
>
> ADVERTISEMENT FOR MORGAN & PANCOAST, LAWYERS AND LAND ATTORNEYS
> *Perry Daily Times*, NOVEMBER 21, 1893

BY THE TIME PRESIDENT HARRISON got around to signing the Organic Act in May 1890, Guthrie was already a thriving city destined to end the year with eleven schools, three daily newspapers, and five weeklies. According to the census of 1890, its population of 5,333 compared favorably to Oklahoma City's count of 4,151 souls.[1] Although estimates vary, we can be sure that a disproportionate number of the inhabitants (perhaps more than two hundred) were lawyers, and they had all the work they could handle. "It is estimated that as much as one-half of the land was in title disputes of one kind or another," explained David Morgan. "The homestead laws were confusing, surveys were poorly marked, and of course, they had to deal with the 'sooners' who had entered the territory prematurely and made claims that were later challenged."[2]

Legal imbroglios that flared during Guthrie's early days were no impediment to the cosmopolitan culture that began to take root in the first days of non-Indian settlement. Residents were not interested in becoming just another frontier village. They wanted a civilized metropolis whose commercial activity, architecture, and cultural refinements would rival whatever cities "back in the States" had to offer. Their city was to be "progressive"—a description that everybody understood as "eastern"—and they wasted no time in making it

happen. In May 1889, residents took time from their building frenzy to organize a chapter of the Knights of Pythias and establish a Masonic Lodge, and the Young Men's Christian Association (YMCA) set up shop and began to hold meetings. A chamber of commerce sprang into being on July 20.

By then, women had begun to arrive in Guthrie to meet their husbands, and they brought with them urban refinements that had been sorely missing in a mostly male community. With less time to spend in saloons, gambling dens, and brothels and more time to spend at home, most (if not all) men came to appreciate the settling effect that their wives had on their upstart town.

Whatever their socioeconomic status, everyone knew that their success as a community depended on cooperation. Class distinctions meant little when everyone was facing the same challenges, from the whims of Mother Nature and food shortages to what later generations would call supply chain disruptions.

Street scene in Guthrie, Indian Territory, May 23, 1889. Morgan's office is the second door to the left of the two-story Merchant's Bank building.
COURTESY OF THE OKLAHOMA HISTORICAL SOCIETY, OKLAHOMA CITY

Simply put, there was neither time nor interest in drawing social distinctions that got in the way of building a city. Within six months of the opening, the ladies responsible for entertaining the congressmen during their September visit, to assess the Unassigned Lands' progress, had set up a variety of clubs and organizations: Calumet, a women's social and literary club; the Ladies' Social and Literary Society; the Northside and Pioneer Euchre Clubs; and the Guthrie Whistler Club. Among the most popular additions to Guthrie's social scene was the Arion Dancing Club. Although plenty of ladies and gentlemen flocked to dances, we can be fairly sure that Dick and Orietta Morgan, long since schooled in the improprieties of close contact, declined to attend. But they probably were in the audience when touring theatrical and musical groups made their stops at the McKennon Opera House. They were regulars at worship services and Sunday school meetings at the First Christian Church that Morgan had helped found, one of ten churches listed in the August 1889 city directory.[3]

Guthrie's political prestige skyrocketed with the Organic Act's guarantee that it would be the capital, albeit temporarily, of Oklahoma Territory. As the location of one of the territory's two U.S. Land Offices (the other was located at Kingfisher) and offices of the AT&SF, whose higher-ups were among the city's most ardent boosters, Guthrie was the natural pick for the capital. Funding to set the gears of governance in motion came with a congressional appropriation of $140,000. On May 14, Congress passed an act to incorporate the four towns that constituted Guthrie at the time of the opening into a single town sprawling across 1,280 acres. Oklahoma City, by contrast, remained on the map as a cluster of 320-acre townsites, and it still lacked a U.S. Land Office.[4]

George W. Steele, the man President Harrison had assigned to govern the brand-new territory and whose appointment Dick Morgan likely supported, arrived at his post on May 22 to an enthusiastic welcome. "I am determined as far as in my power to make my coming here both lucky to myself and lucky and useful to the people of Oklahoma," declared the governor as he and his wife and children gazed at the multitudes gathered below the station platform. That evening, Guthrie honored the First Family of Oklahoma Territory with what the *Guthrie Daily News* described as "the most brilliant reception ever given in Oklahoma."

"Governor Steele is a man of remarkable energy of character, and distinguished for sound and practical judgment," continued the *Guthrie Daily News* about the lawyer, former soldier in the Indiana infantry, and four-term congressman from Indiana. "His character and reputation in the civil walks of life, whether as a private citizen or in public position as the choice of the people, or as an army officer, defending the flag of the nation, shows him to be a gentleman of undoubted ability, firm and honest in his opinions, and unimpeachable integrity. He is an uncompromising republican, devoted to his friends, loyal to his party, and fair, courteous and generous to his opponents."

Although Morgan left no record of his presence at the Steeles' arrival at the depot and the reception that followed, we can be sure that he, Orietta, and Porter were among the well-wishers from all parts of the territory who partook in the grand occasion. A few days later, Steele toured the territory, and wherever he went, he was greeted by joyous throngs. But there was much to be done, and as the touring and gladhanding gave way to official business, Steele ordered a census. Completed in June 1890, the census put Oklahoma Territory's population at 60,000 souls. Logan County boasted the largest population with 14,254; at the other end of the scale was Beaver County, which contained the entire Panhandle, with a population of 2,982.[5]

Governor Steele's loyalty to Guthrie, and Guthrie's loyalty to Governor Steele, endured its trial by fire when the first territorial assembly convened at the McKennon Opera House on August 27, 1890. Practically before they took their seats, delegates squared off on locating a territorial capital, a decision that would have far-reaching repercussions when it came time for admission to the Union as a state. At issue was Section 15 of the Organic Act:

> That the legislative assembly of the territory of Oklahoma shall hold its first Session at Guthrie, in said territory at such time as

> the governor shall appoint and direct, and at said first session or as such thereafter as they shall deem expedient the governor and the legislative assembly shall proceed to locate and establish the seat of government for said territory at place as they may deem eligible, which place however shall thereafter be subject to be changed by the said governor and legislative assembly.6

James L. Brown, a representative from Oklahoma City whose nickname, "Lot Jumpin' Jim," did not bode well for amicable relations with his fellow delegates, threw down the gauntlet with Council Bill No. 7. Not only did his bill propose moving the capital to Oklahoma City; it set a deadline of February 1891 to complete the move. Not to be outdone, Kingfisher entered the fray with its bid to become the capital. Although several other communities entered the sweepstakes, none rivaled Oklahoma City. The stage was set for a high-stakes showdown between Guthrie and Oklahoma City.

Council Bill No. 7 was known alternately as "the capital bill" and "the Daniels bill" after Speaker Arthur N. Daniels from Frisco, who was nicknamed derisively (and somewhat opaquely) the "Sockless Statesman of the Canadian." Other than making plans for an election on November 4 to select a territorial delegate to Congress, the territorial assembly's routine business ground to a halt. Under intense pressure from railroad officials determined to keep the capital in Guthrie, Governor Steele had a genuine crisis on his hands that threatened to send Oklahoma Territory back to a state of chaos.[7]

Perhaps inevitably, Governor Steele's close ties to the railroad led to cries of corruption. Such was the anger toward Steele for his favoritism toward Guthrie and cozy relations with the railroad that irate residents in rival cities burned his effigy. Accusations gained traction that $32,500 had been used to buy votes to keep the capital where it was. Those with a conspiratorial bent accused Steele of plotting a trip to Washington, D.C., where, as a former representative from Indiana, he could leverage his influence to prevent Oklahoma City from obtaining the capital.[8] Things took a nasty turn when Guthrie partisans besieged Speaker Daniels in front of the Palace Hotel. Suspected of trying, somehow, to steal the capital from Guthrie, Oklahoma City representative Dan Peery made a mad dash from the opera house to a nearby butcher shop, where he hid behind an ice box and waited for his pursuers to rush by.[9]

There is no reason to believe that Morgan was implicated in improper relations with the railroad or that he was active in the capital location issue. Nor do we know much about Morgan's relationship with his fellow Hoosier Governor Steele, who had received the gubernatorial appointment that Morgan had sought. Morgan's position on the capital location was most likely influenced by his role as an attorney and businessman with deepening ties to Guthrie, a town dominated by Republicans. He had a vested interest in preserving the town's capital status as a surefire catalyst for economic development. Morgan was destined to change his position twenty years later when, as a congressman representing Oklahoma County, he would advocate moving the capital from Guthrie to Oklahoma City.[10]

Guthrie held its collective breath while Governor Steele weighed his options. Finally, in a speech that echoed across the territory, he explained the deficiencies in the Daniels bill and closed with the message that the people of Guthrie had been waiting for: "In consequence of all which I must return Council Bill No. 7 without my approval."

The *Guthrie Daily News* dipped into its mythological repertoire to capture the spirit of a community gone wild:

> Guthrie from her birth has been a city of surprises. Like the mystic temple of Valhalla, she sprung in a single day a magic metropolis, a seething, swarming city of the first class. Many a time have her citizens turned out to celebrate a victory. Many a time have the cannon, bell, gun, pistol, firecracker and the voice of man made the air tremble with their overwhelming noise. But the title of her townsite, the passage of the territorial bill in the halls of congress, the president's naming her the temporary seat of government—this, these all paled before the tumultuous outburst of rejoicing that, like a hurricane, swept and swayed the city from center to circumference. The tempest started in the middle of the afternoon and strengthened and accumulated until at night it boomed like a mighty ocean lashed by the waring [*sic*] winds of every quarter.

Within minutes of Governor Steele's refusal to sign Council Bill No. 7, a rapturous horde, one thousand strong and stretching for half a mile, marched east on Harrison Avenue toward Steele's home. Upon reaching their destination, the parade did not stop, but marched around and around the house. "Cheer after cheer went up, hurrah after hurrah," blared the *Guthrie Daily News*. "One thousand mouths were yelling at the same time, one thousand hands were lifted up, one thousand hats were thrown into the air, their owners careless where they went." At the windows were Mrs. Steele and the Steeles' daughter, Meta, smiling as the citizens of Guthrie expressed their delight in the governor's decision.

Eventually, Governor Steele appeared in the stairway. At his side was E. P. McCabe, Guthrie's most illustrious Black settler, who would spend the 1890s enticing Blacks to migrate to Oklahoma Territory and, perhaps, attend the university he founded in the all-Black community of Langston. Urging the crowd to settle down, McCabe stepped forward with hands uplifted and presented the governor as "the savior of your fireside." McCabe, a one-time candidate for territorial governor, maintained a law office a few doors south of Morgan's office on Second Street. His promotion of Black immigration to the territory, role in establishing all-Black towns, and founding of Langston University were later commemorated in a plaque that stands to this day near his former office.

Governor Steele then addressed the crowd, taking care to remind everyone that Guthrie's good fortune came at the expense of its neighbors. "You must remember that Guthrie is not all of Oklahoma," intoned the governor. "If you do as I will you will work for the good of the whole territory. I would not change this thought but hope that you will work to the end that general good will result to the entire territory."

Meanwhile, in another part of town, an equally exuberant crowd was stoking a celebration that lasted far into the night. With bonfires blazing, the cry went up, "Three cheers and a tiger for Guthrie! Hip hip, hurrah! Hip hip, hurrah! Hip hip, hurrah!"[11]

As stipulated in the Organic Act, Indian reservations near and mainly west of the former Unassigned Lands opened by presidential proclamations to non-Indian settlement would become part of Oklahoma Territory. Even as the residents of Guthrie kept up their frenzied pace of building, their status as a capital city made them keenly interested in subsequent land runs and allotments. The next (the first since the run of '89) came on September 22, 1891, when prospective homesteaders thundered into 1,120,000 acres recently purchased from the Iowa, Sac and Fox, Pottawatomie, and Shawnee tribes. Another land run (the second since the run of '89) on April 19, 1892, turned into the biggest one yet when 4,300,000 acres occupied by the Cheyenne and Arapaho tribes were thrown open to homesteading and townsite development.[12]

The explosion of homesteading and townsite development was tailor-made for Dick T. Morgan. "He became an expert on homestead law," explained David Morgan, whose research led him to brand his great-grandfather as the busiest lawyer in the territory. But herein lay a contradiction that would complicate his political aspirations for years to come. As an attorney and businessman with an unwavering loyalty to the Republican Party, he had a vested interest in the railroad. Whatever his relationship with the company's higher-ups, we can be sure that he was just as relieved as they were when Governor Steele vetoed the Daniels bill and thereby thwarted Oklahoma City's ambition to seize the capital.

Morgan's move from Terre Haute to Garden City and then Guthrie coincided with an agrarian revolt fueled by resentment toward the Republican Party for its ties to Eastern capital in general and price-gouging railroad companies in particular. That revolt crystallized in the short-lived Populist Party, whose supporters included the very people Morgan wanted to represent in Oklahoma Territory: homesteaders fighting for fairness in a lopsided economy. Although the job with the AT&SF that had lured Morgan to Garden City confirmed his commitment to the Republican Party and its model of economic development, it might have made farmers and homesteaders skeptical of his intentions. Simply put, Morgan was caught between the polarities of the Gilded Age, a period of American history unparalleled in its socioeconomic divisions. But it did not take him long to decide which side to stand on: as a lawyer and, later, as a representative in Congress, he came to stand squarely behind homesteaders and others who had been shortchanged in an unforgiving economy.[13]

With the dual aim of building his law practice and shoring up his bona fides among farmers and homesteaders, Morgan relied on the Preemption, Homestead, and Timber acts to write *Morgan's Manual of the United States Homestead, Mining and Townsite Laws*. "Its five editions sold more than 20,000 copies to become probably the most read real estate book in Oklahoma Territory," said David Morgan about his great-grandfather's tour de force. "It was a 'how-to' book for homesteaders and was endorsed by the secretary of the interior and became a guide for determining the validity of homestead claims. *Morgan's Manual* was recognized as an authority by law clerks in the U.S. Department of the Interior."[14] Competition for *Morgan's Manual* came from the prolific Henry N. Copp, whose works included guides to land laws, mining regulations, and other matters of interest to settlers. Morgan was unafraid to engage with him in a contest for readers.[15]

The five editions of *Morgan's Manual* were published over a ten-year period, beginning in 1891 and ending in 1901. To make sure his readers could keep up with laws pertaining to land runs and lotteries, which made Oklahoma Territory ever larger and more populous, Morgan revised and updated each edition. Secretary of the Interior John W. Noble gave the book an invaluable recommendation in the 1891 edition:

> I thank you for the copy of your "Manual of United States Homestead and Townsite Laws," and have to say that on submission thereof to the Assistant Attorney-General assigned to this Department, and the attorneys acting with him, they have expressed their favorable opinion, and think it ought to be well commended as fairly representing the policy of the Department in the administration of the public land laws. I take pleasure in joining this commendation. You can send me, if you please, five additional copies, for which I shall expect to reimburse you.
>
> John W. Noble, Secretary of the Interior, September 11, 1891[16]

OVERLEAF: *Oklahoma and Indian territories, 1892.*

COURTESY OF THE OKLAHOMA HISTORICAL SOCIETY, OKLAHOMA CITY

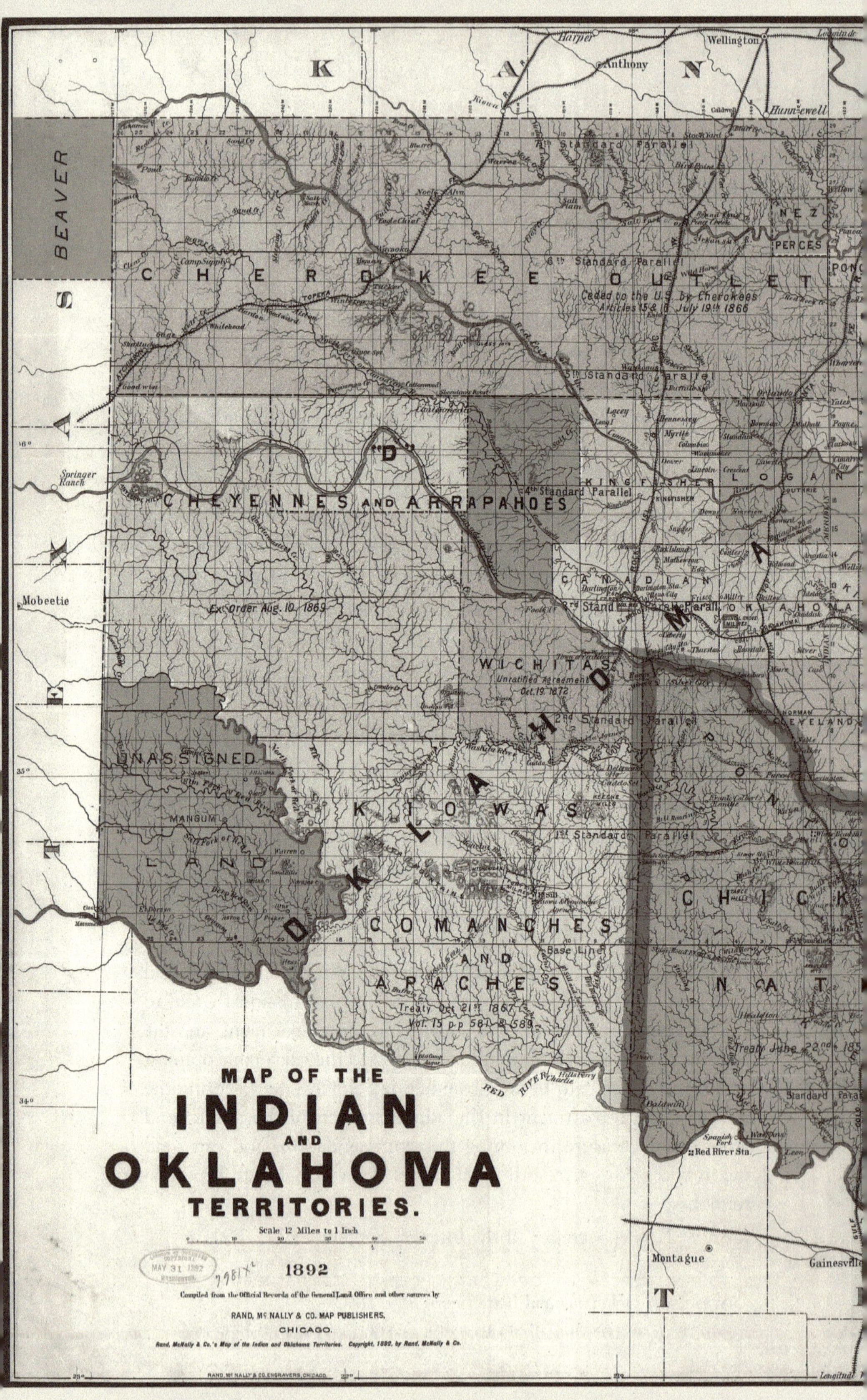
MAP OF THE
INDIAN
AND
OKLAHOMA
TERRITORIES.
Scale 12 Miles to 1 Inch
1892
Compiled from the Official Records of the General Land Office and other sources by
RAND, McNALLY & CO. MAP PUBLISHERS,
CHICAGO.
Rand, McNally & Co.'s Map of the Indian and Oklahoma Territories. Copyright, 1892, by Rand, McNally & Co.
RAND, McNALLY & CO. ENGRAVERS, CHICAGO.
MAY 31 1892
K A N
Harper
Wellington
Anthony
Kiowa
Caldwell
Hunnewell
BEAVER
T E X A S
CHEROKEE OUTLET
Ceded to the U.S. by Cherokees
Articles 15 & 16 July 19th 1866
NEZ PERCES
7th Standard Parallel
6th Standard Parallel
5th Standard Parallel
4th Standard Parallel
3rd Standard Parallel
2nd Standard Parallel
1st Standard Parallel
Base Line
Camp Supply
Springer Ranch
Mobeetie
"D"
CHEYENNES AND ARRAPAHOES
Ex. Order Aug. 10. 1869
KINGFISHER
LOGAN
CANADIAN
OKLAHOMA
CLEVELAND
WICHITAS
Unratified Agreement
Oct. 19. 1872
UNASSIGNED
MANGUM
LAND
KIOWAS
COMANCHES
AND
APACHES
Treaty Oct 21st 1867
Vol. 15 p.p 581 & 589
OKLAHOMA
PONTOTOC
CHICK
NAT
Treaty June 22nd 185
RED RIVER
Red River Sta.
Montague
Gainesville
T

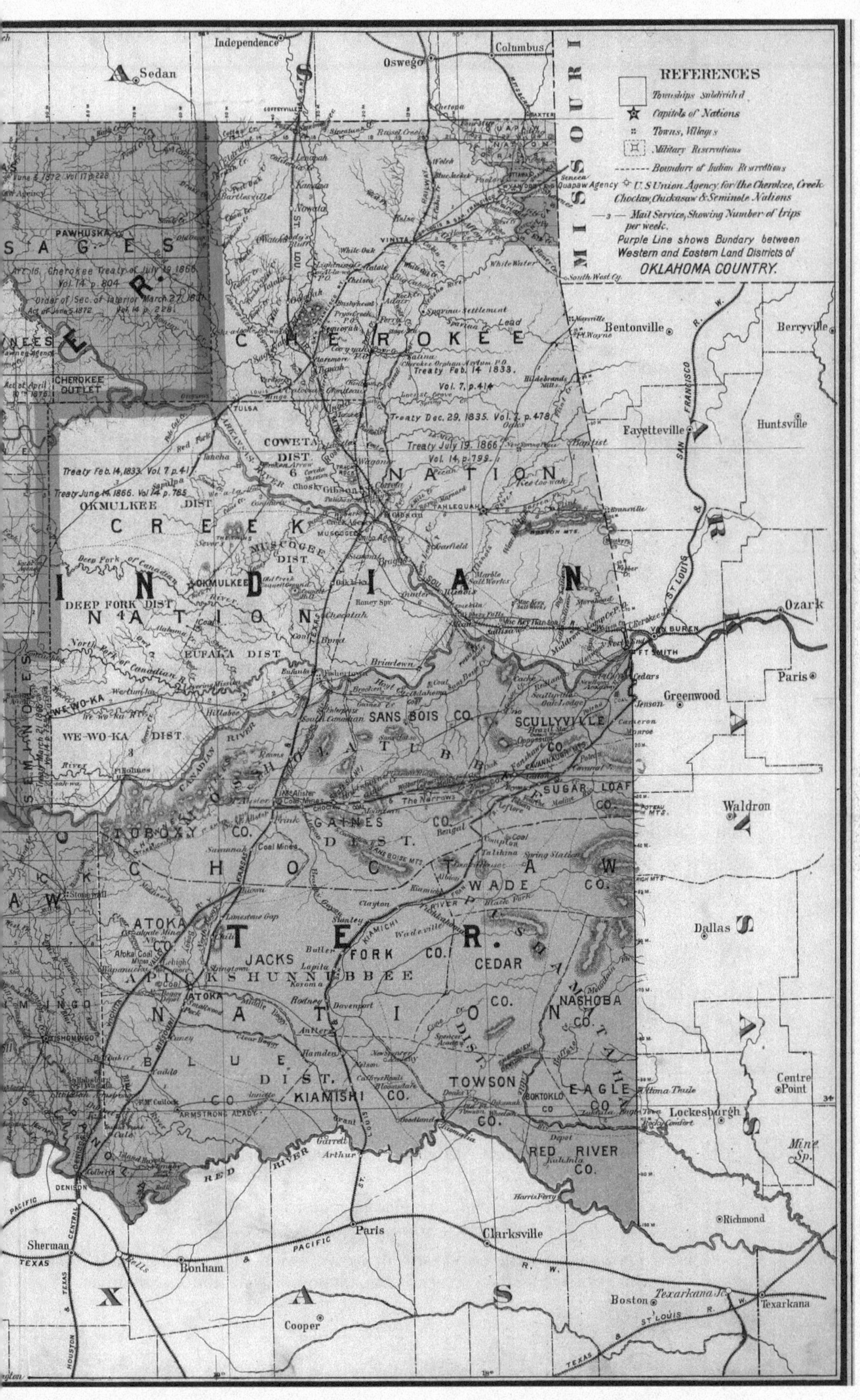
REFERENCES
Townships subdivided
Capitols of Nations
Towns, Villages
Military Reservations
Boundary of Indian Reservations
U.S. Union Agency for the Cherokee, Creek Choctaw, Chickasaw & Seminole Nations
Mail Service, Showing Number of trips per week.
Purple Line shows Bundary between Western and Eastern Land Districts of
OKLAHOMA COUNTRY.
Independence
Sedan
Columbus
Oswego
MISSOURI
Quapaw Agency
Vinita
Bentonville
Berryville
Fayetteville
Huntsville
CHEROKEE
NATION
Treaty Feb. 14 1833.
Vol. 7, p. 414
Treaty Dec. 29, 1835. Vol. 7. p. 478
Treaty July 19. 1866
Vol. 14, p. 799.
TAHLEQUAH
PAWHUSKA
CHEROKEE OUTLET
TULSA
COWETA DIST.
CREEK
OKMULKEE DIST
OKMULKEE
MUSCOGEE DIST.
DEEP FORK DIST
EUFALA DIST
WE-WO-KA DIST.
INDIAN
NATION
Treaty Feb. 14, 1833. Vol. 7 p. 417
Treaty June 14 1866. Vol 14 p. 785
Ozark
VAN BUREN
FT SMITH
Paris
Greenwood
SANS BOIS CO.
SCULLYVILLE
SUGAR LOAF CO.
GAINES CO.
DIST.
Waldron
CHOCTAW
WADE CO.
ATOKA
TER.
JACKS FORK CO.
CEDAR CO.
APUCKSHUNNUBBEE
NASHOBA CO.
Dallas
NATION
BLUE CO.
DIST.
KIAMISHI CO.
TOWSON CO.
EAGLE CO.
RED RIVER CO.
Lockesburgh
Centre Point
Mine Sp.
Richmond
RED RIVER
DENISON
Sherman
Paris
Clarksville
Bonham
TEXAS
Cooper
Boston
Texarkana
TEXAS & PACIFIC R. W.

When he wasn't building his law practice with his new partner, J. L. Pancoast, a former legislator and county attorney from western Kansas, or jockeying for political position, Morgan was working on behalf of the Christian Church. The Christian Church's governing board, the American Christian Missionary Society (ACMS), had been caught flat-footed by the run of '89 and had neglected to assign a pastor to Guthrie. It was not until late July 1890 that the ACMS's Home Board sent Edgar Forrest Boggess, an Illinois native then living in Barber County, Kansas, to Guthrie to serve as missionary pastor. What he found was not encouraging: a congregation that had dwindled to thirty-nine disheartened members with no fixed place of worship.

Boggess did what he was assigned to do, and by the end of August, membership had grown to sixty-three and plans were underway to build a church. Boggess's success was due in no small measure to Dick Morgan's incessant organizing and proselytizing. In an article published in the *Christian Standard* in 1890, Morgan expressed his

---

Two missionaries, Brother and Sister Smedley, pause for a meal during their travels on behalf of the American Christian Missionary Society.

PHOTO DONATED TO THE UNIVERSITY OF OKLAHOMA BY DICK T. MORGAN, N.D. COURTESY OF THE CARL ALBERT CONGRESSIONAL RESEARCH AND STUDIES CENTER, NORMAN, OKLAHOMA

vision not only for Guthrie, but for the entire territory, which was in dire need of Christian leadership: "Should this meet the eye of any Disciple in Oklahoma with whom I have not met, I extend to such a one an invitation to call at my law office in Guthrie. I think the time has come when the Christians in Oklahoma should perfect an organization to take active steps to take Oklahoma for Christ."[17]

There was no way for Oklahoma Territory's tiny churches to summon the resources to establish such an organization. But with God, through the guidance and funding from the ACMS, all things were possible. In 1892—the same year that the First Christian Church of Guthrie was dedicated—the Oklahoma Christian Missionary Society (OCMS) sprang into being. Twenty-three delegates gathered for its organizational meeting and elected Dick Morgan as president, E. F. Boggess as vice president, E. M. Chester as secretary, and John F. Stone as treasurer. Through the OCMS, churches and their ministers throughout Oklahoma Territory channeled ACMS funds into growing congregations and building churches. Collaboration between the ACMS and the OCMS paid off, and within a decade, the Christian Church was the largest denomination in the territory. With 16,000 members in 1903, it ranked ahead of its closest rivals: the Roman Catholic Church, with 15,000 members; and the Methodist Episcopal Church, with 13,900 members. As ACMS corresponding secretary J. M. Monroe, a Civil War veteran whose war wounds made it hard to get around, put it without a trace of humility, "We are the dominating spiritual force in Oklahoma."[18]

"Dick T. was elected as president of the organization for fifteen consecutive years," wrote David Morgan. "It is impossible to determine how many churches he helped to found, but we know that several still include him as part of their church history." Whenever a congregation needed a preacher to officiate at a Sunday service, Morgan was happy to fill in. By all accounts, he could be counted on to deliver "a very good sermon." About the same time as the OCMS was founded, Morgan was also serving as president of the newly created Sunday School Association.

"I recently visited the state office of the Disciples of Christ and the First Christian Church in Perry," continued David Morgan. "It appears that Dick T. had a hand in the opening of most, if not all, of the Christian Churches established in Oklahoma Territory from 1890 to 1907."[19]

By 1893, dreams of transforming Guthrie into a modern metropolis were coming to fruition. Businesses were prospering, a telephone system was up and running, school bond issues were passing by respectable margins, and lavish balls and theatrical performances were pushing Guthrie's rough beginnings from day-to-day reality into the history books.

Guthrie's journey into modernity coincided with the Panic of 1893, a full-blown banking disaster occasioned by a rapid increase in the nation's cache of silver and, in keeping with the inexorable law of supply and demand, a precipitous drop in its price. Convinced that silver coinage was to blame, jittery folks back East went into panic mode and made a beeline for their banks. Westerners who favored the coinage of silver to increase the money supply were equally convinced that Eastern "gold bugs" were behind the panic because they wanted to maintain a strict gold standard and discredit the coinage of silver. Either way, the Panic of 1893 came at the end of a string of panics that roiled the nineteenth-century economy every couple of decades, and it was a reminder that the nation's financial system was never far from a meltdown. Guthrie's good fortune in weathering the panic stemmed from its booming real estate market and overland freighting contracts to supply Indian agencies and military outposts with food and supplies.[20]

But history was not quite done with Oklahoma's unusual beginnings. A fourth land run was in the offing, in September 1893, and it promised to dwarf its predecessors. The area up for grabs this time was the Cherokee Outlet, whose undulating grasslands comprise most of present-day northwestern Oklahoma. The Cherokee Outlet was (and still is) often confused with the Cherokee Strip, known in frontier vernacular simply as "the strip." It is a belt two and a half miles wide that ran just south of the Kansas border along the thirty-seventh parallel. The Cherokee Outlet's incomparable grasslands attracted

cattlemen by the score, and from the 1870s to the early 1890s, they contracted with the Cherokee Nation for grazing rights. The Outlet's brief but illustrious history as a cattleman's fenceless dreamscape ended as prospective homesteaders showed up with their own ideas about economic development. Whatever remained of Cherokee claims to the Outlet were extinguished when Congress purchased the land for $8,505,736, or about $1.40 per acre.

And then, at noon on September 16, 1893, in a melee captured in one of Oklahoma's most iconic photographs, tens of thousands of prospective homesteaders and townsite developers dropped the curtain on the Cherokee Outlet's ambiguous status. Within days, Enid, Perry, Alva, and Woodward dotted the map. Counties carved out of the grazing Mecca included Garfield, Grant, Kay, Noble, Pawnee, Woods, and Woodward. Woodward and Woods counties were later divided into most of Ellis County and Harper, Alfalfa, and Major counties.[21]

Dick Morgan was among those who decided to take their chances

---

Prospective landowners waiting for the signal to begin the run into the Cherokee Outlet, September 16, 1893. COURTESY OF THE CHEROKEE STRIP MUSEUM, PERRY, OKLAHOMA

Oklahoma and Cherokee Strip "THE HOME-SEEKE

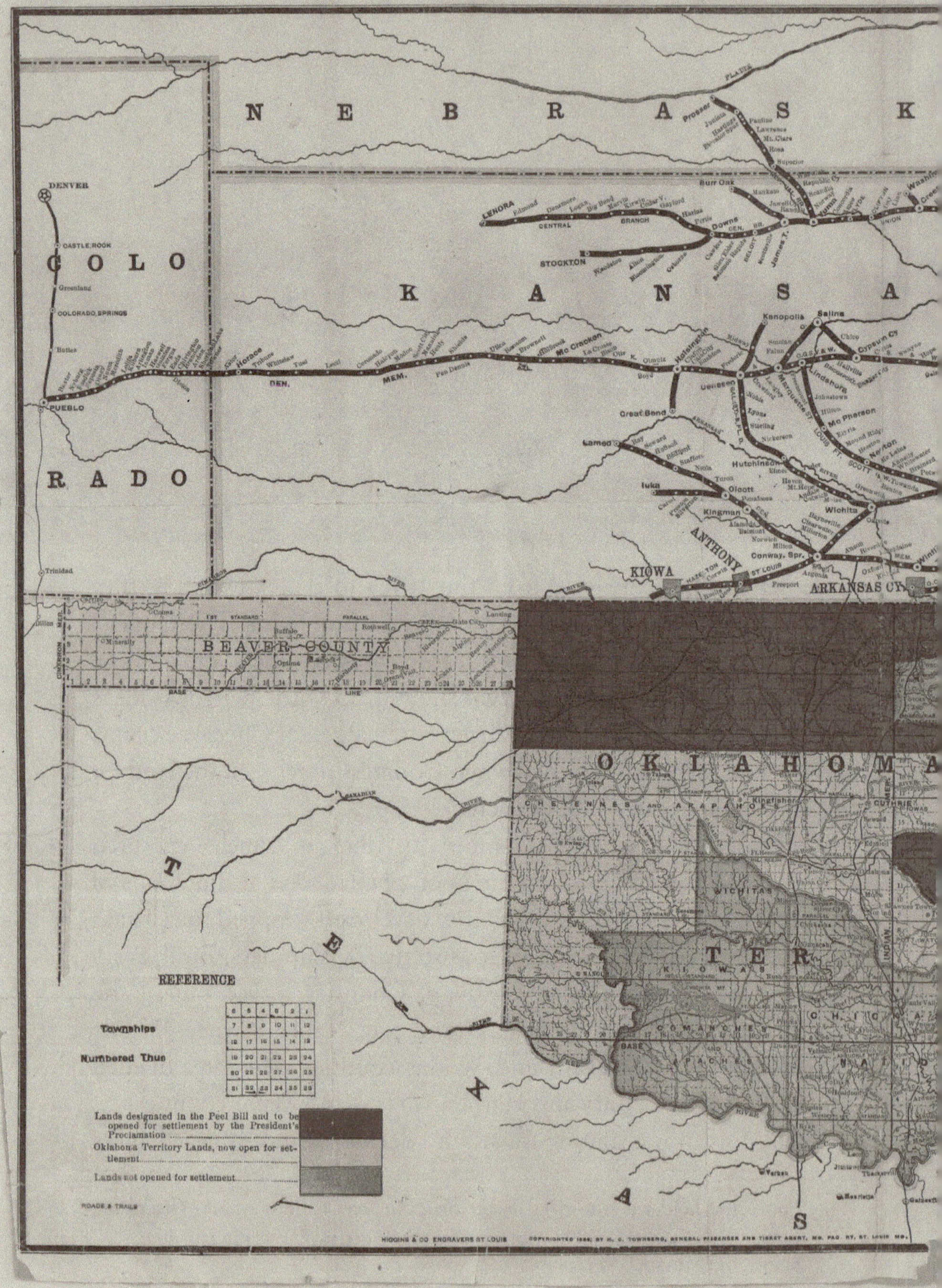

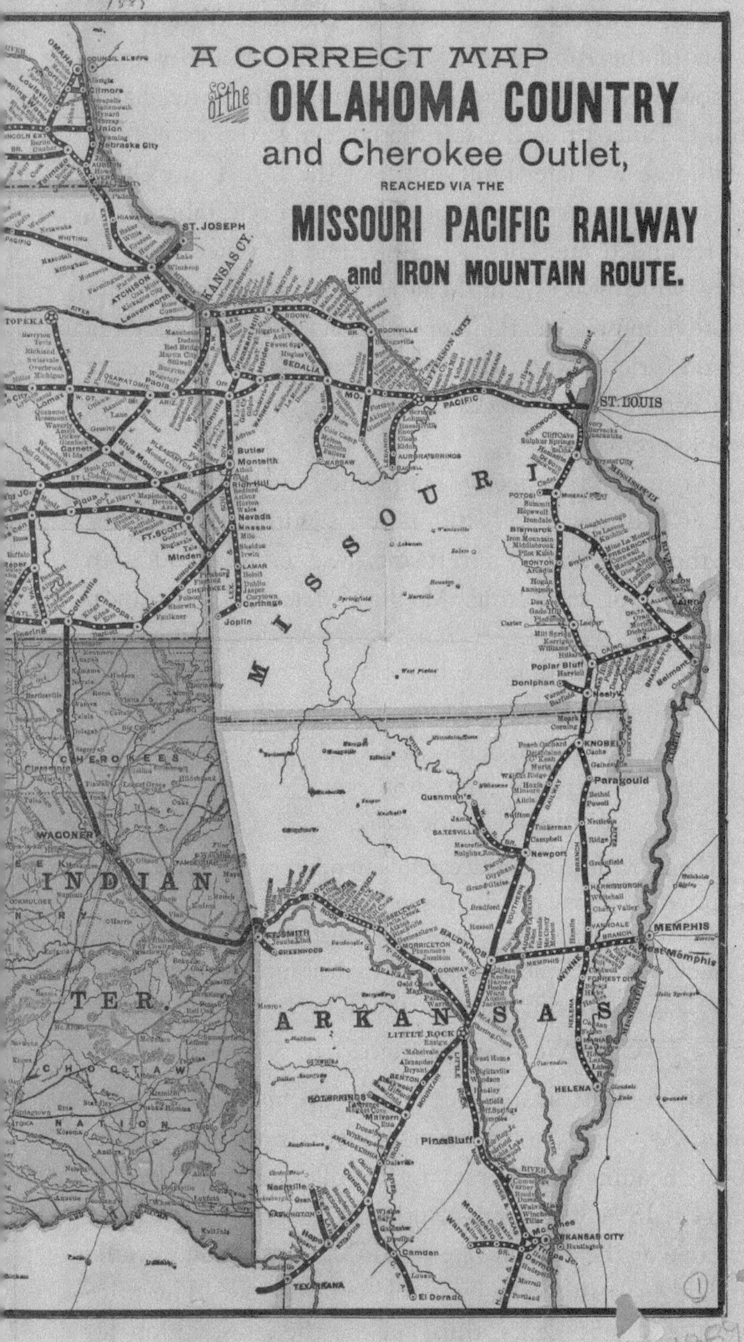

A railroad advertisement of routes to available land in Oklahoma Country and Cherokee Outlet Via the Missouri Pacific Railway and Iron Mountain Route, 1889. COURTESY OF THE OKLAHOMA HISTORICAL SOCIETY, OKLAHOMA CITY

in the former Cherokee Outlet. "We know from statements made less than three weeks later, that he arrived on the second train into Perry on the day of the run," wrote David Morgan about his great-grandfather's move from Guthrie to Perry. As in Guthrie, he shared his office with J. L. Pancoast, and it was directly across the street from where the courthouse was later built and near the U.S. Land Office on the town square, the current site of Perry's Carnegie Library. As David Morgan reminded me, Dick T. "always had an office near the U.S. Land Office, which was one of the factors that would enable him to represent more homesteaders than any other attorney in Oklahoma Territory." He and Orietta eventually built a home near the corner of what became Eighth and Elm Streets. That was the last house that he and his wife would ever own.[22]

Although Morgan and Pancoast maintained their presence in Guthrie, they now had their hands full in Perry. Within two months of their arrival, they were already advertising their services (and, with Morgan's usual flair for marketing, *Morgan's Manual*) in the local newspaper:

> Dick T. Morgan author of the
> *Morgan's Manual of the U.S. Homestead and Townsite Laws.*
>
> Morgan & Pancoast,
> Lawyers and Land Attorneys
> Perry and Guthrie, O.T.
>
> The above firm will give careful attention to all business placed in their care, and give special attention to business before the United States Land Office. Settlers will find it to their interest to call on us for information and counsel.
>
> Office West of Land Office.[23]

By the end of 1893, Morgan was ramping up his marketing for *Morgan's Manual*. As noted in an advertisement in late November under the alluring heading "Free! Free!" he was offering his book at no cost until January 1, 1894, with a subscription to the *Perry Weekly Times*, which was available at the annual rate of $1.00. "Every homesteader in the strip should have this valuable book," ran the ad. "The price of the manual alone is 50 cents, thus making the subscription for

the best weekly newspaper in the strip for 50 cents a year. Cash must accompany all orders." Money was to be sent to the Times Publishing Company's office.[24] Clearly, Morgan's experience with the *Terre Haute Daily Courier* was paying off in opportunities for marketing and business networking.

As Morgan settled into his new home, he must have experienced a sense of déjà vu. Like Guthrie, Perry was a magnet for lawyers. Between 100 and 125 lawyers, barristers, and judges, some legitimate and some with only the thinnest of résumés, were available at all hours to help settlers sort out their claims. Like Morgan, many of them had arrived in Perry during the run of 1893 and set up makeshift offices, with plans to find more comfortable accommodations as the townsite developed. To build their businesses, lawyers could take advantage of Perry's ninety-day divorce law. The law (or, more accurately, the scheme) was set in motion when an entrepreneur set up a boarding house for clients seeking a divorce. After signing the boarding house register, clients had the option to leave town and return after the required ninety-day waiting period to prove their residency and be

---

Prospective landowners waiting to file their claims at the U.S. Land Office in Perry, Oklahoma Territory, 9:00 am, September 28, 1893. COURTESY OF THE A. J. BARASH COLLECTION, OKLAHOMA HISTORICAL SOCIETY, OKLAHOMA CITY

granted a divorce. But when the U.S. Land Office closed and Congress passed a law requiring a year's residency for a divorce, the gambit no longer worked, and lawyers had to look elsewhere for business-building opportunities.[25]

As he had done in Garden City and Guthrie, Morgan complemented his law and real estate businesses with church-building activities. His close collaborator in Perry was E. F. Boggess, the missionary pastor who had helped to lift Guthrie's congregants out of the doldrums. In what went down in church lore as Boggess's Ride, the pastor took a leave of absence from his church in Guthrie and, with funding and blessings from the Board of Church Extension, acquired the funds to purchase a horse and a town lot in Perry, already designated as a government townsite. As Boggess explained in a 1925 retrospective about planting churches in Oklahoma Territory, experiences in the first three land runs taught valuable lessons in how to secure lots, and he was more prepared than most when he entered the fray on Saturday, September 16, 1893.

According to church lore, repeated so often it has been accepted as gospel, Boggess's horse was a real charger that had been training hard for the run of '93. However, that's not quite how a twelve-year-old Porter Morgan remembered it. As he noted many years later in a letter to the Reverend Carl Covey with the Oklahoma Christian Missionary Society, "in truth and in fact, Boggess had a little, round, roly-poly pony which he drove around hitched to a phaeton there at Guthrie, and as I remember about it at this time I wonder how his pony got as far as Perry let alone with Boggess on his back."[26]

After a sluggish ten-mile ride from Orlando to Perry, Boggess, surely tired and clearly unschooled in the art of surveying, missed Perry entirely and staked a claim not only outside the government townsite, but in someone else's homestead, leaving his mission to claim a lot for the church unfulfilled for a year. Meanwhile, the Morgans showed up in more comfortable accommodations, aboard the second train, to arrive at the Perry townsite.

Within hours of the opening, Morgan had his tent-office up and running, complete with a desk, chairs, and legal blanks, and he was close enough to the U.S. Land Office to lure settlers as they lined up

to file their claims. But the Lord's work was never far from his mind. As the duly appointed chairman of a committee to locate church lots, he was responsible for finding people throughout the Cherokee Outlet to secure property in their chosen townsites.

At some point, Boggess straggled into town, set up his church headquarters in Morgan's tent, and prepared for the next day's services. Left to fend for himself while the adults went about their business, Porter bedded down for the night on a saddle blanket with Boggess's saddle for a pillow. And what was there for the twelve-year-old boy on the adventure of a lifetime to complain about? As he wrote in his letter to Covey, "I remember I certainly felt overcharged when I paid ten cents that afternoon for a glass of water."[27]

No record has survived of the Disciples' first service the day after the land run, and for good reason—it never happened. After Boggess made his famed ride on Saturday, he secured a temporary place of

Church service in Perry, Oklahoma Territory, October 8, 1893. COURTESY OF THE JOSEPH THOBURN COLLECTION, OKLAHOMA HISTORICAL SOCIETY, OKLAHOMA CITY

worship and, with Morgan's help, erected a tent over a temporary frame. Satisfied that all was in order, he took the train back to Guthrie to fetch his communion service and hymnbooks. No sooner did he arrive back in Perry the next morning than a dust storm came howling through town and blew down the tent that he and Morgan had erected. Consequently, the first service had to wait until the following Sunday under clearer skies. Morgan, who agreed to serve as superintendent, presided over what was surely a well-attended service.[28] As late summer gave way to fall and cooler weather set in, Morgan invited parishioners to hold services in his office.

Boggess eventually managed to purchase a lot from its first owner at the bargain-basement price of $150.00—far less than the First Christian Church of Guthrie's original lot, which cost about $1,000. Boggess's success in Perry became a model for church expansion in subsequent openings. When lots were purchased in such towns as Anadarko, Hobart, and Lawton, the Home Board held them in trust until congregations could be established.

The First Christian Church of Perry, Oklahoma Territory, was formally organized on October 22, 1893, with thirty-six charter members, including Morgan, who was elected to the board as a church elder. The first minister, Reverend Powers, earned twenty-five dollars per month. A building committee was formed on May 14, 1894, and tasked with building a proper church on a legal claim at the corner of Eighth and Fir Avenues. Scraping by on a budget of $1,500, the committee oversaw completion of the foundation in July 1894. Brother Buzzard, the "boss carpenter," was hired for $2.00 per day and was required to donate three-eighths of his wages to the church.

When the committee's shoestring budget ran out, members voted to borrow $750.00 from the Board of Church Extension. That was enough to complete construction, and the First Christian Church of Perry, Oklahoma Territory, was duly dedicated. A Ladies Aid Society was organized to purchase a communion set and collection baskets, install seats and a carpet for the pulpit, and—wonder of wonders!—bring electricity into the building. The church acquired an organ with funding from the Christian Endeavor, a nondenominational association dating back to 1881 whose mission, originally targeted toward youth and later expanded to include all ages of evangelical Protestants, was to encourage members to "work together to know God in Jesus Christ."[29]

Another notable tale from Morgan's church-building days comes from the First Christian Church of Stillwater. As president of the OCMS, Morgan was called upon to help find a new minister for the church. He was pleased when an application arrived from Virtes Williams, a twenty-seven-year-old seminary graduate. Their first meeting went well—so well that Morgan accepted his application, assigned him to the church in Stillwater, and sent a letter of endorsement to lay leaders of the church. To begin his tenure, Virtes drove his buggy to Stillwater to meet his congregants, blissfully unaware that some of them were resisting his appointment. "Their first meeting did not go well," explained David Morgan. "Fortunately for Virtes and the church, their relationship improved, and Virtes served the church for twenty-eight years." A century later, Morgan's and Williams's descendants attended the First Christian Church's hundredth anniversary celebration.[30]

While Morgan was doing his part for the church, the Republican Party, together with the *Perry Daily Times*, was touting him as a candidate for the territorial legislature. The newspaper's endorsements started gaining traction in the fall of 1894. In an open letter to the newspaper editor on September 29, Morgan, now just shy of his forty-first birthday, played coy about his candidacy: "I highly appreciate the good opinion of my fellow citizens and would gladly render any service to the public of which I am capable." Even though he had not announced his candidacy, he made it clear that if attendees at the upcoming Republican convention chose to nominate him, he would certainly not decline, "but would accept said nomination and put forth the best efforts in my power to elect the entire republican ticket."[31]

The next day, the *Guthrie Daily Leader* claimed that he had announced his candidacy.[32] Once he confirmed that he was, indeed, a candidate for office, the *Perry Daily Times* cut to the chase with an endorsement originally published in the influential *Guthrie State Capital*:

> It would be a sensible thing for the people there to send him. He would stand out ablest among the members, command respect and pass much needed legislation. A lawyer of established reputation, of fixed integrity and good nature, his influence would be felt. If there is anything to be had for his constituency, Dick Morgan can come nearer than anybody to secure it. A legislature made up of such men as Morgan would elevate our laws and establish legislative dignity in harmony with Oklahoma's high citizenship.[33]

When Election Day 1894 rolled around, Noble County voters thwarted Morgan's first foray into territorial politics by electing another Republican to the legislature.[34] Although the loss was the first of several setbacks, his candidacy raised his profile among voters and empowered him to run for office another day. As the *Tulsa Daily World*'s Omar Benedict observed in his 1917 review of Morgan's career, he was already known throughout the territory for appealing "to the better side of man." More than that, he was "temperate, logical, religious, and conservatively open-minded," and "was supported and respected for his clean character and absolute sincerity."[35]

Denied a seat in the territorial legislature, Morgan spent the next year building his business and tending to his church responsibilities. In November 1895, he and Orietta joined Mrs. Will Glenn and Miss Mittie Bryan on a trip to Dallas to attend the Christian Church's annual convention. Their travel plans included a post-convention detour to Galveston, where they remained for a few days before returning to Perry. Shortly after they got home, an audience gathered at the First Christian Church to hear their report on the Dallas convention and enjoy a performance by the church choir. Following Miss Bryan's address on the Christian Endeavor's progress in promoting spirituality among evangelical Protestants, Orietta Morgan read from a sermon that had been delivered at the convention. The final speaker was her husband, who gave an upbeat assessment of the goings-on. As noted in the *Perry Daily Enterprise*, "Col. Dick Morgan closed with a very interesting talk about the convention at Dallas and of the church in general, noting its rapid material and spiritual progress in the world." After songs and a benediction, the meeting was adjourned.[36] Although Morgan had never served in the military, newspaper reporters often referred to him as a colonel out of respect, a common practice in the late nineteenth and early twentieth centuries to single out men held in high regard.

The Morgans' travels on behalf of their church continued with a trip to Guthrie to attend the Territorial Sunday School Convention, where officers for 1896 were elected and Morgan was chosen to serve on the executive committee. Upon their return to Perry, Morgan was pleased to report that he and Orietta "spent a very pleasant time at the Sunday School convention at Guthrie."[37] Back at the First Christian Church, party invitations were sent to parents whose children were in Sunday school. More than two hundred people responded and crowded into the church to show their enthusiasm for what the church was doing for their children. "Col. Dick Morgan, who is an enthusiastic Sunday school worker, and his equally enthusiastic corps of teachers had delightful surprises for all," ran a cheerful article in the *Perry Enterprise* about the Parents' Day celebration. "The children were all as happy and bright as the birds and the sunshine and they sang sweet songs in harmony with nature's brightness and melody."[38]

Some of David's and Kenyon's earliest childhood memories were stories from their grandfather, Porter, reminiscing about his childhood in Perry. "Those were happy times for Grandpa and his parents," said David. Porter amplified that sense of contentment in an interview that David had requested for a sixth grade Oklahoma history project at Putnam Heights Elementary School in Oklahoma City. "I interviewed Grandpa the year he died," continued David. "He told me stories about his childhood in Perry. The event that stood out was the time he traded his saddle to a friend for a gun. His parents were not happy! Guns were not part of the Morgan family. Grandpa said that he was punished severely and had to return the gun."

That same year, David and Kenyon met Sadie Hill, one of Porter's teenage girlfriends. Asked to share her memories of early-day Perry, Sadie recalled Dick Morgan's influence over the young folks. As superintendent of the Sunday school, he trained Sadie and her friends to be teachers.

Sadie also recalled Porter's sense of humor. At a Christian Endeavor meeting, everyone was racking their brains to recite Bible verses from memory. Porter, clearly not worried in the least, rose from his chair and, with a straight face, said "John 11:35: Jesus wept" and promptly sat down. After holding back for what seemed like an eternity, the whole class burst out in laughter.

As David concluded, with a touch of bravado, about his debonair grandfather, "Sadie said that every girl in town was honored when Grandpa asked them out for a buggy ride!"

Some of those girls might have had to wait for a buggy ride. Dissatisfied with Perry's nascent educational system, the Morgans sent their son to Norman, where he attended high school classes at University High, a division of the University of Oklahoma, where students could beef up their academic skills before enrolling in the university. "We have letters from Porter to his parents indicating that he was quite a tennis player," said David. "One letter—a real anachronism from today's perspective! —reads like a formal thank-you note, and it shows how deeply he appreciated his parents' gift of a tennis racket. And, not surprisingly for a future lawyer, he became known as a skilled debater and public speaker."[39]

Eighteen-ninety-five ended on an upbeat note when, in November, Morgan served as musical director for a Thanksgiving cantata, open for general admission at a price of fifteen cents. The story revolved around Israelites who prayed to God for deliverance from the oppressive rule of the Ammonites and around Jephthah's return from banishment. Under Morgan's direction, the orchestra, complete with a cornet, piano, first and second violins, and flute, "rendered the sweet pathetic music of the opera excellently." When the curtain dropped, the audience signaled its delight with rapturous applause and demands for encores. Such was the take on opening night ($68.00, according to the ladies in charge of ticketing) that a repeat performance was scheduled. Rave reviews included one from the *Perry Daily Enterprise-Times*: "The opera house was filled to its uttermost with a large audience of the elite of the city, who were delightfully entertained for more than two hours, by the rendition of this beautiful cantata, in a pleasing and happy manner by our home talent opera company."[40]

No sooner did Morgan finish his work on the Thanksgiving cantata than he got busy organizing a Christmas cantata under the title "Palace of Santa Clause." The building was standing room only; those fortunate enough to find seats were thrilled to hear ten children clad as Eskimos sing "We Will Make a Snowman" and other seasonal favorites in Santa Clause's home. Special effects included an ascending balloon symbolizing a trip to the North Pole and a snowman's transformation into old Saint Nick. Once again, the *Perry Daily Enterprise-Times* published a cheery review of the performance: "The music and scenery were very pretty, and the girls and all connected did well, and the audience were [*sic*] highly entertained."[41]

Holiday cheer notwithstanding, a showdown was looming in faraway Washington, D.C., and as the New Year dawned, it drew the wrath of Morgan and like-minded leaders who were determined to reduce the gap between the haves and have-nots. Under the banner "Justice Is Our Battle Cry!", settlers struggling to carve out a living in Oklahoma Territory were beginning to voice their opposition to Congress's latest ploy to balance the nation's books, this time on the backs of homesteaders in the form of exorbitant fees hidden in the fine print of their homestead claims.

What those homesteaders needed was leadership to fight for justice. What they got was Dick T. Morgan's attention.

Dick T. Morgan's law office in Perry, Oklahoma Territory. Standing in the doorway are Guerney Sawyer (left) and Dick T. Morgan (right). COURTESY OF THE JOHN E. SHANAFELT COLLECTION, OKLAHOMA HISTORICAL SOCIETY, OKLAHOMA CITY

CHAPTER SIX

"Justice Is Our Battle Cry!"

> Land for the landless and
> homes for the homeless
>
> HOMESTEAD ACT OF 1862

OKLAHOMANS KNOW EXACTLY WHERE THEY WERE, and what they were doing, when the Alfred P. Murrah Federal Building exploded on April 19, 1995. Within minutes of that sickening low point in American history, everyone not in proximity to ground zero was glued to their televisions, struggling to imagine a monster who could visit such violence on people as they went about their routines in a downtown office building. Most imagined a perpetrator from the Middle East bent on bringing down America, which was excoriated in terrorist circles as the Great Satan. None doubted that he (or, less likely but remotely possible, she) would be brought to justice.

Then came the televised footage, played over and over again, of a pleasant-looking ex-soldier from Lockport, New York, who had been pulled over for a traffic violation on Interstate 35 north of Oklahoma City, as he was led in handcuffs from the county courthouse in Perry, Oklahoma.

Exactly one hundred years before Timothy McVeigh became a household name for committing the deadliest homegrown terrorist attack in American history, lawyers and public officials gathered in Perry in 1895 to launch the Oklahoma Territorial Free Home League, a grassroots campaign to relieve homesteaders of a financial burden that threatened to bring many to ruin. Nobody was more determined to make that movement succeed than Dick T. Morgan, who officed near the public square where the courthouse was later built, directly across the street from the U.S. Land Office.

"His office was across the street from the building where Timothy McVeigh was held after his arrest," said David Morgan. "Photos went viral of McVeigh being hustled out of the courthouse where Dick T. conducted a lot of his business. The original courthouse is no longer standing, and most of the nearby buildings have long since been demolished and replaced. But it's not hard to imagine the public square and the surrounding business district teeming with land lawyers and settlers in the early days of non-Indian settlement."[1]

David Morgan let that bizarre historical juxtaposition sink in and continued: "Just like the name says, the League called for a waiver from Congress of the final payment for the land title. This was the perfect organization for Dick Morgan. He was representing the people he loved the most—the farmer, the land holder, the middle-class worker, all trying to make a living in rural and small-town Oklahoma."[2]

Whatever their disagreements in those heady first years of non-Indian settlement, the lawyers and public officials who gathered in Perry were on the same page when it came to the heart of America's promise: access to cheap land as the surest route to prosperity. The Founding Fathers knew all about wealth creation in Europe, where feudalism had given rise to an aristocracy whose stability and social status depended on land ownership. Absent feudal restrictions that maintained Europe's rigid class structure, immigrants to America were encouraged to see land ownership as a guarantor of individual rights, and the less it cost the better. America's commitment to liberal land policies was codified in the Northwest Ordinance of 1787, whose long-term effect was to make cheap land, often available through installment payments, a cornerstone of democracy and engine of economic growth.

That commitment, renewed in the Homestead Act of 1862 and celebrated by land reformers ever since, was applied to non-Indian settlement of the Unassigned Lands in April 1889. For that opening, homesteaders paid a modest administrative fee, ranging from ten to twenty-five dollars, to the U.S. Land Office. After that, they were free to fulfill their five-year residency requirements and prove up their claims, en route to full ownership, without any further payments.

But then, Congress came up with the idea to reimburse the federal treasury for the money paid to Indian tribes to extinguish their claims in preparation for homesteading in the Iowa, Sac and Fox, Pottawatomie, and Shawnee reservations in 1891, the Cheyenne and Arapaho Reservation in 1892, and the Cherokee Outlet in 1893.

Aiming to balance the nation's books, officials did an end run around the Homestead Act of 1862 by charging settlers who obtained claims in those three land runs from $1.00–$2.50 per acre. To add insult to injury, homesteaders were required to pay a 4 percent per annum interest charge on unpaid balances. By 1893, each settler was saddled with a payment obligation ranging from $160 to $400.[3] The price differential was based on estimated land values. Blessed with a climate conducive to agriculture and abundant water, eastern land was more valuable than land in the west.

Realizing that only Congress could provide the needed relief, Oklahoma Territory's delegates expressed their constituents' fury in Congress and, beginning in 1892 and continuing throughout the 1890s, lobbied for what became known as the Free Homes Bill. David Morgan explained his great-grandfather's crusade on behalf of homesteaders: "This became a huge political issue in Oklahoma and other western states in the mid-1890s, as those payments were coming due after five years of homesteading."[4] Unless they made their payments, homesteaders could not obtain patents for their land.

While Dick Morgan and his like-minded colleagues were mustering grassroots support for free homes, Oklahoma Territory's delegate to Congress, Dennis Thomas Flynn, was carrying their message to Congress. Born on February 13, 1861, in Phoenixville, Pennsylvania, Flynn was raised in a Catholic orphanage and attended common schools and Canisius College in Buffalo, New York. Like Morgan, he went west to grow up with the country, first to Iowa, where he established and edited the *Riverside Leader* and was admitted to the bar, and then to Kiowa, Kansas, where he served as postmaster and city attorney and published the *Kiowa Herald*. He moved to Guthrie at the same time as Morgan and served as postmaster until his election as a Republican delegate to Congress in 1892.

Elected every two years, territorial delegates were second only

to the governor in wielding political clout. Although territorial delegates did not have voting privileges, they were members of the U.S. House of Representatives and could introduce legislation and speak upon any measure. Only thirty-one years old at the time of his election, Flynn served as territorial delegate for a total of eight years (1893–97 and 1899–1903), longer than any other Oklahoman during the territorial period.[5]

His youth and voting restrictions notwithstanding, Flynn hit the ground running. From his arrival in Congress in 1893 through October 1894, Flynn managed to get eighteen bills through the House of Representatives. By contrast, his fellow delegates from Utah, Arizona, and New Mexico territories, all Democrats whose alignment with the Cleveland administration earned them monikers as "harmony" delegates, managed to get only five bills through the House in the same period. And their fellow delegate from Oklahoma Territory? "Flynn, the 'disharmony' delegate, got through *eighteen bills*," boasted the *Perry Daily Times*. "How much more than this do the people want done? Flynn has accomplished everything, and much more than the people expected."[6] In fact, he secured passage of more bills than any congressman since the dawn of the Republic, and more than any five congressmen in the current session, in a comparable length of time.

Despite his successful record as a delegate, Flynn experienced a setback when members of the Public Lands Committee laughed out loud at an early iteration of the free homes bill and accused him of attempting a raid on the treasury. He responded by vowing to make free homes the fight of his life. Thanks to his insertion of riders into

---

As Oklahoma Territory's delegate to Congress, Dennis T. Flynn was a leading spokesman for eliminating fees on homesteads and returning to the principles of the Homestead Act of 1862. COURTESY OF THE JOHN DUNNING POLITICAL COLLECTION, OKLAHOMA HISTORICAL SOCIETY, OKLAHOMA CITY

the annual Indian appropriation bills, settlers in the former Cheyenne, Arapaho, and Pottawatomie reservations received two twelve-month extensions to make their payments; settlers in the Cherokee Outlet were authorized to vote and prove up their land in fourteen months; and settlers in Beaver County were allowed to commute their homestead entries. He also lobbied to open the Wichita, Kiowa, and Comanche reservations to non-Indian settlement. But still, debt forgiveness remained a pipe dream.

Even so, Perry's local newspaper was impressed with what Flynn had accomplished in his first two terms. "Is not this a remarkable record?" continued the *Perry Daily Times*'s paean to Dennis Flynn.

> Mr. Flynn has given the people all they hoped for and more. His faithful and conscientious performance of duty is recognized by all, regardless of party. With such a worker in congress, can the people afford to change for an experiment? Of course not. At the November election Mr. Flynn is certain of a vote of confidence such as he deserves—the appreciative voice of a great people will shout in unmistakable terms, "Thou good and faithful servant!"[7]

Although Flynn was unable to secure passage of his free homes bill, his success in obtaining extensions gave homesteaders ample opportunity to agitate for a return to the principles embodied in the Homestead Act of 1862. Adopting the slogan "free homes for free men," Pawnee, Kay, and Noble counties became the breeding ground for ad hoc organizations to spread across the territory and, ultimately, to other states and territories.

Flynn's work in Washington, together with grassroots campaigning in Oklahoma Territory, set the stage for the Oklahoma Territorial Free Home League's historic gathering in 1895. With six counties represented, delegates adopted a constitution and formed a trilevel organization aimed at turning back the clock to 1862, when the nation's commitment to individual land ownership was empowered by the force of law. James J. Houston, a Perry real estate agent, was elected as the first president. To advance the League's aims, the third Oklahoma territorial legislature appropriated five hundred dollars. League members were further heartened by the support of homesteaders in the Unassigned Lands. Although those homesteaders had secured their claims before Congress imposed its draconian new rules, they opposed unjust payments that would leave settlers who had secured homesteads in later land runs unable to afford improvements and subject to grinding poverty, if not bankruptcy. What is more, both early and later homesteaders knew that revenues collected through land payments would not, in the long run, make much of a dent in the U.S. Treasury.[8]

Morgan complemented his involvement in the free homes movement with his usual blend of business and community building, and that included education. Perhaps having a fifteen-year-old son gave him added motivation, in early January 1896, to attend a board of education meeting, where he offered to furnish sufficient liquid slate to finish installing blackboards in the high school. After the board accepted his offer, the superintendent asked him to procure it.[9]

A couple of months later, Morgan participated in "a very enthusiastic meeting" at city hall to organize the Perry Mining Company. As noted in the *Perry Daily Enterprise-Times*, "A large number of our citizens, who have become deeply interested in mining matters, were present and entered into the spirit of the meeting with a freedom and confidence, which is the best evidence of their faith in the company and the brilliant prospects of ore in large and paying quantities." The newly appointed directors elected Morgan as their president and filed articles of incorporation with the territorial secretary of state with capital stock of a million dollars. With its main office to be located at the northwest corner of Seventh and D Streets, the Perry Mining Company announced plans to open shafts in three locations to procure copper, lead, and zinc ores. Two men with twenty years of experience in mining were hired as foremen. "A large number of shares in this company were taken last night and today," continued the upbeat newspaper report, "and it starts out under the most flattering conditions."[10]

No matter how busy he was, Morgan's thoughts were never far from the First Christian Church. In the spring of 1896, he helped prepare for a concert under the direction of Professor John Brower of Chicago.

The performance "was the finest musical entertainment to which the citizens of Perry have had the pleasure of listening," asserted the *Perry Daily Enterprise-Times*. Morgan was among the sixteen ladies and gentlemen in the chorus who, accompanied by an unnamed pianist, served up the "high-class music" to which the citizens of Perry had become accustomed.[11]

Meanwhile, in May 1896, Orietta Morgan did her part to build a viable community by hosting a reception for a celebrity whose message resonated among evangelical Christians: Clara C. Hoffman, a New York State native who lectured and organized on behalf of the Woman's Christian Temperance Union (WCTU). Organized in 1873 in Hillsboro, Ohio, the WCTU sponsored social reform campaigns based on the application of Christ's teachings. Projects ranged from missionary work and promoting women's suffrage to outlawing intoxicating spirits. For five years, Hoffman served as president of the WCTU chapter in Missouri, a state that became a model for organizing chapters in other states and territories. Hoffman's message was on target for Orietta Morgan and Perry's other leading ladies who attended the reception. As noted in the *Perry Enterprise-Times*, "A large number of the ladies of the W.C.T.U. and other ladies of the city, called on the distinguished lady and tendered her a very cordial welcome to Perry."[12] Orietta rounded out her volunteer activities by joining her husband at Sunday school conventions and, beginning in the fall of 1898, serving as superintendent of the Territorial Sunday School Association's Primary Department.[13]

That same month, the First Christian Church of Perry hosted Noble County's first Sunday school convention to formally establish the Noble County Sunday School Association. About twenty-seven Sunday schools had been organized in Noble County, and more were on the way. Braving torrential rains that had made creek crossings perilous, only fifty people representing about half the county attended. According to press reports, attendees were enthusiastic about their Sunday school programs; the progress reported by some of them was nothing short of "astonishing." Dick Morgan, who had been elected as the association's vice president, delivered an address whose content has been lost to history, but that surely touched on the value of Scripture in building a wholesome community. Among the convention's resolutions was one that must have met with hearty acclamation: "Resolved—That in view of the importance of the Sabbath School as an agency for the upbuilding of the Master's Kingdom, and promoting the highest interests of society, we as an organization and as individuals, record our purpose to labor earnestly, that a Sabbath School may be kept up in every school district in our county."[14]

The Noble County Sunday School Association's next gathering came on August 30, 1896, at the Oak Grove schoolhouse seven miles east of Perry. Its purpose was to organize a permanent township Sunday school association and to elect officers. As an added incentive to attend the meeting, dinner was served. Dick Morgan delivered an address on the benefits to be derived from Sunday school. Other addresses covered such subjects as organizing a Sunday school, securing parental buy-in, instructing children in the main tenets of Christianity, and teaching the Bible. Attendees closed the meeting with a rousing rendition of "God Be with You till We Meet Again."[15]

Now that the Noble Township Sunday School Association was up and running, quarterly meetings were scheduled. One such meeting, on April 4, 1897, at the Willow Creek school house, departed from previous enticements by requiring attendees to bring their own dinner. The meeting proceeded with the usual prayers, songs, and addresses, including two from Dick Morgan. One was on drumming up interest in Sunday schools, and the other was on Sunday schools' effect on a community's intellectual life.[16] His listeners thus had much to ponder as they sang their closing hymn before adjournment. One imagines a pensive Dick Morgan reflecting on his upbringing in Indiana, when family, church, and school had left him with lasting impressions of the good life—a life dedicated to service to others.

Morgan's religious work went beyond service to the Christian Church. In July 1896, representatives from several Protestant churches met at the Methodist Church to organize the Noble County Bible Society, which would be affiliated with the American Bible Society. Reverend J. H. Lockwood of Salina, Kansas, who served as district superintendent for Kansas, Oklahoma, and Indian territories, delivered an address on the organization and work of the American

Bible Society. Attendees were asked to contribute to a collection to establish a Bible depository. Nobody was surprised when Dick Morgan was elected as treasurer for the coming year.[17]

Committed though he was to his community and his church, Morgan had to make a living, and that meant practicing law and continually updating and marketing *Morgan's Manual*. In 1897, he published a compilation of Oklahoma Territory's statutes and supreme court decisions under the title *Morgan's Digest of Oklahoma Statutes and Supreme Court Decisions*. David Morgan explained his great-grandfather's success with his second major publication: "In 1899, the Territorial Legislature authorized the purchase of eight hundred copies to be sent to judges and county officials around the territory."[18]

Not only did *Morgan's Digest* earn money; in tandem with *Morgan's Manual*, it heightened the author's esteem in legal circles. As noted in the *Noble County Sentinel* at the time of publication, *Morgan's Digest* was bound to be a bestseller, as it condensed three volumes of statutes and five volumes of supreme court reports, all published since the run of '89, into a single volume. Those eight volumes contained about six thousand pages and cost more than thirty dollars. "Mr. Morgan's aim has been to present in one volume in condensed form, the pith and substance of all that is contained in these eight volumes," ran the glowing newspaper review. "An examination of the work will show that he has succeeded admirably in his purpose. The work has been prepared with the idea that the people generally are interested in the laws of their own State or Territory, and that if these laws were presented in such form as to place them within reach of all common readers that the people would purchase and read such a book."

In addition to presenting complex topics in a readable format, *Morgan's Digest* included blank forms that could be used to prepare contracts and agreements without legal counsel. To procure a copy, all people had to do was contact Morgan at his office in Perry. Books bound in cloth sold for $2.00; those bound in special law sheep binding cost $2.50. Customary discounts were available to dealers and agents.[19]

On January 10, 1896, the Oklahoma Territorial Free Home League convened in El Reno to adopt resolutions and prepare a memorial to Congress. The purpose of the memorial was unambiguous: to empower Dennis T. Flynn "to use all honorable means to secure to all the settlers of this territory, the full benefits of a free homestead law." In laborious and somewhat repetitive detail, League members laid out their case, beginning with the essential fairness of homestead laws that had been in effect for more than three decades and that had suddenly, and without justification, been abrogated to the detriment of Oklahoma settlers. After Indian claims were extinguished and/or their occupancy was terminated, those lands became part of the public domain and were subject to general homestead laws. Simply put, those lands should never have been made the subject of special legislation. The League's memorial reminded Congress that, since 1862, settlers on public lands had been granted 160 acres at no cost other than land office fees; those who opted for commutation under preemption laws acquired their land at a minimum cost of $1.25 per acre. Above League president J. J. Houston's signature, the memorial closed as unambiguously as it began: "We therefore respectfully ask congress, to extend to the settler of the whole Territory of Oklahoma the full benefit of the free homestead law, and all other relief herein indicated."[20]

The League's lobbying was causing a stir and had all the hallmarks of a successful campaign. On January 14, 1896, Delegate Flynn sent a brief telegram to League President Houston indicating that his Free Homes Bill had been reviewed favorably by the House Public Lands Committee.[21] Flynn rose to the podium on March 16 to expound on the Oklahoma bill (H.R. 3656). The key passage, duly read by the clerk of the house, declared that any settler who had acquired a homestead by all legal means would be required to pay a modest application fee to the local land office; "no other or further charge of any kind whatsoever shall be required from such settler to entitle him to a patent for the land covered by his entry." Caught in the squeeze of an economic downturn brought on by the Panic of 1893, settlers realized too late that the Oklahoma country and its environs were not quite the Garden of Eden that promoters had promised. Relief from onerous expenses would save them from losing their homesteads, an eventuality that was inevitable for thousands in the absence of a free homes bill.

Flynn reserved special opprobrium for the secretary of the interior who, through either ignorance or misrepresentation or a combination of the two, insisted that the U.S. Treasury had bled too much already to extinguish Indian claims in preparation for the openings and needed to be replenished. Among other things, the secretary neglected to consider the money pouring into the Treasury from settlers who had opted for commutation. Citing figures readily available in congressional records, Flynn estimated that the U.S. Treasury had already collected between one and two million dollars, mostly from homesteaders who had commuted their claims. In 1894 alone, homesteaders had sent nearly a half million dollars to Washington.

Summoning the fiery oratory of Galusha Grow, Flynn reiterated the Homestead Act's bedrock principle: by residing upon and cultivating their homesteads for a minimum of five years, settlers enhanced the nation's wealth and contributed to the body politic in ways beyond measure. Like the League's memorial to Congress, Flynn's closing was unambiguous:

> Mr. Speaker, I have taken more time than I intended in urging the passage of this bill. It is of transcendent importance to the people of Oklahoma. The future welfare of thousands of families depends upon the relief it affords. As I have said before, they have gone there to repair their shattered fortunes. With the relief which this bill gives they will emerge from the adverse conditions by which they are now surrounded, and will do their part faithfully and well in founding the institutions and developing the resources of the new State of Oklahoma.[22]

Even though the Free Homes Bill continued to languish, spirits were running high when Republicans convened in Oklahoma City in late March to elect delegates to the 1896 national convention in St. Louis. "The convention was a very tame affair," reported the *Guthrie Daily Leader*. "The machinery was in good working order and the usual committees were quickly ground out." Part of that good working order was in evidence when Dick Morgan was selected as an alternate delegate. He no doubt led the applause when resolutions were adopted for Republicans to renew their commitment to their party "under whose wise guidance the nation has always had progress and prosperity" and to condemn the Democratic party "as a destroyer of prosperity, as a retarder of progress, as a total failure in all the departments of government." For proof of Democratic malfeasance, all Republicans had to do was point to the bank panic three years earlier, which had toppled banks and businesses nationwide just a few months after Grover Cleveland's inauguration as president. Republicans, asserted the committee on resolutions, stood for "America and Americans, first, and the world afterward."[23]

The applause at the Oklahoma City convention continued when resolutions were read in praise of Flynn, a "popular, active and earnest" delegate who embodied Republican Party principles. "His passage of eighteen measures through the last congress, on which he made a triumphant campaign at the last territorial election, has been immeasurably added to by his effective work in the present congress," asserted the *Guthrie Daily Leader*. "The passage of the free home bill through the house shows his earnest determination that the promises made by himself and the Republican party in the fall of 1894 shall be fully carried out." Thanks to Flynn's efforts, Republicans estimated that homesteaders' aggregate savings might reach $18 million. Republicans further resolved to thank the lower house of Congress "for the hearty and unanimous support and passage of the free home bill and express the hope that the Senate will pass the same at the earliest opportunity and with equal unanimity."[24]

"Flynn and Free Homes" was the catchphrase at another convention in late August 1896. Noble County Republicans convened this one at the opera house in Perry in preparation for the November elections. Dick Morgan, still sporting the whiskers that had made him instantly recognizable even as facial hair was on its way out, was elected permanent chairman of the convention. In a speech oozing with eloquence, patriotism, and Republicanism, Morgan made two predictions: first, that Major William McKinley would soon take up residence in the White House; and second, that the Republican Party would bring a free home to every homesteader in Oklahoma Territory.[25] Both of Morgan's predictions came through in McKinley's win over Democratic contender William Jennings Bryan and (spoiler alert!) passage of the Free Homes Bill in 1900.

In a later speech in Pawnee, Morgan asserted that Flynn's focus on free homes made him the candidate "best fitted to represent the territory." He concluded his speech to "a great ovation" and assurances that Pawnee County was foursquare for Flynn.[26]

Readers in a later age of uber-toxic politics might be surprised to know that Republicans and Democrats found some common cause in the free homes movement. A year after his first defeat to McKinley (and three years before his second defeat to McKinley), Bryan responded to a letter from Judge Louis Davis, register of the U.S. Land Office in Perry, who wanted to know what Democrats thought about the Free Homes Bill that was working its way through Congress. Bryan, known as "the Great Commoner," whose crusade on behalf of farmers and laborers helped sow the seeds of the Populist Party, was unequivocal in his reply: "Our platform contained these words: 'The Democratic party believes in home rule and that all public lands of the United States should be appropriated to the establishment of free homes for American citizens.' That plank applies to Oklahoma as well as the States and I believe in the doctrine."[27]

For Republicans, second in urgency to the campaign for free homes was the imperative to maintain the gold standard as the only way to ensure a sound money supply. Presenting their party's principles somewhat tongue-in-cheek as Republicans' Ten Commandments, convention speakers admonished their listeners to have no other God but gold, to never accept silver as legal tender, to remember the power of gold on the Sabbath, and to honor their fathers and mothers, as long as they did not forget that gold was better than either and "vastly better than the prosperity and happiness of thy fellow man."[28] We are left to wonder what Dick Morgan thought about a light-hearted spoof of the Ten Commandments.

Flynn suffered a setback when he lost the 1896 congressional delegate election to James Y. Callahan, a coalition (or "fusion") candidate who appealed to both Democrats and Populists. Sensing that his time had finally come, Morgan threw his hat in the ring and, in April 1898, announced his candidacy for territorial delegate to Congress. "My great-grandfather regularly attended county and territorial Republican conventions," explained David Morgan, "and in 1898, made an attempt to be selected as the Republican nominee to be the territorial congressional delegate."[29] Somewhat nuanced support for Morgan's candidacy came from his hometown newspaper, the *Perry Enterprise-Times*: "Mr. Morgan is a good citizen and is about the staunchest gold standard Republican in this county, which is the requisite quality to entitle him inside the ranks of the Republican kingdom. We are for Dick for the nomination, but for a Democrat for election."[30] The influential *Edmond Republican* was less nuanced in its support: "Dick Morgan is one of the brainy men of Oklahoma, a true and sterling republican, than whom there is none better; should he be the choice of the party, the republicans will have a candidate in whom all have confidence and for whom all could heartily work."[31] The *Perry Enterprise-Times* cited the *Woodward News*'s unequivocal support in extolling Morgan as the most popular candidate: "The sentiment of the territory, expressed through the medium of the press, shows clearly that Col. Dick T. Morgan is the popular choice of the people of Oklahoma for candidate for Congress."[32]

Victory seemed within Morgan's grasp when Republicans in Noble County gathered in August 1898 to select delegates to the upcoming territorial convention in El Reno. Characterizing the gathering as "A Republican Morgan Mass Meeting," the *Perry Enterprise-Times* published a refrain that was making the rounds:

> "Morgan, Morgan, Morgan is all the people hear;
> Morgan will get there the same as he did here."[33]

Attendees expressed their enthusiasm for their candidate and their party in three unambiguous resolutions: (1) to renew their allegiance to the Republican Party and endorse its platform, which had been adopted at the 1896 national convention in St. Louis; (2) to confirm their pride in a party that stood for liberty, intelligence, and humanity, qualities desperately needed to face the nation's challenges as modernity relentlessly advanced; and (3) to affirm every American's justifiable pride in their wise, able, and patriotic leadership, and in a flag representing the principle of human liberty with the backing of a mighty army and navy. Finally, delegates nominated Dick T. Morgan to run for territorial delegate to Congress and empowered him to name his own delegates in El Reno. One imagines Morgan bowing in humility after his fellow Republicans were instructed "to use all honorable means to secure his nomination."[34]

"He seems to be the most available candidate," concluded the *Perry Enterprise-Times*, "and the Republicans of the territory are beginning to realize that with him as their standard bearer success will crown our efforts."[35]

When Morgan's advance guard left Noble County to open their campaign headquarters in El Reno, they relied on martial vernacular to hammer home their message: they were off to the seat of war in what would quickly become a battlefield, with a reserve force not far behind to complete the county's fighting delegation. "The edict has gone forth," intoned the *Perry Enterprise-Times* in its own bellicose messaging, "that Morgan must be nominated tomorrow and if the large number of Republicans who have gone from this county cannot accomplish that result they had better go to the Fort and enlist for immediate shipment to the front."[36]

Morgan arrived in El Reno with high hopes and an entourage of enthusiastic supporters, but he faced a formidable opponent in Flynn, the free homes champion whose accomplishments in Congress were the stuff of legend. Morgan led after the second ballot, but the third time around, Flynn received 156 votes compared to 31 for Morgan, making Flynn the hands-down Republican nominee. "The convention then went clear over the boards," declared the *Guthrie Daily Leader*, "and a perfect wild and wooly time was had, Flynn's nomination being made unanimous amidst the wildest excitement."

Playing coy, Flynn insisted that he would have declined the nomination unless the other candidates supported him. He went so far as to ask the rapturous throng to nominate another candidate. But when Morgan voiced his support for Flynn's candidacy, the cheering went into overdrive. As noted in the *Perry Enterprise-Times*, "Dick T.

Morgan the next highest candidate declined to accept the nomination and said he would heartily support Flynn, all the other candidates expressing themselves in like manner." When Flynn returned to the stage, he humbly accepted the nomination, but not without reminding his listeners that the race for Congress "was no child's play."[37]

Characteristically, Morgan refused to let his disappointment show. The *Guthrie Daily Leader* acknowledged his letdown with a not-so-subtle jab at his religious predilections: "Dick Morgan is mad, but being a Sunday school man he can't think out loud."[38]

Back in Perry, Morgan spoke before a courthouse packed with Democrats and Populists as well as Republicans. He held his audience in thrall for an hour and a half with his honest opinions and cogent arguments. "He is not abusive to the opposition," ran a local newspaper account, "but attempts by persuasion and logical reasoning to convince them that his way of thinking politically is right and will produce the greatest good for the greatest number." Morgan reached his crescendo when he cited twelve reasons why Flynn should be elected to Congress and, in a show of party solidarity, offered to deliver pro-Flynn speeches right up to Election Day. Wherever the venues might be for Morgan's speechmaking, none doubted that "the effect will be beneficial to the Republican cause."[39]

But, of course, Morgan was bitterly disappointed in his failure to secure his party's nomination for territorial delegate. Solace for a lost opportunity came in a letter from seventeen-year-old Porter, who had traveled with his mother to Indiana to visit family and friends and, not incidentally, take a break from Dick's incessant campaigning. During a respite from farm chores on a blazing hot day, Porter encouraged "Papa" to join them for a few days of rest and relaxation.[40] Although Dick declined the invitation, in a letter to Orietta he expressed his appreciation for his family's support. "I assure you that I appreciate all your words of consolation and encouragement, and will treasure your words always," wrote Morgan. "On your account I felt my defeat the more and know you above all would be sincere in your words."

Clearly optimistic about his future in politics, Morgan scrambled for a way to apologize for waiting so long to inform his wife of his defeat, noting that a victory would have spread like wildfire by telegraph. The best he could come up with was, as usual, scrupulously honest, and perhaps it serves as a lesson to us all:

"I guess I have no good excuse."[41]

In early March 1899, Morgan announced that he and Pancoast were dissolving their partnership. Morgan's new office was three doors east of his and Pancoast's former office and on the north side of the public square, upstairs from McCubbin's grocery. Although he continued to specialize in land cases, he was open to whatever the territorial courts might send his way.[42]

Meanwhile, since its inception in 1895, the Oklahoma Territorial Free Home League had grown from scattered clusters of disgruntled homesteaders into a political powerhouse. James Kirkwood, who replaced Houston as league president in April 1897, spent a month in Washington assisting Delegate Callahan in his advocacy. Kirkwood did double duty as president of the Anti–Horse Thief Association, an invaluable partner to law enforcement agencies that ne'er-do-wells antagonized at their peril. Callahan's other reinforcements included Flynn and territorial governor C. M. Barnes. Organized into nine hundred local leagues with a total membership of twenty-five thousand, the League was endorsed by the major political parties and supported by such diverse organizations as the Trans-Mississippi Congress, the Grand Army of the Republic, the Colored Men's Protective League of Oklahoma, and the Oklahoma Press Association. Additional support came from other western states and territories where many saw Indian lands as an impediment to non-Indian settlement. Rallying behind the slogan "Justice is our battle cry, and Victory means a home," League members deluged Congress with petitions and memorials in their crusade against what they deemed a repudiation of America's foundational principle of granting free land to homesteaders.[43]

To make sure Congress got the message, the League enlisted the help of Galusha Grow, the former Speaker of the House of Representatives, who had been reelected (after a thirty-one-year hiatus!) in 1894, and who was still revered as the father of the Homestead Act of 1862. As the only seated congressman from the coterie that had pushed through that historic act, Grow added a powerful voice to the free homes movement. To appeal to more ancient reasoning, League spokesmen summoned the ghost of Solon, the Athenian lawmaker whose wisdom had lost none of its resonance across the millennia: "The ideal state is that in which an injury done to the least of its citizens is an injury done to all."[44]

Intense lobbying notwithstanding, the free home bill never reached a House vote in the Fifty-Fifth Congress (March 1897–March 1899), and all Callahan accomplished was to secure extensions of homesteaders' due dates. Prospects brightened when Flynn won his old seat back in the fall of 1898 and returned to Washington for the 1899 session. In a penultimate push to the finish line, the League held its fifth convention at the opera house in Guthrie in February 1899. Every county in Oklahoma Territory sent delegates to memorialize Flynn and Callahan for their unflagging work in Congress, prepare for another year of lobbying, and elect League officers. To replace James Kirkwood as president, delegates turned to Dick Morgan, whose support for Flynn and involvement in the free homes movement convinced convention delegates that he was the man to finish the job.

Delegates adjourned with assurance that passage of the Free Home Bill was within sight. But even though the unrelenting Flynn was back in Congress, 1899 came and went without it. Nevertheless, delegates were optimistic when the League held its final convention in February 1900, this time in El Reno, and this time under the presidency of Dick T. Morgan.

"My great-grandfather addressed the convention as its last president," wrote David Morgan in a May 2021 article in the *Alva Review Courier*. "His final address to the convention was copied and sent to every member of Congress as well as other prominent Washingtonians. It was also printed in its entirety in the Guthrie newspaper the next day. The theme of the Convention: 'Justice is our Battle Cry.' Within a week after his speech was sent to Congress, he received 35 letters from Congressmen who promised to support the legislation."[45]

Morgan's address, widely acknowledged as the most elegant speech given on the subject, included a history lesson, beginning with the presidential proclamation of March 23, 1889, opening the Unassigned Lands to non-Indian settlement under the provisions of the Homestead Act of 1862. The act's promise to provide "land for the landless and homes for the homeless" had been a cornerstone of public land policy since its historic passage. Subsequent openings between 1891 and 1895 followed similar proclamations. But there was a catch: rather than pay a modest fee to the U.S. Land Office and settle in for a five-year residency to secure ownership, homesteaders were stuck with a bill. And now, after nearly a decade of lobbying and campaigning and petitioning, a cancellation of that bill seemed within reach.

All eyes were on Dick Morgan as he stepped onto the stage to deliver his presidential address. "We ask nothing except what is fair, just, right and honorable," he said as heads nodded and cheers erupted. "This is an unfair discrimination against the Oklahoma settlers. They are entitled to the same privileges granted to settlers in other territories and states of the west." Charging for land was a clear violation of homestead law "that effectually takes out the very heart of that law." Now the government was resorting to "the hairy hands of the old preemption law" in requiring homesteaders to purchase their land. To add insult to injury and without justification, the government made no distinction between town lots and homesteads, and some homesteads were more expensive than others. "No reason can be given," continued

Dick T. Morgan did double duty in the late 1890s as president of the Oklahoma Sunday School Association and the Oklahoma Territorial Free Home League.
COURTESY OF THE MORGAN FAMILY COLLECTION

Morgan. "Think of the utter absurdity of this great Republic, founded upon justice, upon equal rights to all and special privileges to none, and then setting the price of the lands as purely an arbitrary matter, without any reference to equity or fairness."

For Morgan, the Homestead Act of 1862, fashioned under the leadership of Galusha A. Grow and bearing President Lincoln's signature, became law and deserved to be placed alongside the Emancipation Proclamation in establishing America's promise: one made free men; the other made free homes. "The congress of the United States should know our position," declared Morgan with the force of righteous conviction. "We are not mendicants. We ask no special privileges. We want no donations. We seek no bounties. We plead not for charity. We demand simple *Justice*!"

One imagines a cacophony of shouting and cheering and hurrahing drowning out Morgan as he reached his crescendo:

> The hour is at hand. The opportunity is here. The struggle is in progress. The Free Home bill has been favorably reported. The tide is in our favor. The hour to vote is rapidly approaching. Millions of dollars are at stake. Aye! more than this, the homes of our people are at stake. The time has come for action. There must be plans. There must be work. Our actions should be prompt, vigorous, and judicious. I appeal to the delegates of this convention, I appeal to the people of Oklahoma to make one grand, united and determined effort to secure the passage of the Free Home bill.[46]

Galusha Grow's lengthy absence from Congress had done nothing to diminish his passion for free homes. Indefatigable as ever, he rose to the floor in 1900 to repeat his maiden speech, "Man's Right to the Soil," which he had delivered forty-eight years earlier to announce his decade-long crusade in support of free homes and against monopolists and speculators. As noted by his biographers a decade after he died in 1907, "The land cry rang out again. It was remarkable to hear the aged champion of 'Free Homes for Free Men,' after an interim of nearly fifty years since his first speech, again exhorting Congress to uphold the homestead policy."[47]

Clearly, the momentum was unstoppable. On May 17, 1900, President William McKinley signed the Free Homes Act into law. Thanks to Flynn's and Callahan's persistence, Grow's influence as the father of the Homestead Act of 1862, support from the Oklahoma Territorial Free Home League, and Morgan's electrifying speech, both houses of Congress approved the bill without a dissenting word spoken or a dissenting vote cast. With the stroke of the presidential pen, homesteaders in Oklahoma Territory saved an aggregate $15 million, or about $550 million in 2024 dollars. To add to the drama at the eleventh hour, homesteaders from other states and territories were brought under the bill's purview, thereby increasing the aggregate savings to $65 million, or almost $2.4 billion in 2024 dollars.[48]

Flynn telegraphed the good news to Oklahoma Territory, and the good times rolled. Newkirk's dual celebration, originally scheduled for the Fourth of July but held instead on June 30 to avoid conflicts with other hooplas in Kay and other counties, aimed to commemorate free homes and the harvest. "Harvest will be over," ran one announcement, "and everybody is invited; come out and have a good time and show a hearty appreciation of Free Homes." Flynn was billed as the keynote speaker—if, that is, he could make it back from Washington in time. Other speakers included Territorial governor C. M. Barnes, Territorial secretary William M. Jenkins, and the Honorable Dick T. Morgan.[49]

One of the biggest celebrations broke out in Alva over the Memorial Day weekend. Thanks to a five-hundred-dollar donation from Alva businessmen, the party was free and open to all. In addition to the requisite barbecue dinner and parade led by three marching bands, celebrants were treated to trick bicycle riding, a steam-powered merry-go-round, acrobatic derring-do, and a hot-air balloon ascension, topped off with a parachute leap. As daylight faded, weary partygoers gazed skyward for a dazzling fireworks display.

Of course, no celebration of that magnitude would have been complete without a round of speeches, interrupted by cheering and choruses of *hip-hip-hurrahs*. Speakers included Delegate D. T. Flynn,

The homestead is ours; hurrah!
Our delegate towers, hurrah!
Over Adversity,
Flynn wins the victory:
The homestead is ours, hurrah!

To Flynn 'tis accorded, hurrah
The merit awarded, hurrah!
Undaunted energy
Makes our people free:
The homestead is ours, hurrah!

An empire is shouting, hurrah!
Who is left doubting? hurrah
Bright is the coming day,
Dark clouds have rolled away,
The homestead is ours, hurrah!

List' to the thunders; hurrah!
All the world wonders, hurrah!
'Till they have understood
OUR DEEP GRATITUDE,
The homestead is ours, hurrah!

Now watch the horizon, hurrah!
For something surprising, hurrah!
A bright star will royally
Mount to our galaxy;
Twill be "OKLAHOMA," hurrah!

Governor C. M. Barnes, Black leader E. P. McCabe, and League president Dick T. Morgan. "Flynn was praised by Republican and Democratic newspapers alike," continued David Morgan in his article for the *Alva Review Courier*. "Many newspapers suggested that the day of the presidential signing should be made a legal holiday in the territory." Someone got the not-so-bright idea to purchase a home for Flynn. Perhaps more attuned to the propriety of giving such lavish gifts to elected officials, Flynn respectfully declined the offer.[50]

Free Home Poem, by S. H. Peters, Garber, O.T., May 17,1900. Published in David D. Morgan, "Oklahoma Territory Celebrates the Passage of the Free Homes Act," Alva Review Courier, May 16, 2021. COURTESY OF DAVID D. MORGAN

Not to be outdone, Perry put on a show of its own to honor Dick Morgan and all the others from Noble County who had championed the cause of free homes for free men. As soon as news of President McKinley's signing was spread, "happy, prosperous looking farmers with their wives and families, young men and their sweethearts and small boys and firecrackers" flooded the streets. Jaunty tunes filled the air, buildings were festooned with flags and bunting, and store windows enticed homesteaders with wares that were suddenly more affordable. After dinner, celebrants thronged to the northwest corner of the public square to hear Morgan, surely exhausted from a punishing travel schedule, heap praise on Flynn and other congressmen who had worked for the bill's passage. "At every mention of Flynn's name the speaker was loudly cheered," ran a breathless account in the *Perry Daily Journal.*

As in Alva and other towns throughout the territory, fireworks lit up the night sky. If press reports published during those heady days are to be believed, there were no drunks or disorderly people in the streets. According to the Perry newspaper, "Everybody was in a good humor."[51]

"But I guess my favorite celebration," said David Morgan, "was when a man in Cushing agreed to have himself tied to a rope and dragged across the town lake with a friend on his shoulders, which took place in front of six hundred people and the town band."

David went on to describe his great-grandfather's experiences in Perry as a turning point in his life. "He got knocked around quite a bit in the 1890s, but he finished on a high note as president of the Oklahoma Territorial Free Home League, and he was instrumental in getting Congress to return to the principles embodied in the Homestead Act of 1862. He and his family would soon leave Perry for El Reno, where he would continue his quest for high office and lobby for Oklahoma statehood."[52]

By the time David, Kenyon, and I went on our walkabout in Perry, I had just completed the first draft of this chapter, and I was eager to check out the birthplace of the Oklahoma Territorial Free Home

League. Shortly after we pulled into town, we met Cheryl DeJager, a retired CPA whose knowledge of Perry's colorful history had been invaluable in David's deep dive into his great-grandfather's career. As Cheryl guided us around the business district and then introduced us to her friends in the Noble County courthouse and the picturesque library next door (and before she dropped us off at Perry's famed diner, the Kumback Lunch), I tried, somewhat successfully, to picture the League's organizational meeting across the street from the public square.[53]

Although Morgan was almost surely in attendance, no evidence has come to light about who was in charge. Whatever his precise role in the organization's founding, I had no trouble imagining his and the other attendees' indignation over the federal government's betrayal of its compact with the American people. Knowing something about nineteenth-century politicians and their oratorical flourishes, I further imagined the way they would have expressed that indignation, with fists pounding tables and voices raised in righteous anger, all aimed at righting a wrong and bending the arc of history back toward the public lands policies that were key to the American experiment. Knowing something about Morgan's temperament, I was pretty sure he wasn't pounding tables and shouting in outrage over perceived injustice. More than likely, he surveyed the cacophony in pensive detachment, turning over in his mind the arguments that might win over the holdouts in Congress.

So that's why this project was so compelling! As evidenced in the Oklahoma Territorial Free Home League, those founders, for all their faults and prejudices born of another age, were engaged in creating something based on principles of fairness that, to paraphrase Dennis T. Flynn, justified the fight of a lifetime.

And then, unbidden, and certainly unwelcome, came memories of Timothy McVeigh's forced march out of the courthouse. Exactly a hundred years separated an act of creation in the Oklahoma Territorial Free Home League and an act of mindless nihilism in blowing up the Alfred P. Murrah Federal Building. And both were linked to the public square and its environs in Perry, Oklahoma.

Our final stop was at the Cherokee Strip Museum two and a half miles west of Perry on U.S. Highway 64. Touring the exhibits and an equipment shed jam-packed with farming implements and machinery, I found it easier to imagine the world that framed Morgan's dual career in law and politics and avocation in church work. Like the farmers and ranchers who built Oklahoma agriculture from scratch, Morgan participated in the run of '89 with visions of a meaningful life and applied his multitasking skills to make it happen. Success was never guaranteed, and failure was always an option.

David, Kenyon, and I had much to discuss on our way back to Oklahoma City. But I found it hard to concentrate. I couldn't shake the sense that something had gone terribly wrong between Dick T. Morgan's time and our own.

CHAPTER SEVEN

Indiana with a Panhandle

Morgan is conceded to be the best land attorney in the United States and is [*sic*] authority on land law.

Oklahoma State Capital
JULY 15, 1900

"THE FIRST REUNION OF EX-INDIANANS was held in the district court room yesterday afternoon and was a complete and glorious success."[1]

So began an upbeat article in the *Guthrie Daily Leader* about the first Hoosier reunion in Oklahoma Territory in February 1900. Held in Guthrie, the gathering came less than a week after the Oklahoma Territorial Free Home League's final convention in El Reno and just three months before President McKinley signed the Free Home Bill in Washington, D.C. Looking back at their accomplishments since the run of '89, Oklahomans had much to celebrate, and none more so than the Hoosiers who had helped make it happen.

As always, speechmaking was at the top of the agenda. Former governor George W. Steele, whose resignation in 1891 and return to Indiana had spawned speculation that Morgan would be his successor, was applauded in absentia as one of the territory's founding fathers. Governor C. M. Barnes dropped in for the party, and although his birth in New York State and growing-up years in Michigan put him outside the Indiana circle, he delivered his address "in his usual happy style," and it earned a chorus of demands for an encore. Kentucky-born Horace Speed, who had earned his Hoosier credentials in Benjamin Harrison's law firm in Indianapolis before his former boss appointed him as U.S. district attorney for Oklahoma Territory in 1890, was "highly applauded" for his tribute to Indiana's famous sons. Other addresses by Indianans who have faded from the historical record included "Old-Time Hoosierdom," "On the Banks of the Wabash," and "Indiana Poets and Poems," all of which ended to thunderous applause.

Fortunately, one of those speeches has survived in its entirety: Dick T. Morgan's "The Hoosier in Oklahoma."

Like the other addresses at the party, Morgan's rang with pride in his native state–proud of its history, wealth and resources, public institutions and, of course, its illustrious citizens, from statesmen and poets to soldiers who had risked, and sometimes lost, their lives on the field of battle. As though his listeners needed reminding, none of those citizens was more illustrious than Benjamin Harrison, whose presidential proclamation in March 1889 heralded the opening of the Unassigned Lands to non-Indian settlement. Morgan noted, "Being myself only one of the very humble Hoosiers in Oklahoma, I may, with propriety, say that Indiana is, no doubt, also proud of the honorable record of her sons in Oklahoma."

Then it was time for Morgan's civics lesson. The first man to file a claim in the U.S. Land Office in Guthrie was an Indiana farmer; behind the desk to receive his papers was the land register and a fellow Hoosier: John I. Dille. Thirty-five miles to the west, at the U.S. Land Office in Kingfisher, J. V. Admire of Indiana served as receiver of public moneys. Morgan heaped praise on Chief Justice John H. Burford for his length of service, legal acumen, intellectual power, and dignity of character. Among the three men appointed as U.S. Attorneys, two were from Indiana: Horace Speed, who was serving his second term at the time of the Hoosier reunion; and Samuel L. Overstreet, "clear-headed, warm and generous hearted, universally popular, true and faithful."

For four years, C. A. Galbraith, "that able Hoosier lawyer," had filled the position of attorney general. Oklahoma Territory legislators from Indiana, past and present, included Council president J. H. Pitzer, Senator O. R. Feagan ("No one has served with more credit in our legislative halls..."), and J. J. Merrick, who represented his county with distinction. "In every legislature," declared Morgan with the weight of evidence behind him, "the voice of the formerly Indiana man has been heard in behalf of just, wise and equitable laws." Of course, no rundown of eminent politicians would have been complete without a paean to George W. Steele, President Harrison's pick for the first territorial governor.

Morgan went on to praise Indiana's soldiers, including "the broad-shouldered, big-brained, fearless Hoosier, Major John F. Stone," who served with distinction in the Spanish-American War and, at war's end, was appointed as colonel of the territorial militia. Territorial adjutant general Bert Orner, the son of the widely known Indianan George D. Orner, served for several years as special agent of the U.S. Land Office.

It was not only in public service that Hoosiers distinguished themselves. Morgan characterized Leslie J. Niblock, editor of the Democratic-leaning *Guthrie Daily Leader*, as a "talented, versatile, and brilliant Hoosier journalist." In terms of editors more attuned to his own party, Morgan singled out Jim Johnson of Newkirk as a Hoosier who wrote with "grace, force, and originality." When it came to businessmen, Morgan posed a question that was likely greeted with *hurrahs* and shouts of a familiar name: "Who among the business men of Oklahoma, is entitled to rank with the widely known Hoosier Capitalist of Oklahoma City, Hon. Henry Overholser?" Morgan then reminded his listeners that the building in which they were having such a jolly reunion had been built by Major George F. Harriott of—you guessed it!—Indiana.

Morgan wound toward his conclusion by suggesting that an entire volume could be written under the title *Hoosier in Oklahoma*. "In general, therefore, I may say that the Hoosier in Oklahoma, may justly boast of the creditable part he has taken in the affairs of our Territory. No other state in the union can claim for her sons a record more conspicuous, useful, and honorable." To summarize his tribute to Hoosiers in Oklahoma Territory, Morgan rattled off the positions that they had attained: governor, chief justice of the supreme court, U.S. Attorney, attorney general, adjutant general, colonel of the militia, register and receiver of the U.S. Land Office, Council president in the legislature, plus innumerable positions in county and city governments, law, medicine, education, ministry, journalism, farming, construction, and transportation.

"Go where you may in Oklahoma," concluded Morgan, "there you will find the Hoosier—intelligent, industrious, progressive, law-abiding, sociable, generous, independent, loyal and patriotic. He has been a useful citizen and his coming has been a blessing to Oklahoma."[2]

The *Guthrie Daily Leader*'s rhapsody to the Hoosier reunion failed to mention Morgan's claim to fame as the author of *Morgan's Manual of the United States Homestead, Mining and Townsite Laws*. Although *Morgan's Manual* was by no means the only guide to homesteading and public lands laws, it was likely the most successful.[3] Endorsements published in the 1900 edition echoed what Secretary of the Interior John Noble had written in the 1891 edition and ran the gamut of officialdom in Oklahoma Territory and Washington, D.C.:

> "I regard it as the most valuable compilation of the laws and regulations bearing on these questions that I have ever seen."
>
> GOVERNOR C. M. BARNES, EX-RECEIVER OF THE U.S. LAND OFFICE, GUTHRIE

> "I regard it the best work of the kind published. It should be in the hands of every homesteader and every land office practitioner."
>
> JOHN T. DILLE, EX-REGISTER OF THE U.S. LAND OFFICE, GUTHRIE

> "All seekers after correct information should possess themselves of a copy of your 'Manual.'"
>
> J. C. DELANEY, RECEIVER OF THE U.S. LAND OFFICE, OKLAHOMA CITY

> "I know it will be of great value to persons having business before local land offices."
>
> J. C. ROBERTS, REGISTER OF THE U.S. LAND OFFICE, KINGFISHER

> "It should be in the hands of every homesteader."
>
> JOHN W. SCOTHORN, SPECIAL AGENT OF THE GENERAL LAND OFFICE, WASHINGTON, D.C.

> "It seems to me that this work is exactly what is needed for the use of the general public."
>
> J. V. ADMIRE, RECEIVER OF THE U.S. LAND OFFICE, KINGFISHER

> "I regard this work as of much value to those seeking homes on the public domain."
>
> S. L. OVERSTREET, EX-REGISTER OF THE U. S. LAND OFFICE, GUTHRIE

Not by happenstance, publication of the 1900 edition coincided with plans, announced on June 6, 1900, to open the Kiowa, Comanche, and Apache Reservation to non-Indian settlement. A subsequent presidential proclamation, on July 4, 1901, scheduled registration for a land lottery for later that month; the opening was slated for August. To provide background for prospective homesteaders, Morgan reviewed the provisions and requirements set forth in previous land openings. As the free home bill was still winding its way to President McKinley's desk at the time of publication, Morgan specified the fees (typically, between one and two dollars) that homesteaders had been assessed—and hopefully would no longer be assessed! —on each of their 160 acres. With reference to the Kiowa, Comanche, and Apache lands that were about to be opened, Morgan explained the special rights conveyed to ex-Union soldiers and sailors. His further recitation of fees, age and residency requirements, and a host of other provisions leaves no doubt as to why territorial courts continued to labor under a deluge of lawsuits over disputed claims. In essence, Morgan wanted settlers to know exactly what they were getting themselves into when they lined up to claim a homestead or town lot. To make sure his readers had plenty of warning, he defined *soonerism* as the act of entering and occupying lands prior to their official opening.

"Conflicting claims and contests are not infrequent," he wrote, with a flair for understatement. "Every settler should know how to proceed that he may not lose any rights which he may have acquired. A settler should not leave the land until he has done sufficient to constitute valid settlement. Settlers are often in too great haste to get to the land office and make entry."[4]

About the time the third edition of *Morgan's Manual* was published in 1900, Morgan, now forty-six years old, announced his candidacy as territorial delegate to Congress. That was good news to the *Republican News Journal*, published in Kay County. "Hon. Dick T. Morgan, the prominent Perry lawyer, has definitely announced his candidacy for delegate to congress," ran an announcement in the Republican-leaning newspaper on March 23, 1900. "This paper has a strong leaning towards Mr. Morgan by reason of the fact that he is eminently qualified for the position he seeks. Well educated in the law, clear and level-headed, a thorough Christian gentleman, genial and pleasant in all his intercourse with his fellow men, Dick becomes the ideal Oklahoma politician and statesman. His character is without blemish and his dealings consistent with the highest standards of morality."

To amplify Morgan's Hoosier credentials, the *Republican News Journal* made specific reference to his tenure in the General Assembly of Indiana as a fitting prologue to his activities in Oklahoma Territory, where he had devoted himself to his law practice and earned a reputation as a Christian gentleman and an intelligent statesman. But nothing compared to his speech at the Oklahoma Territory Free Home League convention in El Reno in confirming his qualifications as a candidate for high office. As noted in the paper's cheery announcement, "It is universally conceded to be the strongest utterance ever made on the subject."[5]

But in July 1900, Morgan earned the everlasting respect of his party by ceding to Dennis T. Flynn's popularity and withdrawing from the race. "Mr. Morgan has simply cast his bread upon the waters," ran a laudatory explanation in the *Oklahoma State Capital.* "He withdrew to make the nomination of Mr. Flynn unanimous and the voters of this territory will remember him for the graceful act." The article went on to predict that the territory's admission to the Union would make Morgan a shoo-in for a seat in Congress. "At that time this territory will have at least three members of the national house of representatives and the voters of Oklahoma will surely decide that the prosperous and growing city of Perry is clearly entitled to a congressman."[6]

As always in politics, there may have been an additional motivation for Morgan's magnanimous withdrawal. A few weeks before his announcement, the same newspaper reported that two other candidates for territorial delegate, Jerre Johnson and Tom Ferguson, had agreed to leave each other's congressional aspirations alone "and take it all out on Dick Morgan." At issue was the fact that Johnson and Ferguson owned farms, whereas Morgan's farming experience dated back to his growing-up years in Indiana. Perhaps a résumé that included current engagement in farming or ranching remained a key factor in campaigns for high office.[7]

A month after his withdrawal, Morgan returned to a vocation he had enjoyed in Indiana and launched the *Kiowa Chief*, an eight-page, four-column newspaper aimed at providing information regarding the Kiowa, Comanche, and Apache Reservation, which was scheduled for opening a year hence. His inaugural edition featured a half-tone photo of Mount Webster in the Wichita Mountains and included valuable knowledge about the area. In a display of camaraderie, the *Noble County Sentinel* welcomed Morgan to the newspaper club: "We welcome Mr. Morgan into the journalistic field, and hope that the printer's ink he may use in his publication may return to him manyfold of that longing desire of every editor."[8] Such was Morgan's interest in returning to journalism that, in May 1901, he traveled to Blackwell to attend a meeting of the Oklahoma Press Association. As noted in the *Noble County Sentinel*, "members representing newspapers throughout the territory were duly elected to the association. Among them was Dick T. Morgan of the *Kiowa Chief*."[9]

The cozy relationship between Morgan and the *Noble County Sentinel* ran both ways. In the same edition that included the paper's welcoming message, Morgan advertised the *Kiowa Chief* and *Morgan's Manual* as the go-to sources for homesteaders aiming for a slice of the three-million-acre reservation. For the bargain-basement price of a dollar, readers could buy a one-year subscription to the *Kiowa Chief*, with a sectional map thrown in as a bonus. For $1.75, Morgan would sweeten the deal with a copy of *Morgan's Manual*. He was less specific about the fee he would offer to readers who either signed up as sales agents for his publications or referred someone else. Mailing was free; all subscribers had to do was contact "Dick T. Morgan, Land Attorney, Perry, Okla."[10]

On September 27, Morgan honed his message: a year's subscription to the *Kiowa Chief* still went for a dollar, single copies were available for a dime, *Morgan's Manual* and a sectional map were only a dollar, and a sectional map was a quarter. Put it all together, and all it cost was $1.75. "Read and send to your friend back east," advised Morgan in closing.[11]

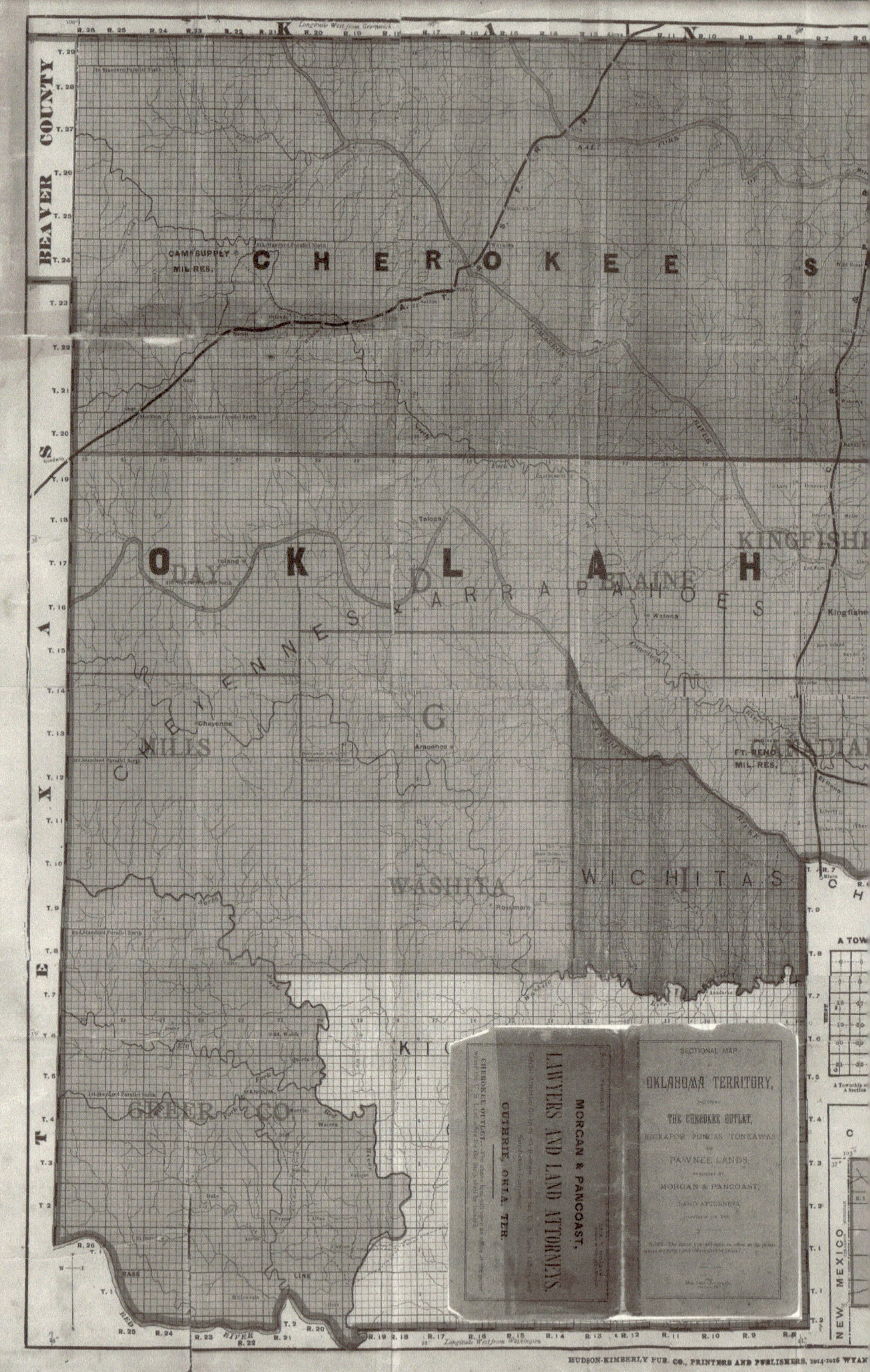

BEAVER COUNTY
CHEROKEE
S
OKLAH
KINGFISHE
DAY
BLAINE
ARRAPAHOES
CHEYENNES
MILLS
G
WASHITA
WICHITAS
CANADIAN
FT. RENO MIL. RES.
CAMP SUPPLY MIL. RES.
GREER CO.
MANGUM
TEXAS
RED RIVER
NEW MEXICO
Longitude West from Greenwich
Longitude West from Washington
Cheyenne
Arapahoe
Taloga
Watonga
Kingfisher
Rossmore
Anadarko
SECTIONAL MAP
OKLAHOMA TERRITORY,
THE CHEROKEE OUTLET,
KICKAPOO PONCAS TONKAWAS
PAWNEE LANDS
MORGAN & PANCOAST,
LAND ATTORNEYS,
MORGAN & PANCOAST,
LAWYERS AND LAND ATTORNEYS.
GUTHRIE, OKLA. TER.
CHEROKEE OUTLET.
HUDSON-KIMBERLY PUB. CO., PRINTERS AND PUBLISHERS,

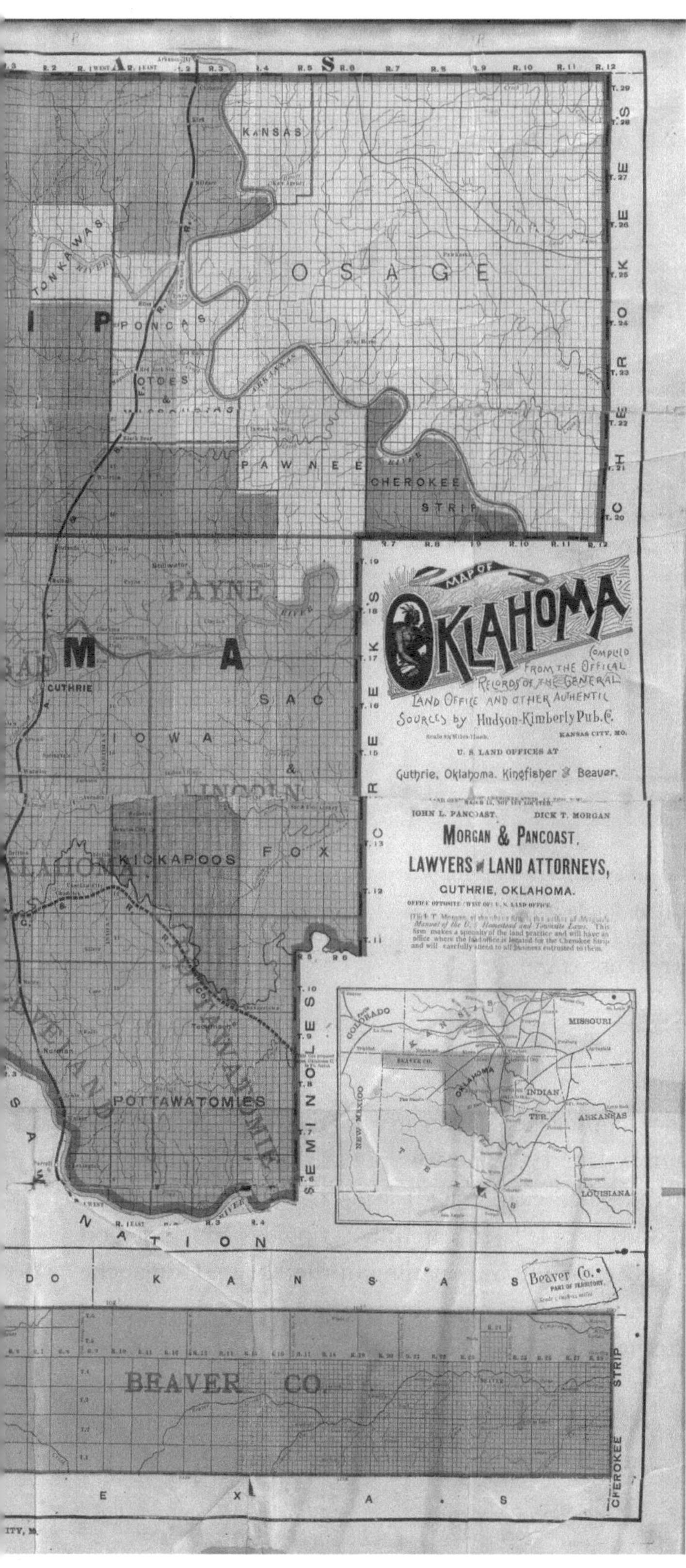

Sectional map of land available for settlement in Oklahoma, Hudson-Kimberly Publishing Company, Kansas City, Missouri, 1893. COURTESY OF THE MORGAN FAMILY COLLECTION

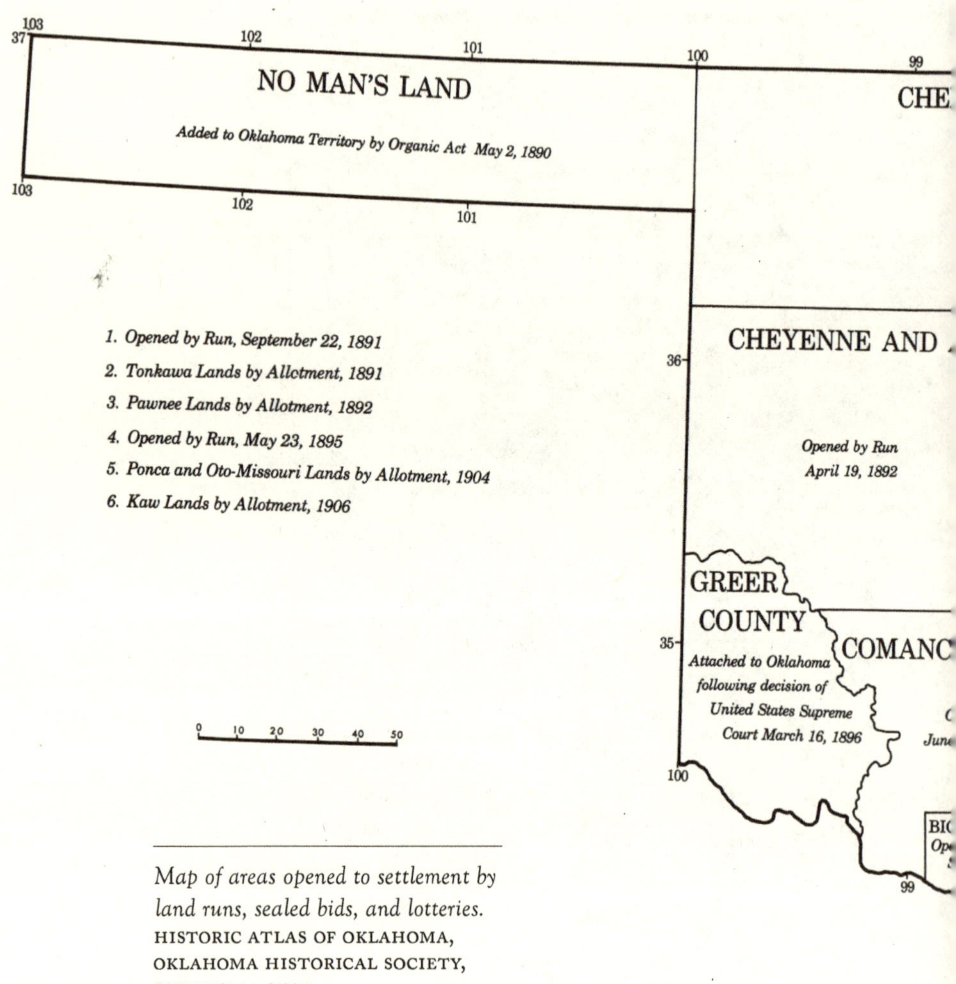

Map of areas opened to settlement by land runs, sealed bids, and lotteries.
HISTORIC ATLAS OF OKLAHOMA, OKLAHOMA HISTORICAL SOCIETY, OKLAHOMA CITY

As opening day approached, Morgan's marketing campaign was in full swing, and by late 1900, he was publishing flyers under the alluring (albeit somewhat exaggerated) heading "Oklahoma offers free homes to 75,000 people!!" In carefully scripted business jargon, Morgan continued to promote the opening of the Kiowa, Comanche, and Apache Reservation as the opportunity of a lifetime. Large cities were in the planning stages, commercial and residential lots as well as homesteads were free for the taking, and minerals—coal, asphalt, lead, copper, oil, gas, and probably gold and silver to boot—were ripe for development under U.S. mining regulations. As always, Morgan

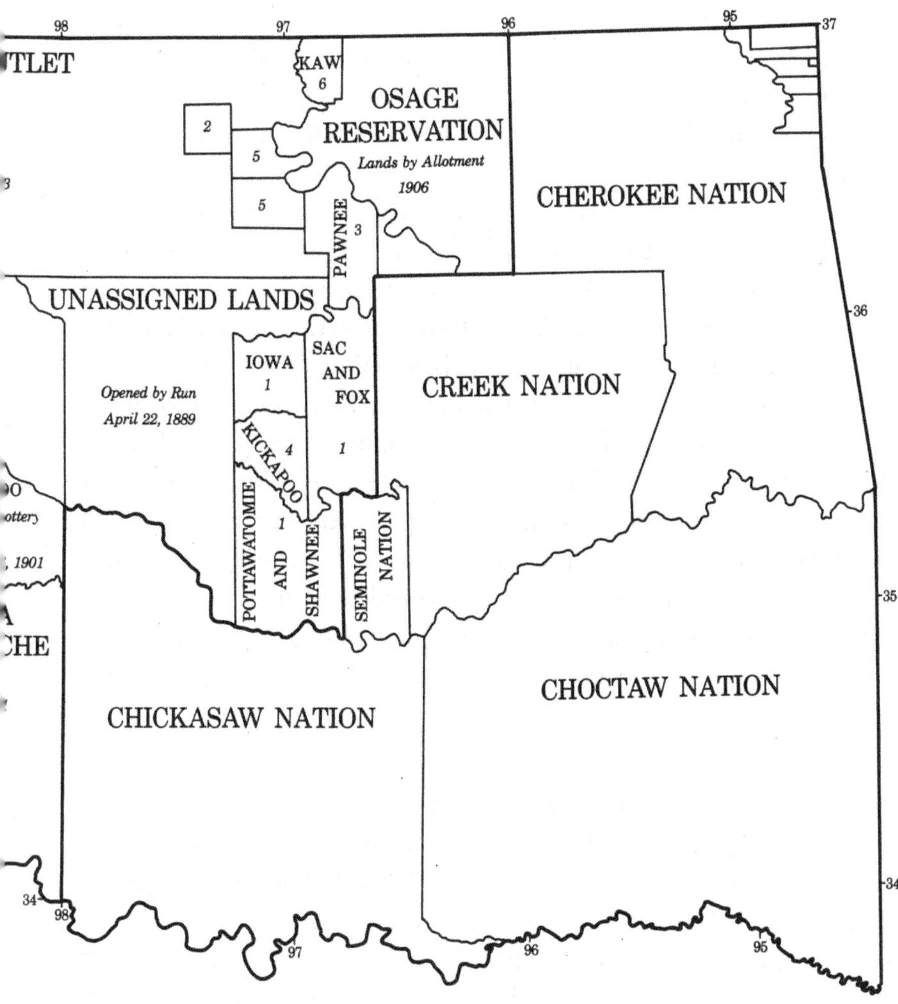

offered readers cost-effective combinations of *Morgan's Manual*, sectional maps, and a subscription to the *Kiowa Chief*. Anyone signing up as a sales agent for his publications could expect to earn handsome commissions, including 40 percent on *Kiowa Chief* subscriptions. To help his agents develop their markets, Morgan promised display cards to hang in their offices, free circulars for distribution, and sample copies of *Morgan's Manual* and sectional maps to show potential customers. He encouraged anyone not interested in becoming a sales agent to pass his solicitation on to others who would surely jump at the chance to profit from the impending opening.[12]

One thing seems certain: Dick Morgan was profiting as an author. In July 1900, the *Oklahoma State Capital*—the same newspaper that published the Hoosiers' happy reunion—included a special boxed message on its masthead: the 210-page *Morgan's Manual*, the "absolute authority on land law," was available for a mere dollar. Under the heading "How to Get Free Homes," the paper reported that the fifteen thousandth edition of *Morgan's Manual* had just been issued. The paper further reported that Morgan was, hands-down, "the best land attorney in the United States and is [*sic*] authority on land law." As the date for the Kiowa, Comanche, and Apache Reservation opening drew near, Morgan doubled down on soliciting sales agents; barring that, readers were advised to buy a copy of *Morgan's Manual*. As noted in other ads and articles in the territorial press, for an additional twenty-five cents, the author would toss in a sectional map. The article, published repeatedly that summer, concluded with instructions on how to obtain Morgan's merchandise: "The manual and map mailed to any address upon receipt of price."[13]

Just as Morgan had moved to Guthrie and Perry to be closer to the action, he set his sights on El Reno, one of two locations (the other being Fort Sill) designated for a U.S. Land Office in anticipation of the opening of the Kiowa, Comanche, and Apache Reservation. According to one estimate (devilishly hard to confirm!), nearly 170,000 people besieged those two land offices between July 9 and July 28 for a chance to buy a winning lottery ticket for a homestead or town lot. The odds were not in their favor, as only 6,500 names selected between July 29 and August 5 came away winners in a territory that, in keeping with the Organic Act of May 1890, now embraced three more counties: Kiowa, Caddo, and Comanche.[14]

"When he moved to El Reno in 1901 at the age of forty-seven, it was already an established city, having been involved in two previous land runs," explained David Morgan. During our walkabout in El Reno, I took a stroll through the Canadian County Historical Museum grounds, where the Rock Island Depot, several railroad cars, and buildings, long since removed from their original locations, provided context for Dick Morgan's activities. A marker placed on the ninety-eighth meridian bears testimony to the town's role in the two land runs that David mentioned: the run of 1889 into the Unassigned Lands east of the meridian, and the run of 1892 into the Cheyenne and Arapaho Reservation west of the meridian.[15] Perhaps deciding that land runs were too fraught with peril and conducive to cheating, officialdom in 1901 settled on a lottery to parcel out land to those lucky enough to win it.

"This time," continued David, "my great-grandfather bought a building, and leased part of the building to the U.S. Land Office. His law office was on the northeast corner of Bickford and Hayes." Just a few blocks from his office was a boardinghouse, built in 1890 and still standing today at the southeast corner of Wade and Barker, where the Morgans lived for three-plus years. It has since been converted to a single-family home, which David visited during a solo walkabout after he retired as general counsel for MidFirst Bank and that he, Kenyon, and I had the chance to visit thanks to the hospitality of its convivial owner, Jill York.

Earlier that day, before we treated ourselves to onion burgers and milkshakes at Sid's Diner, Associate Minister Tara Dew of the First Christian Church gave us a guided tour of the building, whose origins date back to Dick T. Morgan's spate of church building and that, according to architect Kenyon, deserves inclusion on the National Register of Historic Places.[16] In a brochure commemorating the church's seventy-fifth anniversary, Morgan is remembered both as a church member and longtime president of the board of the Oklahoma Christian Missionary Society, a position he held from the early 1890s until about 1905.[17]

After touring the First Christian Church, David drove us a block south to the Fogg Law Firm, owned and managed by Richard M. Fogg. The building was easy to spot as a banner by the entrance announced its founding in 1901, the same year that Dick Morgan moved from Perry to El Reno. After Richard and his wife, Lynda, warmly greeted us in the lobby, we were directed to a conference table in Richard's office. Lynda showed us a framed letter, dated November 16, 1901, from

Dick Morgan to Richard's grandfather, Harry Lee Fogg. That letter is a centerpiece of the Fogg Law Firm's memorabilia.

As Richard and Lynda explained and the letter confirmed, Dick Morgan hired Harry Lee Fogg, then living in Hobart, as an associate attorney for a weekly salary of $12.50, with the promise to be "reasonably liberal" with raises. "Hoping this will be satisfactory," wrote Morgan in closing, "I shall expect to hear from you soon; but if it is satisfactory, all you need to do is to come on and report for duty."[18]

Harry Lee's two sons, William and Rupert, and his grandson and Rupert's son, Richard, followed in the family practice, which lays claim to the longest continually operating law firm in Oklahoma. The current Fogg office is less than a half mile from the one that Morgan opened when he arrived in El Reno in 1901. Morgan purchased three, and maybe more, properties in El Reno—two in the business district and another on Admire Avenue, where the Bethel Methodist Temple Church was later built.

As Morgan acclimated to his newest venue, he was constantly revising his letterhead to reflect the growth of his law and real estate businesses. It carried his curriculum vitae and named two associates: G. W. Sawyer as general manager and Harry Lee Fogg as assistant attorney. Under the heading "Real Estate Department," the letterhead listed branch offices in Lawton, Anadarko, Hobart, Bridgeport, Harrison, Ft. Cobb, Apache, Chickasha, Binger, Sickles, Lone Wolf, and Sayre. Bank references included City National Bank in Lawton, Hobart National Bank, and the National Bank of Anadarko. If that was not enough to instill confidence in his business, he assured his clients that "any territorial or federal official in Okla." would vouch for him.[19]

On January 30, 1901, "a large and enthusiastic gathering" answered the call for a statehood convention—one of several held during the late territorial period—at the opera house in Guthrie. Cheers erupted when convention chairman Sidney Clarke of Oklahoma City announced what everyone already knew: with property valued at $175 million, industrial and agricultural production rivaling and even surpassing that of many states and territories, and educational institutions in full swing, Oklahoma Territory was more than ready to "throw off the uncertainties and impediments of a territorial form of government, and step out into the bright sunlight of a government of the people, by the people of the state of Oklahoma."[20]

Size was no impediment to statehood, as the territory was about as big as Ohio and bigger than thirteen states, including Indiana. Its population, already verging on a half million, was sure to grow by another fifty thousand with the upcoming lottery in the Kiowa, Comanche, and Apache Reservation. As noted by ex-senator and temporary convention chairman H. E. Havens, Oklahoma Territory would then exceed the population of thirteen states "whose stars glitter upon our flag and who participate in governing us."[21]

The question was, would Oklahoma Territory enter the Union by itself, or would it and Indian Territory be forced into a marriage to form a single state? As David Morgan reminded me whenever the subject came up, his great-grandfather stood with most Republicans in favoring statehood for Oklahoma Territory and leaving the less developed and heavily Democratic Indian Territory to make its own decisions whenever it was deemed ready for statehood. "As a Republican, Dick T. wanted the new state of Oklahoma to be more aligned with midwestern states such as Kansas, Nebraska, Iowa, Illinois, Ohio, and especially his home state of Indiana," continued David. "Democrats favored a single, combined state aligned with the South. Dick was very concerned that with the influx of southerners into Indian Territory (by 1900, whites outnumbered tribal members six to one), single statehood would accomplish Democrats' dream of adding another southern state to the Union."[22]

David nodded and laughed when I suggested that what Dick really wanted was Indiana with a panhandle.

Proponents of admitting Oklahoma Territory as a state had a powerful argument on their side, as Indian Territory was nowhere close to its western neighbor on just about every metric, from infrastructure and funding for public buildings to economic development and governmental organization. Also, non-Indian residents were perplexed by the Native American tribes' way of life. Despite efforts to assimilate them into the dominant capitalist economy, they had preserved their own customs, including holding land in common. This made it impossible for non-Native authorities to impose property taxes on them. White residents of Oklahoma Territory believed they would have to pick up the slack, creating an unfair burden. Indian Territory's mixture of separate tribal governments, preserving their distinct tribal cultures, stood in stark contrast to Oklahoma Territory's political organization, which rendered it a de facto state. And even if the so-called Twin Territories had somehow reached comparable stages of development, the consensus in Indian Territory, especially among Native Americans, was to avoid union with Oklahoma Territory at all costs. None doubted that such a union would surely put tribal sovereignty on the road to oblivion.

Objections notwithstanding, the ever-optimistic Sidney Clarke deemed statehood to be in everybody's best interests, no matter which of the Twin Territories they called home. "In a word," declared Clarke to his enthusiastic listeners, "Oklahoma will become a state with a stalwart American and independent manhood, demanding equal rights for all, and special privileges for none." For Frank Gillette of El Reno, who had earned a reputation for never missing a statehood convention, politics had no business getting in the way of immediate statehood, with or without Indian Territory. "If it is necessary to take care of the five civilized tribes let Congress do it," suggested Gillette. "For gentlemen, Oklahoma is fair beyond comparison. Do your duty and make your friends in Congress do their duty and it will not be long until we will be able to hold up our heads as high as the people living in the empire state of New York."[23]

That evening, standing before a hall that was "crowded to its utmost," Clarke read the convention's resolutions calling for an enabling act "at the earliest possible moment" to permit Oklahoma Territory to join the Union, with boundaries that Congress "in its wisdom may see fit to establish." If, in accordance with the Flynn bill, that meant uniting with all or parts of Indian Territory, then so be it. Clarke further called for a committee to present a memorial to Congress, "setting forth the superior qualifications of Oklahoma for statehood, on the basis of these resolutions." Dick Morgan was one of five men elected to that committee. Other committee members included Sidney Clarke of Oklahoma County; A. J. Seay of Kingfisher County, who had been appointed by President Harrison as associate justice of the territorial supreme court in 1890 and as territorial governor in 1892; Frank Gillette of Canadian County, with his perfect record of attendance at statehood conventions; and Robert A. Neff of Kay County.[24]

Ending Oklahoma's territorial status was very much on Morgan's mind when, in February 1902, he represented the statehood committee and the Republican Party on a trip to Washington, D.C., to help Delegate Flynn in his crusade for statehood. In his spare time, he tended to his day job and took care of his caseload of land disputes. As always, Morgan radiated optimism that lawmakers would do the right thing, backed by a conviction that statehood was long overdue. "To deny it," said Morgan in an interview with the *Weekly Oklahoma State Capital*, "would be to deny justice and right." Although he preferred Flynn's bill, he was ready to support any bill that would grant statehood immediately, with or without Indian Territory. Either way, Morgan was confident, for the time being, that Republicans would be the majority party, as most homesteads had been claimed by northern (i.e., Republican) immigrants who espoused conservative, pro-business policies.[25]

A month after his return from Washington to El Reno, Morgan made the short trip to Guthrie to participate in what was billed as a sad farewell to the First Christian Church's original building, which stood in the Choctaw Railway's right of way. As the only charter member in attendance, his eyes surely welled with tears as church co-founder and former pastor E. F. Boggess, then doing God's work in Des Moines, Iowa, described his adventures as a frontier minister. Morgan then entertained his listeners with tales of church building in the early days of non-Indian settlement.

Then it was back to politics. A week after the sad farewell to the First Christian Church building, Morgan was once again in Guthrie attending to legal matters when a reporter queried him about a rumored run for Congress in 1902. "Yes," he said, "I have decided to make the race for the nomination as delegate to congress on the republican ticket, and judging from present indication my name will be presented to the convention when it meets to choose a candidate." Promising a vigorous campaign, Morgan assured his interviewer that the Republican Party was rock solid and teeming with original settlers from northern and heavily Republican states, whereas most of the men who had relinquished their claims were southern Democrats.

"Dick Morgan is the typical republican, always in the harness," wrote his interviewer. Since he had helped organize the Republican Party and attended its first convention, Morgan had earned a reputation as the "number one stump speaker" in Oklahoma Territory. And now, as the 1902 Republican primary drew near, voters from across the socioeconomic spectrum were counting Morgan as one of their own, as he had met and transacted business with more people in the territory than just about anyone. As the reporter concluded, "He is one of the public men in Oklahoma who can always be counted upon at any and all times, and wherever he goes he always addresses a large crowd for the people like to hear a man in whom they have confidence."[26]

Running for Congress did not dampen Morgan's enthusiasm for real estate ventures. A no-nonsense ad in the *Noble County Sentinel* reminded readers in Perry that he was still their go-to realtor: "Attention! Real Estate Owners. If you have a farm or good city residence or business property in Noble County, which you wish to sell for cash, write Dick T. Morgan, El Reno, O.T."[27] Even so, El Reno had become his primary field of action. His purchase of an entire business block for $11,000–in cash, no less! –earned him accolades in the territorial press. "Good for Dick," ran a business brief in the *Norman Transcript*. "He has thousands of friends in all parts of Oklahoma who are glad to hear of his prosperity."[28] Somewhere along the way, he was named president and treasurer of the Western Investment Company, publisher of the *Oklahoma Real Estate Register*.[29]

Morgan's competition from other Republican hopefuls in the Republican primary of 1902 included Bird S. McGuire, an Illinois native who had been appointed as an assistant U.S. Attorney for

Oklahoma Territory in 1897. He was backed by the Rock Island Railway, which made him a formidable opponent. It also included First National Bank of Guthrie president J. W. McNeal and Oklahoma Territory's favorite son, Dennis T. Flynn. As noted in the *Noble County Sentinel*, the strong field of contenders promised to make the Republican primary in Enid on June 25 "a merry chase." Flynn, who had yet to promise that he would accept his party's nomination, knew he could count on the support of President Theodore Roosevelt, who once quipped that their friendship would cease unless he ran for reelection.

Flynn's friendship with the president surely suffered a setback when he announced his retirement from Congress. Even before he dropped his bombshell, word on the street was that he aimed to secure a Senate seat when Oklahoma Territory was admitted to the Union. With Flynn out of the running, Republicans flocked to Enid for their seventh and, by all accounts, most enthusiastic convention yet. Even the weather was on their side. "The day was perfect," ran a giddy account in the *Oklahoma State Capital*, "with weather sublimely republican."

With Governor Ferguson doubling as the party's territorial chairman, delegates nominated Bird McGuire on the third ballot. The crowd went wild as McGuire's supporters hoisted him to their shoulders and carried him to the stage. Whatever decorum was left fell to the wayside when the band struck up its rendition of "Yankee Doodle Dandy," a surefire crowd pleaser in a room packed with immigrants from northern states. More cheers erupted every time President Roosevelt's name was mentioned. Straining to be heard

Bird S. McGuire served as Oklahoma's territorial delegate to Congress (1903 – 1907) and, after the declaration of statehood in November 1907, represented the state's First Congressional District (1907 – 1915). COURTESY OF THE VIRGINIA SUTTON COLLECTION, OKLAHOMA HISTORICAL SOCIETY, OKLAHOMA CITY

above the din, the other congressional candidates announced their loyalty to the party and to McGuire.

Governor Ferguson managed to restore sufficient order for speeches to be heard. Whatever disappointment Morgan felt about losing the nomination was lessened when he was credited for his hard work on behalf of the territory and the Republican Party. As one speaker remarked, Morgan "was closer to the people than any other. Morgan was physician at the birth of the republican party in Oklahoma and had been family doctor ever since."[30] Nevertheless, Morgan was deeply disappointed with his poor showing, as he had campaigned longer, and worked harder, than any of the other candidates. "According to newspaper reports, Morgan was the clear favorite to win the nomination," said David Morgan. "Instead, he hit rock bottom." To make matters worse, Orietta was back in Indiana, and a gap in their correspondence indicates that she was unavailable for campaign advice and consolation.

Even though he was experiencing a dark night of the soul, when it was his turn to address the convention, Morgan expressed no remorse about his campaign, and he left no doubt about where his loyalties lay:

> I am satisfied with the race I made. I am profoundly thankful to my friends for the support they gave me. Canadian county gave me loyal support which I appreciate more on account of the fact that I have lived there so short a time. In my defeat I feel almost as sorry for my friends as for myself. McGuire is an able man and will make a strong candidate. He will be triumphantly elected. He will have the hearty support of Canadian county republicans. I will do all in my power to elect him.[31]

Then it was off to the general election campaign. "There are three issues in the Oklahoma campaign, and nothing else enters into the political discussions there," said Flynn in an interview shortly before he retired from the House. "They are support of President Roosevelt and his administration, statehood and free text books for the school children." Flynn brushed off criticisms that Oklahomans seemed always to be looking for something free. One critic quipped that Oklahomans had just won the right to free homes, and now they wanted free textbooks. Next, they'd be looking for free lunches.

Of those three issues, statehood was the most crucial. The Flynn Bill seemed most likely to carry the day, as it had passed the House with nary a dissenting vote. But when it reached the Senate, the Committee on Territories was split, and the bill was held over until the next session. At issue was not only the likelihood of an unhappy marriage between Oklahoma and Indian territories; there was also the complicating factor of admitting Arizona and New Mexico territories to the Union, a prospect that was bound to upset the sectional balance between Republicans and Democrats. As the 1902 campaign was playing out, the four southwestern territories remained a theater of Gilded Age politics whose terms of admission to the Union were anyone's guess.

"The campaign is one of the most interesting Oklahoma has known," continued Flynn in his interview. "There is no apathy there. I look for the heaviest vote the territory has polled and I expect Republican success." Flynn's prediction was borne out when Bird McGuire defeated William Cross, the Democratic Party's nominee for delegate, who stood with his party in advocating for a single state. Known for his fiery oratory, Cross's candidacy was compromised by his brief and even dubious residency in Oklahoma Territory. A cursory glance at a Kansas City directory showed him not only as a resident, but also as a representative of a business firm in that city.[32]

Losing his party's nomination did not dampen Morgan's penchant for speaking out. In addition to amplifying his unwavering support for Republican candidates, his loss gave him more opportunities to support the Flynn Bill regarding immediate, separate statehood for Oklahoma Territory. He delivered a speech in Pond Creek, three weeks before the November 1902 elections, that summarized the Republican Party's stance on statehood. That speech, published in its entirety in territorial newspapers, survives as a succinct and persuasive paean to Republicans' bedrock principles, a denunciation of Democrats' single-state proposition, and a testament to Morgan's fight for fairness. Morgan's throughline was that the union of Oklahoma and Indian territories (that is, single statehood) could not possibly fulfill his vision of Indiana with a panhandle—a state closely tied to midwestern politics, and far removed from the toxic culture that made the former Confederacy a risky place to do business.

First, Morgan asserted what most folks, with the notable exception of William Cross, already knew: uniting the Twin Territories would mean delay ("a long, lonesome, treacherous highway") because it would require buy-in from Native Americans, who would never surrender their tribal sovereignty without a fight. "This opposition of the Indians stands like a great range of mountains, protecting them from an invasion from Oklahoma," declared Morgan. Moreover, the federal government had no authority to alter or abolish treaties without Native American consent. To violate sacred treaties would be to stain America's democracy and its claim to exceptionalism in the community of nations.

Second, Morgan cited another factor that was common knowledge: that conditions in Indian Territory were simply not favorable to statehood. Not for the first time, Morgan recalled President Garfield's observation that a free government's strength was rooted in families, schools, and churches. He believed that none of these were firmly planted in Indian Territory, where Native Americans practiced their own spirituality and religion, communal living arrangements, and ways of educating their youth. From the perspective of most white leaders, it was a benighted land: infrastructure was "primitive" and, in their view, crime and illiteracy were rampant. Also, white leaders opposed the fact that Native land was held in common, thereby putting it beyond the reach of taxation. "No country can escape the long train of evil influences which must follow such conditions as have existed in the Indian territory for many years," said Morgan. As far as this devoted church leader was concerned, it was certainly not a place amenable to building organizations "which mold the moral sentiment of a community."

Next, Morgan warned that uniting the Twin Territories would place an undue burden of taxation on Oklahoma Territory's farmers. Digging deep into his trove of census data and statistics, he revealed the extent to which Oklahoma Territory dwarfed its neighbor in agricultural output. "These figures are a high compliment to the superiority of Oklahoma farmers," continued Morgan. In his estimation, Oklahoma Territory farmers would wind up paying six times more in taxes than farmers in Indian Territory. "The republican party proposes to stand by the farmers of Oklahoma," thundered Morgan. "We will oppose to a bitter end any statehood that will not be fair, just and equitable to our farmers."

Along the same lines, Morgan cited taxation as a fourth objection to union. Although combining state salaries and expenditures would achieve some economies of scale, the costs for education, the criminal justice system, caring for residents with disabilities, and a host of other obligations would skyrocket. Inevitably, taxes would ratchet up, and none more so than property taxes. With its dearth of taxable property, residents of Indian Territory would lean heavily not only on Oklahoma taxpayers, but also on the federal treasury.

Given his experience in public lands policies, it comes as no surprise that Morgan's fifth objection was the threat that single statehood would pose in funding common schools, public buildings, universities, agricultural colleges, and normal schools that had been built on Oklahoma's public lands. Perhaps later, Congress in its wisdom could devise formulas to compensate Oklahomans for divisions of their public lands. But real equality was a pipe dream: "Whatever may be the advantage of single statehood, the people of Oklahoma will certainly not vote to contribute to the people of the Indian territory, by taxing themselves one half million dollars every year for all time to come."

Morgan's sixth and final objection was that single statehood was "out of harmony with the position of the national democracy." For the past six years, Republicans' position on statehood had been in sync with the basic tenets of the American system of government. Congress's Committee on Territories agreed, and it made its position clear in one of many opinions on the advisability of Oklahoma statehood: "In the opinion of this committee, no territory has been better fitted to enter the Union as a state." Many Democrats, but certainly not all, supported this position. "I feel sorry for our democratic brethren in being divided," said Morgan as he reached the end of his Pond Creek speech, "but I can get consolation in the Scripture which says, 'A house divided against itself cannot stand.'"[33]

As always, Morgan complemented his political maneuvering and speechmaking with building his business in Oklahoma Territory and beyond. In ads published in newspapers nationwide, he enticed homesteaders to follow Horace Greeley's advice and move west to grow up with the country. In a departure from his usual business dealings, Morgan was named as president of the Denver, El Reno, and New Orleans Railway, an audacious enterprise incorporated in Oklahoma Territory that aimed to build a thousand miles of track linking the Gulf Coast to the Rocky Mountains, with its red-hot center in El Reno. To raise money for the venture, Morgan spent two months in early 1903 negotiating with financiers in New York and New England. "I have made arrangements, which are practically complete, to finance the proposition," said Morgan in an interview with the *Woodward Dispatch*, branded on its masthead as a "flat-footed truth teller" and the only Democratic newspaper in Woodward County. "I find in the east a sentiment favorable to Oklahoma investments that is as flattering as it is sound."

Rather abruptly, the reporter switched topics and asked Morgan to comment on D. T. Flynn's position as expressed in the eponymous "Flynn bill" that was circulating through Congress. The bill provided for Oklahoma Territory's admission to the Union without special reference to Indian Territory other than authorizing Congress to admit specific areas as soon as they met with congressional requirements. Morgan did not "fully concur" with Flynn's somewhat ambiguous bill and suggested that economics trumped politics in the decision of whether to combine Oklahoma and Indian territories: "The main proposition is not one of politics. Statehood is of right, due Oklahoma. It will be due the Indian Territory in 1906."

Not surprisingly for a man with ambitions for high office, Morgan reverted to politics to assert his clear preference for Republican rule, no matter what might transpire in the escalating and increasingly acrimonious debate over statehood:

> I believe that the single state to be formed of those two will ultimately be a republican state. The day of solid states has gone. It went with the better education of the people and the forgotten rancor of the war between the states. Oklahoma is now republican. It will probably

> be republican, though joined with Indian Territory, when the latter shall have been settled. But with or without statehood, Oklahoma is making giant strides to the front in a material way. It has an exceptionally good administration of public affairs by Oklahoma men who have been given place by the government. We can wait for statehood and continue to build more railways than any other state in the union. But we ought to have statehood for Oklahoma at once—for we deserve it.[34]

What Morgan did not say, but surely thought, was that many of those Oklahoma men appointed to high office were born-and-bred Hoosiers.

Morgan's multitasking during his years in El Reno extended to higher education. In a letter written in 1949 to an unknown person, Porter recalled overhearing a conversation indicating that his father was instrumental in founding Phillips University in Enid:

> I remember one hot August afternoon at El Reno, Oklahoma, in 1902, when James Monroe, C. M. Jackman, and my father were sitting out in the shade of a residence, they got to talking about the need to have a church college or university in Oklahoma, and I recall very clearly their deciding that something must be done about it in the very near future. No doubt this was perhaps the first conference or talk about the situation which eventually led to the establishment of Phillips University.[35]

Less than a month after Morgan delivered his speech at Pond Creek, delegates from Oklahoma, Arizona, and New Mexico territories arrived in Washington, D.C., to advocate for statehood. Their arrival coincided with the Committee on Territories' investigation into conditions in the three territories. Aside from Oklahoma Territory's strained relationship with its neighbor, factors that would determine their prospects for statehood ranged from population and taxable property to mineral wealth and natural resources. But as with everything in Washington, politics was never far from the surface. Now that his bill had sailed through the House, Dennis Flynn continued to insist that Oklahoma would be a Republican state, and he advised

Republican delegates—a group that would soon include his successor, Bird McGuire—to vote for immediate statehood. Flynn's confidence was about to be tested at a one-state convention slated for December 3, where up to a thousand delegates were expected, and in the Senate chamber on December 10, when statehood for the three territories would be up for debate. Waiting in the wings was President Roosevelt, whose expectations of his partisans in the Senate might have seemed overly optimistic. As noted in the *Evening Star*, "The advocates of statehood are counting on the support of President Roosevelt, whom they are quoting as favoring the admission of the territories without any reference to their future political affiliations."[36]

Debates over statehood were raging from Oklahoma Territory to the nation's capital when, on November 28, 1902, leaders from the Cherokee, Chickasaw, Creek, Choctaw, and Seminole nations (collectively known as the Five Tribes) summoned a conference in Eufaula to make sure that Indian voices were heard. As Dick Morgan had emphasized at Pond Creek, as his first objection to single statehood, Indian opposition did indeed stand "like a great range of mountains" against an invasion from its western neighbor. According to the *Oklahoma State Capital*, tribal delegates in Eufaula were "unalterably opposed to absorption of the Indian territory by any other state or territory." In their resolutions, delegates admonished Congress to hold to its agreement to extinguish Indian land titles no earlier than March 4, 1906. Hopes ran high that Indian Territory would then be ready to support a bill to join the Union as a single state.[37] To paraphrase Dick Morgan, honoring sacred treaties was the least the federal government could do to extend fairness to its most vulnerable citizens.

By late 1903, the Republican Central Committee had heard enough about single statehood and, at a meeting in Guthrie on November 20, decided once and for all to let Indian Territory fend for itself. Under the urging of Governor Tom Ferguson, committee members agreed to enlist their party's support in compelling Congress to pass a separate statehood bill. Otherwise, Oklahoma Republicans would be doomed to domination by Democrats, who ruled supreme in Indian Territory.

"It is now a matter of politics with us," said Ferguson as heads nodded around the room, "as it has always been a matter of politics with Congress." Taking his cue from the governor, former governor A. J. Seay implored committee members to work as Republicans to secure a Republican state. Next up was Sidney Clarke of Oklahoma City, who declared that the statehood fight would, and indeed should, be a Republican fight. Among the committee members who voiced their wholehearted agreement were former governor Cassius M. Barnes and Dick Morgan, who had no doubt that single statehood would consign the Republican Party to minority status.[38]

In January 1904, Morgan's penchant for speaking out took him to Washington, D.C., where he argued his and his party's position.

"Dick T. wanted a midwestern state," David Morgan repeated to make sure I got it. "He was concerned that Indian Territory had been so overrun by southern Democrats that a single state would be dominated by those southern Democrats. He wanted a state that would attract immigrants and capital from the Midwest and northern states."[39]

Given his stance at the Republican Central Committee meeting in November, it comes as no surprise that Morgan was less than enthused about McGuire's bill. Like Flynn's bill that had held such promise in 1902, before its popularity ebbed and then crashed altogether, the McGuire bill included a clause that all or parts of Indian Territory could be added to Oklahoma when Congress deemed it prudent. Morgan acknowledged that Indian Territory's land area, population, and resources met the requirements for statehood. But it came up short on three key metrics. First, its laws were deemed inadequate or nonexistent. Second, it lacked an organized civil government. Finally, its institutions, including education, were not fully developed.

"Mr. Chairman and gentlemen of the committee, these things to which I have called your attention demonstrate my first proposition that Oklahoma is a State in everything but name and the relation she bears to the Federal Government," declared Morgan. "In my humble judgment, this committee should make a favorable report on this bill. The measure should pass both Houses of Congress, receive the approval of the President, and become a law at the earliest possible moment."

Under direct questioning from committee member James T. Lloyd, a Democrat from Missouri, Morgan admitted that proponents of immediate statehood for Oklahoma Territory were willing to compromise on adding all or parts of Indian Territory to the new state because they thought Congress would sign off on it:

> Mr. Lloyd. Is not the real difference in Congress, the real difference at your home; that is, the question of single or double statehood? Is not that really, the difference between your people at home?
>
> Mr. Morgan. Yes, sir; we differ on that some.
>
> Mr. Lloyd. Your argument has been to the effect that Oklahoma is now entitled to statehood?
>
> Mr. Morgan. Yes, sir.
>
> Mr. Lloyd. Without reference to the Indian Territory?
>
> Mr. Morgan. Yes, sir.
>
> Mr. Lloyd. Why do you not make your bill correspond to that view?
>
> Mr. Morgan. We have done this with a view to getting a majority in Congress to vote for it.

Morgan made it clear that neither he nor any other proponent of Oklahoma statehood bore ill will toward Indian Territory, and they wished its citizens nothing but the best. Nevertheless, he was determined to hold Congress to a standard of fairness. "My first duty—after loyalty to the Nation—is to the commonwealth of which I am a citizen," said Morgan. "The people of Oklahoma ought not to be required to bear the burdens of the people of the Indian Territory, and it is unjust for Congress to require it."

In closing, Morgan detailed the deficiencies of territorial status: it denied Oklahomans the benefits of full citizenship in the Union, prevented their participation in national affairs (except, of course, the obligation to pay taxes), and granted only partial representation in Congress and no voice in presidential elections. "Our lips are closed; our voices are hushed; our opinions, our sentiments, our views, our ideas are smothered under the great incubus of Territorial government. Territorial government retards our material growth and progress. Every business halts and hesitates under its paralyzing touch. Commerce feels insecure; capital is timid."

Then Morgan delved into his cache of oratorical flourishes, honed to a razor's edge through dozens of impassioned speeches and sermons in Indiana and Oklahoma Territory, to close his testimony before the Committee on Territories: "A Territorial government is tolerated only through necessity. Its defects are glaring. Its faults are conspicuous. Its drawbacks are numerous. Its burdens are heavy. Its disadvantages are as the sands on the seashore. To further perpetuate it, after the reasons for its creation have ceased to exist, is oppression and tyranny."[40]

Delivering his message to the Committee on Territories in the winter of 1904, neither Dick Morgan nor anyone else embroiled in the statehood debate could have imagined that almost four years would pass before Oklahoma was admitted to the Union as the forty-sixth state, and in ways that were definitely not to everyone's liking.

"Porter and Clem take their usual stroll," ran a caption in the 1903 edition of Quax, the Drake University yearbook, above a drawing of Porter Morgan and Clemmer Deupree, known in their social circle as the Siamese twins. COURTESY OF THE CARL ALBERT CONGRESSIONAL RESEARCH AND STUDIES CENTER, NORMAN, OKLAHOMA

CHAPTER EIGHT

The Right Kind of State

> Promote good business, a positive environment for laborers and educators, and guarantee people's rights and privileges regardless of race, creed, and color.
>
> DICK T. MORGAN, 1907

WHILE DICK AND ORIETTA were making their transition from Perry to their newest field of action in El Reno in 1901, their teenage son was making an entirely different transition: from high school to college.

"Nobody knows for sure, but family lore has it that Porter was sent to Drake University in Des Moines, Iowa, a Disciples of Christ School, because he had been involved in a drinking episode at OU as a freshman," explained David Morgan about the ill-starred beginning of his grandfather's college career. "Of course, Dick T. was a staunch supporter of prohibition throughout his entire life. Porter had also gone to a boarding school at OU, located on the North Oval."

Any misgivings Porter might have had about leaving Oklahoma faded away when he met an attractive girl from the Hawkeye state, Clemmer Deupree. "Grandpa and Grandma were definitely an item at Drake," continued David. "There are two photos of the happy couple in the school yearbook." After Porter graduated, he and Clemmer were married in her hometown of Bloomfield, Iowa, on September 15, 1903. The newlyweds promptly moved to New York City, where Porter attended law school at Columbia University. Some of the saddest letters that Dick and Orietta received from their son and daughter-in-law were during the winter of 1903, as that was the first holiday season that Porter and Clemmer had spent apart from their families. Porter remained at Columbia for a year before transferring to the University of Chicago Law School, which had opened two years before

Porter's arrival. Back in the Midwest, Porter and Clemmer would be closer to their relatives in Indiana and Iowa and have shorter trips to Oklahoma.[1]

Meanwhile, the ever-expanding regions of America's heartland open to homesteading were about to expand once again, this time in South Dakota. About the time Porter was completing his first year of law school at Columbia, word hit the streets that President Theodore Roosevelt would issue a proclamation opening the Rosebud Reservation to non-Indian settlement. That proclamation came on May 13, 1904. Registration for a land lottery was set to begin on July 5 at four communities in South Dakota: Chamberlain, Yankton, Bonesteel, and Fairfax. Other than honorably discharged soldiers and sailors, who had earned the right to register in absentia, land seekers were required to register for the lottery in person in hopes of acquiring one of nearly 2,500 homesteads carved out of the Sioux Nation's 382,000-acre reservation.

Prospective landowners line up on Capitol Street in Yankton, South Dakota, in anticipation of the Rosebud Indian Reservation opening in 1904. Dick T. Morgan's office sign is visible among the jumble of signage at left. COURTESY OF THE YANKTON COUNTY HISTORICAL SOCIETY, PHOTO COLLECTION, YANKTON, SOUTH DAKOTA

It was all too tempting for Oklahoma Territory's most accomplished land lawyer. No sooner did Porter wrap up his spring 1904 semester at Columbia than he joined his parents on yet another adventure on the rapidly fading line of frontier settlement.

In the spring of 2021, David and Ellen Morgan traveled to Bonesteel and Yankton to follow his family's unlikely detour to the northern plains to participate in the opening to non-Indian settlement of the Rosebud Reservation. The entire Morgan family, including Porter and Clemmer, spent most of the summer of 1904 in South Dakota. David found the exact locations of Dick T.'s offices in Bonesteel and Yankton, and he learned even more when he came across a cache of his great-grandfather's letters from the summer of 1904.

"Dick T.'s business letterhead included three principals," explained David in one of our many FaceTime conversations. "Other than himself, he listed his son, Porter, who had completed only a year of law school before being thrust into the Rosebud Reservation land lottery; and Dick's brother, Fred." In addition to their two offices near the reservation and the one in El Reno, their letterhead listed an office in Chicago, where the Morgans conducted what Dick T. referred to as their "soldier business." More than likely, the Morgans represented Civil War and Spanish-American War veterans in the Upper Midwest, who didn't have to travel to South Dakota to participate in the lottery and needed a lawyer to represent them.

"Bonesteel just hasn't changed," continued David. "It literally looks like you could walk in today and register for the 1904 lottery. It's the same town, almost like a western movie set!" There was at least one change that might have surprised Dick T.: as near as David could tell from his and Ellen's walkabout, the registration office where land seekers had lined up for their lottery tickets had taken on a new purpose as the Bonesteel Supper Club. Unfortunately, David and Ellen never sampled the menu, as the eatery was closed on the day they toured Bonesteel. They had better luck after Kelly Wollman, editor and owner of the *Bonesteel Enterprise*, directed them to a café down the street where photos told the story of early-day Bonesteel and a local historian, Doug Spitzenberger, regaled them with tales of the land lottery of 1904.

David and Ellen then traveled ninety-three miles to Yankton, where they found the biggest surprise of their South Dakota trip. At the Mead Cultural Education Center, there was a photo of the Pierce Hotel, where registrants signed up for the Rosebud Reservation lottery. Next door was a small structure that David identified as Dick T.'s law office, where he registered lottery applicants. Later that day, Kelly Hertz, editor of the *Yankton Daily Press and Dakotan*, was receptive when David offered to submit an article about his great-grandfather. It was published on July 2, 2021.

Despite worries that there might not be enough applicants to claim all 2,500 homesteads, business was brisk at the registration sites and the lawyers' offices that served them. More than 106,000 people filed applications–57,434 in Yankton and 37,034 in Bonesteel. Even so, Dick Morgan was having second thoughts. As David Morgan noted in

Dick T. Morgan's law office near the Rosebud Indian Reservation in South Dakota, 1904. Standing from left to right on the front row are Porter, Clemmer, Orietta, and Dick Morgan. COURTESY OF THE MORGAN FAMILY COLLECTION

his article, "My great-grandfather seemed dissatisfied with his venture in South Dakota. It did not seem to measure up to what he had remembered from the exciting 'land-run' days in Oklahoma." For one thing, fierce competition forced attorneys to work for a pittance. Their fee often consisted only of charges for notary services, which ran as low as twenty-five cents a pop. Worse yet, con artists and pickpockets ruled the streets, and storms were horrific even by Oklahoma standards. Nevertheless, when Morgan returned to El Reno for the 1904 political campaign season, he had every intention of returning to South Dakota to pick up where he had left off.

But fate had other plans. While campaigning for Republicans in Oklahoma Territory, Morgan received word that President Roosevelt had appointed him as register of the U.S. Land Office in Woodward, Oklahoma Territory. The *Congressional Record* carried a notice whose brevity belies its huge implications for the aspiring congressman: "Dick T. Morgan, of Elreno [*sic*], Okla., who was appointed November 23, 1904, during the recess of the Senate, to be register of the land office at Woodward, Okla."

So, instead of catching the train to South Dakota, Dick and Orietta moved to Woodward in December 1904 to enjoy the prestige of a political office and the handsome salary of $4,500 per annum that came with it. As noted in the *Woodward Dispatch*, "There is a good deal of satisfaction shown in Guthrie over the appointment of Colonel Dick T. Morgan, of El Reno, to fill the vacancy in the receivership of the land office at Woodward. He is popular with the people without regard to party and his indorsement [*sic*] by so many leading Republicans is taken to mean that there are no factional fights in the Republican party in Oklahoma."[2]

And, as David Morgan wrote in his article for the *Yankton Daily Press and Dakotan*, "It would also provide him a political base that would ultimately lead to a seat in Congress after statehood."[3]

But not everyone in Woodward was thrilled about Morgan's appointment, as he had an unfortunate and undeserved reputation as a latter-day carpetbagger. His previous residences—Guthrie, Perry, and

El Reno—were on the eastern side of Oklahoma Territory, and he was now smack in the middle of the high plains, where trees were rare, water was scarce, and undulating grasslands stretched all the way to the Rockies. What is more, some thought that Woodward had no need for an outsider, as there were plenty of Republicans in the northwest who were qualified to serve in the U.S. Land Office. But President Roosevelt, a wildly popular Republican whose values dovetailed perfectly with Morgan's, wanted him in Woodward, and that was good enough for him.

After a brief stop in Alva, Morgan arrived in Woodward in the evening of December 7 and made straight for the courthouse. As court was in session, he ran into several acquaintances who surely congratulated him on his appointment. Not surprisingly, he dropped by the land office before checking into a hotel, a simple frame building that had at least two advantages: it was centrally located and it was known for fine dining.

Morgan stayed at the Central Hotel, long since demolished to accommodate urban development. During my walkabout (or, more accurately, driveabout) with David in Woodward, we passed by the half dozen lots that Dick Morgan owned and leased out for use as a movie

---

Dick Morgan, third from left, standing in front of the U.S. Land Office in Woodward, Oklahoma Territory, circa 1906. COURTESY OF THE MORGAN FAMILY COLLECTION

theater on Main Street, the Central Hotel's former location, and the site of the U.S. Land Office at the corner of Main and 11th Street. The U.S. Land Office was replaced first by the McDonald photography studio, then by a building that now houses Woodward Main Street.

Fortunately, we have Dick's letters to and from Orietta to tell us about his first days in Woodward.

Before retiring on his first night in Woodward, Dick dashed off a letter to Orietta, who had stayed behind in El Reno to wait for her husband to find suitable lodgings. "All things considered I think it will be better for me to postpone coming home for a week," wrote Morgan on Central Hotel stationery. "You can therefore make your arrangements accordingly." His closing was, as usual, overflowing with fondness for his wife: "With much love & kisses, I remain, your affectionate husband, Dick."[4]

Morgan wasted no time in getting down to business. "I entered upon my duties this morning and everything passed off smoothly," he wrote to Orietta on December 8. "There is plenty of work to do, & things are slightly mixed." Perhaps to assure her that accepting Roosevelt's appointment had been a good idea, he offered an assessment of the community that would be their home for the next sixteen years: "Woodward has improved some since I was here–it is quite a nice little city." And the hotel where he had spent his first night? "They set a pretty good table and things seem very clean & nice. It is the best hotel here."[5]

By the time Morgan moved to Woodward, that nice little city was booming. "Woodward started coming into its own in 1904," explained Robin Hohweiler, former executive director of the Plains Indians and Pioneers Museum in Woodward. Three industries put Woodward on the map: broom corn, which was easy to raise and spawned two factories that shipped it nationwide; creameries; and cattle. "This was a huge hub of commerce," continued Hohweiler, who went on to mention a prized photo of the last cattle drive from the Texas Panhandle that made its way into the museum's collection. A cattle shipping yard and livestock market once defined the town's business district, at First and Main Street, before urban development became concentrated in the current downtown area, some nine blocks to

the west. A highlight of David's and my Woodward walkabout was lunch with the museum's executive director, Mikel Robinson, at Al's Steakhouse, a well-appointed restaurant that occupies the spot where cattle were once herded and shipped to market.

Meanwhile, a less respectable business was muscling its way into Woodward: bootlegging, a genuine growth industry that gained traction as calls for Prohibition became more insistent on the eve of statehood. "Beer and spirits were shipped in from Kansas," said Hohweiler. "Bootleggers wielded real power. In the run-up to statehood, saloon keepers tried to renew licenses before prohibition could put them out of business. There were more saloons, brothels, and dance halls than any other business!"[6]

Surely energized by Woodward's booming businesses (and just as surely vexed by Satan's grip on his most recent hometown), Morgan reported that his second day on the job went even better than the first. Although his colleagues at the land office were running behind on their paperwork, he felt certain that they could catch up within aweek. As he

---

Main Street looking west past 6th Street, Woodward, Oklahoma Territory, circa 1911–14. COURTESY OF THE PLAINS INDIANS AND PIONEERS MUSEUM, WOODWARD, OKLAHOMA

reported to Orietta on December 9, "I am learning some things about the work of the Register, but on most of the questions which arise, I am pretty well-posted." Such was his satisfaction with accommodations at the Central Hotel that he was considering boarding there, as long as he could talk the proprietor down on price.

In his spare time, Morgan formed a friendship with Pastor Ed S. McKinney at the Christian Church. A young man educated in Texas, McKinney apparently had a flair for delivering a good sermon. Morgan was duly impressed, and in the weeks to come, he enjoyed attending Sunday School in a building that doubled as an opera house ("a rather comfortable place") and dining with his new friend. Morgan's only complaint was the absence of a stove in his room. This forced him to spend most of his evenings in the hotel office and left him suffering from a stiff neck.[7]

Although he made friends quickly, Morgan managed to run afoul of a newspaper editor, Billy Bolton, who resented Morgan's decision to post legal notices in a competing newspaper that charged two dollars more than Bolton did. We are left to wonder if Bolton's derisive nickname for the eastern immigrant, "Two Dollar Dick," made much of an impression among Morgan's new neighbors in Woodward. Most of them regarded Morgan as the town's most forceful elected figure and a credit to the community, and his friends included a fair number of Democrats.[8]

Busy though he was building his businesses and sorting out land claims at the U.S. Land Office, Morgan made time to give lectures to his neighbors on work ethics. He had been in Woodward for only seven months when, in July 1905, he delivered a speech (probably one of his ready-made ones that he could pull out on a moment's notice) on the alluring topic "Pyramid of P's for the Potent Pedagogue." The *Woodward Democrat* invited one and all, and especially educators, to come to the Presbyterian Church for what was sure to be an enlightening evening.

Morgan began with a reference to one of the seven wonders of the world—the pyramids of Egypt, immense stone structures erected by the ancient Egyptians to commemorate their pharaohs. Those structures have withstood the ravages of time and the depredations of tourists who, for centuries, had been trampling over them in a daze of wonder. But the pyramids paled in significance to the structure that Morgan was about to build for his rapt audience. His pyramid, hewn "from immaterial substance" and more enduring than any edifice built of iron or stone, was composed of attributes that contribute to a life well lived, all starting with the letter "p."

First came punctuality, and who could argue with the importance of showing up on time? Then came preparation, "indispensable to meritorious and effective work," and a passport to exploring the higher realms of knowledge. Pluck combined "the great moving boulder of push" and the "brilliant diamond of persistency." Those endowed with pluck succeeded; the faint of heart did not. "Let our pyramid be permeated with pluck, push and persistency."

Morgan continued his lesson in geology with a succession of p's, all of which he likened to stones and precious gems: the jewel of promptness, the white marble of patience, the solid granite of perseverance, and the limestone of practicality. In his lexicon, the pure gold of philanthropy was less about giving to charity than expressing kindness and love for mankind. The only exceptions to Morgan's rock-solid imagery were his paeans to the utilitarian sunshine of prudence and the banner of patriotism.[9]

One imagines an energized throng exiting the church and dispersing into the northwest Oklahoma night, bidding one another a good evening, and vowing to brush up on their p's. Meanwhile, gathering his notes at the pulpit, a pensive Dick Morgan was pondering the lessons he had learned on a farm in Vigo County, Indiana, which had brought him all the way to the U.S. Land Office in Oklahoma Territory at the behest of President Theodore Roosevelt. These lessons would propel him to Congress, where he would spend the rest of his life in service to his country.

President Roosevelt's appointment of Dick Morgan to serve as register of the U.S. Land Office in Woodward, and Morgan's eager acceptance of the position as a potential on-ramp to Congress, offers an opportunity to delve into a movement that fought against the inequities of Gilded Age America and shaped public policy for generations to come. Through this movement, Roosevelt and Morgan were united in a common cause: Roosevelt the president, whose bully pulpit gave him immense leverage to promote reforms aligned with Republican principles; and Morgan the lawyer, churchman, and aspiring congressman, whose multifaceted career in Oklahoma Territory, inspired by a deep and abiding faith in Scripture, had caught the attention of higher-ups in Washington. After so many disappointments in territorial politics, Morgan had reason for optimism. With Roosevelt's support, he might finally achieve his dream of winning election to Congress and taking his fight for fairness to a whole new level.

Known to history as Progressivism, the movement that inspired such leaders as Teddy Roosevelt and Dick Morgan emerged from populism and its manifestation in the short-lived Populist Party. Progressivism roared to life in the writings of Henry George, a newspaperman and entrepreneur whose outlook took shape when his businesses were wrecked by Gilded Age monopolies. Recognizing that his misfortunes were the outcome of a crushing economic system that left small businesses defenseless against predatory corporations, George penned one of the most influential books of the early modern period: *Progress and Poverty: An Inquiry into the Cause of Industrial Progress and Depressions and of Increase of Want with Increase of Wealth.*[10] First published in 1879, reprinted countless times, and translated into nearly every language that knew print, George's book revealed the unfairness in unfettered capitalism and opened the floodgates to political and social reform.

Written at a time when Americans were still reeling from the bank panic of 1873 and its attendant miseries, *Progress and Poverty* posited progress not merely as the advance of science and an increase in personal fortunes, but as a social process aimed at improving people's lives regardless of their standing on the socioeconomic ladder. Believing that the "garments of laws, customs, and political institutions which each society weaves for itself, are constantly tending to become too tight as the society develops," George admonished his readers to imagine a community as people in a lifeboat whose chances of survival depended on conserving their energy and charting their course together.[11] Like many writers of his era who mourned the passing of a golden age, real or imagined, George relied on a biblical theme dating back to America's founding: Eden was vanishing, and its loss was nothing less than catastrophic for future generations.

Three decades after *Progress and Poverty* was first published, Herbert Croly seized the mantle of Progressivism in *The Promise of American Life*, a book that served as both a palliative and an instruction manual for a nation hurtling headlong into runaway industrialization and the social ills it created. Unlike George, Croly believed that America was not a tarnished Eden, but a land brimming with opportunity whose "peculiarity consists, not merely in its brevity, but in the fact that from the beginning it has been informed by an idea. From the beginning Americans have been anticipating and projecting a better future. From the beginning the Land of Democracy has been figured as the Land of Promise."[12]

Despite his upbeat interpretation of American history, Croly was not altogether sanguine about the challenges attending the explosive economic growth that defined Gilded Age America. He knew that self-interest was a double-edged sword: even as the nation's single-minded pursuit of profit was creating the conditions for a brighter future, most of that profit was accumulating in trusts and monopolies that gave rise to deep socioeconomic divisions. "The plain fact," wrote Croly, "is that the individual in freely and energetically pursuing his own private purposes has not been the inevitable public benefactor assumed by the traditional American interpretation of democracy." Unless economic freedoms could be subordinated to recognition of a greater good, America would come to resemble the European models that New World immigrants and their descendants had sought so desperately to escape.

George's and Croly's progressive messages surfaced in Dick Morgan's fight for fairness in Oklahoma Territory, and within a few short years, they would work their way into his work as a congressman. As Croly noted with the force of progressive conviction,

> The existing concentration of wealth and financial power in the hands of a few irresponsible men is the inevitable outcome of the chaotic

individualism of our political and economic organization, while at the same time it is inimical to democracy, because it tends to erect political abuses and social inequalities into a system. The inference which follows may be disagreeable, but it is not to be escaped. In becoming responsible for the subordination of the individual to the demand of a dominant and constructive national purpose, the American state will in effect be making itself responsible for a morally and socially desirable distribution of wealth.[13]

Arguably, nobody expressed Progressivism more cogently and forcefully than the man charged with putting it into practice: President Theodore Roosevelt. In an address delivered in 1912 in Louisville, Kentucky, Roosevelt credited progressives with putting Americans in possession of their birthright, just as their creator intended. Like George and Croly, Roosevelt touched on martial themes to drive home his message: "With this purpose in view, we propose to do away with whatever in our government tends to secure to privilege, and to the great sinister special interests, a rampart from behind which they can beat back the forces that strive for social and industrial justice, and frustrate the will of the people."

At the top of the progressive agenda were four key reforms, all aligned with Morgan's ideology: (1) securing the direct election of U.S. senators; (2) allowing people to nominate candidates for office through direct primaries without the corrupting influence of money and patronage; (3) enforcing an eight-hour workday; and (4) putting an end to the exploitation of women and children. Progressives' ultimate aim was to promote legislation to ensure social and industrial justice "so that the work of all of us may be done and the lives of all of us lived under conditions which will tend to increase the dignity, the worth, and the efficiency of each individual."

Roosevelt had a warning for future generations: if Big Business (often capitalized to emphasize its significance as a Really Big Deal) continued to tilt the playing field in its favor, and if privilege and special interests were allowed free rein, the captains of industry would one day reap the whirlwind in the form of revolution: "Most surely if the wise and moderate control we advocate does not come, then someday these men or their descendants will have to face the chance of some movement of really dangerous and drastic character being directed against them." In a passage that surely stirred the souls of listeners with lived memories of the Civil War, Roosevelt credited the Lincoln-Douglas debates for searing into collective consciousness the eternal struggle between right and wrong: "None of us can really prosper permanently if masses of our fellows are debased and degraded, if masses of men and women are ground down and forced to lead starved and sordid lives, so that their souls are crippled like their bodies and the fine edge of their every feeling is blunted."

Roosevelt then called on his listeners to remember that they were, as Scripture demanded and the Almighty expected, their brothers' keepers. "This country will not be a good place for any of us to live in if it is not a reasonably good place for all of us to live in," he said in closing. "Our cause is the cause of justice for all, in the interest of all. Surely there was never a more noble cause; surely there was never a cause in which it was better worthwhile to spend and be spent."[14]

Far from the nation's centers of power and influence, Progressivism endured trial by fire in the run-up to Oklahoma statehood. On August 21, 1905, delegates representing tribes throughout Indian Territory gathered at the Hinton Theater in Muskogee, Creek Nation, for the Sequoyah Convention, named for the Cherokee linguist who put his people's language into writing. They were joined by descendants of slaves, known as freedmen, living in Indian Territory. Native Americans and freedmen who came together on that steamy summer day were united in a single purpose: to prevent the union of Oklahoma and Indian territories. Against all odds, delegates aimed to persuade Congress to admit Indian Territory into the union as the state of Sequoyah, where Native Americans and Blacks could carve out the slice of America's promise that the dominant culture had denied them since the beginning of European settlement. Delegates were acutely aware that time was running out, as Indian land titles were set to expire on March 4, 1906—a milestone that would make union of the Twin Territories all but inevitable.[15]

"Dick T. shared that sense of alarm," wrote David Morgan. "He firmly believed that tribal consent was a prerequisite to statehood. Solemn treaties dating back to the nation's founding could not be ignored."[16]

To serve as vice president of the Sequoyah Convention, delegates turned to one of Oklahoma's most colorful but controversial leaders: William H. Murray. Born to a farming family in Toadsuck, Texas, Murray discovered at an early age that farm chores did not suit him. He ran away from home at the age of twelve and, after a few false starts that typified frontier entrepreneurship, clawed his way to a law practice in Fort Worth. When that failed to meet his expectations, he set his sights on Tishomingo, the capital of the Chickasaw Nation, where he schmoozed his way to the inner circle of tribal and territorial politics. When it came time to choose delegates for the Sequoyah Convention, none was perceived as more qualified to represent Indian Territory's interests than William H. Murray. As delegates got down to business, Murray's stirring orations on the cultivation of alfalfa earned him his enduring sobriquet, "Alfalfa Bill."[17]

Murray made his intentions clear at the outset of the historic gathering. "We knew that it must stand before Congress above ridicule," wrote Murray in a 1931 retrospective about his role in the dual-state movement, "and in harmony with the best modern thought for the protection of life, liberty, property, and the citizens' highest estimate of intelligence and progress. That our own futures in the political world depended upon just that."[18]

To help hammer out a constitution, Murray called on two of Indian Territory's most prominent leaders: Charles N. Haskell, destined to become Oklahoma's first governor; and Robert L. Owen, a native Virginian of Scots-Irish and Cherokee descent who, like Dick Morgan, had honed his debating skills as a student. Owen had attended Washington and Lee University, where he earned a Master of Arts degree in 1877. He and his wife, Narcissa, had relocated from Virginia to Indian Territory in 1879 to capitalize on her prominence in Cherokee affairs and participate in what was sure to be a booming economy.

Owen's dual skills in business and the law earned him a plum job as Indian agent in Muskogee. This prestigious appointment, lasting from 1885 to 1889, made him accountable to members of the Five Tribes scattered across some 26 million acres.[19] When the National Banking Act was extended to include Indian Territory in 1890, Owen re-careered to organize the First National Bank of Muskogee, an institution that he served as president of for a decade. As bank president, he became acquainted with businessmen and politicians throughout the territory, and he was an obvious choice to assume leadership in the Sequoyah Convention. As a dyed-in-the-wool southern Democrat, Owen was a natural pick for the subcommittee charged with drafting a constitution.[20] His mission was to help draft a constitution that would reflect his party's populist distrust of Big Business and the elected officials who did its bidding.

None of the Sequoyah Convention's leaders truly believed that the Republican administration would admit a Black and Native American state, as it would surely pave the way for more Democrats in Congress. Although campaigning for separate statehood was a classic Hail Mary pass, the convention's leaders were confident of two things: first, their proposals were necessary to convince Congress that Native Americans were capable of self-government; and second, that its constitution would influence Oklahoma's constitution. As Murray noted without a trace of ambiguity, "without this experience the work so well done in the Guthrie Convention later, would have been impossible. The Sequoyah Convention gave us the outlines of an organization."

In the short term, the convention forced Native Americans to accept the inevitability of statehood, and it compelled federal authorities to answer, once and for all, the contentious Oklahoma question. It was left to later generations of historians to expose Democrats' duplicity in framing the Sequoyah Convention as a Black and Indian project. Knowing that Congress would never admit a separate Black and Indian state into the Union, Democrats who controlled the convention convinced attendees that a sincere effort had been made to promote statehood for Sequoyah. Naming it after a Cherokee cultural hero was touted as further evidence of Democrats' sincerity. But clearly, there was more to the story. Knowing that whites outnumbered Native Americans in Indian Territory by a factor of six to one and that Blacks remained subject to the tyranny of Jim Crow, Democrats' real goal was to cement their alignment with the South and augment their party's influence in Congress. Native Americans and Blacks thus faced two overwhelming obstacles as territorial governance reached its denouement: first, southern whites were bent on controlling Indian Territory politics; and second, the federal government had set a deadline for ending tribal sovereignty.[21]

Sequoyah Convention delegates had no doubt that Republicans of Dick Morgan's ilk, regardless of their grudging willingness to compromise so that Congress would finally act, would try to exert overpowering influence over Indian Territory when it came time to draft a constitution. As Murray noted in his retrospective, "The politicians of Oklahoma City and Guthrie will try to dominate the convention and shut out the Indian Territory along with western Oklahoma."[22] But Indian leaders were determined to preserve what was left of tribal sovereignty, guaranteed in treaties with the federal government, and they kept up their crusade in the weeks leading to the November 7, 1905, vote on the Sequoyah Constitution.

Turnout was light, but decisive: 56,279 people voted in favor of the constitution and endorsed a petition to Congress; 9,073 voted in opposition. Early in the Fifty-Ninth Congress, Representative Arthur Phillips Murphy of Missouri, who also acted as attorney for the Creek Nation, and Senator Porter James McCumber of North Dakota filed Sequoyah statehood bills. None was surprised when Congress refused to consider them.[23]

March 4, 1906, came and went, and with the dissolution of Indian land titles, the Twin Territories entered the endgame of their contentious courtship. Less than four months later, Congress set forth the conditions for uniting the odd couple in the Oklahoma Enabling Act of June 14, 1906. Those conditions included forming a state government and submitting a constitution for presidential and congressional approval. Section Six of the Enabling Act's twenty-two sections dealt with the state's representation in the U.S. House of Representatives. This provision would remain in effect until 1913, when the state's congressional representation would be revised to conform with the 1910 federal census, which put Oklahoma's population at 1,657,000 in a nation of 91,972,266. Oklahoma thus became the first state since the original thirteen to be admitted into the Union with as many as five representatives.[24]

Oklahoma's congressional districts were defined as follows: District One–Grant, Kay, Garfield, Noble, Pawnee, Kingfisher, Logan, Payne, and Lincoln counties, and the territory comprising the Osage and Kansas reservations; District Two– Oklahoma, Canadian, Blaine, Caddo, Custer, Dewey, Day, Woods, Woodward, and Beaver counties; District Three–all territory then comprising the Cherokee, Creek, and Seminole nations, and the reservations lying northeast of the Cherokee Nation; District Four–all territory comprising the Choctaw Nation and parts of the Cherokee, Creek, and Chickasaw nations; and District Five–Greer, Roger Mills, Kiowa, Washita, Comanche, Cleveland, and Pottawatomie counties, and part of the Chickasaw Nation.[25]

Partisanship went toxic in the weeks before the Constitutional Convention, and nowhere more so than over what was known in turn-of-the-twentieth-century vernacular as "the Negro Question." On September 22, 1906, E. J. Giddings, who would represent Oklahoma six years later at the National Democratic Convention in Baltimore, laid out the differences between the parties in a speech in Oklahoma City. "The issue is clearly drawn," declared Giddings, who went on to accuse Republicans of pandering to Blacks for no other reason than to ensure their votes. "We know that Republican spellbinders constantly remind negroes of the auction block and similar alleged agencies of torture." Was it merely coincidence that theatrical performances of *Uncle Tom's Cabin*, adapted from Harriett Beecher Stowe's blockbuster novel, had been playing in Indian Territory? And was it true that Blacks were admitted for free? "We are not abusing *Uncle Tom's Cabin*," said Giddings in reference to Stowe's book. "We are merely criticizing those who use it, and other means, to inflame the passions of the negro and line up all negroes for Republican candidates. We are also forcibly reminded of the fact that the Republican Gerrymandering Board has evinced a great deal of love for the negro [*sic*] vote in the laying out of the Constitutional Convention districts."[26]

It seems unlikely that Dick Morgan attended Giddings's speech. But if he had, he would have been squirming in his seat at the accusation of gerrymandering, a process that had effectively ended his political career in Indiana and was now rearing its head on the eve of Oklahoma statehood.

Giddings continued: "The negro [*sic*] has been a faithful ally of the Republican party. Whatever honors he attains in the kingdom of politics, whether it be a golden diadem, or a silver crown, a janitorship or some high elective office, he must receive it at the hands of the Republican party." He went so far as to accuse Republicans of sponsoring a colonization plan to bring Blacks to Oklahoma, where they could circumvent Jim Crow laws by marrying Whites, sending their children to mixed-race schools, and riding carefree in integrated railway cars. The possibility of greater equality for Black people had been articulated by none other than Booker T. Washington, who was spreading the word that Oklahoma was the last, best place for America's Black citizens. Giddings further insisted that his party was not as blatant in seeking their votes: "If the state goes Republican for the constitutional convention, it will go by virtue of the fact that the Republicans have carried the negro districts." Giddings further asserted that all eyes were on Oklahoma in the countdown to the election of delegates, slated for November 6, to the Constitutional Convention.

"Mark it, the people of the Union know that the negro question is being fought out in the new state of Oklahoma," declared Giddings as Democratic heads surely bobbed in unison. "God grant, when the election returns come in on the night of the sixth of November, that the wires will flash the news everywhere that the people of Oklahoma have satisfactorily settled the negro question!"[27]

The nation's eyes remained fixed on the Twin Territories when voters went to the polls on November 6 to elect delegates to the Constitutional Convention, often shortened to "Con Con." Each territory was to elect fifty-five delegates, with an additional two delegates assigned to the Osage Nation. As Dick Morgan had warned, the results did not bode well for his party's influence on state politics: of the 112 delegates, 99 were Democrats (the "nine and ninety"); 12 were Republicans (the "twelve apostles," a moniker that had a familiar ring to Morgan); and 1 independent (the "renegade"). Reflecting the Twin Territories' dominant economic sector, most delegates were farmers; some were lawyers and laborers; and their average age was about forty. In yet another ill omen for Republicans, Bill Murray and Charles Haskell were elected as president and majority floor leader, respectively.[28]

"Democrats' takeover of the Con Con was the harbinger of six-plus decades of Democratic Party rule in Oklahoma," explained David Morgan. "Reasons for the imbalance included internal fighting among Republicans; Republican complacency after many years of dominance dating back to the early days of non-Indian settlement; negative perceptions of corporate lawyers, and especially those working on behalf of railroads; the loss of Black votes, not only to Democrats, but also because so many sat out the electoral process; the preponderance of southern Democrats in Indian Territory; and finally, the failure of a single past or current Republican office holder to file as a candidate to the convention."[29]

Murray called the convention to order on November 20, 1906. Inspired by William Jennings Bryan's brand of grassroots populism and their own experiences at the Sequoyah Convention, Murray and Haskell played dominant roles in drafting a constitution aligned with Democratic Party principles. Ominously, some of those principles came straight from the Old South's playbook, and they utterly ignored the Enabling Act's requirement that the constitution "make no distinction in civil or political rights on account of race or color." In his inaugural address, Murray made it clear what kind of state he wanted to create: "As a rule [Negroes] are failures as lawyers, doctors, and in other professions... He must be taught in the line of his own sphere, as porters, bootblacks, and barbers and many lines of agriculture, horticulture, and mechanics, in which he is an adept, but it is an entirely false notion that the negro can rise to the equal of a white man."[30]

In December, delegates might have paused in their deliberations to glimpse the passing of the frontier when nearly a half million acres—stretching from just south of Lawton to the Red River, and comprising present-day Comanche, Cotton, and Tillman counties—were opened to homesteading. Known as the Big Pasture, the area had been used for grazing by the Kiowa, Comanche, and Apache tribes after their reservation was opened to non-Indian settlement. The U.S. Land Office accepted sealed bids for quarter sections between December 3 and 15, 1906, thereby dropping the curtain on Oklahoma Territory's piecemeal absorption of Indian reservations that had begun with the run of 1889.[31]

The convention adjourned on March 15, 1907. But before the constitution was put to a popular vote, Murray summoned delegates to a series of meetings to make revisions. In July, President Roosevelt weighed in with his objections to the constitution. Murray responded by bringing delegates together once again to make yet more revisions. The final document included the initiative and referendum, prohibition, strict regulation of corporations, and women's suffrage in school elections—all shaped to the contours of Progressivism, and all with no input from Black citizens and precious little from Republicans. Those progressive reforms notwithstanding, Oklahoma's founding fathers left no doubt about their consensus: white political power would be guaranteed, just as extinguishing Indian land titles and parceling out land in individual allotments had guaranteed white economic power.

The date set for a popular vote, September 17, was the same month and day on which another assembly of founding fathers had affixed their signatures to the U.S. Constitution in 1787.[32]

In the spring of 1906, Porter Morgan graduated from the University of Chicago Law School and moved with Clemmer to Oklahoma City. By the summer of 1907, he was about a year into his law career and increasingly impatient for statehood. In contrast to his father's and many Republicans' opposition to uniting with Indian Territory, Porter wanted a state no matter what form it took: a single state or one united with Indian Territory. He expressed his contrary views in a letter to

TURN IT DOWN

DELEGATE

Woodward County

THE BEARER OF THIS CARD IS A
DELEGATE OR ALTERNATE
TO THE
REPUBLICAN STATE CONVENTION
AT TULSA, AUGUST 1, 1907
AND IS ENTITLED TO A SEAT IN THE CONVENTION

Countersigned:

J. L. Hamon
State Chairman

Campaign material from the "Turn It Down" campaign and Republican Convention in Tulsa discouraging voters from approving the Oklahoma Constitution, August 1, 1907. COURTESY OF THE CARL ALBERT CONGRESSIONAL RESEARCH AND STUDIES CENTER, NORMAN, OKLAHOMA

his parents on June 10, 1907, in which he announced his intention to vote for the constitution. "Interestingly, he admitted that he hadn't actually read all fifty thousand words of the constitution, but as near as he could tell, it was acceptable," explained David Morgan. "Porter applauded many of the constitution's progressive provisions, including the initiative and referendum, regulation of corporations, methods of taxation, and judicial matters." In that same letter, Porter dismissed his father's complaints about Democrats' gerrymandering. Republicans did it too, so what was the problem? Ever the pragmatist, Porter saw statehood as the key to a better business environment, or what he called "money in my pocket."

Disagreements notwithstanding, Porter counted on the elder Morgan's counsel to guide him in the fledgling law practice that he had established with his brother-in-law, Harlan Deupree. In one of his many letters to his father describing his caseload, Porter cited *Morgan's Manual*– "about the only authority I have"–as the go-to source for real estate questions.[33]

Although Dick Morgan was not a delegate to the Constitutional Convention, he was not about to sit on the sidelines while Oklahoma's future was at stake. Just days before voters went to the polls, he delivered a speech under the uber-patriotic title "Our Country: What Made It Great"—a speech that spawned the anti-constitution campaign slogan "Turn It Down!" Repeating his mantra from the free homes campaign of the 1890s, Morgan judged the Homestead Act as second in importance only to the Emancipation Proclamation, both signed by President Lincoln, and both aimed at ensuring fairness to all Americans. One made free men; and the other made free homes.[34]

"I like this speech," wrote David Morgan, "because it shows his thought process about the Homestead Act in comparison to the Emancipation Proclamation. He first puts them equal in importance, but then expresses thought that the Emancipation Proclamation was a greater act." Lincoln coupled his Emancipation Proclamation with an insistence, surprising to all and infuriating to most Republicans, that Confederates who swore an allegiance to the Union should be welcomed back into the fold. "Many northerners were expecting and hoping for a vindictive President," continued David, "but instead saw a forgiving President."[35]

For Dick Morgan, identifying the number-one reason for America's greatness was a no-brainer. "My answer is this," he declared in response to his own question. "The Republican Party made this country great; Republican principles, Republican policies, Republican statesmanship, Republican legislation and Republican management of national affairs—made this country great—great in its population, great in its wealth, great in its industries, great in its trade and commerce, great in its transportation and communication facilities and great in its prestige and power and influence throughout the world." When it came to specifics, Morgan paraphrased his party's platform, ratified at the Republican Convention of 1860 in Chicago, and the fundamental principles that it expressed: (1) preservation of the Union; (2) human liberty and freedom; (3) encouragement of foreign immigration; (4) free homestead law; (5) federal aid in constructing a transcontinental railroad; and (6) protective tariffs. All this and more would have been destroyed if the Union had dissolved and slavery had spread across the continent.[36]

Morgan was not done yet. As the upcoming elections on September 17 would include a full slate of state and county officers and legislators,

Morgan delivered another speech to denounce the proposed constitution and clarify the issues so that voters could make informed decisions. His main point (no surprise here!) was that Democrats were not to be trusted, and certainly should not be elected. Reverting to scripture, he admonished his listeners to remember, "By their fruits ye shall know them." He further admonished them to beware of false prophets, "which come to you in sheep's clothing, but inwardly they are ravening wolves."

Then, like a good lawyer, he broke his argument down into propositions. First, he insisted that the proposed constitution, drafted by "incapable, untrustworthy, unreliable and dangerous politicians," conflicted with the Enabling Act in that it failed the test of republicanism and was repugnant to the nation's founding texts, the Declaration of Independence and the U.S. Constitution. He reserved special opprobrium for the future governor, Charles N. Haskell, "the man who by his dictatorial policy earned and obtained the appropriate title of 'boss' is now the nominee of his party for governor."

Second, Morgan attacked the substance of the constitution, which was so full of dangerous and unwise provisions that Bill Murray had been compelled to reconvene delegates and make more than thirty amendments. Due to delegates' "disastrous, disgraceful and unfortunate failure," voters had a responsibility to "forever bury them in deserved oblivion." Democrats' perfidy was particularly puzzling considering their access to forty-five state constitutions, many of which were models of enlightened governance. Instead of seizing the potential to exercise real statecraft, they squandered a historic opportunity. In a related third proposition, Morgan accused Democrats of deceiving the electorate and, in some instances, members of their own party through obfuscation and downright lies.

In his fourth proposition, Morgan shifted from attacks on the constitution's framers to a critique of its structure. Most notably, the framers made it possible for the legislature to take away protections that were allegedly in place, including: (1) the control of corporations (one article gave the legislature the power to "alter, amend, revise or repeal" sections that it deemed offensive); (2) caps on railroad fares (the Corporation Commission was granted the power to exempt railroads from this provision); and (3) the initiative and referendum (again, subject to the whims of the legislature). Morgan was particularly alarmed at the prospect of a Democratic legislature with the authority to regulate business and commerce: "If the Legislature, comprising one hundred or more men, may be controlled and influenced by corporation power, how much more easily will it be for these great and grasping corporations to control two out of three comprising the Corporation Commission." Hobbled by these and other structural weaknesses, the constitution did nothing to prevent the legislature from curtailing basic freedoms by pandering to an electorate dominated by Democrats.

Morgan then aired a grievance that had hounded him since his stillborn political career in Indiana and now constituted his fifth proposition: Democrats had committed a "great moral crime" in resorting to gerrymandering. To ensure victories at the polls, Democrats had drawn electoral districts that robbed certain sections of their fair and just representation. In laborious detail, Morgan cited districts whose size and boundaries and convoluted combinations all but guaranteed Democratic majorities. "These Democratic politicians talk loud and long about the corporations and trusts robbing the people of their money, and yet these politicians with brazen effrontery, in broad daylight as it were, rob the people of their elective franchise, discriminate against one section of the State on account of the politics of its inhabitants, and violate the rule 'that there shall be no taxation without representation.'" Morgan's outrage extended to the constitution's preamble insofar as it invoked the guidance of Almighty God. A more honest preamble would have asserted that the Constitution aimed to perpetuate the power of the Democratic Party.

Given his abhorrence of territorial governance, it comes as no surprise that Morgan, in his sixth proposition, blamed Democrats for delaying statehood. Whereas Republicans had done all they could to hasten statehood under the auspices of the Enabling Act, Democrats had dragged their feet. So, like a ship at sea, the process of admission to the Union had drifted from its course. Even though they had been vastly outnumbered, Republicans had followed Congress's mandate to draft a constitution in sixty days. But Democrats were so inefficient that

Bill Murray had been compelled to summon post-convention meetings to make revisions, some occasioned by Democratic partisanship and incompetence, and others by President Roosevelt's objections. As Morgan noted with disdain, "Eight months were consumed in doing what should have been done in two months."

Even though the Constitution seemed to be destined for approval by a vote of the people, Morgan insisted that Republicans had never been willing to settle for statehood at any price. Digging into his repertoire of historical precedents, Morgan reminded listeners, in his seventh proposition, that the Founding Fathers had spurned peace with Great Britain because the price had been too high. Nor had Lincoln been willing to make peace with the Confederacy at the cost of the Union. In that same tradition, Republicans in the Twin Territories were not in harmony with the statehood-at-any-price crowd—that is, statehood that would disenfranchise thousands of voters and deprive large swaths of the population of their basic rights as citizens. In short, Morgan's party did not want statehood that was not Republican in form or that was "repugnant to the Constitution of the United States and the principles of the Declaration of Independence."

The crux of Morgan's argument can be found in his eighth, ninth, and tenth propositions, in which he described the right kind of statehood, whose leaders would promote good business, foster a positive environment for laborers and educators, and guarantee people's rights and privileges regardless of race, creed, and color. Democrats, by contrast, seemed bent on creating a state that was openly hostile to business and aligned with Jim Crow laws, which left Blacks at the mercy of the dominant white culture. Those contrasting visions of statehood had been on display in Oklahoma Territory since the run of 1889. Republicans had been in the majority for thirteen of the previous seventeen years, and the fruits of their labors could be seen in progressive legislation, successful farms and businesses, thriving industries, good schools, and intelligent statesmanship. To perpetuate its growth, Morgan once again cited the North and Midwest as a model for Oklahoma's growth and most promising source of capital.

"Capital will not come from the South," said Morgan. "We must go north for additional capital. Capital will not go to a State where the people are slow-going and non-progressive." With a nod to scripture, Morgan inspired his listeners to express gratitude for the Republican Party's leadership: "Well done thou good and faithful servant; thou hath been faithful over a few things, I will make you ruler over many things."

Morgan wound toward his conclusion with a warning that voters' rejection of the constitution on September 17 would certainly delay statehood, but it had already been delayed "by the inefficiency and duplicity of the Democratic leaders." And even if the people were to ratify the constitution, President Roosevelt was empowered to shoot it down. Either way, Republicans bore no responsibility for its shortcomings, and if it were not for their criticism at the Constitutional Convention, the constitution would have been even worse. "Through these criticisms, the constitution was greatly improved," concluded Morgan. "It is not what it should be but it is much better than it would have been except for Republican criticism."[37]

"September 17, 1907, was probably the most important election day in Oklahoma history," explained David Morgan. "It set the political climate in Oklahoma for the next hundred years. The results of that election made Oklahoma a southern state politically, put the Democrats in power for the next sixty years, and started the state down the road of Jim Crow laws." David went on to cite Democrats' success in branding Republicans as carpetbaggers and allies of the railroads and Big Business. Both of those charges had been leveled at Dick Morgan since his arrival in Guthrie in April 1889, and they were, at least in part, responsible for thwarting his quest for high office.[38]

Knowing that voters would likely support Prohibition, Morgan wrote to Orietta to ask if she would assure her father, who was convinced that the Republican Party's fortunes rested on banning intoxicating spirits, that "we are doing something out here to get Prohibition in Oklahoma. You can explain to him that in voting <u>for</u> or <u>against</u> our Constitution we also vote separately as to whether we will have Prohibition."[39]

As Morgan feared, voters approved the Oklahoma Constitution

by a landslide margin.[40] The success of the measure to ban liquor provided some consolation. In the races for Congress, Democrats elected to serve truncated terms until, after the general elections of 1908, they outnumbered Republicans four to one. The results were as follows: District 1 - Bird McGuire (Republican); District 2 - Elmer L. Fulton (Democrat); District 3 - James S. Davenport (Democrat); District 4 - Charles D. Carver (Democrat); and District 5 - Scott Ferris (Democrat).[41]

For the time being, Dick Morgan was content with his position as register of the U.S. Land Office in Woodward and had decided not to enter the congressional race in 1907. That was the last time he would sit out an election to Congress.

CHAPTER NINE

Mr. Morgan Goes to Washington

It is a dangerous thing to begin
the work of disenfranchisement.

DICK T. MORGAN
"A PARTISAN MEASURE," CIRCA 1909

VOTERS APPROVED THE OKLAHOMA CONSTITUTION on September 17, 1907, with 71 percent approval. But this was not enough to dissuade its detractors from fighting to the bitter end to scuttle it. Two weeks after the election, African Americans representing the Suffrage League convened in Oklahoma City to select delegates to deliver their objections to President Roosevelt and Congress. None doubted that the constitution would make Oklahoma an appendage of the Deep South and consign Blacks to subjugation under Jim Crow. As noted in Indian Territory's leading Black-interest newspaper, the *Muskogee Cimeter*, "The entire people are a unit in the matter of sending the delegation to Washington."[1] The delegation's reason for optimism was that President Roosevelt, a fellow Republican whose progressive policies were mitigating the most egregious abuses of Gilded Age America, would stand with African Americans to fight a state constitution that restricted Black suffrage and sanctioned white supremacy.

The delegation arrived in Washington to find a president with serious reservations about Oklahoma's proposed constitution. According to an upbeat article in the *Muskogee Cimeter*, Roosevelt had opined that it "was not fit for publication," and if he could be convinced that it contradicted Republican Party principles, he would reject it. "With this ray of hope, the Republicans of Oklahoma have renewed the fight," declared *Muskogee Cimeter* editor W. H. Twine. "It is now up to us to convince the President of the rottenness of the constitution." Republicans went so far as to submit a brief showing that the constitution was "un-republican in form" to U.S. Attorney General Charles J. Bonaparte, a descendant of the French Bonapartes and, more relevant to Oklahoma history, President Roosevelt's pick to investigate land fraud in Indian Territory. Bonaparte promised the delegates that he would render his final opinion as soon as the president returned to Washington from a bear hunt.

In the end, all was for naught. Convinced that 71 percent approval was nothing to trifle with and encouraged to find that the most obnoxious provisions had been excised from the original draft, Roosevelt signed off on the constitution.[2]

There's no better place to reflect on Oklahoma's tortuous path to statehood than Guthrie, the state's original capital. Imagining what it must have been like to experience those heady days, David, Kenyon, and I began our walkabout in Guthrie with a visit to the Oklahoma Territorial Museum and Carnegie Library, where we toured the exhibits and discussed our project with Museum Director Nathan Turner and Assistant Curator Michael Williams. After receiving their assurances that they would help in any way they could, we said our goodbyes and made for the exit. Before climbing into David's SUV and heading downtown, we lingered in front of a statue near the museum entrance commemorating the marriage of Oklahoma and Indian territories on November 16, 1907. That marriage was more than a metaphor. It was an actual wedding ceremony, and it happened in the exact spot where David, Kenyon, and I were standing.

Festivities preceding the exchange of vows kicked off with Oklahoma Territory secretary of state Charles H. Filson's recitation of President Roosevelt's proclamation declaring the creation of the Union's forty-sixth state. Roosevelt signed the proclamation at 10:16, Washington time, that morning. To signal his affinity for the west, he affixed his signature with a quill plucked from the wing of an American eagle. That quill eventually made its way to the Oklahoma Historical Society's vast collection of artifacts.

Governor-Elect Charles N. Haskell was the first to get word of the signing. As soon as he made the announcement, and even before

Filson read the proclamation, the good times started to roll. "The word spread like wildfire, and it was but a few moments before pandemonium reigned supreme," declared a breathless article in the *Beaver Herald*, self-branded as Oklahoma's oldest newspaper and Republican to the core. "Every bell in the city rang out the glad tidings, scores of factory whistles screamed piercing blasts of overwhelming joy, and the hotel lobbies were filled to overflowing by cheering men. Guns were fired, giant crackers exploded and the air was rent with the general gladness."

After Secretary Filson finished reading the presidential proclamation, *Guthrie Leader* editor Leslie G. Niblack struggled to be heard over the din as he administered the oath of office to Haskell. Less enthused than the people on stage were Republicans like Dick Morgan who were certain that the uber-populist from Muskogee with a distaste for Black people was about to confirm their worst fears of Democratic Party rule.[3]

But this was a time not for politics, but for nuptials. Tall and fair-haired, Oklahoma City businessman and chairman of the statehood committee Charles G. "Gristmill" Jones, sporting striped trousers and a black coat in keeping with the solemnity of the occasion, personified Mr. Oklahoma Territory. The role of his bride, Miss Indian Territory, was played by Mrs. Leo Bennett, a Cherokee and wife of the U.S. marshal in Muskogee, described in the *Guthrie Leader* as one of the most beautiful women of Native American descent in the Southwest. She was clad not as an Indian princess, but as a fashionable bride decked out in a floor-length lavender satin dress with long sleeves and a high collar, a large picture hat, and gloves.

Miss Indian Territory waited patiently backstage as her husband-to-be stepped to the front of the platform, bowed graciously to the crowd, and delivered his wedding vows. "Though he was born in tribulation, in the city of Washington in 1889, his life of 18 years on the plains has been one of tremendous activity and he has grown to the size of a giant," declared the gallant groom. "On account of his youth and inexperience, he is possessed of an unconquerable modesty and has asked me to propose marriage to the Indian Territory."

Heads surely nodded when Jones acknowledged that their romance had not been a case of love at first sight: "A lady by the name of Sequoyah at one time interfered with the courtship and at first tried to break up the match. But having failed to do so, and tired of the loneliness of single blessedness, she gracefully surrendered to the inevitable, and has ever since been in favor of the marriage."

The wedding march blared as Miss Indian Territory, cradling a mauve chrysanthemum and shielding her eyes from the midday glare, took her place at Mr. Oklahoma Territory's side. Attention then turned to William A. Durant, a young Choctaw from Bryan County who had served as sergeant-at-arms during the Constitutional Convention and went on to become Speaker in the Oklahoma House of Representatives. In giving Miss Indian Territory away in marriage, Durant flattered her as "a beauteous maiden" who brought to the marriage fertile fields, productive mines, and sterling and upright citizenship. It was up to Mr. Oklahoma Territory to care for his bride and conserve her resources "to the unending glory of our new state and the untold benefit of her people." An ensemble of Cherokee girls added a patriotic flair with a rendition of the Star Spangled Banner.

And then, amid the whoops and hollers that one might expect from the last generation of pioneers, the Reverend W. H. Dodson, a Confederate veteran and pastor of the First Baptist Church of Guthrie, joined the couple in holy matrimony.[4] If anyone objected to the union, their protests went unrecorded. One imagines a pensive Dick Morgan caught up in the revelry, but also shaking his head at what would likely be a troubled marriage.

I knew all about the hoopla of November 16, 1907, from previous research, and I could not help but look at the statue outside the museum with skepticism. Standing before me was not the stylish couple described by witnesses and historians with an eye for accuracy, but a groom dressed in the Western garb of his day, complete with a string tie and cowboy boots, and an Indian princess outfitted in buckskin and moccasins. I mentioned that to David and Kenyon on our way downtown, and after I was back in my Charlottesville office, I emailed Nathan Turner about it. Turns out that the sculptor was Fred Olds, the museum's first director, whose paintings and bronzes were on display in the museum. His statue was installed in 1975, and as Nathan wrote in his email, it was "an artistic interpretation of the ceremonial marriage."[5]

With all due respect to artistic interpretation, the statue conjures scenes from a classic grade-B Western, with a handsome and paternalistic cowboy towering above an Indian maiden who, figuratively if not literally, was unable to stand on her own two feet.

Not for the first time and surely not the last, historical accuracy had taken a back seat to later generations' preferred narrative. That's something to ponder in our own age of hyper-partisanship and battles over symbols that have lost their connection to the history they aim to commemorate.

The sun rose on November 17, 1907, to cast its radiance on the newest state in the Union. The Twin Territories, bound by sacred vows, were now equal partners, ready to embrace challenges and opportunities as the frontier faded to collective memory and modernity relentlessly approached.

Or not. As Dick Morgan had testified before Congress's Committee on Territories in early 1904, and reiterated throughout the tortuous run-up to statehood, what was now eastern Oklahoma had little in common with the western half of the state. Although there is no evidence that Morgan went on extensive tours of Indian Territory, his dire assessment reflects a sad but inescapable reality. Almost a decade into the new century, the former Indian Territory still lacked law and order, had yet to organize civil governance, and had few of the institutions that accrue to the common good. Equally damning was eastern Oklahoma's alignment with southern Democrats and allegiance to Jim Crow, a toxic mix that made a mockery of America's promise to all its citizens. Toss in the crushing poverty that infected the region, and you had a witch's brew of impediments to a happy marriage. Those impediments had less to do with Native American governance than the haphazard influx of non-Indian immigrants, many of whom appropriated land and upended Native cultures with impunity. At the risk of abusing the analogy, Miss Indian Territory was not so much Mr. Oklahoma Territory's willing partner as a troubled bride forced into an arranged marriage.

For a glimpse into the real Miss Indian Territory and its stark contrast with the rapidly developing Oklahoma Territory, we turn to the spring of 1907, when an unassuming German from the tiny Bavarian village of Achstetten showed up in Oklahoma City. He made straight for the office of Otto Branstetter, a one-time homesteader in the Cherokee Outlet and trade unionist in Kansas City who had been appointed secretary of the Socialist Party of Oklahoma in 1906. The newcomer needed to get the scoop on Oklahoma farmers and assess the likelihood of wooing them into the Socialist fold. Branstetter had no illusions about reformers at the radical fringe of Oklahoma politics, and he was not altogether sure if they would accept centralized party authority. As the visitor to Branstetter's office wrote many years later in his memoir, *If You Don't Weaken*, "The secretary confessed there wasn't much of a proletariat in Oklahoma to build a proletarian revolution on, and with."[6]

The visitor was Oscar Ameringer, and to follow his trail through eastern Oklahoma shortly after statehood is to discover the vast underbelly of the American Dream. Forty years of single-crop farming, soil erosion, and the absence of civil governance, combined with unregulated capitalism, which was thriving in the central and western parts of the state, had pushed untold thousands into poverty and the endless grind of tenancy.[7] In 1910, tenants operated 54.8 percent of farms in the state; by 1925, the percentage had risen to 58.6. Some counties in eastern Oklahoma groaned under the weight of 75–80 percent tenancy.[8] Oklahoma City's leading business newspaper, *Harlow's Weekly*, was unambiguous in identifying tenant farmers "whose family are ill clothed, inadequately fed and squalidly housed, and whose children are growing up uneducated" as a major drag on the state's economy. "What we need to recognize," ran a story about the scourge of eastern Oklahoma's economy, "is that we have with us a type of incompetent, present in large numbers; the economically incompetent, just as truly incompetent as the intellectually or morally incompetent. And the state owes them some kind of responsibility."[9]

Known as "the Mark Twain of American Socialism," Ameringer was born to the thunder of artillery during the Franco-Prussian War. He spent his youth steeped in rural poverty and rigid class structure, a toxic blend that led him straight to the most radical writers and agitators of his day. After he immigrated to America, he synthesized the democratic principles of Jefferson with the frontier culture of rugged individualism and sprinkled them with a tolerant, nonsectarian brand of Marxism. Thus, he formulated what he called "industrial democracy": industry of the people, by the people, and for the people. Raising storytelling to an art form, Ameringer wrote and spoke about the plight of dispossessed Oklahomans, but not without a folksy wit that earned him accolades in the tradition of southwestern humor.

As predatory businesses spread their tentacles across Gilded Age America, some farmers sought refuge in the Farmers' Alliance, an organization founded in Texas in the 1870s as a vehicle for collective action against monopolies. One of the Alliance's main goals was to form cooperatives to strengthen farmers' influence in buying their supplies and marketing their products. Hamstrung by lack of capital, poor management, and insufficient patron support, cooperative enterprises fell by the wayside, and farmers whose grievances remained unresolved flocked to the banner of Populism. With the demise of the Populist movement in the late 1890s, farmers had a choice: they could either cast their lot with a Democratic Party that was losing touch with farmers and working-class constituents; or they could march under the banner of Socialism, an ideology stewed in the juices of European social theory and homegrown frustrations, and one that Ameringer used to rally dispossessed Oklahomans to his cause.[10]

Ameringer spoke for many in the Socialist movement when he linked farmers with laborers in their struggles against exploitation: "The city wage worker is exploited because he does not own the tools with which he must work, and the farmer is exploited because he does not own the land he must till." In the countryside and to some extent in the city, the movement aimed to remove parasitic bankers, landlords, and other artificial forces from productive processes so that people could exert their natural energies to harvest nature's bounty. Unlike their ideological kin in Europe, who shaped their grievances to the contours of scientific Marxism, Oklahoma Socialists never strayed far from their Bibles. Like modern-day marketers who know their customers, local Socialists built their base in Oklahoma on old-time religion, a proven morality, and a sense of righteous conviction.[11]

Such was the extent of Socialist strength in Oklahoma that Ameringer, running under the banner of the Socialist Party of Oklahoma (SPO), garnered 23 percent of the vote in a three-way race for mayor of Oklahoma City in 1911. More than a hundred Socialists were elected to local office, including six to the state legislature.[12] Further evidence comes from the three national elections after statehood, including the one in November 1908 that sent Morgan to Congress for the first time. From a base of fewer than 10,000 votes in 1907, Party membership grew to more than 21,000 in 1908, nearly 25,000 in 1910, and more than 41,000 in 1912. In 1910, the Party's dues-paying, "red-card" membership was not only the largest in the Southwest; it was the largest in the nation. With 5,482 members, Oklahoma's Socialist Party had precisely 800 more than the number two state, New York, and paid more dues to the national office ($3,800) than any other state, thereby supplying Oklahoma Socialists with an impressive war chest to fund elections.[13]

In a final measure of Socialism's allure, Oklahoma led the nation in subscriptions—22,276 at their peak—to the movement's leading journal, *Appeal to Reason*. In 1908, its publishers in Crawford County, Kansas, rewarded the banner state with a special Oklahoma City edition. Served by fifty-five weeklies in Oklahoma, Texas, Louisiana, and Arkansas, Socialists had plenty to talk about at summer encampments that drew them by the thousands to rail against the unfairness baked into Gilded Age America.[14]

Growing in tandem with the SPO was the Working Class Union (WCU). Formed in 1914, the WCU was commended in *Appeal to Reason* for the same rapidity of growth that had fueled the sansculottes in Paris in their assault on the Bastille and their ideological kin in the countryside who had burned and murdered their way through feudal estates and brought the French monarchy to its knees. Unlike the SPO, the WCU operated under a veil of secrecy, vowing to abolish rent and prevent foreclosures "by any means necessary," including the use of dynamite, its weapon of choice. The WCU's targets included landlords, creditors, agricultural merchants, scabs, and collaborators—in short, anyone who stood in the way of revolutionary change. Although many in the SPO sympathized with the WCU, the party declined to endorse its tactics for fear of suppression and reprisal.[15]

From his home in northwestern Oklahoma, Dick Morgan reflected with mixed feelings on the new state's political prospects. Now that the territories were forever joined, he feared that Oklahoma would be more aligned with southern Democrats than midwestern Republicans and face obstacles in attracting capital. He was further troubled by Democratic legislators bent on chipping away at progressive clauses in the state constitution, thus perpetuating white supremacy. His dire predictions were borne out when the Democrat-dominated legislature wrote segregation into law with Senate Bill No. 1—the state's first law! —mandating racial separation in railroad cars and depots.[16]

Still, Morgan had built a solid reputation throughout northwestern Oklahoma, and he was convinced there was a place for him in the new political arena. Until the next census could be completed in 1910, Congress granted Oklahoma five congressional districts. His hometown of Woodward was centrally located in District Two, which stretched from Oklahoma County to the New Mexico and Colorado borders. What is more, the district included two communities whose support he could count on: El Reno, his former home and place of business, for three and a half years; and Oklahoma City, an exploding population center, where Porter was practicing law and where Black voters typically flocked to Republican candidates.

To compete in the September 17, 1907, elections, Republicans had chosen former territorial governor Tom Ferguson as their District Two Congressional candidate, not in a primary, but in a caucus. Ferguson lost to Elmer Fulton, the Democratic candidate from Oklahoma City, who went to Washington knowing that his shortened term was set to expire on March 4, 1909. Surely haunted by his string of past failures, Morgan aimed to replace Fulton as soon as Oklahoma could be integrated into the nation's normal electoral cycle, set to begin with the elections of November 3, 1908.[17]

Morgan's campaign roared to life on February 26, 1908, when Republicans from the Second District convened to endorse his candidacy, but not before heaping praise on the Party faithful who were already in office. First to be praised was "that noble statesman," President Theodore Roosevelt, whose fight for a square deal for everybody and against predatory corporations defined the progressive agenda. Next came endorsements for Dennis T. Flynn for the U.S. Senate and Bird McGuire, "who had fulfilled every pledge he has made," as the First District's candidate for the House. And then came the moment Morgan had been fighting for: "We congratulate the Republicans of the Second Congressional District upon their wise selection of a nominee for Congress and recognize in the Hon. Dick T. Morgan, of Woodward, Okla., a man in every respect fitted to represent our people in Oklahoma."

Citing Morgan's residency in Oklahoma since the run of 1889, chairmanship of the Free Home League, and consistent support for "plain, common people" at the expense of "the special few," Republicans' paean continued:

> We recognize in Mr. Morgan a moral and intellectual model of manhood; a man who has an acute sense of honor and duty; a conscientious desire to serve his constituents; a nature sensitive to right, fairness, and justice; a heart in sympathy and accord with men who live by the sweat of their brow; an able conception of the particular needs of our people, and the tact and ability to get the legislation needed for their welfare; a man whose efforts in Congress would be actuated by noble impulses and an earnest desire to do right and to be right.

One imagines a beaming Dick Morgan and a chorus of *hurrahs* as attention turned to confirmation of the Republican Party's principles, including the sale of public lands by the state; strict regulation of corporations, especially the railroads, and punishment of top brass who violated the people's trust; liberal pension laws for veterans; and legislation aiming to attract capital, promote population growth, and increase prosperity for everyone regardless of race, creed, color, or socioeconomic status. The convention closed with a reminder (as though anyone needed it!) that progressive Republicanism was the wave of the future: "The Republican party from its birth has been the friend and protector of labor; we are in hearty sympathy with all organizations of labor and employees of all kinds which have for their object the securing for labor of higher wages and protecting the members of such organizations in all their just rights in all controversies between capital and labor."

Morgan was further praised for resigning his position when the U.S. Land Office in Woodward was closed and consolidated with the office in Alva as a cost saving measure. For three-plus years, he had served as land register "in a highly competent manner; rendering fair, impartial and intelligent judgment on all matters coming before him." Rather than fight to save his job, he "voluntarily and unselfishly" traded the security of a federal position for a political campaign whose outcome was far from certain.[18]

The run-up to Election Day continued when Republicans met in Woodward on May 14 to form a Dick T. Morgan Republican Club, whose purpose was to secure their candidate's nomination. Officers and an executive committee were duly formed, and based on resolutions passed at the February convention, attendees renewed their support for Morgan's candidacy. "We submit to the republican voters that Dick T. Morgan is the man above all others to become the republican candidate for congress in this district," ran the resolution. "He is in entire harmony with his party and belongs to no faction. He has been a resident of Oklahoma, since the date of its birth in 1889, and has a wide personal acquaintance throughout the entire state. He is known personally and by reputation by almost every man in the district." Morgan was credited for resigning his position in the U.S. Land Office in a spirit of selfless sacrifice and in the interest of the public good. Known for his moral, social, and political purity, he was deemed perfectly suited to further the aims of progressive Republicans and bring balance to a playing field that had tilted for too long in the direction of special interests.

After accepting his nomination, Morgan delivered a brief speech and thanked everyone who had worked on his behalf, and especially members of the Dick T. Morgan Republican Club. Like the previous convention in February, this one ended with an optimistic flourish: "Mr. Morgan is known to have positive strength in every county in the district and good judges believe he will win the nomination."[19]

The momentum continued in Morgan's adopted hometown of Woodward, where supporters crafted a banner of reversible silk, thirty-eight inches long by thirty inches wide, bordered with gold lacing and festooned with tinsel. On one side, large gold-leaf letters bore the inscription "Dick T. Morgan" above an oval bust in a circle bordered in gold. Below was the caption "The People's Choice for Congress." On the reverse side, in a four-inch box bordered in gold leaf, was another message straight from campaign headquarters: "Woodward, Ok., Dick T. Morgan Republican Club." The banner was hung from an ornamental lateral bar and supported by a ten-foot polished staff with a bronze top knob.[20]

"Nineteen-eight was the first full-term election in Oklahoma," explained David Morgan. "Now fifty-four years old, Dick T. entered the primary and won both the primary and then the general election over Fulton, the incumbent, to become the first full-term congressman representing Oklahoma City and the Second District. It was a razor-thin margin (a difference of 924 votes, to be exact), with Dick T. winning only a plurality, not only because of the Black vote, but also because so many people voted for the Socialist candidate and siphoned votes from the Democrat." By then, Socialism was earning the allegiance of voters far beyond its breeding ground in eastern Oklahoma to become a seductive lure for anyone who felt left out in an unregulated economy and was fed up with the two-party system.[21]

After squeaking by with his narrow margin of victory, Morgan traveled to Washington in the company of Barritt Galloway, a sixteen-year-old high school dropout who had left his hometown of Vinita to become Morgan's secretary. They arrived in Congress to find that Morgan had been given a plum seat. "In what was basically luck of the draw, Dick T. got a very good seat assignment in his first session in Congress, number 218," continued David Morgan as he proudly displayed a seating chart for the Sixty-First Congress (March 4, 1909–March 4, 1911). That number put Morgan in the middle of the second row on the western side of the Chamber and left of Speaker of the House Joe Cannon, a Republican from Illinois who was widely

deemed the most dominant speaker in U.S. history.[22] As Speaker Cannon gaveled the session to order, Morgan was surely aware of speculation swirling on the other side of the aisle that he owed his election to Black voters, whose fealty had been so assiduously courted by Oklahoma Republicans, and Socialists, who had siphoned votes from the Democratic candidate.

To clarify his position on race and push back against Democrats' allegations that Republicans' coziness with Blacks was all about politics, Morgan denounced the "grandfather clause" amendment to the Oklahoma Constitution. It effectively denied their right to vote by imposing literacy tests at the polls and inserted a provision that effectively waived the requirements for all except Blacks. "Incredibly, of the more than fifty-seven thousand Blacks then living in Oklahoma, only fifty-five would have been allowed to cast their ballots," said David Morgan. Local voting registration officials interpreted the Voter Registration Act to mean that they could flatly refuse to administer literacy tests to Blacks or, at the very least, refuse to impose unreasonable ones. David continued: "As Dick noted in one of his

Dick Morgan (right) and his secretary, Barritt Galloway (left), in Morgan's congressional office. COURTESY OF THE MORGAN FAMILY COLLECTION

speeches, election laws should enable voters to register their will in a manner that preserves the dignity of every American citizen. As he said, 'It is a dangerous thing to begin the work of disenfranchisement.'"

Despite his objections, the amendment passed into law as Article 3, Section 4a of the state constitution, as passed by a popular vote on August 2.[23]

Oklahoma had plenty of company in rolling back Black voting rights after Reconstruction. Beginning with Mississippi in 1890, most southern states passed statutes or adopted constitutional provisions aimed at disenfranchisement. In an article for the *Harvard Law Review* in 1912, Julien C. Monnet, dean of the University of Oklahoma College of Law from 1909 to 1941 and dean emeritus from 1941 to 1951, compared Oklahoma's constitutional amendment to similar measures in the Deep South and made a startling observation: "A comparison of this clause with its predecessors shows the Oklahoma amendment to be the most sweeping attempt yet made constitutionally to include all whites and exclude all blacks from the privilege of voting."

Was this latest phase of retrograde legislation constitutional? That was for the courts, not Congress, to decide. At the time of Monnet's analysis, a decision on the validity of Oklahoma's amendment was pending in two jurisdictions: the Eighth Circuit Court of Appeals, in a criminal case; and the U.S. Supreme Court, in a civil case. At stake was nothing less than the Fourteenth and Fifteenth Amendments to the U.S. Constitution, which guaranteed the right to vote and equal protection under the laws regardless of race, color, or previous condition of servitude.[24]

Monnet concluded his article on a downbeat note:

> Congress thus pushes the shuttle back to the courts. Neither seems inclined to take jurisdiction, for the perhaps unconscious but nevertheless apparent reason that public sentiment in neither the north nor the south would sustain a policy of radical enforcement. Public sentiment in the north is apathetic, while in the south the racial feeling is so powerful that endless new expedients would be resorted to in order to maintain the supremacy of the white race.[25]

Vindication for Morgan and his fellow progressives who resisted Oklahoma's slide into the clutches of Jim Crow would come a few years later when the U.S. Supreme Court declared the amendment unconstitutional in *Guinn v. United States.* The state legislature responded by devising other schemes that kept Blacks from voting for the next half century. "From today's perspective, Dick T. might not be seen as a great civil rights pioneer, but he certainly was for his time," explained David Morgan. Morgan's opposition to restricting the Black vote dated back to his term in the Indiana legislature. Listening to inaugural speeches by two of his most influential role models—Governor Albert Porter and President James Garfield—Morgan was more convinced than ever that Blacks deserved the right to cast their ballots. In his own speeches against the proposed Oklahoma constitution, Morgan followed their lead and insisted that citizens of every race, creed, and color deserved equal treatment under the law, and he had no qualms about speaking out against the Jim Crow laws that were gaining traction in Oklahoma.[26]

In two of his elections (1910 and 1912), and even before the grandfather clause was ruled unconstitutional, Morgan would defend the right of Blacks to vote. In both elections, he would withstand charges of conspiracy and collaboration with the U.S. Attorney (his former campaign chairman) in their defiance of a law that had been upheld by the Oklahoma Supreme Court.

The first order of business of the Sixty-First Congress, seated on March 4, 1909, was to elect a Speaker of the House, which was not without controversy in Oklahoma. As a Republican in a House controlled by his party, Morgan was practically duty bound to vote for Joe Cannon's reelection. Since attaining that position in 1903, Cannon had exercised dictatorial control over legislation, meaning that bills were doomed without his approval. Predictably, Cannon was reelected, leaving Morgan with the strongest ally that a freshman congressman could hope for while causing his constituents to doubt his commitment to progressive reform. With that piece of business out of the way, Congress turned its attention to what was arguably the most contentious issue of the entire session: the Payne-Aldrich tariff.

Named for Republicans Sereno E. Payne of New York in the House and Nelson W. Aldrich of Rhode Island in the Senate, the bill called for the first increases in import duties since the Dingley Act of 1897. The debates that ensued revealed ideological positions that split along party lines. Republicans, dubbed "standpatters" for resisting the changes attending the galloping pace of modernity, saw the tariff as a vehicle to protect their benefactors in business and industry from imports. Democrats, in support of the much-touted common man, were dead set against the tariff and wanted to shield farmers and laborers from artificially high prices. Although progressives had yet to coalesce into a genuine party, they framed the tariff issue as part of their wider war on trusts and monopolies and fought to put certain items on the free list to exempt them from duties. Disagreements over the tariff bill compelled President William Howard Taft to call Congress into a special session, shortly after his inauguration, to deal with it. Meanwhile, representatives lined up to deliver speeches on the House floor.

Morgan was one of the first to take the floor. In his maiden speech before the House of Representatives, he argued vociferously against reductions in duties on gypsum, a mineral that was spawning one of western Oklahoma's most profitable industries. In his analysis, tariffs were vital to protecting infant industries. Under the tariff that had been in place since 1897, seven gypsum mills had been established in his district to foster dozens of supporting businesses and provide employment for thousands. Morgan further opined that protective tariffs did not, as Democrats believed, raise commodity prices. On the contrary, they reduced prices by fostering competition, improvements in machinery and manufacturing, and the acquisition of skills among mechanics and artisans. Morgan's proof was in the price of gypsum, which had dropped 37 percent after a duty was imposed.

For Morgan, the tariff had a dual purpose: first, it furnished revenue; and second, it "scatters its blessings to every section of the country and to the people in every occupation and calling." He sided with his Republican brethren in citing tariffs as key to the nation's unparalleled industrial development insofar as such duties encouraged and stimulated the development of natural resources. The trick was to identify resources that needed protection, a factor that depended on whether they existed in sufficient quantities to supply domestic demand. In his view, gypsum met that requirement in spades, as there was enough gypsum in his district and, indeed, throughout the nation to fuel a homegrown industry. "In view of the inexhaustible quantity of gypsum in every section of the United States, I believe proper encouragement should be given to the development of this industry."

Morgan's maiden speech in Congress ended to applause from his side of the aisle.[27]

That applause was not replicated in the Democratic-leaning *Daily Oklahoman*, whose editors branded tariffs as "the mother of trusts." In a series of broadsides against Morgan and the other Republicans in the state's congressional delegation, the newspaper blasted supporters of the tariff bill as enemies of the people, particularly those who still lived in soddies out on the prairie and whose lives depended on cheap supplies. Morgan fought back against accusations that he had voted for a duty on lumber when, in fact, he had recommended it for the free list to satisfy farmers' need for building materials. He continued to insist that whatever short-term benefits might be achieved through lower consumer prices would be offset by reductions in manufacturing and employment. At the same time, the *Daily Oklahoman* castigated Morgan for voting to reelect Joe Cannon as speaker, thereby ensuring a continuation of his "tyrannous House rules." Even Porter cautioned his father that "being a Cannon man" might hurt him.[28]

Congress passed the Payne-Aldrich Tariff Act on August 5, 1909, with Oklahoma's delegation voting along party lines. President Taft affixed his signature on the same day. The *Daily Oklahoman* wasted no time in excoriating Taft and his partisans in Congress, who would surely be tossed out of office, along with his Republican henchmen, for siding so squarely with trusts and monopolies. Other than injecting Congress with a heavy dose of toxicity, the most long-lasting effect of the Payne-Aldrich tariff was to showcase America's preference for isolation over a robust and mutually beneficial foreign trade. Another unfortunate legacy was leaving Big Business with outsized influence in Congress, a situation that Democrats and progressives vowed to combat with everything they had.[29]

Passage of the Payne-Aldrich tariff was one of the Sixty-First Congress's five significant accomplishments. The other four, all of which Morgan endorsed, included (1) a constitutional amendment to levy an income tax; (2) instituting changes in House rules to curtail the speaker's power to control legislation; (3) passing the Mann-Elkins Act, which strengthened Congressional authority over railroad rates and expanded its jurisdiction to cover telephones, telegraphs, and radio; and (4) authorizing the creation of postal savings banks.[30] Of less import to history were Morgan's vote against a motion to strike from the Urgency Deficiency Appropriation Bill the provisions allowing President Taft to spend $25,000 for traveling expenses (and no wonder—the presidential salary had been increased from $50,000 to $75,000 per year, "with the solemn promise that no additional amount should be allowed or asked for, for traveling expenses") and his vote to allow the vice president and speaker of the House to spend $12,000 for automobiles.[31]

As Morgan's freshman term entered its final months, his constituents back in northwest Oklahoma had reason to wonder if he really was the progressive Republican that he claimed to be. Voting to retain Joe Cannon as Speaker of the House sent an early signal that he was working his way to the inner circle of old-guard Republicans. Then came his vote for the Payne-Aldrich tariff. As if that were not enough to raise eyebrows, in late October 1909 Morgan joined President Taft, other dignitaries and businessmen, and newspaper reporters on a presidential flotilla down the Mississippi River, from St. Louis to the Gulf of Mexico. If Morgan intended to assert his independence from the standpatters, he would have to do it soon or risk going down in history as a one-term congressman.

Clearly vexed by what he considered unfair publicity, Morgan bristled at suggestions that he was in Speaker Cannon's pocket and, more to the point, that he was not a progressive. "I have a pretty good record as against Cannon because I voted against him in the republican caucus," wrote Morgan to his son on January 15, 1910. "On questions of legislation I am not a stand-pater [*sic*] but a progressive of progressives, and in my judgment the real thing that the people will finally be interested in is how a man votes on the important questions before Congress."[32]

One thing was for sure: Democrats knew he was courting trouble from the progressive wing of his party for seeming to cozy up to Taft and Cannon and supporting the tariff, and sending Elmer Fulton back to Washington was looking like a real possibility. "Did [Morgan] at any time ever vote in your interests?" ran a message from the Second District Democratic Congressional Committee in June 1910. "We defy him to point out a single instance when there was a division in Congress, with the trusts and the special interests arrayed on one side and the people on the other, where he did not vote for and go to the assistance of the trusts and special interests." Fulton, on the other hand, had used his truncated session in Congress to vote consistently in the interests of the people. "The only way the people of this country will rule is to have in Congress men who will stand like flint against Cannon and 'Cannonism' and at all times vote in the interests of their constituents."[33]

But there's likely more to the story. David Morgan suggested that his great-grandfather spent his freshman term acclimating to Congress, wary of making enemies (especially with Speaker Cannon!) and testing the limits of his influence. "Dick T. didn't really cast his lot with progressivism until his second and third terms," said David Morgan.

Speaker of the House Joe T. Cannon (left) and Congressman Dick T. Morgan (right), July 1916. COURTESY OF THE MORGAN FAMILY COLLECTION

"He definitely drew fire from Democrats, and maybe even progressive Republicans, for supporting the Payne-Aldrich Tariff Act because they objected to the higher prices that come from a tax on imports. What they didn't acknowledge was how hard he fought to put key imports on the free list."[34] Morgan continued to argue that farmers needed tariff protection from Canadian imports that were flooding the market.

Morgan complemented his work in crafting national legislation with bills aimed at helping his constituents. A short list of bills that he shepherded through Congress includes: (1) an appropriation of $230,000 for a federal building in Oklahoma City; (2) an appropriation of $100,000 for a federal building in El Reno; (3) setting aside land near El Reno for a Masonic orphanage home and industrial school; (4) providing for the platting of an Indian allotment near Anadarko as an addition to the city; (5) opening the Fort Reno military reservation to settlement; (6) securing two terms of federal court annually in Woodward in order to relieve congestion; and (7) securing and, in some instances, increasing pensions for soldiers. In a July 1910 interview with the *Wichita Eagle*, Morgan revealed a commitment to underserved constituents when he explained that selling the Fort Reno military reservation for approximately $300,000 and opening it to settlement would accrue to the benefit of Cheyennes and Arapahoes, as they would draw 4 percent interest per annum.

"I estimate that in actual cash my district is a million dollars better off by reason of the service which I have rendered," said Morgan. "For a first term member, I feel that I have served my constituents successfully."

Morgan went on to tell his interviewer that he held the unique distinction of answering every roll call in the recently closed session of the Sixty-First Congress. One suspects that he cut his interview short, as he was on his way to Woodward and had scheduled speeches every day from mid-July to the statewide primaries in August. And his prospects for reelection? Morgan expected "no trouble" in defeating Joe Sherman, the progressive candidate running against him.[35]

A couple of weeks before his interview with the *Wichita Eagle*, a correspondent with the *Indianapolis News* caught up with him on a swing through Indiana to visit family and friends. Having shaken "Indiana dust from his feet" twenty-five years earlier, he had plenty to say about his adopted state, from its vast mineral resources to its incomparable farmland. Although he was more interested in describing Oklahoma's future than political machinations, he could not resist making rosy predictions for his party:

> The general belief is that Oklahoma finally will switch around and get into the Republican column. Immigration from the northern states will have much to do with this. As the commercial interests of the state develop many people are coming from the north and this increases the number of Republican votes, for the most [*sic*] of them are Republicans. Many of the early immigrants were from the south.

Morgan went on to express his support for moving the state capital from Guthrie to Oklahoma City, a prospect that polarized the two cities and gave lawyers lots to argue about. He then rattled off facts and statistics from the 1910 census: Oklahoma's population was approaching two million; assessed property valuation was nearly a billion dollars; the benighted eastern part of the state was brimming with coal, oil, gas, limestone, lead, and zinc; and agricultural output was staggering in both its quantity and variety.

And then he was off to Terre Haute before continuing to Oklahoma, where a tough campaign season awaited him. One imagines a pensive Dick Morgan spending his travel time writing and rewriting speeches that he hoped would convince Republicans to send him back to Washington for a second term in Congress.[36]

Congressman Dick T. Morgan, n.d. COURTESY OF THE VIRGINIA SUTTON COLLECTION, OKLAHOMA HISTORICAL SOCIETY, OKLAHOMA CITY

CHAPTER TEN

The Million-Dollar Congressman

Control must begin where competition ceases.

DICK T. MORGAN, 1912

DICK MORGAN'S CONFIDENCE IN WINNING the August 2, 1910, Republican primary was vindicated when he trounced Joe Sherman by 7,632 to 2,564 votes. Also-rans included James H. Norton, with 1,487 votes; and George W. Partridge, with 1,031 votes. Now that he was his party's candidate, Morgan turned his attention to the general election, slated for November 8.[1]

Morgan kicked off his general election campaign, a few days after the primary, when the Second District Republican Congressional Committee met to adopt resolutions renewing the state platform adopted four years earlier and endorsing Morgan's record. Additionally, the committee credited President Taft with enacting more laws for the public good than any other president in a comparable time period. The committee also gave its stamp of approval to the Payne-Aldrich tariff bill. In his brief remarks before the committee, Morgan emphasized the need to listen and respond to his constituents if he had any hope of winning the next election and helping his fellow Republicans secure a majority in Congress. With his usual optimism, he assured his listeners that he would earn more votes than he had in 1908. More evidence of confidence in Morgan's reelection came in September when Homer N. Boardman, prosecuting attorney for Blaine County, resigned and took charge of Morgan's campaign, which was headquartered in the Baum Building in Oklahoma City.

Morgan's campaign itinerary ended with a stop in Custer County, where he stood before a sizable crowd in Clinton to review his achievements. His listeners knew enough about his first-term accomplishments in wooing federal dollars to his district to nickname

VOTE FOR

HON. DICK T. MORGAN

FOR CONGRESS

A BUSINESS PROPOSITION:--Oklahoma City should send a Republican Representative to a Republian Congress.

Times-Journal Pub. Co. Oklahoma City, Okla.

Campaign poster, 1910. COURTESY OF THE CARL ALBERT CONGRESSIONAL RESEARCH AND STUDIES CENTER, NORMAN, OKLAHOMA

him the Million-Dollar Congressman. "No other member of the Oklahoma congressional delegation did so well," ran one laudatory account of his Custer County tour. Singled out for special recognition were his five votes for free lumber and retention of the duty on gypsum, one of the state's most profitable industries.[2]

Morgan likely drew special applause for his promotion of good road legislation, an issue of paramount importance to farmers and ranchers struggling to get their produce to market. As he had declared at the Second National Good Roads Congress in Baltimore in May 1909, "The building of good roads, the improvement of our public highways and the betterment of the means of communication, of travel, of transportation throughout the country districts, will in a thousand ways add to the profits of farming and contribute to the comfort, dignity and well being of all those engaged in agriculture." Good roads were a panacea not only for agriculture, but also for parents looking to send their children to good schools, attend church, and enjoy luxuries and cultural refinements "heretofore unattainable." In Morgan's telling, the movement to build good roads was "inspired by the highest benevolence and the purest patriotism," and it deserved the full backing of the federal government that he now represented.[3]

But not everything was smooth sailing. In a spirited two-and-a-half-hour debate in the Anadarko opera house, more than a thousand people were on hand when Morgan squared off against his Democratic opponent, Elmer Fulton, who was determined to regain the seat he had lost to Morgan in 1908. According to the Democratic-leaning press, Anadarko was the last place Morgan wanted to be. His effort to avoid a debate with Fulton had been thwarted when the two men met by chance on the campaign trail. Fulton promptly threw down the gauntlet. Morgan could not say no, and the stage was set for a showdown in Anadarko. Tensions rose when Fulton brought up the Payne-Aldrich tariff bill, which was sure to raise prices on imports vital to western Oklahoma farmers and ranchers. Morgan had to go on defense, leaving Fulton with a clear advantage. An article, likely from an unfriendly newspaper, about the mid-October clash left no doubt about the winner: "A huge crowd filled the stage after the session to congratulate Mr. Fulton."[4]

As the campaign of 1910 entered its endgame, Oklahoma pundits cited three issues of importance to the state and nation: first, the likelihood that Oklahoma would remain "unshakably Democratic"; second, whether the three Republicans in the state's congressional delegation—Bird McGuire of the First District, Dick T. Morgan of the Second District, and C. E. Creager of the Third District—could hang onto their seats; and finally, whether the state legislature's upcoming redistricting, set to begin as soon as it convened in January 1911, would bring drastic changes to voting patterns.

Morgan had seen enough of partisan gerrymandering in his home state of Indiana and his adopted state of Oklahoma to be wary of Democratic machinations. According to the federal census of 1910, Oklahoma's population had shot past 1,600,000, which was more than enough for the state to gain three seats in Congress, for a total of eight. If the legislature were to retain its Democratic majority, which it almost certainly would, then Republicans up and down the ballot would be in serious trouble. Some went so far as to predict that seven out of Oklahoma's eight districts would be safely in the Democratic fold. Morgan had only to reflect on his own slim margin of 924 votes over Elmer Fulton in 1908 to realize the tenuousness of his and other Republicans' grip on power. An analysis in mid-October came as no surprise to Morgan, who had labored in vain to keep the Twin Territories from getting hitched: "Since in the past elections the heavy southern democratic vote has more than offset the heavy northern Republican vote."[5]

As a new state racked by old-fashioned partisanship, Oklahoma gave pundits an opportunity to gauge how voters would respond to the fight between standpatters and progressives. Judging from their records in the Sixty-First Congress, neither Morgan nor the other incumbent Republicans, Bird McGuire and C. E. Creager, seemed willing to jeopardize their careers by standing up to Joe Cannon and his coterie of standpat Republicans. All three were perceived as mainstream Republicans in thrall to the status quo. And all three came under harsh criticism not only from Democrats, but also from the progressive wing of their own party for voting on the side of privilege.[6] For a taste of the invective directed at Messrs. Morgan, McGuire, and Creager, we turn to the *Oklahoma Farmer and Laborer*, a progressive newspaper published in Guthrie that had little use for standpatters:

> The republican leaders have been arguing that Oklahoma's three standpat congressmen should be reelected because no congressmen can be of any service to his people unless he is a member of the majority party in the House. Let them continue the same argument. The next congress is as sure to be democratic as it is sure to meet. What good can three standpat republicans from Oklahoma accomplish in the House with a democratic majority against them?[7]

Attacks on Morgan escalated in the Second District's most influential newspaper, the *Daily Oklahoman*. Citing Morgan's votes to retain Cannon as speaker and pass the Payne-Aldrich tariff bill, one editorial branded Morgan "an avowed member of the Standpat-Cannon-Aldrich element" who represented "only a small part of the people, the privileged classes." Despite his campaign pledges from 1908, that same newspaper insisted that every time the standpatters signaled for his vote, Morgan had "delivered it as graciously as a royal flunkey hands a card to his master." Fulton, on the other hand, had voted against Cannon and his machine and, during his short tenure in Congress, had done what he could to wrest control from the Republican machine and return governance to the people.[8] The *Daily Oklahoman* then continued its mudslinging in criticizing Morgan's procurement of 35,000 packages of garden seeds—free of charge! —for his constituents. Readers were called on to imagine Representative Morgan toiling away, meticulously labeling and delivering all those packages to the grateful farmers of western Oklahoma. "It is doubtful if either Cannon or Aldrich with all their reputed power and influence were ever able to bestow upon their constituents such a munificent gift as thirty-five thousand packages of garden seed." Morgan's labors earned him the nickname "Garden Seed Dick," a moniker that resonated among his detractors until Election Day. It probably elicited more laughs than his designation, likewise attributed to Bird McGuire and C. E. Creager, as a "System Republican."[9]

Morgan did not take the *Daily Oklahoman*'s attacks lying down. Under the heading "An Upright and Fearless Public Servant," his campaign brochure reminded voters that he had voted for Roosevelt's and Taft's policies and that he had insisted on exempting lumber from the tariff and putting it on the free list with an eye to mitigating the influence of special interests. The brochure called attention to Morgan's two overarching achievements during his first year in the House: he had secured more than a million dollars' worth of legislation for his district in less than six months, earning him renown as the Million-Dollar Congressman; and he had never missed a roll call.[10] Morgan exhibited his own flair for negative campaigning when he criticized Fulton, his Democratic opponent, for accepting his government salary of $7,500 per annum eight months before he was elected to office and, as he had been elected in the waning days of Oklahoma's territorial status, before the office even existed.[11]

Election Day arrived on November 8, 1910. Morgan survived the negative campaigning and barrage of negative newspaper articles and was sent back to Congress for a second term, but just barely. With 25,134 votes, he came out slightly ahead of Fulton's 24,062 votes and the Socialist candidate, H. I. Bryant, with a respectable 5,382 votes. Morgan's margin was about the same as it had been in 1908, when he defeated Fulton by 924 votes. Apparently, Democrats' fixation on Morgan's standpatterism (an inelegant term, even for political jargon) could not stand up to Morgan's characterization of Fulton as a salary grabber.

But Fulton was not done with the election. The next month, he filed a protest in Washington, D.C., alleging that Morgan had broken three election laws to clinch his victory. First and foremost was his accusation that Morgan had received at least eight hundred Black votes in violation of the grandfather clause, which had been accepted by a vote of the people and approved by the state supreme court. Fulton admitted that some Blacks might have passed the literacy test. Yet, as he stated in his lawsuit, most of them "were ignorant and illiterate and could not have so qualified." Fulton's other grounds for protest were that ballots in many Oklahoma City precincts had not been counted correctly and that some precinct boundaries did not conform to population requirements.[12]

Fulton's contest caught Morgan by surprise, and he declined requests for interviews on the matter until he could obtain counsel.

For that, he called on Porter to head up his defense. Then officing in the American National Bank Building in Oklahoma City, Porter received his father's Western Union telegram, in which he fulminated against Fulton's "vague, indefinite, and uncertain" allegations. Morgan assured his son that he had been "legally and lawfully elected" and denied, categorically, all his former opponent's grounds for protest. Any doubts that Morgan might have had about enlisting his son in his defense were put to rest when he asked his attorneys in Washington to review Porter's answer to Fulton's complaint. "We have read carefully the enclosed answer in your election case," ran a January 11, 1911, letter to Morgan from his Washington counsel, Michener & Pence. "We consider it an admirable document from end to end and would not know how to improve upon it. Please convey our appreciation of it to your lawyers in Oklahoma."[13] One imagines the elder Morgan bursting with pride over his son's sound legal advice and political acumen.

By April of the following year, Fulton's contest was fading into history. An investigation into the contested election of 1910 by the House Committee on Elections lay in Morgan's future.

On the bright side, so did his exoneration.[14]

By the time the Sixty-Second Congress (March 4, 1911–March 4, 1913) convened, Morgan was ready to launch his crusade against progressives' enemy number one: trusts and monopolies. Convinced that Big Business was choking progress and putting the American Dream beyond the reach of most Americans, Morgan had dedicated his off hours in Washington to studying the economic system and figuring out how to make it more equitable. As David Morgan explained, "When Dick T. entered Congress on March 4, 1909, he recognized that the trust question was one of the nation's most pressing unresolved problems. He at once began a careful and systematic study of the question and looked for inspiration from every available source, including the Library of Congress, the U.S. Constitution, federal statutes, and Supreme Court decisions. While others were talking, he was working." Morgan's goal, which he had shared with constituents during his campaign of 1910, was to prepare a bill to create a federal corporation commission aimed at bringing trusts and monopolies to heel.[15]

Not that Dick Morgan was the only one with predatory trusts and monopolies in his crosshairs. Success in reining in corporations dated back to the Sherman Antitrust Act of 1890, a seminal piece of legislation named for its principal author, Republican senator John Sherman of Ohio. Broadly speaking, the Sherman Antitrust Act prohibited anticompetitive agreements and unilateral conduct aimed at monopolizing markets. Its purpose was not to protect competitors from legitimately successful businesses or prevent companies from turning an honest dollar, but to foster healthy competition and protect consumers from abuse.[16] But Big Business was not about to cede its power without a fight, and over the ensuing two decades, enforcement of the Sherman Antitrust Act waned as companies devised ever more devious end runs around it. It was left to President Roosevelt and his "bully pulpit" to enact legislation from his progressive playbook to curb corporations' insatiable pursuit of profit at the expense of the public welfare.

Although the president and his progressive allies in Congress were certainly effective in curbing abuses, there was still no federal agency tasked with enforcing laws and meting out punishment. Moreover, there was nothing in the U.S. Constitution to protect consumers from companies that dictated prices and manipulated markets. As David Morgan explained, Dick T.'s goal was to create an agency with the power to impose a code of business ethics, create the conditions for a competitive marketplace, compel corporations to sell their products at just and reasonable prices, and punish higher-ups who acted against public policy and endangered the people's welfare.[17]

With that lofty goal in mind, Morgan introduced his bill (H.R. 18711) on January 25, 1912. To explain the bill in detail, he rose to the podium on February 20 to deliver a speech under the unambiguous title "Control of Corporations: Control Must Begin When Competition Ceases." The purpose of the bill, said Morgan, was "to provide a practical and effective method by which the National Government may exercise proper and effective control over our great industrial corporations."

And then came his call to arms:

> Let us keep the fire of competition burning brightly and brilliantly in every industry and in every section of our country; but should the flame of competition in any industry grow dim, or should it, under stress of monopolistic power, become extinct, let us not leave the people in darkness and despair. Let us have a great commission and place in its hand the blazing torch of authority to reinforce competition, to perpetuate its life, and preserve its power and potency in our industrial system.

After giving due credit to the Sherman Antitrust Act, Morgan told his colleagues what they already knew: no laws had been passed since 1890 to strengthen federal authority over corporations, and increasing concentration left them with massive power to control prices. Although the Founding Fathers had taken every precaution to protect political and property rights, those protections were threatened if companies could minimize competition and, in effect, repeal the law of supply and demand. If the U.S. Treasury could routinely spend millions on defense during peacetime, was it not reasonable to allocate a fraction of those outlays to protect citizens from trusts and monopolies? As Morgan insisted, House Bill 18711 was far from radical, and his speech contained nothing but accolades for corporations whose "splendid achievements" had made the United States the envy of the world. All he wanted to do was impose restrictions that would ensure continued prosperity for industries and increased protection for consumers.

And how, exactly, was this proposed agency supposed to work? With his customary eye for detail, Morgan used his speech to outline the creation of a seven-member commission with jurisdiction over industrial corporations, much like the Interstate Commerce Commission (ICC) had jurisdiction over railways and public utilities. First, Morgan said the commission would be empowered to declare which prices were just, fair, and reasonable. Second, corporate practices would be "just, fair, and reasonable, and not contrary to public policy or dangerous to the public welfare." Third, corporations would be required to deal justly and fairly with their competitors as well as the public— "that is, to offer no special privileges or advantages, and enter into no special contracts or agreements, that might result in discrimination against individuals, competing companies, or localities." Fourth, commissioners would have the authority, either in response to complaints or on their own initiative, to prescribe just, fair, and reasonable prices for merchandise and products, which would align corporate policies with the public welfare. Finally, commissioners would be required to act in accordance with the U.S. Constitution. With the support of the courts, they would be granted authorization to enforce their orders and exercise strict supervision over corporations with gross annual receipts of more than five million dollars.

"Free, open, honest competition must continue to be the great factor in controlling and regulating prices," said Morgan as he wound toward his conclusion. "In my judgment there is nothing impractical, nothing revolutionary, nothing dangerous to society, to the State, or to the people for the National Government to exercise such control over such corporations as will require them to dispose of their products at reasonable prices."[18] In an argument that dates back to the dawn of free-market capitalism, Morgan thought it was unreasonable, and certainly unrealistic, to expect corporations to regulate themselves.

The Q&A session following Morgan's speech began with skepticism about the efficacy of price controls. Two representatives cited efforts to control the price of bread during the French Revolution as a prime example of how *not* to manage the marketplace. "They hanged a few bankers to lamp posts on account of the price of bread," said Republican Edward L. Hamilton of Michigan. Brushing aside Hamilton's nod to Clio, which seemed lacking in relevance, Morgan insisted that his goal was to strengthen the Sherman Antitrust Act by empowering the federal government to destroy monopolies. Historical precedent more relevant than the French Revolution could be found in Republican and Democratic party platforms, dating back to 1884, that called for regulating commerce and restraining Big Business from abusing consumers. After all, William McKinley and his trust-busting vice president, Theodore Roosevelt, had been elected on the strength of the Republican Party platform of 1900. "Let us act the part of a wise physician," suggested Morgan in a shift from history to medicine, and "continue our efforts to destroy the disease, but in the meantime apply some remedy that will keep it under control."[19]

Questioning then turned to the thorniest issue of all: what, exactly, constituted a monopoly? Disclaiming expertise in the matter, Morgan singled out the three hundred or so corporations with gross revenues of more than five million dollars annually as subject to regulation. Economic growth would no doubt push that number higher. Determining how much higher, and what other factors might warrant adjustment in a rapidly modernizing economy, would be up to the "quasi-court" agency envisioned in Morgan's bill.

But wouldn't putting legislative and judicial functions in the same agency spawn endless conflicts of interest and open the door to corruption? Not necessarily. Morgan's model, the ICC, was the nation's first regulatory agency, and it had been doing a good job, since its creation on February 4, 1887, of regulating railroads, express services, and telegraph and telephone companies even though it was vested with purely legislative powers. Besides, anyone unhappy with the agency's rulings had access to appeal through the courts. The point was to make laws in harmony with public sentiment, which was clearly in favor of tighter regulations to promote fair competition.

"Control is the only substitute for competition," declared Morgan. "Control must begin where competition ceases."

Morgan ended his speech as he had begun, with a clarion call for congressmen to stand shoulder-to-shoulder with their constituents, who wanted nothing more than fairness to build better lives:

> By so doing we will have promulgated a higher law for the guidance of our gigantic industrial corporations engaged in interstate commerce; we will have set in motion the governmental machinery that will be able to cope with these great corporations; and we will have put the people and the corporations upon a highway that will lead them to reconciliation and unite them in an effort to bring to our country a reign of industrial peace, which is essential to our industrial prosperity.

Rousing applause erupted as Morgan returned to his seat.[20]

Although the census of 1910 qualified Oklahoma to elect three additional representatives to Congress, the legislature failed to complete its redistricting in 1911, which meant that the three additional congressmen would be elected at large in 1912. The five original districts would keep their same boundaries. The at-large candidates attracted little notice, with the notable exception of "Alfalfa" Bill Murray, whose political appeal and notoriety made him a magnet for the press and, as it turned out, a successful candidate.[21]

Far more interesting were the district races, and none more so than in District Two. "The election of 1912 was crucial for Dick T.," said David Morgan. "He was making a transition from getting his feet wet as a 'leaning' conservative supporter of President Taft and Speaker Joe Cannon to a maverick progressive. He was also becoming a national leader because of his hard work and passion in his beliefs, and his ability to communicate thoughts to others."[22]

Maybe so. But Morgan's rise to leadership was by no means assured in the run-up to the 1912 election. He was caught off-guard by the vindictive campaign between Roosevelt and Taft, which would influence the Republican primary in his remote congressional district. In March, Republicans who gathered in Clinton for the Second District convention paid scant attention to Morgan's candidacy and refused to endorse him because he made it so hard for people to know where his loyalties lay. As noted in the *Guthrie Daily Star*, "Mr. Morgan, who has repeatedly announced himself in favor of Taft's renomination appeared today with a Roosevelt button on his coat."[23]

News that Morgan's renomination was in jeopardy set off alarm bells among Republicans in Washington. Writing two days after the Republican County Convention, party partisan H. G. Eastman informed Representative William B. McKinley of Illinois that attendees had voted about thirty to one for Roosevelt. What is more, they admonished delegates to withhold their support from anyone "who was not an avowed Roosevelt supporter." Although Eastman expressed great admiration for Morgan, he feared that Morgan's loyalty to Taft might end his congressional career. "I sincerely trust it will not prevent his renomination," wrote a downcast Eastman, "yet we may as well face the fact that his constituents are overwhelmingly for Roosevelt."[24]

Struggling with split loyalties, Morgan was in a precarious position. But in a letter to Porter from the Dewey Hotel in Washington, he exhibited a naivete that seems surprising in a seasoned politician. "Being for Taft it seemed to me I was honor bound to stand by him in his hour of trial," he wrote to his son, who served as his campaign manager in Oklahoma City. "I hope Roosevelt men will not become too easily offended, and that I may have their support."[25]

To win that support, Morgan requested Porter's help in compiling a mailing list of Republicans in Oklahoma City to help them "get a good idea of the sentiment of the city." Morgan's campaign strategy included keeping costs down by relying on volunteers as much as possible and enlisting only people who could be counted on to maintain confidence. "The men who you have to assist you in this matter should be persons whose loyalty is known."[26]

His vacillation notwithstanding, Morgan ran uncontested in the Republican primary. That would not be the case in the general election, where Democrats were poised to secure a congressional majority both nationwide and in Oklahoma. To shore up his defenses, Morgan returned to Oklahoma from Washington ten days before the primaries to clarify his positions and remind voters of his accomplishments over the previous four years. He made his case before a sizable crowd on July 23: "I have shirked no responsibility, neglected no duties, evaded no issue, and I have not dodged a single vote. I have given the people the best service of which I was capable." He then delved into the specific bills that had earned him his moniker as the Million-Dollar Congressman, claiming that there was scarcely any part of his district that had not benefited from his legislation. In terms of national legislation, Morgan had voted for a slew of bills that carried the progressive seal of approval: an income tax; postal savings banks; conservation of natural resources; taxes on big corporations; enhancement of the ICC's power to fix rates on railroads and express, telegraph, and telephone services; employers' liability; exemptions of agricultural products from the tariff; direct election of senators; limits on campaign expenses; good roads; and an eight-hour workday.

Some listeners were no doubt aware of his support for labor unions in their fight against unfair judicial injunctions and contempt orders. "With organized capital now supreme in the land, labor unions are essential," declared Morgan to his fellow congressmen on July 9, 1912.

"Such organizations have done much to shorten the hours of labor, increase wages, improve conditions under which labor is performed, and to educate public sentiment to understand the rights of labor." To preserve peace and harmony between labor and capital, Morgan urged his colleagues to join him in shaping legislation "so as to recognize any reasonable demand of labor and make those who create the wealth of the Nation feel that their rights and interests are fully recognized and that they reap a reward commensurate with the labor performed."[27]

And his plans for a third term? Not surprisingly, regulating Big Business and fighting monopolies topped his list. He also vowed to vote in the interests of agriculture– "to promote its prosperity, to extend its growth, to make farm life more attractive, and to add to the comfort, convenience and prosperity of our farmers." Other items on his congressional to-do list included improving wages and working conditions, continuing to promote protective tariffs, and ensuring veterans the pensions they had so honorably earned.[28]

Morgan amplified his message on August 23, 1912, with a speech imploring his fellow legislators to do what he had been doing since his first day in Congress, and through the Committee on Public Lands: promote legislation to ensure fairness in producing, conserving, taxing, controlling, and distributing wealth. To make sure that the U.S. Treasury had sufficient funding, he had voted to amend the Constitution to enable the federal government to impose a tax on incomes based on a guarantee that "the just, proper, fair, and equitable share of taxation" would be levied on those most able to afford it. In addition, he had voted, in August 1909, to place a 1 percent per annum tax on corporate profits above $5,000, a measure that was bringing $30 million annually into the U.S. Treasury. It was only fair, declared Morgan, "that the wealthy corporations of the Nation should pay a special tax to relieve to some extent the burden which would otherwise come upon those less able to bear it." More recently, he had voted to levy an excise tax on individuals who earned more than $5,000 annually. After all, if they were truly patriots, they would welcome the additional burden and "not grumble at the payment of this additional tax."

Returning to the theme of his "Control of Corporations" speech,

Morgan reminded his listeners that a quarter century of revolutionary change across the economic spectrum had wrested control from individuals and vested it in corporations with the clout to manipulate prices. "Free, fair, effective competition is no longer the controlling factor in the prices of many products in common use," said Morgan as progressive heads nodded in unison. As wealth devolved into fewer hands, Congress was left with an option to either destroy monopolies or control them.

Legislators had chosen option two, beginning with the creation of the ICC. Congressional oversight had expanded, with the Mann-Elkins Act, giving the ICC added authority to regulate express, telegraph, and telephone companies. All of these were "natural monopolies" whose rates "should not be left to the greed of their managers." But as Morgan had emphasized in his "Control of Corporations" speech and reiterated at every opportunity, those regulatory milestones had done little to curb monopolies, leaving it to the increasingly anachronistic and ineffectual Sherman Antitrust Act to mitigate wealth concentration. "Whatever may be said in favor of this law," said Morgan, "it is a fact that since its enactment our corporations have been growing in size and in monopolistic power." Predictably, Morgan touted the bill, H.R. 18711, that he had introduced earlier that year. Surely looking for applause from his side of the aisle, Morgan cited former President Roosevelt's plug for an interstate trade commission in his "Charter of Democracy" speech before the Ohio Constitutional Convention. Additional support for relieving people from "unjust, unfair, and unreasonable" prices came from the Republican and Progressive (a.k.a. Bull Moose) Party platforms of 1912.

Citing the Census of 1910, Morgan then described the size and distribution of the labor force– "an army of toilers that gives this country its wealth, its prosperity, its prestige abroad, and its real strength at home." According to the census, the U.S. was home to some thirty-five million laborers and farmers. They demanded, and deserved, a level playing field. "The proper distribution of wealth is, therefore, not only a question of doing justice to the men who earn the wealth, but it involves also the very life and perpetuity of the Republic and its free institutions."

Finally, Morgan spoke up for policies that had been part of the Republican Party's playbook since its inception to encourage and stimulate wealth production: "The policies which have been pursued by the Republican Party and the laws which have been enacted by Republican Congresses have been the most favorable to the production of wealth among our people." As the world leader in mining, manufacturing, and agriculture, the U.S. had grown from crude settlements along the Atlantic Seaboard to a global powerhouse with annual production of manufactured goods surpassing $20 billion, $4 billion more than the national wealth in 1860. "I hope in this free Republic it will be in the years to come as it has been in the years gone by that the humblest boy may rise to positions of the highest distinction and honor," concluded Morgan. "Not only are we better off than any other people, but in all the 125 years of our history as a Nation we never before were so well off as we are to-day... Take our entire population as a whole, there has never been an hour in our history when the average man among us had more of the good things of life, more to make him contented and happy than he has in 1912."[29]

Regardless of Morgan's accomplishments and promises, he could not shake perceptions that he was a standpatter at heart, less interested in progressive reforms than in cozying up to Taft, Cannon, and Aldrich and voting on behalf of Big Business. "The mask is removed and the face of Dick T. Morgan shows clearly," ran a typical screed in the *Daily Oklahoman*. "His countenance reflects a standpat expression. Dick T. Morgan is for Taft." Progressive Party of Oklahoma chairman Alva L. McDonald was unequivocal in his rant about supposed reactionaries of Morgan's ilk who stood for the status quo and against progressivism. "No republican of that stripe will be recognized as other than the arch enemy of the progressives," quipped McDonald in an interview with *Harlow's Weekly*. "It will be progressives first and democrats next, at least, so long as the democrat is progressive."[30] Even Theodore Roosevelt, now running as a third-party candidate for president under the Bull Moose banner, admonished Republicans not to vote for Taft, claiming that no honest man would vote for the Republican ticket.[31]

So, who was the real progressive in the District Two race for Congress? Running on the Democratic ticket, El Reno judge John J. Carney was anything but bashful in claiming that mantle. Speaking before a packed lobby in the Lee-Huckins Hotel in Oklahoma City, Carney branded himself as "an ultra-progressive" who had been leaning in that direction ever since he knew what the word meant. In Carney's telling, Democrats were the true progressives, as they had always stood foursquare for justice and human rights. In the absence of genuine progressive reforms, Carney predicted that the United States would follow the downward spiral of nations whose leaders had eschewed the will of the people. Republicans would surely reap the whirlwind in the upcoming elections for subordinating the public good to private interests.[32]

In a typically close vote, Morgan squeaked past Carney by a margin of 24,349 to 23,773 votes. Suffering from his "usual dread of being counted out," Morgan wrote to Orietta a few days after the election to explain that the close vote might cause a delay in certifying his victory.[33] At the far end of the political spectrum, the continued appeal of Socialism was evident in Socialist Party candidate P. D. McKenzie's tally of 7,453 votes, which siphoned support from Carney and, as third-party candidates often do, helped Morgan win the election by 576 votes. Further evidence of Socialism's allure to Oklahomans came when Eugene Debs (Morgan's former near neighbor in Terre Haute), who ran on the Socialist ticket in 1912, captured 16 percent of the presidential vote in Oklahoma, compared to 6 percent nationwide. In several states, Socialist candidates had enough popular support to defeat their Republican opponents. Over the next few years, more than a thousand Socialists were voted into office across the land, including 175 in Oklahoma. Alert to any movement that threatened his vision of America's fighting spirit, Theodore Roosevelt once quipped that the Socialist Party's growth was "far more ominous than any populist or similar movement in times past."

Morgan's victory left him with just one Republican ally among Oklahoma's new apportionment of eight representatives: incumbent Bird McGuire in District One, whose margin over Democrat John J. Davis of Chandler was similarly tiny (579 votes). Morgan and

McGuire surely had much to discuss as they braced for a Sixty-Third Congress (March 4, 1913–March 4, 1915) dominated by Democrats.[34] Morgan now faced a Democratic president and a Congress controlled by Democrats. Clearly, he would have to develop a new strategy to maintain his influence in the legislative process.

"All of Dick T.'s election victories, until 1918, were close votes, with his getting less than fifty percent because of the votes for the Socialist candidate," said David Morgan. "In fact, it is safe to say that in his first three elections, in which he ran in the Second District, he only won because he got almost all of the Black votes and the Socialist candidate siphoned off some votes that otherwise would have gone to the Democrat."[35] Morgan had another stroke of luck when the brand-new Progressive Party entered its candidate too late to qualify for a place on the 1912 ballot.[36]

As with the election of 1910, winning those Black votes did not come without controversy. Two days after Morgan eked out his win, Carney filed a protest, alleging that Morgan had collaborated with the newly appointed U.S. Attorney and his former campaign manager, Homer N. Boardman, to intimidate election officials into ignoring the grandfather clause in the Oklahoma Constitution and certifying illegal Black votes. Perhaps most damning was Carney's allegation that Boardman, who owed his appointment as U.S. Attorney in no small measure to Morgan's support, had warned precinct workers that they might face federal charges and even imprisonment if they tried to enforce the grandfather clause.

In charges that composed nineteen clauses in his lawsuit and touched on every county in the Second District, Carney laid out his argument: the grandfather clause, sanctioned in the state constitution and upheld by the Oklahoma Supreme Court, excluded illiterates from voting, and that included a (supposed) majority of African Americans. Nevertheless, registration officers had allowed thousands of Blacks to cast their ballots, knowing that they could not read and write and were thereby excluded from the franchise. Morgan and Boardman's alleged conspiracy to circumvent the law, carried out through "fraud and intimidation," had allowed "vast numbers of illegal negro voters to vote" and thereby steal Carney's election.

Morgan pulled no punches in his answer to Carney's accusations and, once again, enlisted his son to represent him in the contest. Citing "the insufficiency, incompetency, irrelevancy, immateriality, vagueness, and uncertainty" of each and every charge, Morgan geared up for a battle to keep his seat in Congress. More than a year would pass before he was exonerated from wrongdoing in his second contested election.[37]

While Morgan was fighting to keep his seat in Congress, former Princeton University president and, later, New Jersey governor Woodrow Wilson was campaigning to take his progressive predilections to the White House. In his inaugural address as governor in January 1911, Wilson had expressed the trepidation that many of his countrymen felt at the dawn of a new age: "The whole world has changed within the lifetime of men not yet in their thirties; the world of business and therefore, the world of society and the world of politics. The organization and movement of business are new, and upon a novel scale. Business has changed so rapidly that for a long time we were confused, alarmed, bewildered in a sort of terror of the things we had ourselves raised up."[38]

During his ensuing single term as New Jersey's Democratic governor, Wilson met the challenges of a shifting paradigm head-on, and he earned accolades by forcing a reluctant state legislature to accept measures that progressives had been demanding for a decade. These included direct primary elections, anti-corruption legislation, workmen's compensation, and stricter regulation of railroads and public utilities. As the nation geared up for the presidential election of 1912, Wilson became a passionate spokesman for progressivism and was acknowledged as the leader of the Democratic Party.[39] He was rewarded with an easy win over Republican incumbent William Howard Taft and third-party nominee Theodore Roosevelt, who had founded the Progressive Party after he lost the Republican nomination. On account of his passion for shooting woodland creatures, Roosevelt's short-lived Progressive Party was better known by its official mascot and emblem, the bull moose.[40]

Party differences notwithstanding, Dick Morgan and Woodrow

Wilson were on the same side when it came to public service. Wilson laid out his philosophy of governance in *The New Freedom: A Call for the Emancipation of the Generous Energies of a People.* Published in 1913, Wilson's book branded progressivism as the "New Freedom," and it provided a blueprint for lawmakers to bridge the gulf between the haves and have-nots, which was ripping the nation apart at its seams. Dedicating his book to those who gave their lives to public service, Wilson gave readers a hint of what to expect from his presidency in his preface:

> The book is not a discussion of measures or of programs. It is an attempt to express the new spirit of our politics and to set forth, in large terms which may stick in the imagination, what it is that must be done if we are to restore our politics to their full spiritual vigor again, and our national life, whether in trade, in industry, or in what concerns us only as families and individuals, to its purity, its self-respect, and its pristine strength and freedom. The New Freedom is only the old revived and clothed in the unconquerable strength of modern America.[41]

Claiming that society was in the throes of a revolution, Wilson dismissed old party platforms as hopelessly out of step with the zeitgeist of the Progressive Era. "The life of the nation has grown infinitely varied," wrote Wilson. "It does not centre now upon questions of governmental structure or of the distribution of governmental powers. It centres upon questions of the very structure and operation of society itself, of which government is only the instrument." No longer did most men and women work in small organizations that offered them a modicum of control over their lives. With the rise of giant corporations, workers were now faceless employees, and they were subject to the whims of untouchable employers and the whims of global commerce. As Wilson put it, "There was a time when corporations played a very minor part in our business affairs, but now they play the chief part, and most men are the servants of corporations."[42] What employers knew about their employees came not from personal contact, but from ledgers and timesheets and superintendents' reports. Everyone, Wilson asserted, from officers and managers to wage-earners on the factory floor, was trapped in a heartless economic system. America had developed from a cluster of backwater colonies to become the envy of the world, but it had done so at the cost of its soul.

Although Wilson might justifiably be accused of looking backward through rose-tinted glasses, he drew a distinction between Jefferson's ideal of the yeoman farmer and his own era of galloping industrialization. Whereas Jefferson had promoted small government attuned to the rhythms of a primarily agricultural economy, the Progressive Era called for broad government powers to protect the weak from the strong. "We are in a new world, struggling under old laws," continued Wilson. "As we go inspecting our lives today, surveying this new scene of centralized and complex society, we shall find many more things out of joint." For Wilson, the most alarming development was the extent to which Big Business had spread its tentacles into government, thereby "laying unfair and impossible handicaps upon competitors, imposing taxes in every direction, stifling everywhere the free spirit of American enterprise."[43]

Like Morgan, Wilson watched with growing alarm the rise of Socialism among farmers and laborers who had lost faith not only in the two-party system, but also in the ideals that had set America apart from other nations—the much-touted "American exceptionalism." Wilson was also in sync with Morgan in embracing progressivism as a roadmap to aligning governance with changes in the economic and political landscapes. What progressives were asking was permission to interpret the Constitution according to Darwin's theory of evolution and to treat the nation not as a machine, but as a living organism. Those who stood in the way of that natural evolution—that is, standpatters—were blissfully unaware of the changes unfolding around them. "The standpatter doesn't know there is a procession. He is asleep in the back part of his house. He doesn't know that the road is resounding with the tramp of men going to the front."[44]

So, where did Morgan and Wilson differ? Two differences stand out: first, unlike Wilson, Morgan remained steadfast in his support for protective tariffs. Second, Morgan championed racial equality, whereas Wilson, born in Staunton, Virginia, and raised in Georgia, remained mired in the segregationist policies of his southern homeland. Not only was Morgan in Wilson's opposition party, but he was also in the minority party in both houses of Congress with no voice in the most influential committees. For the foreseeable future, whatever clout he could muster would depend on his powers of persuasion and the strength of his arguments, backed, as always, by meticulous research into the issues that consumed him.

In 1914, two years after Morgan delivered his "Control of Corporations" speech, he was still working on his bill to take on Big Business through creation of an interstate trade commission. The bill gained further traction when President Wilson endorsed the concept of a federal trade commission in a special message to Congress, thereby ensuring the Democratic Party's commitment to it.[45] As it wound its way through Congress, Morgan's bill "to regulate the commerce of certain corporations, and for other purposes" had been recast as H.R. 1890, referred to the Judiciary Committee for consideration, and rebranded once again as H.R. 12931. Having introduced the most recent iteration of his bill on February 4, 1914, Morgan was now ready, three days later, to explain what it was all about.

"No doubt most of you, if not all, have given this question more study and investigation than I have, and it may be difficult for me to enlighten the committee very much, yet I am somewhat of an enthusiast in favor of an interstate trade commission."[46]

So began Morgan's somewhat self-deprecating testimony before the Committee on Interstate and Foreign Commerce on February 7. Heads on his side of the aisle surely nodded as Morgan reminded his listeners that the Republican Party platform of June 1912 had supported antitrust legislation, discouraged monopolies, and called for rigorous punishment for offenders. In September of that same year, legislators who identified with the Progressive Party had followed suit, demanding "a strong national regulation of interstate corporations." There was ample precedent for an interstate trade commission in the ICC, an agency that Morgan had often cited as an effective regulator of railroads and public utilities. "So that it now appears that all the great political parties are in favor of such a commission," said Morgan as he launched into a recap of his "Control of Corporations" speech.[47]

Congressmen still wanted to know which corporations would fall under the purview of an interstate trade commission. Committee chairman William G. Adamson asked Morgan why he thought that only large corporations were susceptible to evil. Morgan responded with his original suggestion that corporations with annual receipts of more than five million dollars should be regulated. Other criteria might include the value of a corporation's output, its capital, the percentage of business that it controlled in its market (say, 40 percent?), and the nature and character of the business. After consulting the thirteenth federal census, Morgan concluded that about 250 corporations would come under the commission's supervision.

The bottom line? Size really mattered. Small corporations did not pose the same menace to society as giants. Reflecting on his youth on the family farm, Morgan devised an apt analogy: "Let us separate the sheep from the goats. The sheep may be permitted to gambol unmolested upon the public industrial commons, but the goats must be placed in a corral under the surveillance of representatives of the Federal Government."

Morgan was convinced that public sentiment favored antitrust legislation. "I believe the people in this country believe that the large business concerns do possess an undue amount of monopolistic power," said Morgan, and "that they possess such monopolistic power that they can manipulate and arbitrarily control prices, and this legislation is in response to that public opinion." As the states lacked authority to protect citizens from corporate abuse, it fell to the federal government to beef up the Sherman Antitrust Act by appointing an agency to enforce fairness in corporate policies, outlaw preferential treatment to individuals and businesses, and prevent unreasonable and unjust discrimination in pricing.[48]

And how, exactly, would an interstate trade commission determine if a corporation's policies were reasonable and just? Morgan suggested applying the same standards that governed common carriers and other quasi-public agencies. And what about adjudicating disputes? As the courts were already hopelessly mired in business cases, Morgan further suggested that the interstate trade commission be granted quasi-judicial powers: "It is a fact that the courts are powerless to enforce the laws

of this Nation because of overcrowding of business. Administrative commissions to expedite the administration of the laws have become a necessity."[49]

Like President Wilson, Morgan viewed with alarm the social and economic forces that were upending the body politic. Some branded those changes as nothing less than revolutionary and predicted dark days ahead. Brushing aside skeptics who thought an agency empowered with executive, legislative, and judicial functions might even be unconstitutional, Morgan insisted that his bill was consistent with legislation passed over the past quarter century, including the Sherman Antitrust Act, and that Congress had a duty to combat the evil posed by monopolies. "Finally," concluded Morgan with his flair for biblical oratory, "I plead for a great commission to stand like an armed sentinel to jealously guard the mighty hosts of intervening

While Morgan was crafting legislation to benefit the nation's businesses, he remained active in his hometown's economic development. As the Ringling Brothers Circus paraded westward along Woodward's Main Street in 1914, it passed the Pastime Theater whose sign is partially visible at the far left. Morgan owned most of the block where the theater was located. COURTESY OF THE PLAINS INDIANS AND PIONEERS MUSEUM, WOODWARD, OKLAHOMA

corporations plying between the producer and the consumer and see that these corporations do not exact excessive, exorbitant, or unrighteous charges for the service they render to the public."[50]

> The Chairman: "Mr. Morgan, we are very grateful to you for your very valuable discussion."
>
> Mr. Morgan: "I thank you, Mr. Chairman, and gentlemen of the committee."[51]

The interstate trade commission, now officially the Federal Trade Commission (FTC), was signed into law by President Wilson on September 26, 1914, and opened for business on March 16, 1915. Its seal, designed by Tiffany and Company, symbolizes the values that Dick Morgan had been promoting since he introduced H.R. 18711 on January 25, 1912. The seal has since served as the agency's formal emblem and is the centerpiece of the agency's flag, which was created in 1977.

Since its inception, the FTC has acted as an independent agency whose principal mission has been to enforce civil (i.e., noncriminal) antitrust laws and promote consumer protection. Headquartered in the Federal Trade Commission Building in Washington, D.C., the agency shares jurisdiction over federal civil antitrust enforcement with the Department of Justice Antitrust Division. It is composed of five commissioners who are nominated by the president. Subject to Senate confirmation, they are restricted to seven-year terms, and no more than three can belong to the same political party.[52]

"Dick T.'s original bill covered fourteen pages of printed matter, every section, paragraph and line of which had been prepared with the utmost care," said David Morgan about his great-grandfather's contribution to antitrust legislation. "Other representatives followed his leadership and introduced similar bills." The climax came when President Wilson went before Congress to recommend the creation of such a commission, thereby committing his party to the proposition. After that, all Congress needed to do was work out the details and determine what powers should be conferred on the commission.[53]

Three weeks before President Wilson signed the FTC into law, Senator Albert B. Cummins, a progressive Republican and former governor of Iowa, addressed the Senate in words that conveyed supporters' hopes and dreams for their groundbreaking legislation: "I predict that in the days to come the Federal [T]rade [C]ommission and its enforcement of the section with regard to unfair competition... will be found to be the most efficient protection to the people of the United States that Congress has ever given the people by way of a regulation of commerce...I look forward to its enforcement with a high degree of confidence."[54]

Cummins's sanguine prediction was vindicated as the FTC evolved into one of the nation's top watchdog agencies. Although the FTC has endured plenty of challenges, as one would expect, in the century-plus since its inception, it thrives today as testimony both to the success of the Progressive movement and Morgan's vision. Although business writers and academics tend to focus on the agency's contemporary cases and controversies, some take a longer view and allude to the FTC's foundation story. In a 1982 article in the *Tulsa Law Review*, William E. Kovacic analyzed the FTC's successes and failures that occasioned midcentury calls for reforms molded to the needs of a vastly enlarged and increasingly complex economy.[55] Although Kovacic does not mention Morgan specifically, it is clear that he and his allies in the progressive movement saw the federal government as a vehicle to effect change that would curtail the power of large corporations. Theirs was a war on wealth and privilege, with the federal government playing offense for the common man.

In its early history of the Federal Trade Commission, Wikipedia cites Morgan's seminal speech in Congress promoting an agency to ensure fairness in business and commerce: "Following the Supreme Court decisions against Standard Oil and American Tobacco in May 1911, the first version of a bill to establish a commission to regulate interstate trade was introduced on January 25, 1912, by Oklahoma congressman Dick Thompson Morgan. He would make the first speech on the House floor advocating its creation on February 21, 1912."[56] Writing for *Politico* in September 2012, Andrew Glasser commemorated the agency's anniversary with a nod to its founder.

Although Glasser's dates were off by a few days, he left no doubt as to Morgan's leadership in founding the commission:

> Wilson saw the commission as a necessary tool to combat trusts, a political feature of what historians have come to call the Progressive Era. At the time, trust-busting efforts enjoyed wide bipartisan support. The first bill to establish such a commission was introduced on Jan. 12, 1912, by Rep. Dick Thompson Morgan (R-Okla.). He also made the first speech on the House floor urging its adoption on Feb. 21, 1912, and introduced an amended version of the bill in 1913.[57]

During their walkabout in western Indiana, David and Ellen Morgan conferred with journalist and local historian Mike McCormick. His article in the *Terre Haute Tribune-Star*, published on April 22, 2018 (a date whose significance might have been lost on most Hoosiers) and cited several times in this biography, carries the unambiguous title "Dick Thompson Morgan: 'Father of the FTC.'"[58]

"It's interesting how Dick was able to influence legislation after Democrats seized power in 1913," said David Morgan. "I don't know if this was purposeful or not, but he switched his role from legislative oversight (where, beginning in 1913, he had no power) to being an expert witness to the committee overseeing creation of the FTC. As a member of the minority party, that's the only way he could have input."[59]

The Federal Trade Commission Act of 1914 was undeniably a milestone in progressive legislation, and its passage confirmed Dick Morgan's evolution from a freshman congressman struggling to forge his identity in a Republican Party dominated by standpatters to a dyed-in-the-wool progressive with increasing clout in Congress. David Morgan identified passage of the Federal Trade Commission Act as an inflection point in his great-grandfather's career: "He became identified with the agency, and it earned him another moniker as 'Father of the FTC.' In his subsequent speeches in and out of Congress, he reminded his listeners that the FTC was his baby."[60] One wonders what Morgan would have thought about his baby's probe into OpenAI and its artificial intelligence app, ChatGPT, in the summer of 2023. Without a doubt, he would have applauded calls on the FTC to launch an investigation to "ensure the establishment of necessary guardrails to protect consumers, businesses, and the commercial marketplace."[61]

"Dick T. never quite got over the fact that, when Democrats swept the elections of 1912 and 1914, they assumed more credit than they deserved for creating the FTC," continued David. "But I guess that's what you expect in partisan politics!"[62]

As the bill made its way to the president's desk, Morgan wanted Congress to know what an honor it had been for him to introduce its original iteration, on January 25, 1912, and deliver his "Control of Corporations" speech the next month. As a member of the minority party with limited influence on the committee to which his bill had been assigned, he had never wavered in his determination to bring Big Business to heel. Applause erupted as Morgan concluded his comments with both a caveat that more work needed to be done and an expectation that Congress would continue its control of corporations into the future:

> The measure does not go so far as I think it should. The bill which I introduced goes much further; but as time goes on, as we shall develop business along this line, you will find that from time to time Congress will give this great commission additional power, not to harass, not to destroy the business of this country, but to give the business of this country real liberty and freedom and to indicate to business the lines which it shall follow and along which it can proceed.
>
> In my judgment not in half a century has the Congress of the United States enacted a law that is of equal importance to the one we are now enacting.[63]

Among Morgan's role models were presidents from both major political parties who stood shoulder-to-shoulder when it came to issues of fairness: the trust-busting Republican, Theodore Roosevelt, who had appointed Morgan as register of the U.S. Land Office in Woodward, Oklahoma Territory, a position that became a stepping stone to higher office; and Democrat Woodrow Wilson, whose New Freedom became a progressive rallying cry, and whose signature on the bill that Morgan had worked so hard to pass demonstrated his commitment to reform.

During the rest of his tenure in Congress, Morgan would continue to work on progressive legislation on behalf of his constituents in Oklahoma and for the benefit of the entire nation.

Dick T. Morgan's congressional office, n.d.
COURTESY OF THE MORGAN FAMILY COLLECTION

CHAPTER ELEVEN

From (Alleged) Standpatter to Progressive

Our land-credit institutions should be public, or semi-public, non-profit-sharing institutions, designed primarily to serve borrowers, not lenders, to aid farmers not investors, and to promote agriculture, not to provide profits for private banking institutions.

DICK T. MORGAN
Land Credits (1915)

IN 1913–1914, WHILE CONGRESS was figuring out how to protect consumers from predatory corporations without jeopardizing the nation's roaring economy, two additional issues loomed large on its agenda: first, revising the Payne-Aldrich tariff, which continued to generate controversy; and second, reforming laws pertaining to banking and currency.

Leadership in revising the Payne-Aldrich tariff fell to Senator Oscar Wilder Underwood, a Democrat from Alabama who had run unsuccessfully for the Oval Office in 1912 and would run again in 1924. As House majority leader, he was a strong supporter of Wilson's progressive agenda, which included tariff reduction. Underwood sponsored the Revenue Act of 1913 (H.R. 3321, a.k.a. the Underwood tariff), which aimed to reduce the cost of living by placing a range of consumer items on the free list and declaring industrial imports duty free. Underwood's bill, which included a proposal to impose the first federal income tax in American history, ignited fierce debates when President Wilson summoned a special session of the Sixty-Third Congress on April 8, 1913. Although the Underwood tariff never intended to abandon protection altogether, it did propose the first downward tariff revisions since the Civil War.[1]

Dick Morgan was the first member of the Oklahoma delegation to speak on the tariff. In an impassioned defense of protection, he rose to the House floor, on April 28, 1913, to denounce Underwood's bill. "The real purpose of this bill is not a reduction of tariff duties, but the introduction of a new tariff system," declared Morgan. "If this bill shall become a law, we will have abandoned the great national policy of protection; we will have committed this Government to the policy of a tariff for revenue only. Such a change is not revision; it is revolution." Morgan believed that the bill threatened the nation's industrial independence and endangered prosperity. He believed it would drive down employment and wages and, ultimately, "lead the country from its splendid position of safety and security out upon the perilous rocks and reefs of an ocean of doubt and uncertainty." Repeating a favorite mantra, Morgan insisted that competition from abroad was not a remedy for monopoly at home. Monopolies and trusts were the offspring of corporations that abused their power, a form of corruption that he aimed to alleviate with his proposed interstate trade commission.

Morgan was unequivocal in his insistence that tariff reduction would hurt everyone, whatever their line of work or socioeconomic status, and would do nothing to militate against predatory business practices that were widening the gap between the haves and have-nots. Despite Morgan's objections, Underwood's bill sailed through the House on May 8. All six Oklahoma Democrats voted for the bill; Republicans Morgan and McGuire voted against it. Attention then switched to the Senate, where the Democratic margin of control was small, and a tough fight was certain.[2]

The Senate passed the Underwood bill, with revisions, by a vote of 44 to 37. The revised bill went back to the House, where it was approved on September 30, 1913. On the day it passed, Morgan made a last-minute plea on behalf of farmers and manufacturers. With his northwest Oklahoma constituents in mind, he predicted that the tariff would threaten farmers with the loss of their markets in a scramble to survive global competition without compensation. "By this transaction you take from the American farmers one of their most valuable assets," concluded Morgan. "It is the markets of the United States that give value to land, profits, to farms, and encouragement to agriculture. Destroy the farmers' market and you have ruined their business." The same argument applied to manufacturing, as he was convinced that the tariff would deter investors from putting their capital in mills and factories.[3]

President Wilson signed the Underwood Tariff Bill on October 3, 1913. The president's support for tariff reductions confirmed his dominance of the Democratic Party and won the admiration of progressive Republicans. Despite their progressive leanings on other issues, Morgan and McGuire refused to abandon their support for tariff protection, which they had established in the previous two congresses. In his insistence that tariff reduction worked against the interests of farmers and laborers, Morgan seemed to be signaling his affiliation with Big Business, and he risked alienating his progressive constituents by siding with the standpatters. Nevertheless, Morgan would not budge from his position that eliminating tariffs was not progressive, as they hurt farmers and workers struggling to compete in a global marketplace. Whatever benefits consumers might receive in lower prices was offset by the damage inflicted on American farmers and laborers.

Such was not the case when it came to Washington's latest scourge: corporate lobbyists. Throughout the summer of 1913, debates on the Underwood tariff and other important matters of state were derailed by lobbyists who commanded ever increasing attention from legislators. In fact, President Wilson once quipped that "a brick couldn't be thrown without hitting one of them." Progressives in both the House and Senate agreed that lobbying had gotten out of hand. When Democrat Robert L. Henry of Texas introduced a bill (H.R. 198) to limit lobbying, Morgan voiced his support not only for restrictions, but also for appointing a committee to investigate whether lobbyists, particularly those representing the National Association of Manufacturers, had exerted undue influence in elections. As undue influence did not necessarily involve cash payments, Morgan offered an amendment to Henry's resolution to account for nonmonetary forms of coercion. "I have heard of men being given things of value other than money," said Morgan. "I see no reason why this amendment should not be adopted. There might be some quibble about what 'money' meant, what it was, what it included." Although Morgan's amendment failed to gain traction, it certainly showed his objection to corporate influence peddling. By the time the House adopted Henry's resolution, on July 9, 1913, one had to wonder: Was Dick Morgan a standpatter in thrall to Big Business, or was he the progressive Republican he claimed to be?[4]

Progressive Republicans' philosophy of governance was put to the test in a challenge that dwarfed the Underwood tariff in its importance to the nation's economy: how to modernize the nation's antiquated banking system. Since the Republic's infancy, financial crises had been baked into the financial system, and every couple of decades, the chaos spawned by unstable currencies and an unregulated hodgepodge of lenders (the most pernicious among them known derisively as "wildcats") erupted into full-blown panics. The ensuing wreckage left a trail of failed banks, business bankruptcies, and farm foreclosures. The first panic of the twentieth century arrived in the form of a particularly nasty downturn that few saw coming, and for good reason: prices for farm produce were on the upswing, businesses were thriving, and commodities were flowing through the marketplace, from warehouses to retailers to consumers, unhindered by inventory bottlenecks or price resistance. Such was the pace of economic activity that the annual growth rate from the mid-1890s to late 1906—that is, the eve of Oklahoma statehood, and two years before Dick Morgan's first congressional campaign—was an astonishing 7.3 percent. This demonstrated that industrial production had doubled in a scant ten years. Although capital markets in the U.S. and abroad were showing some strains, they were not enough to signal trouble. As one scholar noted, in the stilted prose of a turn-of-the-twentieth-century economist, "it would be difficult to find an equally long period of business activity at the close of which the relative development of different industries would seem to have been similarly satisfactory."[5]

But trouble was coming, and it crashed into history on April 18, 1906, when San Francisco was rocked by an earthquake of epic proportions. Fueled by wood-frame buildings, massive fires incinerated about half of the urban area. Five hundred people perished, and a half million people were made homeless. This natural disaster was followed by a financial one as stocks plummeted and cash and gold flowed to the stricken city. Outflows of gold from England raised fears of a liquidity crisis and fanned rumors that British banks were on the brink of insolvency. The Bank of England and central banks throughout Europe responded to the depletion of their gold supplies by raising interest rates. By the winter of 1906–07, a credit crunch was in the making.

In the ensuing months, markets, and the confidence they courted, were buffeted by declining stock prices and tightening credit. Adding to the turmoil was a swashbuckling New Yorker named Fritz Augustus Heinze, whose investments in copper were his ticket to ownership of his hometown's Mercantile National Bank. He rose to the bank's presidency in February 1907; directorships of other financial institutions were soon to follow. Now that he was on a roll, Heinze bought seats on the New York Stock Exchange for his brothers, Otto and Arthur, and established a brokerage house under the name Otto C. Heinze and Company. Relying on his experience and contacts in the copper business, he and his brothers unleashed an audacious scheme to corner the copper market.

The Heinze brothers' scheme promptly went down in flames and sent the rumor mill into overdrive as the usual constellation of factors—impending bank failures, revelations of swindles, money hoarding, and precipitous drops in security and commodity prices—coalesced into a perfect storm. As frantic depositors swarmed to their banks to grab what coin and currency they could, the Panic of 1907 was making history as yet another consequence of a broken financial system. Total disaster was averted when J. P. Morgan (no relation to Dick T. Morgan), the colossus of Gilded Age finance, summoned the presidents of major New York banks to his Italian Renaissance–style palace on Madison Avenue, locked the doors to his fabled library, and made them sit there until they agreed to pony up a collective $25 million. In deciding which firms would succeed and which ones would fail, the cigar-chomping titan engineered what amounted to a financial bailout of New York City, thus adding his considerable heft to the "too big to fail" argument.[6]

Meanwhile, far from the epicenter of banking and finance, Oklahomans were no more in the mood for a financial meltdown than anyone else, and they had to factor the anxiety that was casting its pall across the land into their statehood celebrations.

Congress's response to the Panic of 1907 was the Aldrich-Vreeland Act of May 30, 1908, named for notorious standpatter Senator Nelson W. Aldrich and Edward B. Vreeland, a banker, businessman, and Republican who represented western New York in the House of Representatives from 1899 to 1913. In addition to legalizing and regulating what had happened spontaneously during the panic, the act created the National Monetary Commission to investigate the nation's finances and propose reforms. The commission's twenty-four volume report, published on January 11, 1911, blamed the national banking system and its inelastic currency as the cause of panics. Although no precise policy prescriptions were offered, everyone knew the fundamental problem: the United States was the only major industrial power without a central bank to serve as a lender of last resort and to monitor currency flows.[7]

Cloaked in secrecy, the lords of finance who served on the commission knew what they were up against: antipathy toward centralization in any guise was part of America's DNA, and centralized banking was sure to encounter a firestorm of opposition. What came to be known as the Aldrich Plan proposed the creation of a "Reserve Association of America" or "National Reserve Bank," a central bank in all but name whose branches would be authorized to issue currency and extend loans to commercial banks. Although the federal government was to be represented on the board of directors, the association would be owned and controlled by banks to constitute a sort of bankers' cooperative.[8]

Shortly after moving into the White House, President Wilson asked the chairman of the House Banking Committee, Carter Glass of Virginia, to spearhead legislation in accordance with the National

Monetary Commission's report. Glass's coalition included two Democrats from Oklahoma: Claude Weaver, who had been elected in 1907 to represent the Fifth District and quickly earned membership on the House Banking Committee; and Robert L. Owen, elected to the Senate in 1907, whose business experience and political savvy made him an ideal candidate to take on banking and currency reform.[9]

Ever since the Sequoyah Convention of 1905, Owen had leveraged his prominence in Indian affairs and Democratic politics to become a formidable candidate for the U.S. Senate. Known for his fierce independence, Owen announced a guiding principle in his first campaign speech that would have had a familiar ring to Dick Morgan: "Equal rights to all, special privileges to none." As expected, Owen trounced his opposition in the Democratic primary, and the state legislature formally selected him as one of the new state's two senators. On December 16, 1907, Owen and western Oklahoma's favorite son, Thomas P. Gore, were sworn in and sent packing to Washington.[10]

Owen arrived in the Senate as an authority on Indian affairs and champion of populist causes, including the redress of public grievances through initiative and referendum. As a founder and former president of the First National Bank of Muskogee, Owen knew better than most the dangers posed by corruption and unrestrained private monopolies. One of his first legislative efforts in finance was to introduce a bill to assess a small tax on deposits to create a guaranty fund as protection against bank failures. When Democrats returned to power in 1913, Owen was an obvious pick to serve in Glass's coalition, and he was named as the first chairman of the Senate Committee on Banking and Currency (Senate Banking Committee), which was established to oversee the nation's monetary policy. Owen would retain that post until Republicans regained control of the Senate in 1919. Relying on what he deemed to be the best provisions of the Aldrich Plan, Owen pushed for an overhaul of the nation's finances under the purview of a federal banking board.[11]

The Owen-Glass Federal Reserve Act, now debated under its most recent iteration as House Bill 7837, was headed for a showdown. Dick Morgan had weighed in with four objections that he had been voicing since September 18, 1913, when the bill was introduced in the House and passed by a vote of 287 to 85. "I have concluded that I shall not vote for this bill," declared Morgan, no doubt bleary-eyed from debates on the currency bill that were lasting far into the night. His first objection—what he deemed the bill's "fatal defect"—was its failure to protect depositors, a concern shared by Robert Owen. After reasonable dividends were paid to bankers and surpluses had been accumulated in the reserve banks, Morgan saw no reason to withhold money from some "great national purpose" that would contribute to the public good. And in no instance did he want reserve banks' profits to go toward paying down the national debt.

Citing Oklahoma's bank guaranty law, which had passed with a resounding majority in the state's first legislative session in 1908, Morgan read his proposed amendment: "All earnings derived by the United States from Federal reserve banks shall constitute a fund to protect the depositors from loss from the failure of any member bank, under such provisions as Congress may hereafter enact." Just before the House rejected his amendment by a wide margin, Morgan made a bold and, as it turned out, prescient prediction: one day, the federal government would follow Oklahoma's lead and guarantee bank deposits.[12]

Second, Morgan believed that the bill under consideration discriminated against the public insofar as individuals were barred from depositing money in, and borrowing money from, the reserve banks. Those privileges, together with stock ownership, were reserved for member banks. "We have heard much and very often from the other side of the House about equal opportunities to all and special privileges to none," said Morgan. "Under the provisions of this bill, in allowing no one except banks to subscribe to this stock, are you not giving them a special privilege that is granted only to the bankers of the United States?" Morgan's second amendment likewise went down in defeat, but only after he castigated his fellow congressmen for denying common people the same opportunities they saw fit to bestow upon bankers. One imagines Morgan in consultation with Owen and nodding his head in agreement about their shared principle: equal rights to all, and special privileges to none.

Third, Morgan addressed a shortcoming that cut to the heart of his ongoing fight for fairness: the bill made no provision for farmers, whose collective output constituted nearly half of the nation's wealth. Included in his proposed amendment was the formation of two organizations that would revolutionize American agriculture. First, farm-credit associations would enable farmers to fund their operations with adequate capital at low interest rates. Second, national rural banks would extend low-interest loans and establish credit protocols that recognized farmers' unique circumstances. Estimating that four-fifths of his constituents in northwest Oklahoma were farmers, Morgan was understandably passionate about integrating rural credit into banking and currency reform.

"Agriculture is our chief industry," declared Morgan as representatives from rural districts surely voiced their agreement. "You are providing a currency for merchants, for manufacturers, for businessmen, for bankers, for speculators, for capitalists, taking care of this great class and letting the farmers go. It seems to me you are putting the cart before the horse, and that the first thing you should care for would be the great agricultural interests of this country." Although Morgan's third amendment was rejected by a substantial margin, he had set the stage for a serious debate on rural credit, an issue that Congress had neglected for far too long.

Morgan's fourth and final objection, like his first, was that the bill discriminated against the public by allowing banks to accumulate surpluses without creating a deposit insurance fund.

After castigating House members for prioritizing monied interests at the expense of farmers, he warned his listeners that history would judge them harshly:

> Now, Mr. Speaker, I have made proper effort to perfect this bill along lines which I regarded as important to the people. But my amendments have been voted down, my suggestions have not been heeded. The majority in this House has turned a deaf ear to my warnings. But the voters of this country will hold the majority responsible for its acts. The people, who pass judgment upon all we do here, will at the first opportunity condemn you for not adequately protecting their rights and punish you to the extent of their power for betraying their interests.[13]

The Senate had passed its version of the bill on December 19, 1913, just three days before Morgan presented his objections, by a vote of 54–34. More than forty important differences between the House and Senate versions remained to be settled, leaving the bill's opponents to anticipate more weeks of wrangling in both houses of Congress. Assuming that the Conference bill would not be brought up until the following year, many congressmen packed their bags for the Christmas recess, blithely unaware that the bill's financially savvy proponents were planning their master stroke. In a single day, all forty of the disputed passages were resolved and the bill was brought to a vote.

On Monday, December 22—the same day that Morgan made his eleventh-hour appeal to amend the bill—the House voted 282–60, and the Senate voted 43–23, to create the Federal Reserve System. Correspondence between Morgan and his wife reveals his sadness at spending a lonely Christmas in Washington. All he could do was hope that his constituents would understand his principled vote against the currency bill, and that Orietta would forgive his absence as a consequence of public duty.[14]

The Federal Reserve System (better known simply as "the Fed") was a game changer insofar as it wrested control of the nation's money supply from capitalists of J. P. Morgan's ilk and bestowed it upon a presidentially appointed and senatorially approved board of directors. The board of directors was charged with overseeing twelve regional Federal Reserve banks and a far larger number of branches. Arguably, no single reform has ever shifted the balance between capitalism and democracy more decisively than the Federal Reserve Act of 1913. Once appointed, the Federal Reserve governors were beyond recall and effectively insulated from political pressure. Yet as stewards of what was, in effect, a central bank, they answered not to shareholders of the Federal Reserve System's member banks, but to the people of the United States.[15]

As a retired bank attorney, David Morgan was particularly interested in his great-grandfather's participation in debating a bill that became the cornerstone of the nation's banking system. "And of course," added David Morgan with a wry smile, "his proposed amendment to guarantee deposits was passed twenty years later as part of FDR's New Deal!"[16]

When the 1910 census qualified Oklahoma to have three additional seats in Congress, the legislature went to work drawing district lines to guarantee Democratic votes. As they were not quite done with their gerrymandering in time for the 1912 election, district lines remained unchanged, and the state's additional representatives (almost certain to be Democrats) were elected at large. Completed before the 1914 election, the legislature's partisan redistricting put Dick Morgan in the newly formed District Eight, which still covered the northwest but embraced three fewer counties. Morgan could now count on more farmers' votes but far fewer from Blacks, as racially diverse Oklahoma County had been switched to District Five.

Sprawling across 14,775 square miles, District Eight was the state's largest and most sparsely populated. With 200,402 almost universally white and Protestant residents who earned their livings from farming and ranching, its population density was a scant 13.5 people per square mile. Some 90 percent of the region was dedicated to agriculture, which, along with his experiences on the family farm back in Indiana, explains Morgan's persistent advocacy for agricultural interests. The twelve counties that fell within District Eight's boundaries, stretching west from the Arkansas River to the New Mexico and Colorado borders, included Kay, Noble, Grant, Garfield, Alfalfa, Major, Woods, Woodward, Harper, Beaver, Texas, and Cimarron.[17]

Included in Morgan's new district was Noble County, where he had resided for eight years and, most famously, spearheaded the Free Homes campaign. As the 1914 political campaign heated up, he found himself squaring off with the county's favorite son, Henry S. Johnston, a popular attorney and Democratic office holder who had served as the first president pro tempore of the Oklahoma State Senate and, thirteen years later, would become Oklahoma's seventh governor. Morgan was also at a disadvantage because Congress remained in session late into the fall. As such, Morgan had to depend on friends to keep his campaign alive.[18] As in the campaign of 1912, Morgan was committed to labor: "Mr. Chairman, if there be a conflict between capital and labor—and, in a broad sense, there should not be—but if there be or is such a conflict, so far as I am concerned, after the most careful and deliberate consideration on my part, I propose to place myself on the side of labor."[19]

In his fourth narrow victory, Morgan defeated Johnston by a vote of 13,294 to 12,439. Far behind the top competitors were three minor-party candidates: G. M. Green of the Socialist Party, with 4,231 votes; Charles R. Alexander from the Progressive Party, with 1,645 votes; and Charles Brown from the Prohibition Party, with 216 votes. That narrow victory set the stage for the Eighth District's distinction as the only district that would be seen as a likely Republican congressional seat for nearly forty years.[20]

Among Morgan's accomplishments in the Sixty-Third Congress was to reaffirm the federal government's responsibility to protect Native Americans' rights. Ever since their land, once held communally, was allotted in severalty, Native Americans had been guaranteed the rights and privileges of citizenship and protection under federal law, and their land was exempted from taxation for up to twenty-one years. But what accrued to the benefit of Native Americans came at a cost to the state of Oklahoma. Morgan estimated that nontaxable Indian lands were costing the people of Oklahoma upward of $50 million in lost revenue. "To relieve one piece of property from taxation is equivalent to increasing the tax upon all other property," declared Morgan on the floor of Congress on February 19, 1914. "Revenue lost from exempted Indian property must be made up by revenue from other property."

Morgan was by no means blaming Native Americans for skewing the nation's books. On the contrary, he called on Congress to reaffirm the nation's duty toward its indigenous people by appropriating funds to compensate for an imbalance that was none of their doing. Moreover, dipping into the federal treasury would relieve non-Indians in Oklahoma of unfair and burdensome taxes. Morgan continued: "The Indian is the ward of the Nation. It is clearly the duty of the Federal Government to provide for his care, protection, education, and training; to see that he is exempted from such duties and responsibilities of citizenship as he is unable to assume; and to pay whatever it costs to provide such care, protection, and exemption. I assume that this proposition is so self-evident that it will not be denied."[21]

The Sixty-Third Congress was not all about politics and bringing the nation's finances into balance. President Wilson's declaration of Mother's Day as a new national holiday, on May 9, 1914, gave legislators an opportunity to think about their upbringing. Reflecting on his youth in Vigo County, Morgan commemorated the occasion by regaling House members with his thoughts on the power and lasting impact of a mother's love.

Under the simple title "Mother's Day," Morgan alluded to his numerous speeches and claimed that none of them rivaled in importance the topic of motherhood. "In honoring our mothers, in emphasizing their virtues, and recounting their splendid qualities of mind and heart, we are made better boys and girls, better men and women and go out into the world better prepared to discharge our duties as citizens and as Disciples of Christ."

In Morgan's telling, a mother's love transcended all boundaries of wealth and power and fame. To illustrate, he cited President Garfield's elderly mother, Eliza, whose horror upon hearing that her son had been shot can scarcely be imagined.

Choking back tears, all she could say was, "How could they hurt my boy?"

"He was still his mother's boy," said Morgan. "So we never go too far away or get too old to have the love and sympathy of our mothers."

Morgan did not have to remind his listeners that Washington was packed with public servants who wielded great influence. Yet their influence was "infinitesimal" next to the real power brokers who held sway in households across the land. Given his penchant for statistics, it is hardly surprising that Morgan found a way to bring up Americans' indebtedness to fund their farms and businesses. "But combine all public and private indebtedness in one grand total and it does not equal the debt of gratitude we owe to our mothers; for that debt is so precious, so pure and so sacred that it cannot be measured in dollars and cents." That debt extended to education. Even as he rhapsodized about the nation's "splendid educational institutions," he reserved his highest accolades for mothers who dispensed their knowledge and wisdom at the firesides of America's twenty million homes.

In all areas of human endeavor, mothers had earned a debt of gratitude that could never be repaid. As a musician, Morgan understood better than most the transformative effects of music. Yet whose songs were the most profound, and who warranted the most careful listening? Mothers, of course, "for, after all, the sweetest songs in the world are those that our mothers sing." Mothers were among history's "best exemplars" and "the safest and truest models" of virtue, and "the uplifting power of mother's love" was the fountain of inspiration behind humanity's greatest achievements, from buildings, railways, and canals to mighty corporations. With a nod to history's sages and philosophers, Morgan lauded mothers as the wisest counselors of all, and the ones to whom a son or daughter could always go with troubles big and small, "with perfect trust and confidence," knowing that they could count on her to be "a trustworthy monitor, a true guide and devoted friend." For all its whizbang technology, even the Bureau of Standards lacked the tools to measure the breadth and depth of a mother's sympathy.

Recalling his own childhood, Morgan quoted his mother's final words of instruction before he set out from Prairie Creek to begin his life's journey: "Be a good boy." As the years passed, he often dropped by the family farm on his trips between Oklahoma and Washington, and each visit brought more words of wisdom and encouragement as he fought "the battles of life." And even though years might pass between visits, he never doubted that his mother's love "was strong enough, her interest in my welfare was deep enough to reach out across the prairies to my home a thousand miles away."

"So it is with all mothers," said Morgan in closing. "The boy or girl, the son or daughter, can never get too far away to get beyond the reach of mother's interest."[22]

The Sixty-Third Congress adjourned on March 4, 1915. The Sixty-Fourth Congress (March 4, 1915–March 4, 1917), elected in November 1914, was not slated to convene until December 1915. Most legislators returned to their home states for the nine-month recess, but not Dick Morgan. He was busy pondering rural credits, an issue that Congress had thus far failed to adequately address, and one that he had tried unsuccessfully to incorporate in the Federal Reserve Act of 1913. "Even though he was not on the Banking and Currency Committee, Dick T. took special interest in an issue that affected his constituents, most of whom were farmers," explained David Morgan. In addition, Morgan was dissatisfied with recommendations offered by a congressional commission that had traveled abroad to study rural credits. So, what else was he to do but stay in Washington and research the subject on his own?[23]

As the progeny of Indiana farmers, Dick Morgan had a head start, as he already knew plenty about the trouble farmers and ranchers had in accessing credit. But nobody expected him to write a book about it. Taking advantage of Washington's unparalleled research facilities, Morgan spent much of his nine-month hiatus writing a three-hundred-page treatise under the unassuming title *Land Credits: A Plea for the American Farmer*. Congressmen returning to Washington in December 1915 were greeted with complimentary copies of Morgan's book. Additional copies were sent to Oklahoma's most prominent bankers.

In his preface to the book, Dick Morgan stated what the banking cognoscenti already knew, but had so far failed to address: the inadequacy of farm-credit facilities and often usurious interest rates were a serious drag on agricultural development and levied a tax on people making their living from the land. Given agriculture's importance to the overall economy, that made no sense. According to the 1910 census, farmers and their families constituted a third of the U.S. population, and farm products were valued at nine billion dollars, putting agriculture on the same level as manufacturing. Other industries—mining, forestry, and fisheries, for example—did not even come close. As Morgan put it, "This has, in effect, placed an annual tax of immense proportions upon agriculture, imposed upon our farming population unnecessary and unjust burdens and hardships, retarded the expansion of agriculture, our greatest industry, and thus held back the growth of our country, reduced its wealth, and weakened the fabric of our national government."[24]

Morgan's fixation on rural credits came at a propitious time. In 1908, President Roosevelt had appointed a Commission on Country Life, an initiative aimed at improving rural living conditions by preserving traditional lifestyles and, at the same time, alleviating poverty and the social problems that it spawned. The commission's chair, Professor Liberty Hyde Bailey of Cornell University, had been lobbying for state-supported agricultural education since 1893. He described what was known as the country life movement as "the working out of the desire to make rural civilization as effective and satisfying as other civilization." Under his direction, the commission held hearings and circulated questionnaires nationwide. Its report, printed in 1911, offered three recommendations that dovetailed with the progressive agenda: (1) a nationalized extension service allowing rural counties to establish advisers through land-grant universities, a program formalized in the Smith-Lever Act of 1914; (2) fact-finding surveys that fostered the development of agricultural economics and rural sociology in universities and federal agencies; and (3) a campaign for rural progress. Conferences held at the state level led to the creation of the American Country Life Association in 1919.[25] Further evidence of the country life movement's influence can be found in the writings of Willa Cather, Laura Ingalls Wilder, and Senora Babb. Outrage toward railroad companies whose abusive rates and practices threatened rural livelihoods crystalized in Frank Norris's iconic novel, *The Octopus*.[26]

The unavailability of rural credit was a dominant theme not only in turn-of-the-twentieth-century farm fiction; it was also a hot topic in Congress when Morgan began writing his book. All three major parties (including Roosevelt's short-lived Progressive/Bull Moose Party) had called for a better system of farm credit in their 1912 platforms. Then, in his first message to Congress, President Wilson had referenced the importance of rural credit. This resulted in several bills (the Commission Bill, the Sub-Committee Bill, and the Senate Committee Bill) circulating in both houses during the Sixty-Third

Congress. A solution had seemed to be in reach when the president had appointed a seven-person commission to see what they could glean from a tour of Europe. But Morgan would have none of it, as nobody was addressing what he deemed to be the fatal flaw in the bills and proposals that came under his scrutiny: they all sought to create "purely private, profit-sharing, dividend-paying, surplus-creating land banks as the instruments to direct, control and manage the land-credit system for the farmers of the United States."[27] Moreover, one proposal recommended only twelve district banks, and another recommended an uncertain number. These proposed district banks would have combined capital of only six million dollars. Thus, none of the bills in the Sixty-Third Congress included a guarantee that there would be enough banks, spread equally across the country, to satisfy credit needs at low interest rates.

Unlike successful land-credit systems in Europe, the congressional plan seemed bent on prioritizing the interests of lenders and profit-seeking investors at the expense of borrowers. Inevitably, cash-strapped farmers would wind up with insufficient credit and more interest than they could afford, all the while leaving lenders and investors with undeserved profits. To top it off, nobody could promise farmers who were representing diverse regions, and who were producing an infinite variety of products, that they would all be treated fairly and equitably.

Morgan noted that the recently created Federal Reserve System had been a boon to manufacturers and urban interests, but that it held little promise for agriculture. "Twelve banks with a combined capital of $6,000,000 to meet the demands for farm-mortgage credit of 6,500,000 farmers! This seems like trifling with the farmers."[28] Reverting (as always) to his statistical playbook, Morgan cited figures to show that farmers constituted about one-third of the population but received only one-ninth of the nation's bank credit. Moreover, even though farms constituted a fourth of the national wealth, they commanded only a fortieth of the nation's credit. One can almost hear Morgan shouting to his readers: "Have not the farmers a right to charge discrimination when our credit institutions extend to corporations $10 in credit for every one dollar extended to them?"[29]

Morgan was clearly enthralled by European land-credit institutions, some of which had been in operation for centuries, and all of which accrued to farmers' benefit, not some distant cabal of bankers and government functionaries. He summarized these institutions' common characteristics: (1) they were authorized by law and supervised by federal authority; (2) they precluded private participation; (3) they extended long-term loans from ten to seventy-five years, compared to the five-year limit that typified loans in the United States; (4) they used bonds and debentures as instruments to promote land credit and guaranteed their security; and (5) they required annual or semi-annual principal payments, known in banking parlance as amortization. Morgan found none of those institutions more appealing than the German Landschaften, founded by Frederick the Great of Prussia in the eighteenth century. "The Landschaften are not simply supervised by the Government," wrote Morgan; "they are in a large degree, government-controlled institutions."[30] As Dr. Kapp-Königsberg, a well-known expert on European land-credit institutions, remarked in a presentation about the Landschaften to the Sixty-Third Congress, "In their unselfish, public-spirited labors, free from every tendency to profit-making, they render the most important services to the State by preserving a vigorous and healthy agriculture."[31] Kapp-Königsberg's assessment was echoed by opinion leaders from such diverse places as Norway, Italy, Egypt, Japan, Australia, and several countries in South America. Regional differences notwithstanding, countries with centrally controlled systems of rural credit were universally mystified by America's infatuation with privatizing everything and seeking profit everywhere.

So, what was Morgan looking for? Anything but the three bills that were circulating through Congress. In proposing for-profit institutions, their authors were seeking to create the last thing that farmers needed: middlemen siphoning off profits and ensuring that the farmer would remain on his own in a complex and multilayered system of finance, marketing, and distribution. Farmers "took the crumbs," wrote Morgan, who went on to distill his preference to a single sentence: "Our land-credit institutions should be public, or semi-public, non-profit-sharing institutions, designed primarily to serve borrowers, not lenders, to aid farmers not investors, and to promote agriculture, not to provide profits for private banking institutions."[32]

Another key failing of the bills under consideration was that they limited loans, which would ultimately be packaged and sold as bonds, to a percentage of a bank's capital, a restriction unheard of in Europe and one that would doom congressional proposals to failure. "Any system of land credit which limits the amount of loans to a certain percentage of the capital of the institutions, is not capable of supplying credit according to the demand therefor. Its credit power lacks elasticity. In times of stress, when more credit is needed, the tendency will be to restrict credit." Congress had addressed the problem of inelastic currency in the Federal Reserve Act by enlisting the U.S. Treasury Department as a source of credit. Why couldn't anyone see that agriculture needed the same mechanism to provide farmers with sufficient credit at reasonable interest rates, no matter what their location or market sector? "This point can hardly be made too emphatic. Adequate credit is essential."[33]

Equally essential was a reserve fund to secure the safety and security of investments, much as Morgan's proposed (and rejected) bank deposit guaranty amendment to the Federal Reserve Act would have created a hedge against bank failures. And under no circumstance should a land-credit bank's capital be counted as part of its reserves. "As the reserve funds grow, the security of the bondholders is increased, the credit of the farmers is enhanced, the institutions administering our land-credit system grow in the confidence of investors and the public generally, and become every year more capable of rendering service to the farmers, to the public and to the nation."[34]

One detects a hint of religiosity in Morgan's insistence that rural credit managers be of impeccable character. Unlike private companies, which prioritized profits and depended on officers' reputations, public and semi-public institutions came with ready-made status as government agencies. "The private institution must first establish a reputation. The public or semi-public institution enters upon business with the reputation of the State or Government behind it. This is an invaluable asset."[35] And no matter who was put in charge, he would have to exercise strict economy in office overhead, as all fees, commissions, charges, and expenses would be factored into interest rates. Once again, Morgan cited the Landschaften as a model of how to keep administrative costs and interest rates to a minimum.

Morgan was also concerned about the effects of competition between farmers to secure the best deals from their regional land-credit banks. The idea was to transform farmers' mortgages into bonds—that is, liquid securities to be bought and sold, much like cattle are turned into beef and pigs are turned into pork. As mortgage bonds were farmers' securities, and because interest rates on those bonds would control the interest rates charged to borrowers, it was clear that permitting land-credit banks to sell their mortgage bonds in competition with each other would force farmers to compete in the sale of their securities. "Competition in the sale of mortgage bonds favors the investors; non-competition favors the farmers. The bank or banks are simply the sales agencies for farm mortgage bonds."[36] Morgan was surely thinking about his experience with the FTC in suggesting that cooperation among land-credit banks was only a step removed from monopoly. Cooperatives had always been formed to facilitate marketing and control expenses and prices. The proposed land-credit banks would follow suit in cooperating to maximize profits for shareholders and bond buyers, not the farmers they were supposed to serve.

Above all, Morgan saw the federal government as the rightful guardian and promoter of agricultural interests. As he noted toward the end of his book, the United States was the wealthiest and most enlightened nation on Earth. Surely it could do at home what Frederick the Great had done for Prussia. Much as the U.S. government leveraged its resources to change the course of rivers to facilitate navigation and commerce, so, too, it could utilize credit to encourage agricultural development. "It is not a question of satisfying the farmers. It is a question of aiding all, through aid to the farmers."[37]

Praise for *Land Credits* was quick in coming. Senator Duncan U. Fletcher from Florida, who had written a book on agricultural credits in 1913 and had led the fact-finding trip to Europe, was effusive: "You have given a most valuable contribution to the discussion of the problem. You show a thorough grasp of it—particularly as to its importance and the need of a proper solution of it. You express clearly and forcibly the reasons calling for a sound system of Rural Credits and your historical tracing of the movement and the work on it is the most accurate and fairest yet given." Senator John W. Kern from Morgan's Indiana homeland congratulated him for writing a creditable piece of work. "You have collected and presented a mass of pertinent facts and statistics and set forth so fairly the arguments in favor of the several systems proposed, that all men in public or private life who desire to investigate the main question will find their labors greatly lessened by an examination of your work." The press chimed in with positive reviews, including a lengthy article in *The Nation* that read in part, "Mr. Morgan has produced a work of many excellencies and one which students of a pending political question will find exceedingly useful."[38] The *St. Louis Globe-Democrat* described Oklahoma as a backwater Nazareth where *Land Credits* came as a surprising addition to the economic literature; indeed, it was "one of the fairest, most illuminating and convincing discussions of land credits to appear since President Taft began to press this neglected question upon the attention of Americans." Now that *Land Credits* was in the hands of politicians, journalists, and bankers nationwide, it was bound to be a factor in pending legislation.[39]

It was surely more than coincidental that a leading agricultural journal, *The Farmer's Open Forum*, published Morgan's article on rural credit in December 1915, the same month that the Sixty-Fourth Congress was reconvening after its nine-month recess. Although opinion had seemed "hopelessly divided" in the prior Sixty-Third Congress, Morgan wrote that he remained hopeful that men "with honest and sincere views" would find common ground in solving the rural credit problem. Perhaps his book, published that very month (coincidental?) to rave reviews, would help shape the debate to the contours of his proposals.

In the article, after summarizing the main points from his magnum opus, Morgan clarified his aversion to deploying private capital to agriculture. As businessmen with a laser-like focus on the bottom line, investors could not be expected to prioritize farmers' interests. "It is no reflection upon them to say that they, like men engaged in other kinds of private business, will look first to their own profits and that the welfare of the farmers and the prosperity and expansion of agriculture must be secondary considerations." Only the federal government could rectify the "two evils" that were strangling farmers: lack of credit and high interest rates. "And any national land credit system which does not give equal credit facilities, at uniform rates of interest to all our farmers throughout the length and breadth of the land would be unjust, unfair and sectional and unworthy of this great Republic."[40]

Two months after his article was published in *The Farmer's Open Forum*, Morgan took a break from rural credits and traveled to Portland, Maine, where he had been invited to address the Lincoln Club at its annual gathering of Republican Party stalwarts. After acknowledging the statesmen from Maine who had "aided in guiding this great young party along the highway of liberty, freedom and the union," Morgan told his audience what they already knew: theirs was the party of Lincoln, a president who had never wavered during the Republic's gravest challenge, and who had predicted that the Confederacy's defeat would presage, with God's grace, "a new birth of Freedom."

> Through it all, Lincoln never faltered, never complained, never despaired. Supremely conscious of the justness of the cause which had been placed in his keeping, he remained serene, confident, hopeful, kind and forgiving. His life was spared until the Union was safe, slavery was doomed, and liberty and freedom were vouchsafed to every American citizen, regardless of race, color or previous condition of servitude.

Even though war was raging in Europe, Morgan saw no reason why Americans should abandon their optimism. Much as the nation had endured a horrific civil war, so, too, would the current generation unite as patriots and, inspired by Lincoln's example, help restore peace in Europe and recommit to the Republican Party's economic principles. "The future, I believe, is full of hope, for our country is bright and shining," said Morgan in closing. "There is no substantive reason why American citizens should not be optimistic as to the future of the Republic."[41]

The new year dawned to find the rural credits bill bogged down in the Committee on Banking and Currency. Fearing that the bill was about to die a premature death due to inaction, Morgan took to the press to complain about the delay and urge his friends to rally to the farmers' cause. "It has now been nearly two years since the Banking and Currency Committee received the report of the joint commission that went abroad to study rural credits," railed Morgan to the *Washington Times* in late March 1916, "but so far, neither in the Sixty-third nor Sixty-fourth Congress has the committee reported a bill to the House." Although Morgan stopped short of criticizing the committee, he was sounding an alarm to prompt immediate action. "The delay has already been so great as to place rural credit legislation in jeopardy at this session. Valuable time has been lost and other measures are now being crowded to the front."[42]

Given his minority status, Morgan had to go to extraordinary lengths to get his points across, and that often included requests for more time to speak. On the last day of debate, he asked for an additional thirty minutes to describe his proposed amendments to the bill. He was offered five. Exasperated, Morgan quipped, "Well, if I knew no more about it than some gentlemen I could tell all I knew in five minutes." Members from his side of the aisle were aware of the months that Morgan sometimes spent on research compared to the hours spent by others, and they responded to his caustic remark with a hearty round of applause.[43]

Morgan's persistence and participation in floor debates were vindicated three and a half months later when he received an invitation from the White House to attend a signing ceremony for the rural credits bill. "The President plans to approve the Rural Credits Bill on Monday, July 17th, at ten o'clock, and would be glad to have you present if it is agreeable to you," ran the invitation from President Wilson's secretary. "He is asking a number of gentlemen who are interested in this legislation to drop into the Executive Office at that time." Included in the Morgan Family Collection is a copy of Dick T.'s invitation and a photo of the signing ceremony, proudly displayed in David Morgan's home office near his tattered copy of *Land Credits*.

"Dick T. is right next to the flowers in the center of the photo," said David with a flourish. "His success in pushing the bill through Congress is remarkable when you consider that he was in the minority

party; he did not sit on the banking committee to which the legislation had been assigned; and he was not part of the delegation sent to Europe to study rural credit systems. He just muscled his way to an influential position and backed up his proposals with solid research!"[44]

The Federal Farm Loan Act of 1916, enacted with a stroke of President Wilson's pen on July 17, 1916, created a federal farm loan board, twelve regional farm loan banks, and farm loan associations scattered from coast to coast. Borrowers were allowed to borrow up to 50 percent of the value of their land and 20 percent of the value of their improvements, and they were required to amortize their payments over five to forty years. The minimum loan was a hundred dollars; the top limit was ten thousand dollars. At the same time, borrowers purchased shares of the National Farm Loan Association (NFLA), a cooperative agency that facilitated loans between farmers. Morgan was surely gratified to know that his model for this kind of cooperative credit, the German Landschaften, had made its way into the final piece of legislation.

President Woodrow Wilson signs the Federal Farm Loan Act on July 17, 1916. Dick T. Morgan is standing in the center, left of the flower vase. COURTESY OF THE MORGAN FAMILY COLLECTION

The new law specified how mortgage-backed bonds would be issued. The rate of interest on the mortgages could be no more than 1 percent higher than the rate of interest on the bonds. Although this thin margin covered the issuers' administrative costs, it did not produce a significant profit. The maximum interest rate on the bonds was 6 percent, ensuring that borrowing costs would be manageable for farmers, who had long suffered under high, and sometimes usurious, interest rates. To oversee and supervise federal land banks and national farm loan associations, the Act established the Federal Farm Loan Board and empowered it to set benchmark interest rates for mortgages and bonds and intervene whenever specific banks seemed to be acting irresponsibly. Finally, the twelve federal land banks were required to hold at least $750,000 in capital. Stock ownership of the banks was held by national farm loan associations and other interested investors, including individuals, corporations, and funds. As mandated in the Federal Reserve Act, the U.S. Treasury was authorized to serve as a lender of last resort whenever a bank's capital dipped below its prescribed threshold.[45]

In March 2011, I caught a glimpse of my future research into Dick T. Morgan and his lasting influence in agricultural lending when I traveled to Ponca City on behalf of the Oklahoma Historical Society. My destination was the office of American AgCredit, where I had scheduled an oral history interview with bank officers Felix Hensley and Kent Crain. American AgCredit served customers in more than thirty branch offices—including the one where we were sitting, down the street from the Pioneer Women's Museum.

Hensley and Crain reminisced about the bad old days of the 1980s when commodity prices dropped from record highs to abysmal lows. Seemingly overnight, the price of wheat went from six to two dollars a bushel. As commodity prices fell through the floor, inflated land values plummeted by as much as 70 percent. "Everyone in the eighties suffered," said Hensley. "There wasn't anyone that the farm crisis of the eighties did not impact, one way or the other."

Strapped for cash and desperate for relief on interest rates, farmers and ranchers flocked to agricultural lenders. "Back when interest rates at commercial banks here in the eighties got up to 19, 20, 21 percent, we were down pretty low," explained Hensley. "Our all-time high was 13 percent." Why was American AgCredit able to offer such low rates compared to commercial banks? Hensley boiled it down to a single word: stability. Asked to elaborate, he described the farm credit system as extraordinarily well capitalized and utterly attuned to the needs of agricultural borrowers.[46]

Early in our interview, Hensley and Crain wanted to make sure I knew that their organization and its laser-like focus on offering low-interest loans to farmers and ranchers originated in the Federal Farm Loan Act of 1916. What they left unsaid was anything about the progressive Republican from northwest Oklahoma who had written the book on land credit, and who had leveraged his increasing clout in Congress to prioritize agriculture and push through the rural credit bill that he had done so much to shape.

For this biographer, that story would have to wait for another day.

CHAPTER TWELVE

Duty of the Hour

In enacting war legislation Members of Congress
should say to their political prejudices,
"Get thee behind me, Satan," move out
into the higher and purer atmosphere of loyalty,
and stand squarely upon the solid, immovable, and
imperishable rock of patriotism.

DICK T. MORGAN
THE PRESIDENT AND CONGRESS IN WAR TIMES

BUOYED BY HIS SUCCESS in pushing through the Federal Farm Loan Act, Morgan was his party's obvious pick to run for reelection in 1916. His opponents included Democrat Z. A. Harris, Socialist Joseph Otti, and Progressive G. M. Henson. Bracing for a trip across his sprawling district, Morgan grabbed some sleep at Porter's house before spending a day with Charles W. Fairbanks, Indiana senator from 1897 to 1905, vice president under Theodore Roosevelt, and vice presidential candidate in 1916. According to Morgan, their meetings in Oklahoma City were "large and successful." Energized by enthusiastic voters, the duo boarded a train to Tulsa at midnight to launch an old-fashioned whistlestop campaign. After the usual fanfare in Oklahoma's second largest city, they traveled west to the Eighth District, first to Pawnee and Perry for Fairbanks to deliver ten-minute speeches, and then to Enid, where Morgan likely attended a trustee meeting at Phillips University, for more meetings and speeches. It was not until 10:30 p.m. that Morgan found time to dash off a note to Orietta. "Well, this is an outline of my doings," concluded Morgan before he turned off the light. Pleading with her to excuse his "bad pen and haste," he signed off, as usual, "Your affectionate husband, Dick."[1]

Election Day fell on November 7, and if Cimarron County was any kind of bellwether of voters' behavior in northwest Oklahoma, it came off without a hitch. "Tuesday's election passed off quietly without fights or fusses," ran a post-election synopsis in the *Cimarron News*. "It was the quietest campaign and election on record for a presidential year. More booze was used in the campaign and at the polling places than ever before in this county but it failed to create any disturbance." The final tally left Morgan with 16,691 votes compared to 14,816 for Harris, 5,218 for Otti, and 352 for Henson.[2] As noted with little fanfare in the *Guymon Herald*, "Mr. Morgan is given a safe majority in the district and will be returned to congress."[3] Once again, Morgan owed his reelection, at least in part, to Socialist partisans for siphoning votes from the Democratic candidate.

When Morgan arrived in Washington to begin his fifth term, on March 4, 1917, federal farm loan bonds were already attracting investors' attention. An advertisement described the Federal Farm Loan System as the only government program authorized to offer high-grade securities that promised to revolutionize American agriculture. Its goal was nothing less than saving the world by financing farmers through twelve federal land banks, all supervised by the Federal Farm Loan Board operating as a bureau of the U.S. Treasury Department.

The first of those banks received its charter on March 1, 1917; others followed suit in rapid succession. Farmers obtained their loans through national farm loan associations, the first of which received its charter on March 27, 1917. Over the ensuing year, about 56,000 farmers joined 2,808 associations to borrow money on their mortgages. Altogether, the banks approved more than 30,000 loans for an impressive total of $160 million. "It is a mighty movement to put farming on a better financial basis," ran the solicitation aimed at

Dick T. Morgan's congressional portrait, n.d. COURTESY OF THE MORGAN FAMILY COLLECTION

potential bond buyers. "You can enlist in it to your own profit and to the good of the Nation by buying Federal Farm Loan Bonds." As a bonus, income derived from farm loan bonds was exempt from federal, state, municipal, and local taxes.

Bonds were issued in denominations of $25, $50, $100, $500, and $1,000, matured in twenty years, were redeemable after five years, were lawful investments for all fiduciary and trust funds, and could be accepted for all public deposits. Printed at the Bureau of Engraving and Printing, farm loan bonds offered the same protection against counterfeiting as the currency in people's wallets.

The bottom line for investors looking to fatten their portfolios? "You can offer your banker no better collateral."[4]

Woodrow Wilson won a close race in 1916 with a promise to maintain American neutrality in what was drifting into the common vernacular as the Great War. But then, less than a month into his second term, he went to Congress seeking a declaration of war. "The president asked Congress to declare war on Germany," wrote Morgan matter-of-factly to Orietta in the late-night hours of April 2, 1917. "Congress will no doubt do it. So as I anticipated, we will have war with Germany. As much as I detest war, I expect to vote for the declaration, and this will of course be by far the most important vote I have cast as a Representative."[5]

As David Morgan explained, his great-grandfather spent his first four terms focused on domestic issues that defined the progressive agenda and mitigated Gilded Age inequities: control of corporations, farm credit, banking and currency reform, popular election of senators, imposition of an income tax, laws protecting laborers and increasing their wages, protective tariffs, women's suffrage, good roads, and prohibition. Then came the paradigm shift from domestic reform to waging war. "His final two terms," said David, "would be almost all about the war and its aftermath."[6]

Morgan signaled his support for servicemen by introducing what the *Tulsa Daily World* deemed his "crowning victory" in wartime legislation: a civil rights bill for soldiers and sailors protecting them from civil suits during their deployment to Europe. In a speech on the House floor, Morgan left no doubt about his commitment to America's warriors:

> To enable us to win this war, our soldiers and sailors should be as efficient as possible. We select the most fit. The young and vigorous manhood of the country is called. We take the best—the strongest physically, intellectually and morally. We give them the best equipment obtainable. We train them for the severe task before them. We seek to make them, man for man, superior to the soldiers and seamen of the enemy. We send them forth to battle. Upon their efficiency, their courage, their fortitude, their bravery and their heroism depends the fate of the nation.

For Morgan, that efficiency extended to the home front, where challenges ranging from family crises to financial difficulties awaited their return and threatened to distract them from their mission. "So far as possible these men should be relieved of any encumbrance at home," continued Morgan. "They should be protected from annoyance, anxiety and embarrassment about all private affairs." Morgan further advocated installment plans for servicemen to pay their debts to ensure that they would not lose their homes and savings while they were serving their country.[7]

Party differences notwithstanding, Morgan remained a staunch supporter of the Wilson administration's war policies. In a campaign letter to an anonymous "Friend," Morgan wrote, "In all war measures, I have given President Wilson, as the Commander-in-Chief of the Army and Navy, my hearty support. I shall continue to do so."[8] The only exception was Morgan's early opposition to the draft, as he found common cause with legislators who preferred a volunteer system.

"Initially, Dick T. was against the draft," explained David Morgan. "He was concerned about forcing young men to be sent to foreign lands against their will. He also questioned the effectiveness of conscripts compared to volunteers." Fending off criticism from Oklahoma newspapers for being the only member of the state's delegation to oppose the draft, Morgan eventually decided (or, perhaps, was persuaded to accept) that an all-volunteer army and navy would never reach the critical mass needed to wage effective war against the German juggernaut. Once he accepted the necessity of sending young men into the line of fire, he was better equipped to make tough decisions.[9]

While Dick Morgan was fighting for soldiers' and sailors' rights, others were fighting to get them out of the war, and nowhere more resolutely than in Oklahoma. Leading the charge to bring American boys home or, better yet, prevent their deployment, were three organizations whose clout was growing by the day: the Socialist Party of Oklahoma, a force to be reckoned with in local and state elections; the more bellicose Working Class Union; and the Industrial Workers of the World (IWW), whose belligerent members, known as "Wobblies," aimed to strengthen workers' solidarity in their revolutionary struggle to overthrow the ruling class. Thanks to nonstop publicity attending their battle to bring down the established order, Wobblies exerted a far greater influence than their relatively small membership (about 5 percent of all American labor unionists) might have expected. According to one estimate, they were responsible for one out of every six workdays lost to strikes in the six months following America's entry into the war. Theodore Roosevelt struck a patriotic chord when he branded IWW members as "unhung traitors." As far as the ex-president and former Rough Rider was concerned, clergymen who refused to put the flag above the church would be well advised to close their doors—and keep them closed.[10]

In a speech under the title "Entered the War Reluctantly," Morgan acknowledged that not everybody was on board with the war effort. "There were those who opposed the war," said Morgan. "So it has always been. So it will always be." But for the vast majority, the only answer to German aggression was to fight. Morgan continued:

> So when the Imperial government of Germany, contrary to the law, justice and right, sunk our ships, destroyed our property, murdered our citizens, and ordered us off of the high seas, there were those among us who said, "don't fight." But the Commander in Chief of our Army and Navy, President Woodrow Wilson, voicing the overwhelming sentiment of the American people, said, "We will fight." We are fighting for our rights, we are fighting for our honor, we are fighting for humanity.[11]

To illuminate the culture that was spawning anti-war sentiment, journalist and publisher John Kenneth Turner picked up where Socialist firebrand Oscar Ameringer had left off and traveled through southern Oklahoma to report on the conditions of tenant farmers. His report, published in the Socialist weekly *Appeal to Reason*, echoed what Ameringer had discovered on his forays into Oklahoma's back country and explains why tenant farmers and the organizations representing their interests would refuse to fight for a capitalist system that had betrayed them. "On this little journey," wrote Turner after his trip in the winter of 1915,

> I did not find anybody enjoying the benefits of modern civilization in any degree. A man of wealth would not stable his horse in such houses as these people live in; the food they eat would be spurned by a well-fed dog. Many of them at this moment are in the actual throes of acute starvation. Many have already been stripped of their poor possessions and turned out in the cold, with no shelter, nowhere to turn, and not a penny in their pockets.

Conditions for tenant farmers worsened when war broke out in Europe. And then, after running a successful reelection campaign on a promise to keep America out of the war, President Wilson signed the Selective Service Act of May 1917. As if the collapse of cotton prices were not enough, young men made more conscious by the Socialist Party of Oklahoma and more combative by the WCU and IWW were recruited as rich men's cannon fodder in distant lands. Writing in the *Appeal to Reason* in 1915, Dick Morgan's fellow Hoosier and Socialist Party leader Eugene Debs expressed what millions of farmers and working men were thinking: "I will refuse to obey any order to fight for the ruling class, but I will not wait for a command to fight for the working class."[12]

Wartime demands and rumblings of dissent notwithstanding, Morgan never lost touch with his family. On May 30, he commemorated his thirty-ninth year of wedded bliss with a heartfelt letter to Orietta: "Thirty-nine years ago, we started our life's journey together. We have had our ups and downs in life. On the whole, we have had many things to be profoundly thankful for." Morgan assured his wife that their journey was far from over and that, in whatever time they had left, he would try to be the kind of husband she deserved to "make the closing years of your life, the happiest of all." He closed with an outpouring of "love and kisses in the greatest of abundance."[13]

No sooner did the United States declare war on Germany and its allies than Congress resumed debate on a bill that had been shelved when the Sixty-Fourth Congress adjourned in March. H.R. 291, known more prosaically as the spy bill and officially as the Espionage Bill, aimed to punish those who spoke and acted against the government during wartime. On May 2, Morgan made his position clear at the outset of his thirty-minute allotment: "I believe that this bill should be passed at the earliest date possible."

Morgan began by asking his listeners to think back to the early days of the war, when the difficulty of maintaining neutrality had been exacerbated by war resisters who wanted no part of the conflict. Then came President Wilson's request on April 2 that Congress declare war on Germany and subsequent passage of the Selective Service Act on May 18. Practically overnight, peaceful protests turned violent, and in the absence of laws to curtail freedoms of speech and assembly that were guaranteed in the U.S. Constitution, law enforcement was ill equipped to keep the peace. As Morgan put it, "We found also that the conditions which developed here in our own land were such that many crimes were committed in the United States which this Government was powerless to punish by reason of the lack of law." He went on to remind his fellow legislators of their obligation not only to wage war effectively, but also to protect citizens' rights and property and to punish those whose crimes were "dangerous to our peace and welfare and our honor." The so-called spy bill did not aim to strip citizens of their freedoms, but to protect those freedoms against enemies, both foreign and domestic, during a time of great national peril. Simply put, people needed to surrender some privileges for the greater good.

Was the spy bill directed at law-abiding citizens?

"Not at all," said Morgan. "It is intended only to affect the criminal classes. And we have them in the United States."

Morgan continued: "Now, then, it is to control and subdue these criminal classes, these men who are unfriendly to the United States, these men who perhaps are not citizens and who would not hesitate to hinder our success in this war. I repeat it is the criminal classes that this act is intended to deter from crime, and to punish if they violate the law."

In closing, Morgan spoke up for strengthening the judiciary, the courts, the Department of Justice, and any other government agency whose prosecution of enemies of the state would "help the boys at the front, and that will aid this Nation to win a glorious victory, the influence of which will live on and on through the ages and be a blessing to all mankind."

Not for the first time, Morgan took his seat to thunderous applause.[14]

With overwhelming bipartisan support, the Espionage Act was enacted on June 15, 1917. The law's threefold purpose was to prohibit interference with military operations or recruitment, prevent insubordination in the military, and block America's enemies from soliciting support during wartime. The Espionage Act was designed as a club to smash left-wing forces of all descriptions. One North Carolina senator suggested that the act could serve as a tool to stamp out propaganda urging Blacks to foment insurrection. Violators could expect a fine of $10,000 or imprisonment for up to twenty years, maybe both. Among the "aye" votes for that historic act of Congress was that of Dick T. Morgan.[15] A year later, Congress would ramp up its crusade against dissenters with passage of the Sedition Act, on May 16, 1918, a sweeping and easily abused piece of legislation whose goal was to crack down on speech that criticized the war effort and discouraged the purchase of government bonds. Under the Sedition Act, the postmaster general was authorized to refuse mail that fell within the bounds of forbidden speech and expression of opinion.[16]

The Espionage Act notwithstanding, anti-war sentiment coalesced two months after its passage when draft resisters gathered at John "Old Man" Spears's farm in Seminole County, Oklahoma, toting rifles and squirrel guns and ready to march the 1,300-plus miles to Washington, D.C., under the red flag of Socialism. Along the way, they intended to enlist more angry young men and cause as much mayhem as they could. Assuming they could survive for weeks on unripened corn, the rebels planned to storm the capital, arrest the "Big Slick" (a.k.a. President Woodrow Wilson), end the war, and restore dignity and decent wages to people who were hanging from the socioeconomic ladder by a thread.

Trouble began when night riders fanned out across Seminole County, burning railroad bridges, cutting telephone and telegraph lines, and raiding ranches and stores, all in an effort to compel Governor Robert L. Williams to rescind the president's draft order. As noted in the *Tulsa Daily World*, the outlaw militia included "Indians, Negroes," and tenant farmers, with a sprinkling of agitators from the WCU, no-holds-barred IWW combatants, and a much smaller organization known rather mysteriously as the "Jones family." They announced their reign of terror in grammatically challenged posters designed to lure recruits into their ad hoc militia:

> Now is the time to rebel against this war with Germany boys. Get together boys and don't go. Rich mans war. Poor mans fight. If you dont go J. P. Morgan Co. is lost. Speculation is the only cause of the war. Rebel now.

The catalyst for violence had come on August 2, when a sheriff's posse on the lookout for draft dodgers had been ambushed near Lone Dove. A deputy sheriff had suffered head and neck injuries but was expected to survive. Having fired the first shot, rebels scattered across the Canadian River valley and dug in for a fight.[17] What they did not know was that townspeople had been alerted to their doings and were determined to end their rebellion before it began. Reinforcements came in a thousand-member posse recruited from Seminole, Hughes, Pontotoc, Okmulgee, and Pottawatomie counties. They launched their attack near Sasakwa, near the South Canadian River and twenty-five miles north of Ada.[18] Resistance was spotty and anticlimactic; nobody was killed, and in the ensuing week, law enforcement and volunteers rounded up all the insurrectionists they could find in what came to be known, tragicomically, as the Green Corn Rebellion.

Repression, including multiple arrests and imprisonments of Green

Corn rebels, was severe. At the same time, law enforcement nationwide was busy putting an end to the perceived Socialist threat once and for all. Among those convicted under the Espionage Act was labor leader and five-time Socialist candidate for the presidency Eugene Debs. His arrest came following an anti-war speech at his party's convention in Canton, Ohio, in June 1918, in which he praised imprisoned Socialists not only at home, but even in Germany. Sweating in his three-piece suit under a blazing sun, he practically begged the authorities mingling in the crowd to arrest him. "I would rather a thousand times be a free soul in jail," thundered Debs as he paced back and forth across the stage at an open-air rally, "than to be a sycophant and coward in the streets." Jurors at Debs's subsequent trial were unimpressed with his compassion for jailed socialists and swiftly found him guilty. Likewise unimpressed, the judge sentenced Debs to ten years in prison.[19]

The Socialist firebrand's imprisonment signaled a swift and brutal crackdown on dissidents nationwide, and nowhere more so than in Oklahoma, where the Socialist Party had threatened, however briefly, the state's two-party system.

Aside from acres of uneaten corn, the uprising's most important consequence was to associate Socialism with treason. Socialist leaders tried to distance themselves from the imbroglio, but to no avail. In a prelude to the Red Scare that followed the Bolshevik Revolution of October 1917, Socialist newspapers were denied mailing privileges, activists were hunted down and prosecuted like common criminals, and vigilantes escorted rabble-rousers to the state borders. The editor of the *Ada Star-Democrat* concluded that if law-abiding citizens continued to tolerate "this revolutionary and anarchistical [*sic*] movement," they would be as foolish as the citizens of France who had "wallowed in luxury" while the vagabond Rousseau penned "the bloodiest page in all history."[20]

As a staunch supporter of the Espionage Act, Morgan took a dim view of anyone who disrupted the war effort, and nothing could dissuade him from supporting Wilson's war policies and the soldiers and sailors who carried them out. Like President Wilson, Morgan was apparently willing to tolerate the draconian punishments meted out to dissidents under the Espionage Act if it meant minimizing the loss of life on distant battlefields, defeating Germany, and enhancing America's stature as an exceptional nation.

"During the Great War, there was a debate over what powers a president should have during wartime," wrote David Morgan about his great-grandfather's uber-patriotism. "President Wilson took the position that he needed to control the U.S. economy, from transportation and food distribution to manufacturing, to bring the war to a successful conclusion. Many Republicans did not trust President Wilson, and they took the position that Wilson was asserting too much control over the economy. As far as Wilson's opposition was concerned, Congress had the ultimate power over the general welfare and common defense."

Rising to the president's defense, Morgan admonished his fellow legislators to eschew politics, as their duty to protect the public welfare did not extend to interfering with the commander in chief's conduct of the war. "In times of emergency, Dick T. believed that Congress should relinquish certain legislative powers to the president," continued David Morgan. "Therefore, he supported legislation giving the president broader powers."[21]

To hammer home his message, Morgan took to the House floor, on May 13, 1918, to deliver a speech under the title "The President and Congress in War Times." In his preamble, he relied on scripture to emphasize the need for a united front against the kaiser's war machine: "In enacting war legislation Members of Congress should say to their political prejudices, 'Get thee behind me, Satan,' move out into the higher and purer atmosphere of loyalty, and stand squarely upon the solid, immovable, and imperishable rock of patriotism."

War was now the nation's chief business, and every other issue was subordinate to defeating and annihilating the enemy. Such a monumental undertaking required that all resources be placed under presidential authority and beyond the toxic influence of party politics. By every appropriate means, declared Morgan, "we must uphold the hands of the Commander in Chief of the land and naval forces of the United States."

As a member of the House Judiciary Committee since March 1913, Morgan had been studying the war powers bill then under consideration. Although he remained as committed as ever to Republican Party principles, he knew that patriotism trumped partisanship during wartime. In a particularly stirring passage of his speech, Morgan called on legislators to put their party allegiances aside and do their duty:

> I am a Republican. I am a strong believer in the principles and policies of the Republican Party. But during the continuation of this war it is the duty of both the great political parties to hold their peculiar political principles and policies in abeyance. All minds and all political parties and all the energies of the Nation should be concentrated on winning the war. We can all stand on a platform of loyalty and patriotism.

Morgan further threatened to vote against amendments to the War Powers Bill, especially those based on fears that the president would abuse his powers. "I will not vote for any amendment which reflects upon the ability, the judgment, or the patriotism of the President," declared Morgan to thunderous applause. "A divided nation can hardly conduct a war successfully."

But was granting a president extraordinary power in wartime constitutional? As Morgan reminded his listeners, almost every important measure that came before Congress was subjected to constitutional scrutiny. "I do not question the good faith, loyalty, or patriotism of those who do not agree with me," said Morgan. "I have great veneration for the Constitution, but while this war lasts, on war measures I shall take a chance on their constitutionality if I am convinced that thereby I can save the life of one American soldier or sailor."

Citing the Constitution, some legislators resisted giving the president more control of federal commissions and boards, even if that control was rescinded at war's end. Morgan begged to differ, particularly when it came to the Interstate Commerce Commission and his own pet project, the Federal Trade Commission. "If the President, upon whom more than any other man rests the responsibility of winning the war, believes he can utilize the Interstate Commerce Commission or any of its employees to aid in winning this war, I am in favor of him using it." Likewise, "until our foe shall have been vanquished, until our brave troops shall have returned home waving the banner of victory, I am willing, if the President thinks it necessary, that the Federal Trade Commission shall be utilized solely in the work of subduing German autocracy."

In closing, Morgan called on his colleagues to be bold in the face of a global emergency. Just as individuals never accomplished anything out of fear, so, too, did nations shrink from bold action at their peril. "Our forefathers took a chance when they promulgated the Declaration of Independence. Lincoln took a chance when he declared himself unreservedly for the preservation of the Union. So Congress may well take a chance in trusting the President."

Morgan closed his speech to more rousing applause from his fellow patriots:

> So I say to President Wilson, here is the Interstate Commerce Commission, here is the Federal Reserve Board, here is the Federal Farm Loan Board, here is the War Finance Corporation, and here are all the other governmental commissions, bureaus, and agencies–trusting in your wisdom, trusting in your statesmanship, trusting in your patriotism–here are all these governmental agencies, take them and use them as weapons with which to whip Germany.[22]

A week after Morgan's speech, President Wilson signed the Department Reorganization Act of 1918. Sponsored by Democratic senator Lee S. Overman from North Carolina, the Act gave President Wilson sweeping powers to reorganize government agencies for the duration of the war and for six months after its termination. Under its authority, Wilson created the War Industries Board, the National War Labor Board, and the Committee on Public Information.[23]

Morgan's "The President and Congress in War Times" speech was a big hit in Oklahoma. Under the headline "Duty of the Hour," newspapers throughout District Eight quoted his clarion call for congressmen to put their political prejudices behind them and, just as Jesus dismissed Satan's seductions as distractions from a higher calling, stand behind the president in facing the greatest challenge of their generation.[24] Most newspapers went on to endorse Morgan in his reelection campaign. "Congressman Morgan has supported the administration consistently in this crisis, still retaining his fealty to the republican party, and ably looking after the best interest of his constituents," ran a story in the *Alva Review Courier*. "He is always one of the hardest workers in Congress, and is always faithful to the people he represents. He is a loyal American citizen and his vote has always been for the best interests of his country, his state and his district."[25] Branding him as a "farsighted patriot," the *Carmen Headlight* cited his lack of opposition in the Republican primary as testimony to his popularity: "Oklahoma and the nation needs Morgan in Congress and he should be returned."[26]

Several newspapers quipped that if the United States had more congressmen like Morgan, the nation would be in better shape, "and President Wilson's program of price fixing, etc., would have been a fact."[27] Citing Morgan's nine years of service, the *Fairview Republican* credited him with building constructive relationships with his fellow congressmen with nary a thought about political affiliation.[28] The *Morrison Transcript* in Noble County, where Morgan had moved to participate in the Cherokee Outlet run of 1893 and build his real estate business, expressed what many of his constituents had come to believe by the eve of his sixth run for office: "Congressman Morgan is one of the best-known men in congress. His straight-forward, efficient manner combined with his ability, and strength of purpose, have made for him a niche in the estimation of his constituents. We all feel in Dick Morgan a personal regard over and beyond the line of partisanship. He gives personal attention to the needs of the people of his district, so far as it is possible to do so."[29]

Morgan's nemesis and the state's most influential and decidedly partisan newspaper, the *Daily Oklahoman*, was so impressed by Morgan's speech that it endorsed him for reelection. "Dick T. must have been shocked by the endorsement," said David Morgan. "But then reality set in, and a week later, the paper withdrew its endorsement. I guess the editorial board decided that it was more important to elect a Democrat than a true patriot!"[30]

Sadly, even the exigencies of wartime were not enough to mitigate mudslinging. In October 1918, the *Guymon Herald* lambasted "pettifogging politicians" for accusing Morgan of refusing to support Wilson's war effort. But everyone knew what a staunch supporter he was and, moreover, that Wilson's strongest opposition came from members of his own party. As noted in the decidedly Republican newspaper, Morgan's name was being "dragged into the mire of a petty political scrap" that defied comprehension. "Mr. Morgan has sought always to hold the confidence of his constituency; and the malicious lies that are being circulated against him as a last-hour resort will only tend to instill deeper into our minds his clean record in congress and his reputation for honesty and fairness."[31]

Election Day on November 5, 1918, left Dick Morgan as the only Republican in Oklahoma's congressional delegation.[32] "The truest sentiments of the American people were expressed in strongest terms thru the ballot," declared the *Guymon Herald*. "Tuesday's vote depicts clearly that a free-born American will give up quite gladly any or all of his God-given rights in a crisis like this for the winning of a just victory." Predictions of a resounding victory were vindicated when Morgan was returned to Congress by the widest margin he had ever received. "And," said David to emphasize his ancestor's increasing popularity, "it was the only time he received a majority, not just a plurality, of votes!"[33] In neighboring Beaver County, Republicans bucked the downstate tradition of trending Democratic—hardly unusual for a northwestern county, but perhaps notable considering Wilson's popularity as a wartime president.[34]

As the saying goes, "All things come to him who waits." That was certainly true for Dick Morgan, Oklahoma's lone Republican in the Sixty-Sixth Congress (March 4, 1919–March 4, 1921). For eight years, "Uncle Dick" had bided his time on the minority side of the aisle while important committee assignments and chairmanships passed him by. That was not for lack of ability, but a consequence of Democrats'

takeover in 1911, in the middle of President Taft's term, which had confounded Republicans' ambitions for eight long years. Wielding whatever influence he could as a minority member of the House Judiciary Committee, Morgan never let up in promoting progressive legislation, remaining active in floor debates, and fighting on behalf of his constituents.

"But things have changed," ran an article in the *Oklahoma State Register*. "The day after the memorable sixty-fifth Congress came to an end, Congressman Morgan took his place on the Committee of Committees. This committee chooses the floor leader, a steering committee of five and the Republican membership of all the committees."[35]

Now empowered with more clout than ever, Morgan ramped up his support for servicemen. To show his appreciation for answering the call of duty, he traveled to New York with Oklahoma governor James Robertson to welcome servicemen home from Europe. As he explained in a letter to Orietta, several companies included soldiers from his district, and he wanted to be part of the official delegation to greet them as they stepped off the boat. Always the politician, he reminded Orietta (as if she needed reminding!) that those servicemen were also voters.[36] Further support for servicemen came in a speech on Memorial Day, May 30, 1919. "Our soldiers, seamen, and marines are clearly entitled to the profoundest thanks we can express," declared Morgan.

> They richly deserve the highest praise we can bestow. They are eminently worthy of the deepest gratitude we can feel. They performed a service to their country under circumstances and conditions which commands our highest admiration. Their service was rendered in a great crisis—in a time of need, in an hour of danger, when all we had was at stake. In this critical juncture these men donned the uniform of their country, marched forth at the call of duty, guided their country safely through the perils which beset it, and carried the flag to victory.[37]

Morgan's support for soldiers and sailors went far beyond speeches and public displays of patriotism. On June 5, 1919, he introduced his "Homes for Soldiers" bill, formally designated as "A Bill to Provide

Homes for Soldiers, Seamen, and Marines, and for Other Purposes" (H.R. 5545). In a speech under the title "Soldier-Aid Legislation," Morgan accused Congress of downplaying veterans' need for housing. "Congressmen generally have agreed that something must be done, but have disagreed upon what should be done," declared Morgan as his listeners surely squirmed in their seats. Disagreement was on display in the seventy-plus bills in circulation to provide various forms of postwar benefits to veterans. To break the logjam, Morgan raised the issue with the Republican Steering Committee in the House. Hoping to "start the ball rolling," he presented a plan based on three principles rooted in his core belief in fairness: first, legislation should help the largest number of soldiers; second, taxpayers should not be overly burdened; and finally, benefits should be spread equitably to every state and community.

Specifically, Morgan proposed the creation of a corporation controlled by the government that would be capitalized with $100 million and authorized to make loans up to $4,000 to honorably discharged soldiers, seamen, and marines, for the express purpose of purchasing a home. The loan period would not exceed sixty years. Borrowers would be charged 4.5 percent interest annually, a figure that included 3.5 percent actual interest, 0.5 percent amortization of the principal, and 0.5 percent payable to a guaranty fund. Loans would be based on 100 percent of the home's appraised value up to the $4,000 limit. As Morgan went on to explain, appraising homes at their full value was fundamental, as it was the only way to avoid discriminating against the poor in favor of the well-to-do. Those interested in buying a farm could take out an additional loan of $1,200 to purchase livestock and equipment.

Morgan admitted that his bill was not perfect, and he fully expected amendments. At the least, he expected congressmen to think seriously about compensating servicemen for their extraordinary sacrifices. "For this purpose nothing more appropriate could be done than to place within the reach of those men a home, in which, throughout their lives, they may reside under the protection of the flag they honored and upheld. A home is the best pension a soldier can possess."

The new corporation would supplement the U.S. Treasury's

capitalization through the sale of bonds. The government's only role would be to guarantee the bonds' principal and interest. In Morgan's usual effort to make everyone a winner, he asserted that his bill would accrue to the public good by multiplying the number of homeowners, mitigating the scourge of tenancy, encouraging thrift and savings among home and bond buyers, and promoting good citizenship. Taking a broad view, he characterized his bill as a bulwark against revolutionary movements that were sweeping the globe, from the Communists in Russia and China to the Green Corn rebels in Oklahoma. Clearly, this was no time to be complacent about America's role in the emerging world order.[38]

Endorsement of Morgan's bill came from none other than *Stars and Stripes*, the military's most prominent publication. In its October 25, 1919, issue, the paper stated that H.R. 5545 was "the soundest and best plan yet proposed for giving the ex-service man a permanent boost and at the same time would reach a large percentage of the men who served." On January 17, 1920, *Stars and Stripes* reported on the status of Morgan's bill as it wound its way through Congress: "Soldier legislation was brought to the front in the House through the efforts of Representative Dick T. Morgan, of Oklahoma, author of the Morgan Home-owning bill." More than fifty representatives who attended a steering committee meeting reached a consensus that some kind of legislation on behalf of veterans was long overdue.

Another crucial endorsement came from the American Legion of Oklahoma. Writing in *Harlow's Weekly*, State Adjutant William B. Siple was gratified to know that Oklahomans wanted to reward veterans for doing their patriotic duty. Shortly after it established its headquarters, the American Legion of Oklahoma let it be known that Morgan's bill was far superior to the dozens of others in circulation and advised the rest of the state's congressional delegation to support it. Among the proposals that fell by the wayside was Secretary of the Interior Franklin K. Lane's plan for veterans to settle on farms, thereby discouraging those who came from urban areas from claiming a home. At its convention in Minneapolis, the American Legion passed resolutions urging passage of what had drifted into common usage as "Morgan's homes for soldiers." State conventions followed suit not only in Oklahoma, but also in Iowa, South Dakota, Colorado, Nebraska, Arkansas, Delaware, and Washington.[39]

In recognition of Morgan's work on behalf of veterans and other constituencies across northwest Oklahoma and the nation, which all but guaranteed his seat in Congress, *Harlow's Weekly* introduced a new expression to the political lexicon: "the Morgan Standard."[40]

And what, exactly, was the Morgan Standard? *Harlow's Weekly* put it this way: "We respect Dick Morgan because he sails under republican colors and never poses as anything else but a republican. He is what he is. And he is what he claims to be. We have no respect for any man who claims to be one thing till after the votes are counted and then straightaway becomes something else."[41]

A final constituency was bankers. Writing to Morgan on April 2, 1920, State Bankers Association secretary W. R. Samuel requested a copy of the soldiers' relief bill, together with any additional comments that Morgan cared to make, for publication in the *State Banker*. Morgan did that and more—he delivered a speech to clarify the financial soundness of his bill, particularly the unorthodox provision that his proposed corporation would be authorized to make loans in amounts equal to 100 percent of the appraised value of the home. His purpose was to enable any veteran to buy a home, regardless of his financial condition. He emphasized that the government's guarantee would not make the bonds good—they were already rock solid! —but it would help keep interest rates low and bond sales brisk. Strengthened by a guaranty fund, the corporation would be able to meet its financial obligations and remain "a perfectly sound financial institution."[42]

Clearly, the Morgan Standard resonated with bankers who stood at the crossroads of their communities, and whose opinions mattered. "Dick T.'s proposal received national attention in the *New York Times* and the *Saturday Evening Post*," added David Morgan. "Although it did not become law at that time, the effect on veterans would have been similar to the Veterans Administration's loan procedures established by Congress twenty-five years later during the last year of World War II."[43]

War was still raging in Europe when Congress was distracted by an issue that surely reminded Morgan of Oklahoma's history of racial injustice: the lynching of Black citizens. Aiming to establish lynching as a federal crime, Leonidas C. Dyer, a Republican from Missouri, introduced H.R. 11279, better known as the Dyer Anti-Lynching bill.[44]

"It's hard to believe that, in 1918, there was still a need for an anti-lynching law," wrote David Morgan. "It's also hard to believe that so many politicians, including several future speakers of the House and a future vice-president of the United States, were against it."[45]

Although Blacks constituted a tiny minority in the Eighth District, Oklahoma's most influential Black newspaper, the *Black Dispatch*, published in Oklahoma City and owned and edited by Roscoe Dunjee, offered Dick Morgan a bully pulpit to express his support for Dyer's bill. The invitation came from Charles B. Wickham, grand chancellor of the Knights of Pythias in Tulsa, which used the *Black Dispatch* as its official news outlet. The need for people in authority to speak out gained urgency when a mob burned two Black churches and scores of homes north of Tulsa, in Dewey. Among the wreckage were several homes owned by Black servicemen who had been deployed to Europe. "How do you think they feel about the 'Kultur' exhibited at Dewey?" asked Wickham rhetorically in his open letter to Morgan. "The Government should break up once for all time mobbing and lynching and the Dyer bill is an advance step in that direction—hence we are asking you to support the same heartily."

Morgan's reply, published above Wickham's letter on page one of the *Black Dispatch*, was unequivocal: "I beg to acknowledge your letter of the 10th inst., inclosing [*sic*] a copy of a resolution adopted by your Grand Lodge at Muskogee, Oklahoma, and you may count on me to lend my whole-hearted support for the Dyer bill. Thanking you for writing me, and hoping that this bill may soon become law."[46]

It didn't. The Dyer Anti-Lynching Bill passed by a vote of 230 to 119 in the House, but southern Democrats in the Senate orchestrated a filibuster to block it. Their reasoning came straight out of the Jim Crow playbook: as lynchings were a legitimate response to rape, the matter was best left for the states to deal with. A century would pass before passage of an anti-lynching bill.

Morgan displayed additional support for Black causes in his correspondence with Roscoe Dunjee's brother, Irving. Then affiliated with a different news outlet in Chicago, Irving Dunjee had sent the congressman copies of resolutions adopted at a recent meeting of Black servicemen. Their topic of discussion was Morgan's Homes for Soldiers Bill. The purpose of the letter was to ask Morgan to consider Dunjee's ideas in crafting his legislation. Morgan's response was published on the front page of the *Black Dispatch* on October 31, 1919.

"Dear Friend," wrote Morgan in an open letter to Dunjee on October 22, 1919, "I have received your letter of the 16th instant in which you enclosed copy of the resolution adopted by the colored soldiers of Oklahoma in a meeting held in Okmulgee, September 24, 1919. I am pleased to receive this expression of your views on these different questions and assure you that I shall be glad to give them careful consideration and attention."

Morgan went on to express how gratified he was to read the letters from Black soldiers and state organizations that had been pouring into his office in support of H.R. 5545. "The plan meets with the hearty approval of our service men wherever it is brought to their attention," continued Morgan. "Thanking you for your aid and cooperation in this matter, I am Very sincerely yours, Dick T. Morgan."[47]

"There are two things that stand out to me about the letter," wrote David Morgan. "First, Dick T.'s letter begins with, 'Dear Friend'; and second, Morgan promised to give Black soldiers' suggestions all due consideration. These may not seem like big things in today's world, but it showed a respect that Morgan had for Black citizens at a time when few elected officials in Oklahoma would have referred to an African American as a friend. Almost nobody paid attention to minority views or opinions."[48]

What British author H. G. Wells dubbed "the war to end all wars" ground on until November 11, 1918, when the Allied supreme commander, French marshal Ferdinand Foch, dictated the terms of an armistice in his own railway car deep in the Forest of Compiègne, near Picardy, France. Facing him in the pre-dawn hours of that bleak November morning was a German delegation representing the Entente's final holdout; previous armistices had been signed with Bulgaria, the Ottoman Empire, and Austria-Hungary. The armistice was concluded after the German government sent a message to President Wilson to negotiate terms based on the Fourteen Points that he had drawn up as the foundation of a formal peace treaty. The guns fell silent at 11:00 a.m.–the eleventh hour of the eleventh day of the eleventh month. "It seemed mysterious, queer, unbelievable," recalled an American medical officer. "All of the men knew what the silence meant, but nobody shouted or threw his hat in the air." Reality slowly sank in that the bloodiest conflict in history was over.[49]

The crown jewel of Wilson's Fourteen Points was a plan to end, once and for all, the scourge of war by establishing a League of Nations. In twenty-six articles, Wilson laid out his plan to guarantee peace among nations, beginning with regular meetings in which representatives of member nations would enjoy diplomatic privileges and the benefits of extraterritoriality. Members would agree to a reduction in arms, rely on an executive council to determine what weaponry was "fair and reasonable," pledge to remain transparent in exchanging information about their military and naval programs, and, above all, prioritize diplomacy and arbitration over war. An act of aggression upon one member would be considered an act of aggression against the entire league.

A permanent court of international justice would be empowered to determine which matters were suitable for arbitration. Breaking covenants would be tantamount to an act of war. Members would entrust the league with supervising the arms trade and contributing military resources to protect covenants. To safeguard the interests of colonies and territories, members would deploy their resources and experience to serve as mandatories.

In essence, Wilson envisioned a community of nations whose north star would be "the moral force of the public opinion of the world." Subject to the glare of public scrutiny, "intrigues can no longer have their coverts, so that designs that are sinister can at any time be drawn into the open, so that those things that are destroyed by the light may be promptly destroyed by the overwhelming light of the universal expression of the condemnation of the world." Designed with the flexibility to react to unforeseen events, the League of Nations would mitigate conflicts and usher in an era of mutually beneficial relations among the nations of the world. "It is a definite guaranty of peace," declared Senator Henry Cabot Lodge as he thundered toward his conclusion. "It is a definite guaranty by word against aggression. It is a definite guaranty against the things which have just come near bringing the whole structure of civilization unto ruin."[50]

As a member of the House of Representatives, Morgan did not participate in the Senate's ratification process. Yet he was enthusiastic about Wilson's proposal, and he claimed to share that enthusiasm with most Americans. "The proposed League of Nations is a theme of almost universal interest," wrote Morgan. "Its importance can hardly be over-estimated. It means a complete change of policy on the part of the United States. Indeed it means a change of policy among all the nations of the earth."[51] One can only imagine his disappointment in the Senate's refusal to ratify America's membership in the League of Nations.

Now that the war was over, Morgan could return to domestic issues that meant the most to him, and that included agriculture. In December 1918, he traveled to Baltimore to participate in the tenth annual convention of the Southern Commercial Congress, a gathering of businessmen and statesmen whose threefold purpose was to reflect on the South's achievements over the preceding decade, acknowledge southern contributions to the war effort, and discuss world commerce since the conclusion of hostilities. In his proclamation welcoming delegates to the convention, Baltimore mayor James H. Preston cited his city's support for agricultural lending: "It was the pioneer that laid down the lines upon which the Farm Loan Banks have been organized, one of which is located in Baltimore." In an evening session dedicated to agricultural finance, Morgan delivered a speech under the title "Short Term Farm Credits." Officers representing federal land banks from coast to coast reported on farm lending in their respective regions. The closing address was delivered by Federal Farm Loan Commissioner George W. Norris.[52]

Another issue on Morgan's priority list was the war on liquor. Since taking his seat in Congress in 1909, he had made no secret of his abhorrence of alcohol. On December 22, 1914, he rose to the floor in support of H.R. 168, a resolution aimed at ending the traffic in liquor, except for pharmaceutical and scientific purposes, by amending the constitution: "Personally, I am in favor of utilizing every legitimate means or method that will restrict, limit, or lessen the consumption of intoxicating liquor for beverage purposes. I believe total abstinence is the only safe rule for the individual, and that prohibition is the only wise policy for the State and Nation." With a nod to his strict upbringing in Prairie Creek, he credited his parents for teaching him to steer clear of spirits.

But Morgan's stance against alcohol was more than a personal or cultural predilection. As a congressman, he was duty bound to reflect the views of his "intelligent, industrious, and patriotic" constituents who shared his commitment to the church, the school, and the home, and who had voted overwhelmingly for prohibition at the time of statehood. "For myself, in casting my vote I shall be true to Oklahoma, true to her institutions, to her laws, to her policies, and true to the hopes, the ideals, and the aspirations of her 1,700,000 people." Although he regretted the damage that prohibition would do to distillers and brewers, he reminded his colleagues that they could not serve both God and Mammon and cater to an industry that flouted the public welfare. "For my part, I prefer to march under the banner held aloft by the moral forces of the Republic and cast my vote in harmony with the dominant moral sentiment of the Nation."

As evidence of popular support for prohibition, Morgan reminded his listeners that more than half the population lived in the nation's seventeen dry states and that six million people had petitioned Congress to outlaw liquor. To vote against H.R. 168 would be nothing less than un-American and incompatible with the ideals of a free government. As usual, he summoned statistics and economic data to illuminate the extent to which liquor interests not only exerted a lopsided influence on the nation's business, but also fostered a witch's brew of social ills. "It is almost universally admitted that the liquor business is the greatest evil in existence; that it is the greatest source of crime, immorality, disease, idleness, poverty, and national waste; and that it is highly detrimental and injurious to the social, economic, and moral welfare of our citizens."

Ultimately, eliminating the scourge of drinking was a matter of patriotism. Morgan concluded his speech with an impassioned plea for Congress to follow his lead and end, once and for all, the damage wrought by the liquor industry: "Believing, as I honestly do, that the liquor traffic lowers the standard of our citizenship—physically, mentally, and morally—as a lover of my country and its people I cannot do otherwise than vote for its suppression."[53]

The groundswell of support for outlawing intoxicating spirits that Morgan had amplified in 1914 came to fruition when the Sixty-Sixth Congress ratified The National Prohibition Act in January 1919. Better known as the Volstead Act for its primary proponent, House Judiciary Committee chairman Andrew Volstead of Minnesota, the act was meant to carry out the intent of the Eighteenth Amendment to the U.S. Constitution, which established the prohibition of alcoholic drinks. The purpose of the Volstead Act was threefold: (1) to outlaw intoxicating beverages; (2) to regulate the manufacture, production, use, and sale of high-proof spirits for purposes other than alcohol consumption; and (3) to ensure an ample supply of alcohol and promote its use in scientific research and in the development of fuel, dye, and other lawful industries.[54] Morgan hailed the Eighteenth Amendment and the attendant Volstead Act as harbingers of "a greater nation, a brighter day and a better world." Such was Morgan's stature in the Sixty-Sixth Congress that, in September 1919, he was appointed to a House conference committee to work with the Senate in putting teeth into enforcement of the Volstead Act.[55]

Surely vexed by his party's intransigence in postwar peace negotiations, Morgan could do little to prevent the Senate's rejection of the League of Nations and its refusal to sign the Treaty of Versailles, which formally (but, tragically, not permanently) ended the hostilities in Europe. Nor could he do much to alleviate people's angst as a postwar depression sent interest rates skyrocketing and forced

businesses into bankruptcy. What he could do was gear up for another congressional campaign. Election Day was set for November 2, 1920.

Now that the war was over and Prohibition was in full force, Morgan returned to his roots in a campaign to help farmers, a surefire way to guarantee his reelection. At issue was H.R. 13931, a resolution offered by House Judiciary Committee chairman Andrew Volstead of Minnesota, who had won Morgan's gratitude as the author of the Volstead Act of 1919. Titled "A bill to authorize association of producers of agricultural products," Volstead's bill aimed to allow and, in fact, encourage farmers to form associations to collectively

---

During their last three years in Washington, Dick and Orietta Morgan lived in the Congress Hall Hotel on New Jersey Avenue between B and C Streets. The Hotel was demolished in 1929 to make way for the Longworth House Office Building. COURTESY OF THE NATIONAL PHOTO COMPANY COLLECTION, LIBRARY OF CONGRESS, WASHINGTON, D.C.

market their products. Even though farmers had banded together in cooperative associations for decades, some questioned the legality under national antitrust laws.

To settle the matter once and for all, Morgan rose to the floor on May 28, 1920, in support of farmers' right to organize. At the outset, he made it clear that farmers' associations benefited everyone, as they enabled farmers to gain clout in the marketplace and consumers to enjoy lower prices through reductions in the cost of transportation, manufacturing, marketing, and distribution of farm products. No one was surprised when he offered a history lesson, beginning with the Sherman Antitrust Act of 1890, which had stood the test of time as the basis of federal laws against "trusts, conspiracies, combinations, and monopolies" whose effect was to restrain domestic and foreign trade. The next major piece of legislation was the Clayton Antitrust Act of 1914, which included an opaque provision seeming to exclude agricultural organizations from antitrust prosecution. As a member of the House Judiciary Committee, Morgan had tried to eliminate vagueness in antitrust legislation. Six years later, he was more adamant than ever that farmers had a right to organize, particularly considering agriculture's pivotal role in supplying troops with the wherewithal to win the war.

With an eye on the upcoming elections, Morgan reached a conclusion that surely resonated among the farmers and ranchers in northwest Oklahoma:

> In conclusion, I will state that this bill should be enacted into law. It should be made clear beyond question that farmers have a right to form business organizations for the purpose of selling their products. The farmers should be organized for the purpose of making their business profitable, for the purpose of promoting the expansion of the great fundamental industry of agriculture, and for the purpose of making their influence felt in the public affairs of the community, the country, the State, and the Nation.[56]

None doubted that Morgan's reelection was practically foreordained. Such was his popularity that he was encouraged to challenge Thomas

P. Gore for his seat in the Senate.[57] The *Ponca City News* reflected the sentiments of voters throughout the Eighth District in a June 1920 paean to their representative:

> Dick Morgan has been on the job in Washington as far back as most of us can remember. And when we say on the job we mean eternally at it. Every request from the people back home receives his instant attention. He numbers his friends among all parties. And nearly all of these admit that for the present at least he cannot be beaten. In fact, very few wish to see this happen. It seems to take several years before a man becomes well enough known and influential enough to make his power felt in a legislative way. Dick Morgan is a power in his quiet, conservative way and the people of this district feel that he actually represents them in our national legislative hall.[58]

Congress adjourned on June 5, 1920. On their way from Washington, D.C., to Oklahoma to launch a seventh campaign, the Morgans took a detour to Niagara Falls and Ottawa, Canada, to learn about the Canadian government's treatment of soldiers as they returned from Europe. Their next stop was Covington, Indiana, where they planned to spend a few days visiting Heath family and friends. But after they arrived in Covington, Dick contracted pneumonia, possibly brought on by the Spanish flu, which was raging across the globe. Orietta hustled him onto a train for a quick trip to Lakeview Hospital in Danville, Illinois, some fifteen miles west of Covington and sixty miles north of Terre Haute, the city where he had begun his career in public service.

Three hours after checking into the hospital and with Orietta at his side, Dick Thompson Morgan died on Sunday, July 4, 1920. He was sixty-six years old.[59]

At a time when telegraphy was the quickest means of communication, the Morgan household in Oklahoma City was in a frenzy over unconfirmed reports that Dick had died. As late as Tuesday, July 6, Clemmer was still trying to learn what had happened to her father-in-law. But in northwest Oklahoma, the news was already out. "The wires flashed the news to Woodward on July 5th that Hon. Dick T. Morgan, while enroute to Woodward, died of pneumonia in a hospital at Danville, Illinois on the day we celebrate our Independence–causing a day of rejoicing to turn into a day of sorrow," ran the *Woodward Democrat*'s mournful account of the tragedy. "We can hardly believe that never again will the people of Oklahoma see the kind face of the man we all loved."

Praising his faithful attendance at roll calls, the newspaper's tribute cited his homes for soldiers bill as his most recent and, as it turned out, final effort to ensure fairness for deserving and potentially vulnerable people. As a virtual shoo-in for reelection and the ranking member of the House Judiciary Committee, he would likely have entered the Republican-controlled Sixty-Seventh Congress (March 4, 1921–March 4, 1923) as committee chairman.

"He never failed to answer when the Roll was called, and when the last call was made he answered present," concluded the *Woodward Democrat*. "We will miss him."[60]

Morgan's body was loaded onto a train and shipped to Oklahoma City. Porter, who did not know about his father's illness until he received a telegram, was on hand to greet it. At the governor's invitation, the body was whisked away to the Capitol to lie in State. A funeral service, presided over by the president of Phillips University, was held the following day at the First Christian Church in Oklahoma City. Morgan was then laid to rest at Rose Hill Cemetery, also in Oklahoma City.

As noted in the *Black Dispatch* with a touch of pathos, "He requested long before his death that whenever he should die, he might be placed to rest in the center of the state he had helped to build."[61]

Dick T. Morgan's congressional portrait, circa 1918.
COURTESY OF THE MORGAN FAMILY COLLECTION

EPILOGUE

With Malice toward None; with Charity for All

A MONTH AFTER DICK T. MORGAN'S PASSING, Sherman M. Smith, a leading attorney in Woodward, sent a special gift to the Oklahoma Historical Society: the banner that the Dick T. Morgan Republican Club had crafted for the late congressman's 1908 campaign against Elmer Fulton. In his transmittal letter to OHS founder William P. Campbell, Smith commended him for his commitment to preserving Oklahoma history: "I congratulate you on being broad minded enough to preserve the history of the state, and doing justice to the memory of one whose life intimately connected with the history of the state, even if the banner partakes of politics in a way, his life work and all things connected with him are now history."

Smith went on to describe Morgan as a sort of anti-politician in the sense that there was nothing tricky or disingenuous about him. His successes in politics came from "unswerving fidelity to whatever trust fell to him." As "one of the earliest of earlies in Oklahoma," Morgan had seemed like a real possibility for territorial governor. If he felt any resentment toward President Harrison for overlooking him, it has yet to surface in the historical record. What Morgan did was gain enough expertise in homestead law to establish a brisk business across from the U.S. Land Office in Guthrie and then relocate to Perry in time for the Cherokee Outlet run of 1893. Two years later, he championed settlers' rights in the Territorial Free Home League, all the while writing books, building churches, directing musical performances, and vying for the chance to win election to public office. His persistence paid off in 1908, when he won a seat in Congress.

"As congressman he was broader than party," continued Smith in his letter to Campbell, "and worked in harmony with his colleagues regardless of party ties, 'giving and taking' with successful effect." And now that Morgan was "laid away to peaceful rest" and his lifetime of service was fading into history, it was left to his son, Porter, "one of the reliable law practitioners of Oklahoma City," to do his part in making sure that his father's legacy was not forgotten.[1]

The lame duck Sixty-Sixth Congress convened at noon on Monday, December 6, 1920. On January 18, 1921, Representative Charles D. Carter announced an appropriate time to commemorate "the life, character, and public services of the late Representative Dick T. Morgan, of Oklahoma." With no objections, House members scheduled a day of remembrance on Sunday, February 27, 1921.[2] Their comments were later bound in leather and given to family members. One of those leather-bound books remains a centerpiece of the Morgan Family Collection

Although representatives from several states offered testimonials on that somber day, none was more poignant than those offered by Morgan's fellow Oklahomans. First up was Everette B. Howard, a Democrat from Tulsa who represented the First District. As a youthful printer who had helped with the publication of *Morgan's Manual*, Howard wanted his colleagues to know about the book that had been "of great benefit to the early settlers of Oklahoma" and, more to the point, about its author, who had taken an interest in him at an early age. "I have never forgotten the kindly interest that this good man took in me as a boy at that time," said Howard, "and have on numerous occasions had reason to remember the good advice given me by him in the days in which I was passing from boyhood to manhood." Describing Morgan as strong, courageous, and patriotic, Howard wished his former colleague and mentor Godspeed on his final journey: "Dick T. Morgan has passed to the great beyond, but he leaves many behind who will long mourn his loss and always keep his name in pleasant memory. So on this Sabbath morning I say peace to his ashes and rest and happiness to his soul."[3]

The next to speak was William W. Hastings, a former attorney general for the Cherokee Nation, a Democrat from Morgan's old Second District. Hastings recalled seeing Morgan just before he left Washington "to enjoy a well-earned vacation"—which, of course, was not altogether a vacation, as he and Orietta had taken a detour to Ottawa to learn how Canada's government was treating veterans upon their return from Europe. Hastings made special reference to his predecessor's "intense loyalty to the farmer," which motivated him to write his magnum opus, *Land Credits: A Plea for the American Farmer*. Regardless of his workload, Morgan remained committed to his family's welfare. As Hastings said in closing, "He was a faithful and affectionate husband, a loyal and consistent friend, and a patriotic and beloved public servant. The district, State, and Nation that he so loyally and patriotically served will miss him."[4]

Scott Ferris, a Democrat representing the state's Sixth District, had been one of Morgan's collaborators, as Ferris chaired the Committee on Public Lands from 1913 to 1919 and sat on the Indian Affairs Committee. "No one would or could challenge one step in his spotless life," declared Ferris. "No one could or would detract from his brilliant record of devotion to duty and usefulness in life." In a Congress often racked by dissension, Morgan never lost his respect for other legislators; "only those of small stature and inferior mentality would ever exact a different rule." Waxing spiritual, Ferris pondered the mystery of great men laid low before their time, even as he assured his colleagues that there was life beyond the grave, and that Dick T. Morgan's soul was "safe and secure in the arms of his Maker" in that land "where all is peace, hope, joy, and rest."[5]

John W. Harreld, a Republican from the Fifth District, served in the House of Representatives from 1919 to 1921 and the U.S. Senate from 1921 to 1927. In his lengthy tribute, Harreld characterized Morgan's nickname, "Uncle Dick," as a term of affection that reflected his constituents' confidence in him and the respect they felt for his Christian piety and gentlemanly demeanor. Like Representative Hastings, Harreld cited Morgan's work on rural credits as an example of his commitment to farmers. He went on to commend Morgan for his last great crusade to provide homes for veterans. "It is remarkable how he had ingratiated himself into the affections of his constituency," said Harreld. "I have never seen a people who were so fond of their Representative as the people of his district were of him. There, after all, is the test of a man's success."

Harreld went on to acknowledge Morgan as the strictest observer of the Sabbath he had ever known. To illustrate, Harreld recalled the time when a House member invited Morgan to a reception on Sunday afternoon. "I am going to the reception," Harreld said to Morgan, "and if you and your wife would like a seat in our car I would like to have you go."

Morgan thanked him but politely declined the offer.

"That is rather strange," I said; "this is the only reception this officer has given this year. I should think you ought to make a special effort to go."

And Morgan's modest response? "Mrs. Morgan and I do not attend public receptions on Sunday."

"It illustrated the character of the man," concluded Harreld. "When he believed in a thing he was firm in that belief and had the courage to make known his conviction when pressed for a reason."[6]

Thomas D. McKeown, a Democrat from Ada, served the Fourth District from 1917 to 1921. McKeown had met Morgan twenty years earlier in southwestern Oklahoma, "just before the opening of that wonderful country," as McKeown was traveling in a covered wagon to file a homestead. Essential to his success was *Morgan's Manual*. "At that time Mr. Morgan was a striking figure," recalled McKeown; "he had a long, black, flowing beard, which directed one's attention to his attractive personality." Less visible, but far more important than his copious facial hair, was his Christian character, complemented by educational attainments and cultural refinements that were "quite noticeable in that western country at that day." As a freshman congressman representing an opposing party, McKeown wondered how Morgan would treat him. "I was agreeably surprised at the welcome I received at his hands," said McKeown, "so much so that I could not realize for a few minutes that he was of a different political faith." Echoing Representative Ferris's certainty in Morgan's deliverance to God's heavenly kingdom, McKeown had no doubt that Morgan had found his just reward: "But I have an abiding faith that he is happy in the living presence of the Savior of men, who will say to Dick Morgan, 'Thou good and faithful servant, enter thou into the joy of thy Lord.'"[7]

In his review of Morgan's service, the Democratic representative from District Seven, James V. McClintic, dubbed "Sunny Jim" by his constituents in southwest Oklahoma, zeroed in on several of his former colleague's areas of expertise and concentration: his proficiency in agricultural lending and authorship of *Land Credits: A Plea for the American Farmer*; and his unflagging support for President Wilson's war policies. On the home front, Morgan revealed his complementary interests in education and religion by serving as a trustee of the Christian Church–based Phillips University in Enid. As a Republican in Oklahoma's Democrat-dominated congressional delegation for many years, Morgan was committed to bipartisanship and cooperated with Democrats at every opportunity. "He was a true Christian in every sense of the word," said McClintic in closing. "His death will be mourned by his thousands of friends and colleagues, and in departing this life he has truly left his footprints on the sands of time."[8]

The last word fell to Charles Swindall, a Republican attorney from Woodward (with an impressive record of bringing cattle rustlers to justice) who had been elected in November 1920 to serve the remainder of Morgan's term. Swindall, who lived two blocks from Dick and Orietta in Woodward, had become acquainted with Morgan during the latter's service as register of the U.S. Land Office. Confronted with a tangle of land contests, Morgan had done yeoman's work in deciding cases and reducing the backlog. As Swindall recalled, Morgan was so efficient that, when the Alva and Woodward offices were consolidated in 1908, Morgan lost his job. So, what did he do? Run for Congress, of course! Swindall had no doubt that Republicans would have nominated Morgan in 1920 and, moreover, that he would have been elected by a landslide.

"In politics, as in private life, he believed in dealing fairly and justly with every citizen," said Swindall about Morgan's fight for fairness. "He would respond as promptly to the call of the most humble citizen of his State as he would to the most powerful and influential member of his own party." In closing, Swindall borrowed a few beautiful lines of verse from Longfellow:

Do your work as well,
Both the unseen and the seen,
Make the house where God may dwell
Beautiful, entire, and clean.[9]

Following Morgan's death, only one Republican remained on the ballot: Manuel Herrick, a self-described Messiah from Perry who had run against Morgan as an independent in 1918. Although he had received a paltry fifty-six votes, and none from his own precinct, Herrick was not about to give up on spreading the Word in Congress. Wary of Herrick's evangelism, Republicans tried to reopen the filing deadline so that they could find a more acceptable candidate, only to be thwarted by Democrats who saw an opportunity to send one of their own to Congress. Democrats' efforts notwithstanding, Herrick was elected to the Sixty-Seventh Congress in the Republican landslide of 1920. Nicknamed the Okie Jesus congressman for his incessant proselytizing, Herrick went down in history as one of Oklahoma's most eccentric representatives to Congress, who distinguished himself with his ignorance in matters of governance. His brief dalliance in national politics ended with a resounding defeat in his bid for a second term. Subsequent attempts at reelection went down in flames. Herrick spent his final years in a cabin near Quincy, California, where he worked at odd jobs, panning for gold, picking fruit, and surely reminiscing about his glory days in Congress.[10]

On the domestic front, Orietta never got over her husband's death. "She loved Washington," said David Morgan. "She liked to dress up and wear fancy hats. Clothing stores would send her stuff and tell her that, if she didn't like it, to send it back. And all of a sudden, that's over." Adding to her bereavement was the loss of the prestige of being a congressman's wife and the $7,500 annual salary that went with it. "She was sixty-four years old when he died," continued David Morgan. "It was a real shocker to her!"

Now that her life in Washington was over, Orietta returned to Oklahoma City and moved to the third floor of Porter and Clemmer's house, across the street from Classen High School. Lonely and

depressed, she entertained few visitors other than Porter, Clemmer, and their four children, who knew her as "Little Grandma": Dick Deupree, Martha Merle, William Maxwell, and the youngest, two-year-old Porter Harlan, called Junior by his family.[11]

"I have always seen Orietta as a post–World War II woman in a pre–World War I era," said David Morgan about his great-grandmother. "She gave up the advantages of her education to marry an ambitious attorney and aspiring politician. And think of this: Although she was fully capable of leadership, she lived most of her life without even the right to vote! Her frustration was evident as far back as the summer of 1902, when she preferred to visit family and friends in Indiana while her husband was on the campaign trail. She had no interest in whiling away her time in El Reno, waiting for Dick to come home on weekends."[12] She vented her frustration in a letter to a church friend

Dick and Orietta Morgan with their grandchildren, 1919. The grandchildren, from left to right, are William Maxwell, Porter Harlan, Dick Deupree (standing), and Martha Merle. COURTESY OF THE MORGAN FAMILY COLLECTION

who she felt had snubbed her by talking to Dick about a project that was really hers. "We are no longer friends," wrote Orietta to her erstwhile friend.[13]

Porter, not yet forty years old, was also left reeling from his father's death. "I think he enjoyed working with his father in the contested elections and using him for support on some of the cases he was working on," said David Morgan.[14]

Porter's distress over losing his father was compounded by the unsettled state of his finances. In a letter to his father dated May 31, 1920, five weeks before Dick's death, Porter confided that he was indebted to the tune of $700 and had earned less than $200 per month for the first four months of 1920. That made it tough to support his wife and four children, let alone care for his mother, whose congressional pension was set to run out in March 1921.[15] Nevertheless, in one particularly poignant letter written about a year after Dick's death, Porter assured Orietta that nothing was more important to him than her happiness, and that he wanted her to feel "more free than ever" to call on him for assistance, just as she had always called on her husband. "In other words," continued Porter, "I feel that I want to take his place as far as is possible." Porter closed with a prayer that God the Father would comfort her, "as none other can."[16]

Apparently, God's grace was not enough to alleviate Orietta's pain, and whatever frustration Porter might have felt over his mother's decline on the third floor of his home and its effects on his wife and children has been lost to the passage of time. What was not lost were more than a dozen boxes stuffed with her late husband's effects—a treasure trove of books, correspondence, speeches, congressional testimonies, newspaper clippings, and photos dating back to their youth in Indiana. "Aren't we grateful that Orietta hung onto those storage boxes!" said David. "The Morgan family will be forever indebted to Orietta. It was

---

Porter Heath Morgan (1880–1959), the only child of Dick and Orietta, circa 1955. COURTESY OF THE MORGAN FAMILY COLLECTION

she who opened the communication between my great-grandfather and me. She told us what was important in their lives."[17]

Meanwhile, Porter was following his father's footsteps into the practice of law, church leadership, and public service. His first bid for office came in 1922 with a campaign for state attorney general. Support came from Okmulgee County attorney Jim Hepburn, who described Porter as "a natural enemy of the crook, grafter, and thief" who would rely on the lessons he had learned at his father's side to fight for fairness.[18] But voters disagreed. Porter lost his bid for attorney general twice, first in 1922, and then in 1928. In 1940, he set his sights on Congress, only to suffer defeat in the Republican primary. In his other forays into politics, Porter turned out to be a better campaign manager than a candidate, and he complemented his law career by serving as chairman of Oklahoma County's Republican Party and helping oilman and banker Ulysses S. Stone win election to Congress.[19]

Unfortunately, things were not going so well at home between Porter and Clemmer, and after many years of separation, they divorced. Unlike Orietta, Porter rebounded and, in 1943, married Faye Roblin, ironically a Democratic Party stalwart and chairperson of the State Industrial Commission.

The year after Porter and Faye were married, and the day after Christmas, Orietta died, leaving her son to wonder what to do with all those boxes.

"I don't know where all this stuff was stored while Orietta was still alive," said David. "It would have taken a lot of storage space!"

Five years later, and nearly three decades after his father's death, Porter collected those boxes and took them to associate professor of history Gilbert C. Fite at the University of Oklahoma, who assured him that his parents' memorabilia would be in good hands. In the last decade of Porter's life, when he wasn't working or enjoying the company of family and friends, he was likely to be serving his fellow parishioners at First Christian Church at 36th and North Walker in Oklahoma City. "I never knew a lay person who spent more time at church than my grandfather," said David Morgan. Dick would have applauded his son for attending to his spiritual needs.

Porter died on August 17, 1959, at the age of 78, and was laid to rest at Rose Hill Cemetery in Oklahoma City, where he joined his parents, Dick and Orietta, and would be joined seven years later by his first wife, Clemmer.[20]

"From my perspective, it doesn't seem like Dick T. Morgan has received his appropriate place in Oklahoma's written history. In most Oklahoma history books, his name does not even appear in the index. I have tried to guess what has kept him from being a more prominent part of Oklahoma history."

So began David Morgan's letter to Dr. Bob Blackburn, former executive director of the Oklahoma Historical Society. By the time he wrote that letter seeking Blackburn's counsel, David had followed Kenyon's advice and made several trips to the Carl Albert

Dick T. Morgan (third from left) and his siblings, circa 1919.
COURTESY OF THE MORGAN FAMILY COLLECTION

Congressional Research and Studies Center in Norman, and he had gleaned enough from the Dick T. Morgan Collection and walkabouts in Oklahoma and several other states to suspect that their great-grandfather's career might be of interest to more than family and friends. As David explained in his letter to Blackburn, "I kept thinking to myself, is this just important to me, because he's our relative, or is it something that's really important?"

Blackburn's answer was unequivocal. Reading David's summary of his great-grandfather's life and career and witnessing one of his PowerPoint presentations gave Blackburn a fresh perspective on early Oklahoma history, and somebody should finally write a book about it.

With validation from a respected historian, David continued his research and began giving talks around the state. On occasion, he was asked to contribute guest articles to local newspapers, and he started to think about the best way to frame Dick's narrative. "At first, I referred to him as Oklahoma's first progressive Republican," explained David. "But he really wasn't. He was kind of a maverick Republican. I thought about a title for a book—*Maverick Republican*." In contrast to Republican ideologues of another era, Morgan believed in a strong government empowered to do good things for the people at a time when Big Business reigned supreme and ran roughshod over the public welfare.

"Wasn't it Madison who said that if men were angels, no government would be necessary?" I asked during one of our FaceTime interviews.

"Yes, it was," said David, "and that's just what Dick believed. This might sound naive in today's world, but he also believed in people's essential goodness, and that most people, when tempted to do the wrong thing, would ignore the calling of their darker angels, and not take advantage of their government." To encourage public officials to live up to their high calling, Dick Morgan set an example of hard work, infused with passion and commitment to bedrock principles that he had learned as a farm boy in Indiana.[21] To borrow from his favorite president, Dick T. Morgan's philosophy of governance—and indeed, his approach to life itself—is perhaps best expressed in an immortal line from Lincoln's second inaugural address: With malice toward none; with charity for all.

Returning to Congress's day of remembrance, David brought up another memorial address, this one by Representative Jasper Tincher of Kansas, who commented on Morgan's advocacy of bills that were not entirely to everybody's liking. Everyone in Congress knew about Morgan's passion for offering land to ex-servicemen with government assistance. "The most severe criticism I ever heard of that bill," said Tincher, "was expressed by a colleague, who said to him, 'Dick, that bill is based for success upon the absolute honesty of every man who has a transaction with the government under that law.'"

Morgan responded, "Yes, I always assume that toward my fellow man."[22]

Of all the materials that David, Kenyon, and I consulted for this biography, none display more evidence of Morgan's passion and commitment to bedrock principles than his speeches. "He appears to always have a handful of speeches in his briefcase or his pocket to be given out at any time," explained David Morgan. "A lot of them had to do with character, and the importance of family, church, and school." Relying on his legal training and experience, Morgan was meticulous in constructing his speeches, and he laid out his arguments to enthrall his audience until he was sure they understood whatever point he was trying to make. "He might not have been the most gifted orator," continued David, "but he was methodical in getting his point across."

Morgan's point, and a throughline that pervades everything he said and wrote, was that people should take their citizenship seriously, and that improvements in the public sphere were everybody's responsibility. That philosophy of citizenship is Morgan's legacy, and nowhere is it more clearly in evidence than in his authorship of *Morgan's Manual*, his work on behalf of farmers and veterans, and his leadership in creating the Federal Trade Commission.

"He's not moralistic in saying, 'Make America great again,'" said David Morgan. "He's just saying, 'Be great.'"[23]

Aside from character and the importance of family, church, and school, Morgan's most consistent theme is his pride in America's greatness—what later generations of historians have referred to as

American exceptionalism. In a speech titled "Fifty Years of Material and Religious Progress," likely delivered several times given his topic's resonance among patriotic Americans, Morgan extolled his country as nothing less than a beacon of hope for all mankind.

His title notwithstanding, Morgan began with Columbus's so-called discovery of the New World, "one of the most important events in the history of the human race" that led to "the uplift, the advancement, the enlightenment, and the freedom of the entire human race." After crediting the Founding Fathers for crafting a new nation on the strength of an ideal, he zeroed in on the nation's accomplishments over the previous half century—that is, since the Civil War. As usual, Morgan drew from his repertoire of statistics: the population had surged from thirty-one million to ninety-two million, wealth had increased from 16 billion to 132 billion dollars, and per capita wealth stood at $1,400 compared to $500 at war's end. "We are the richest nation on earth," intoned Morgan. "The wealth of this country alone approximates the combined wealth of England, Germany, and France."

That astonishing growth derived from the nation's two complementary economic sectors: agriculture and industry. Through their unceasing toil, Americans had cleared forests, subdued the wilderness, conquered the desert, and erected "great commercial, financial and industrial establishments" in cities across the continent. That unceasing toil was fueled by improvements in machinery and tools, better methods of production, and the formation of agencies and institutions to marshal the nation's human and natural resources, all of which created "the golden opportunities of the new world."

Morgan's only lament was that religion and spirituality had not kept pace with the march of civilization, and that too many churchgoers were oblivious to the perils of declining faith. "There are forests of doubt, infidelity, and indifference that need to be cleared to let in the sun light of the gospel," declared Morgan. "There are highways to open that will lead the people to the Kingdom of God."[24]

Morgan returned to the theme of American exceptionalism on June 6, 1917, when he delivered the commencement address at his alma mater, Union Christian College in Merom, Indiana.[25] He likely delivered the same speech at Bethany College in West Virginia, where he also received an honorary law degree in June 1917. All who heard it agreed that it was a speech for the ages, so much so that it survives in the *Congressional Record.* Settling once again into his comfort zone, Morgan presented a history lesson spanning the past four decades, a period marked by unparalleled progress in all fields of endeavor, and whose transformative effects extended to the character of the American people. But even as Americans basked in the fruits of their labors, progress was showing its downside in creating problems and dangers beyond the ken of previous generations.

For better or worse, the march of progress had buried the old nation "in the silent tomb of the past." In its place, a new nation was thrust into the world whose people, a hundred million strong and teeming with immigrants, were abandoning farms for cities and contributing to an industrial juggernaut whose wealth had skyrocketed from $25 billion in 1880 to $200 billion in 1917. "In that wealth there is national strength, national efficiency, and national prestige," declared Morgan to UCC's graduating class. But there was a caveat: "In it there may be national peril and national danger. Dollar signs may multiply until they become danger signals."

To manage that wealth, Congress had been focusing on the two big problems that lay at the heart of Gilded Age America and threatened the progressive agenda: first, how to produce that wealth successfully; and second, how to distribute it equitably. In Morgan's estimation, the first problem had been solved. The second one had not, and solving it would become the defining issue for America's leaders, perhaps for generations to come. Graduates had cause for reflection as Morgan described the world that awaited them:

> The college graduate of 1917 will be confronted with this wealth. Its influence permeates society, business, and politics, affects every calling, profession, and avocation of life, touches every avenue of human activity, extends to every portion and section of the country, and is felt around every fireside and in every home in the land.

Morgan had no intention of denouncing the nation's wealth or underestimating its benefits and blessings. But he did want to express his earnest hope that this great wealth would not become a menace to the nation—that it would not become an instrument of oppression, but would be used "for the glory of our country and for the good of mankind."

As a prime mover behind the Federal Trade Commission, Morgan surprised no one when he described the dangers generated by corporations that, if left unregulated, created monopolies, undermined the public welfare, and pitted capital against labor. His vision for America was a level playing field where corporations served as the people's trustees and instruments of shared prosperity. Thanks to progressive legislation, that vision was coming into focus in a "modified and purified" political atmosphere:

> Corruption in politics has diminished. Fraud in elections has decreased. A higher standard of morals is demanded of public officials. Candidates are limited in the use of money. Publicity of campaign expenditures is required. A secret ballot is in the hand of the voter. The old-fashioned nominating conventions have been abolished. Primary elections are in vogue. The initiative and referendum are in use. The recall is being tested. United States Senators are elected by direct vote of the people. And many other reforms have been adopted.

But of course, the fight for fairness was far from over. "There is still room for improvement. The rising generation should go forth into the world imbued with the spirit of political reform, determined that in this free country we shall have decent politics, honest elections, a free ballot, and a fair count." Morgan credited the press, "one of the great lights," for furthering the progressive agenda. Cheers surely erupted when he cited "America's Christian spirit" as the real force in bringing the nation's promise ever closer to fulfillment, "and for the enlargement of the influence of our benevolent and philanthropic institutions."

Revisiting his "Our Country—What Made It Great" speech on the eve of Oklahoma statehood, Morgan asked rhetorically, what made America great? After acknowledging the importance of natural resources, vast spaces, and a mighty military, Morgan responded to his own question: "Our safety is in our citizenship. Should the time unhappily ever come when this citizenship shall materially deteriorate in physical strength, in intellectual vigor, or in moral stamina the

American Republic will decline, its power will recede, its strength will weaken, its influence will wane, and its glory will fade." He then shared the rush of emotion that surged through him when, as a freshman congressman, he had watched William Howard Taft place his hand on the Bible and swear to protect and defend the nation. At the same time, Morgan was participating in the House of Representatives' swearing-in ceremony.

What was his takeaway from those solemn occasions? "The voter and the citizen are under the same obligation–to perform their duties as the President is to perform his duties. Fundamentally it is not the public officer but the citizen who holds the destiny of the Nation in his hands."

Then came this: "Good citizenship is the basis of' good government. Good laws contribute to good government, but good laws do not necessarily make good government. With good citizens and bad laws there will be better government than with bad citizens and good laws. The laws do not make the citizen–the citizen makes the laws."

What were the chief characteristics of good citizenship? In Morgan's telling, they were simply stated: industriousness, energy, and persistence in working for the good of society; respect for the law, both human and divine; the selection of a life's calling; and a resolve to pursue that calling for the benefit of all. "It is not what you do, but how you do it, that brings success in life, recognition in the world, and earns for you the gratitude of your country."

Graduates of a Christian college probably did not need reminding that citizenship played out in the eternal struggle between good and evil. "It is your duty," said Morgan, "to enlist under the banner of righteousness and resist evil in all its forms, phases, and aspects." If any of the graduates arrayed before him wanted to know where to go to find exemplars of good citizenship, Morgan had the answer: Washington, D.C., where monuments to Washington and Lincoln reminded visitors from around the world what it took to be part of America's ongoing experiment in self-government.

With war raging in Europe and UCC's graduates facing the greatest peril of their generation, it was fitting that Morgan closed with a call to patriotism that Americans had always answered. "They will not fail now," declared Morgan. "Our people will make any sacrifice that is necessary to conduct this war to a successful conclusion." Quoting Lincoln's fervent prayer at Gettysburg "that this Nation, under God, shall have a new birth of freedom," Morgan implored his young listeners to get behind another birth of freedom, so that "forever thereafter peace shall reign among them."[26]

That was good advice for the class of 1917, and for us, too.

NOTES

PREFACE

1 "Stanislaw Brzozowski (writer)," Wikipedia, https://en.wikipedia.org/wiki/Stanisław_Brzozowski_(writer); Agata Bielik-Robson, "Another Conversion. Stanislaw Brzozowski's 'Diary' as an Early Instance of the Post-secular Turn to Religion," *Studies in East European Thought* 63, no. 4 (November 2011): 279–91. Published online October 27, 2011, https://www.jstor.org/stable/41477738.

2 Acting Governor M. C. Trapp to Mrs. Morgan, July 8, 1920, Morgan Family Collection, Oklahoma City (hereafter cited as Morgan Family Collection).

3 "Hundreds View Body of Morgan," *Daily Oklahoman*, July 9, 1920.

4 "Congressman Morgan Laid to Rest," *Christian Evangelist*, July 22, 1920, "Miscellaneous," folder 10, box 5, Dick T. Morgan Collection, Carl Albert Congressional Research and Studies Center, Norman, Oklahoma (hereafter cited as DTMC-CACRSC).

5 "The Building of the Woodward, Oklahoma, Church," *World Call*, September 1920, "Miscellaneous," folder 11, box 5, DTMC-CACRSC.

6 Kenyon Morgan, interview by author, February 17, 2023, Oklahoma City, Oklahoma; Kenyon Morgan to author, June 19, 2023.

7 David D. Morgan to author, June 22, 2023.

8 David D. Morgan's newspaper articles, some used as sources in this book, include "Life of Oklahoma Pioneer Shared," *Ponca City News*, March 14, 2019; "Rotary Members Hear Story of One of State's Early Congressmen," *Woodward News*, March 27, 2019; "Looking Back," *Yukon Review*, April 13, 2019; "Descendant of Oklahoma Territory Attorney, U.S. Congressman Dick T. Morgan Shares Family, County History," *Perry Daily Journal*, May 18, 2019; "Oklahoma Territory Celebrates the Passage of the Free Homes Act," *Alva Review Courier*, May 16, 2021; "Tales of a 'Land-Run' Lawyer," *Yankton* (S. Dak.) *Daily Press and Dakotan*, July 2, 2021.

9 David D. Morgan, phone interview by author, April 5, 2023, Charlottesville and Oklahoma City.

10 Kenyon Morgan interview, February 17, 2023.

11 David D. Morgan, interview by author, February 17, 2023, Oklahoma City, Oklahoma.

12 Frederick Jackson Turner, *The Frontier in American History* (Franklin Center, Penn.: The Franklin Library, 1977), 3; Michael J. Hightower, *Inventing Tradition: Cowboy Sports in a Postmodern Age* (Saarbrücken, Germany: VDM, 2008), 9.

13 David McCullough, *The Course of Human Events*, National Endowment for the Humanities, Jefferson Lecture in the Humanities 2003. *See* Brainy Quote, https://www.brainyquote.com/quotes/david_mccullough_381227.

CHAPTER ONE

1 Outline, Notes, and Typed Copy of an Autobiography, Dick T. Morgan Digital Collection, Carl Albert Congressional Research and Studies Center (hereafter cited as DTMDC-CACRSC), https://dicktmorgan.omeka.net/

items/show/947, accessed February 24, 2022. Hereafter cited under its title, "Indiana My Birth Place." *See also* Dick T. Morgan, "Death of Mrs. Frances A. Morgan," to Editor of the *Christian Evangelist*, n.d., Morgan Family Collection.

2 "Ralph W. Moss (politician)," Wikipedia, https://en.wikipedia.org/wiki/Ralph_W._Moss_(politician), accessed April 20, 2023.

3 C. J. Phillips, "Hon. Dick T. Morgan: An Appreciation by C. J. Phillips," *Osage Magazine* (September 1910): 19; "Morgan, Dick Thompson," Vertical Files, Research Division, Oklahoma Historical Society, Oklahoma City (hereafter cited as OHS Vertical Files); Gene Aldrich, *The Okie Jesus Congressman: The Life of Manuel Herrick* (Oklahoma City: Times-Journal Publishing Company, 1974), 106.

4 Dick T. Morgan, "Prairie Creek, Indiana, Vigo County, November 20, 1911," Family History, folder 27, box 3, DTMC-CACRSC.

5 David D. Morgan to author, November 30, 2021.

6 "James Brown Ray," Indiana Governor History, https://www.in.gov/governorhistory/2374.htm, accessed April 20, 2023.

7 Dick T. Morgan, "Prairie Creek Indiana"; David D. Morgan to author, June 11, 2023.

8 Dick T. Morgan, "Prairie Creek Indiana." For a brief history of the Christian Church of the Disciples of Christ and its characteristic beliefs, *see Year Book 1958–1959: Our Year to Remember, Read and Unite, First Christian Church*, Perry, Oklahoma, Morgan Family Collection.

9 Dick T. Morgan, "Death of Mrs. Frances A. Morgan"; Dick T. Morgan to Editor of the *Christian Evangelist*, November 22, 1913; "Mrs. Frances A. Morgan," *Christian Evangelist*, January 29, 1914, all in Morgan Family Collection *See also* "Honorable Dick T. Morgan: Representative 8th Congressional District of Oklahoma Answered the Last Roll Call at Danville, Illinois, July 5, 1920," *Woodward Democrat*, July 9, 1920; Joseph B. Thoburn, *A Standard History of Oklahoma*, vol. 4 (Chicago: American Historical Society, 1916), 1674.

10 "Whig Party," History, https://www.history.com/topics/19th-century/whig-party, accessed April 20, 2023.

11 John D. Barnhart, Review of *Colonel Dick Thompson, the Persistent Whig*, by Charles Roll, *Indiana Magazine of History* 44, no. 2 (June 1948): 202–4; "Richard Wigginton Thompson," Indiana State Library, https://www.in.gov/library/collections-and-services/manuscripts/indiana-lawyers-and-judges/hoosier-legal-literaries/richard-wigginton-thompson/, accessed April 20, 2023.

12 Dick T. Morgan, "Indiana My Birth Place"; David D. Morgan to author, November 21, 2021, January 18, 2022.

13 Dick T. Morgan, "Indiana My Birth Place"; C. J. Phillips, "Hon. Dick T. Morgan," *Osage Magazine* (September 1910): 18–21; Aldrich, *Okie Jesus Congressman*, 106; David D. Morgan to author, November 21, 2021.

14 Dick T. Morgan, "Indiana My Birth Place"; C. J. Phillips, "Hon. Dick T. Morgan," *Osage Magazine* (September 1910): 18–21.

15 Lucretia's granddaughter, known to David Morgan as Cousin Hazel, lived in Oklahoma City and taught English at several schools well into the 1970s.

16 Dick T. Morgan, "Indiana My Birth Place"; Kosmerick, Todd J., "Morgan, Dick Thompson," The Encyclopedia of Oklahoma History and Culture, Oklahoma Historical Society, https://www.okhistory.org/publications/enc/entry.php?entry=MO019, accessed April 20, 2023.

17 Dick T. Morgan, "Indiana My Birth Place." There are striking parallels between Morgan's and Garfield's biographies, particularly in their rural roots in Indiana and Ohio, respectively, and adherence to Disciples of Christ principles. *See* C. W. Goodyear, *President Garfield: From Radical to Unifier* (New York: Simon and Schuster, 2023).

18 A. James Fuller, "The Great War Governor: Oliver P. Morton and the War of the Rebellion in Indiana," Indiana Historical Bureau, https://www.in.gov/history/4428.htm, accessed April 20, 2023.

19 Dick T. Morgan, "Indiana My Birth Place"; David D. Morgan to author, November 21, 24, 2021.

20 "Morton and Turpie's Speeches in Sullivan," *Wabash* (Ind.) *Express*, July 4, 1860.

21 "Dred Scott," Wikipedia, https://en.wikipedia.org/wiki/Dred_Scott#Dred_Scott_v._Sandford, accessed April 20, 2023.

22 "Morton and Turpie's Speeches in Sullivan."

23 Fuller, "The Great War Governor."

24 C. J. Phillips, "Hon. Dick T. Morgan," *Osage Magazine* (September 1910): 18–21. For a contrast between the civic engagement of Dick T. Morgan's era and the fractured politics of our own, see Evan Osnos, *Wildland: The Making of America's Fury* (New York: Farrar Straus and Giroux, 2021): 303–4.

25 Dick T. Morgan's testimony, "Fulton vs. Morgan," circa 1910, folder 26, box 2, DTMC-CACRSC; "Daniel W. Voorhees," Wikipedia, https://en.wikipedia.org/wiki/Daniel_W._Voorhees#Senator, accessed April 20, 2023; David D. Morgan to author, January 18, 2022. The passage of time did little to diminish the power of Voorhees's oratory. For his debate with Republican Senator John J. Ingalls of Kansas, which made headlines nationwide and likely attracted Morgan's attention, *see* Ray H. Sandefur, "The Ingalls-Voorhees Debate of 1888," *Kansas Historical Quarterly* 17, no. 3 (August 1949): 243–44.

26 "Hon. Dick T. Morgan," unsourced newspaper article, n.d., folder 1, box 5, William H. English Collection No. M0098, Indiana Historical Society, Indianapolis, Indiana (hereafter cited as IHS).

27 Dick T. Morgan, "Indiana My Birth Place."

28 "The Founding of Union Christian College at Merom," *Terre Haute Tribune-Star*, July 29, 2018; David. D. Morgan to author, November 22, 2021.

29 Dick T. Morgan, "Indiana My Birth Place"; "Will H. Hays," Wikipedia, https://en.wikipedia.org/wiki/Will_H._Hays, accessed April 20, 2023.

30 William A. Bell, ed., *Indiana School Journal* 22, no. 12 (Indianapolis: Indiana State Teachers Association, 1877), 461, 519.

31 Dick T. Morgan, "Indiana My Birth Place"; "Hon. Dick T. Morgan," *Noble County Sentinel*, December 23, 1897; C. J. Phillips, "Hon. Dick T. Morgan," *Osage Magazine* (September 1910): 18–21; Thoburn, *Standard History of Oklahoma*, vol. 4, 1674–75; "Honorable Dick T. Morgan," *Woodward Democrat*, July 9, 1920; "Dick Thompson Morgan: 'Father of the FTC'," *Terre Haute Tribune-Star*, April

22, 2018; Kosmerick, "Morgan, Dick Thompson"; Allen D. Fitchett, "History of Noble County, Oklahoma" (Master's thesis, Colorado State College of Education, 1938); David D. Morgan to author, November 21, 2021.

32 Bell, *Indiana School Journal*, 457.

33 Dick T. Morgan, "Indiana My Birth Place."

34 Closing Exercises, Prairie Creek High School, Friday, May 30, 1879, Morgan Family Collection.

35 For what amounts to a sociological study of frontier businessmen's proclivity to seize opportunities and switch careers, *see* Norman L. Crockett, "The Opening of Oklahoma: A Businessman's Frontier," *The Chronicles of Oklahoma* 56, no. 1 (Spring 1978): 85–95; Michael J. Hightower, *Banking in Oklahoma before Statehood* (Norman: University of Oklahoma Press, 2013), 240–41.

36 "Local Matters," *Hagerstown* (Ind.) *Exponent*, April 22, 1880; untitled article, *Hagerstown* (Ind.) *Exponent*, September 21, 1891; untitled article, *Wayne Farmer*, April 26, 1907; "Hon. Dick T. Morgan."

37 Dick T. Morgan, "Indiana My Birth Place"; "Honorable Dick T. Morgan," *Woodward Democrat*, July 9, 1920; David D. Morgan to author, November 21, 2021.

38 For a detailed analysis of the election of 1880, *see* Albert V. House, "The Democratic State Central Committee of Indiana in 1880: A Case Study in Party Tactics and Finance," *Indiana Magazine of History* 58, no. 3 (September 1962), 179–210.

39 For background on Indiana as an October state and Porter's characterization as a skilled politician in his 1880 gubernatorial campaign against Democrat Franklin Landers, *see* Clifton J. Phillips, *Indiana in Transition: The Emergence of an Industrial Commonwealth, 1880–1920* (Indianapolis: Indiana Historical Bureau & Indiana Historical Society, 1968): 6–8.

40 David D. Morgan to author, November 21, 2021, January 9, 2022.

41 Dick T. Morgan, "Indiana My Birth Place"; David D. Morgan to author, November 23, 2021.

CHAPTER TWO

1 Albert G. Porter, Inaugural Address to the Indiana General Assembly, "The Rights of Citizenship," "The Cornerstone of the Capitol," Journal of the House of Representatives of the State of Indiana during the Fifty-Second Session of the General Assembly, Commencing Thursday, January 6, 1881, Regular Session (Indianapolis: Carlon & Hollenback, Printers and Binders, 1881), 79–93, HathiTrust, https://babel.hathitrust.org/cgi/pt?id=uiug.30112108237865&seq=85.

2 Dick T. Morgan's nominating speech for Benjamin Harrison in the Indiana General Assembly, January 18, 1881, Indiana University Mauer School of Law, Brevier Legislative Reports, vols. 19, 20, 56–57, https://libraries.indiana.edu/databases/brevierleg, accessed April 20, 2023.

3 *Indianapolis Journal* quoted in Dick T. Morgan, "Indiana Is My Birth Place"; "Legislative Notes," *Indianapolis Leader*, January 22, 1881; Phillips, *Indiana in Transition*, 17; David D. Morgan to author, November 18, 21, 2021. On May

12, 1912, Congress approved the Seventeenth Amendment to the Constitution providing for the popular election of senators. For the Proclamation of March 23, 1889, which set the stage for the Run of 1889, *see* Michael J. Hightower, *1889: The Boomer Movement, the Land Run, and Early Oklahoma City* (Norman: University of Oklahoma Press, 2018), 154, 160, 183, 238, 251.

4 Phillips, *Indiana in Transition*, 18–19.

5 "Woman's Right to the Ballot," *Indiana State Sentinel*, March 2, 1881. *Ital* in original.

6 David D. Morgan to author, November 18, 21, 2021; Fitchett, "History of Noble County," 226–27.

7 The American Presidency Project, James A. Garfield, 20th President of the United States, 1881, Inaugural Address, https://www.presidency.ucsb.edu/documents/inaugural-address-39.

8 "Hon. Dick T. Morgan"; Dick T. Morgan to Hon. William H. English, July 12, 1888, folder 1, box 5, William H. English Collection No. M0098, IHS.

9 David D. Morgan to author, November 18, 21, 2021; Phillips, *Indiana in Transition*, 18–19.

10 David D. Morgan to author, September 27, 2021.

11 Personal Notebook Journal, Diary, DTMDC-CACRSC, https://dicktmorgan.omeka.net/items/show/1107, accessed March 8, 2022; David D. Morgan to author, September 27, 2021.

12 Phillips, *Indiana in Transition*, 18–19.

13 Thoburn, *Standard History*, vol. 4, 1674; C. J. Phillips, "Hon. Dick T. Morgan," *Osage Magazine*, September 1910, 18–21; Fitchett, *History of Noble County*, 226–27; "Hon. Dick T. Morgan," *Noble County Sentinel*, December 23, 1897; Kosmerick, "Morgan, Dick Thompson"; "Dick Thompson Morgan: 'Father of the FTC'," *Terre Haute Tribune-Star*, April 22, 2018; Dick T. Morgan to Hon. William H. English, July 12, 1888; David D. Morgan to author, November 21, 2021. For Morgan's sale of one-half interest in the *Terre Haute Daily Courier* to John Donaldson, *see* "Minor Notes," *Indianapolis Journal*, January 4, 1884.

14 "The Programme for the Convention," *Indianapolis Journal*, April 17, 1884.

15 "Young Republicans," *Indianapolis Journal*, June 19, 1884.

16 "Nominated for Congress," *Indianapolis Journal*, July 11, 1884.

17 "Vigo County Nominations," *Indianapolis Journal*," July 21, 1884.

18 "Eugene V. Debs," Wikipedia, https://en.wikipedia.org/wiki/Eugene_V._Debs, accessed April 20, 2023.

19 "Eugene V. Debs"; David D. Morgan to author, November 18, 21, 25, 2021; "Dick Thompson Morgan: 'Father of the FTC'," *Terre Haute Tribune-Star*, April 22, 2018. For Debs's election to the Indiana House of Representatives on the Democratic ticket, *see* "The Indiana Legislature," *Indianapolis Journal*, November 10, 1884. For Debs's post office address in Terre Haute, *see* "The Indiana Legislature," *Indianapolis Journal*, November 24, 1884.

20 Phillips, *Indiana in Transition*, 49.

21 Phillips, *Indiana in Transition*, 1–3.

22 Phillips, *Indiana in Transition*, 4–5.

23 Peter H. Argersinger, *Representation and Inequality in Late Nineteenth-Century America: The Politics of Apportionment* (New York: Cambridge University Press, 2012), 4–5.

24 Argersinger, *Representation and Inequality*, 8, 13–14.

25 Argersinger, *Representation and Inequality*, 12, 18–19.

26 Argersinger, *Representation and Inequality*, 20–21, 26.

27 Argersinger, *Representation and Inequality*, 28–29.

28 Phillips, *Indiana in Transition*, 23; Argersinger, Representation and Inequality, 34–41.

29 "The General Assembly: The Political Swindle Proposed by the Unscrupulous Democratic Majority," *Indianapolis Journal*, February 20, 1885.

30 Untitled article, *Indianapolis Journal*, February 21, 1885; "The General Assembly: The Congressional Gerrymandering Swindle Passed by the House," *Indianapolis Journal*, February 25, 1885; "Changing the Gerrymander," "The Rights of the Colored Race," *Indianapolis Journal*, March 3, 1885.

31 Untitled article, (Washington, D.C.) *National Republican*, March 7, 1885.

32 Untitled article, (Washington, D.C.) *National Republican*, March 9, 1885.

33 "Indiana Gerrymanders," (Washington, D.C.) *Evening Critic*, January 24, 1885.

34 Phillips, *Indiana in Transition*, 23.

35 David D. Morgan to author, November 21, 2021.

36 "Personal Mention," *Indianapolis Journal*, February 17, 1885.

37 "Minor Notes," *Indianapolis Journal*, February 28, 1885.

38 "Minor Notes," *Indianapolis Journal*, March 10, 1885.

39 Robert L. Dorman, "Dick T. Morgan, Republican from Oklahoma: Prelude to Congress, 1853–1907," *The Chronicles of Oklahoma* 99, no. 3 (Fall 2021): 262–63.

40 David D. Morgan to author, August 16, 2023.

41 Historian Charles Roll referenced in Phillips, *Indiana in Transition*, 48.

42 "Hon. Dick Morgan Oklahoma's Giant," *Tulsa Daily World*, October 22, 1917.

CHAPTER THREE

1 For a thorough account of Spanish expeditions into the southern plains, *see* Stan Hoig, *Came Men on Horses: The Conquistador Expeditions of Francisco Vázquez de Coronado and Don Juan de Oñate* (Boulder: University Press of Colorado, 2013).

2 Henry Pickering Walker, *The Wagonmasters: High Plains Freighting from the Earliest Days of the Santa Fe Trail to 1880* (Norman: University of Oklahoma Press, 1966), 3–6. *See* also Hightower, *Banking in Oklahoma before Statehood*, 76.

3 James T. DuBois and Gertrude S. Mathews, *Galusha A. Grow: Father of the Homestead Law* (Boston and New York: Houghton Mifflin, 1917), 1–10.

4 DuBois and Mathews, *Galusha A. Grow*, 39.

5 DuBois and Mathews, *Galusha A. Grow*, 281–82.

6 "Galusha A. Grow," Wikipedia, https://en.wikipedia.org/wiki/Galusha_A._Grow, accessed April 20, 2023; Paul W. Gates, "Free Homesteads for All Americans: The Homestead Act of 1862" (Washington, D.C.: Civil War

Centennial Commission, 1962), 5–7, "Homestead Act of 1862," OHS Vertical Files. *See also* Bureau of Land Management, United States Department of the Interior, *Homesteading Past and Present* (Washington, D.C.: U.S. Government Printing Office, 1959), "Homesteads: Oklahoma," OHS Vertical Files.

7 DuBois and Mathews, *Galusha A. Grow*, 84.

8 Robert D. Ilisevich, *Galusha A. Grow: The People's Candidate* (Pittsburgh: University of Pittsburgh Press, 1988), 175–76.

9 DuBois and Mathews, *Galusha A. Grow*, 110–11.

10 Ilisevich, *Galusha A. Grow*, 204.

11 The Homestead Act's commutation clause allowed homesteaders to expedite their claims. Instead of waiting for the residency period to expire, homesteaders could commute their claims by paying a fee. In essence, commutation was an alternative to the standard residency requirement.

12 Ilisevich, *Galusha A. Grow*, 211–12; Hightower, *1889*, 7–8; H. W. Brands, *American Colossus: The Triumph of Capitalism*, 1865–1900 (New York: Anchor Books, 2010), 238–42; Bureau of Land Management, U.S. Department of the Interior, *Homesteading Past and Present*; *Home-Seekers Guide, containing the Indian Treaty, How to File a Claim, Bill Opening Reservation, Full List of Reserved Lands, How to Read Corner Stones, Homestead, Mining and Sooner Laws, Complete List of Unsurveyed Lands, Description of Country by Townships, Changes in Boundary Lines of Reservation, Correct Sectional Map of Kiowa and Comanche Lands*, "Homestead - How to read the marks of the corner stones for land description of homestead," OHS Vertical Files; Homestead Act, May 20, 1862, Avalon Project, Documents in Law, History and Diplomacy, Lillian Goldman Law Library, Yale Law School, http://avalon.law.yale.edu/19th_century/homestead_act.asp, accessed April 20, 2023; The Homestead Act of 1862, Educator Resources, National Archives, https://www.archives.gov/education/lessons/homestead-act.

13 Patrick W. Riddleberger, "George W. Julian: Abolitionist Land Reformer," *Agricultural History* 29, no. 3 (July 1955), 108–10. Julian was elected as the Free Soil (FS) Party candidate to the U.S. House of Representatives in the election of 1848. Active in the elections of 1848 and 1852, the short-lived Free Soil Party opposed the expansion of slavery into the western territories, arguing that free men on free soil comprised a morally and economically superior system to slavery. Julian was one of the party's founders. *See also* "Our Land Policy - Its Evils and their Remedy," Speech of Hon. George W. Julian of Indiana in the House of Representatives, March 6, 1868 (Washington, D.C.: Office of the Great Republic, 1868), folder 51, box 7, Sidney Clarke Collection, Research Division, Oklahoma Historical Society, Oklahoma City. For Julian's influence on Sidney Clarke, an opinion leader in promoting non-Indian settlement in central Indian Territory, *see* Hightower, *1889*, 12–16, 56, 144, 262n22.

14 Julian, "Our Land Policy—Its Evils and their Remedy."

15 Greeley quoted in Gates, "Free Homesteads for All Americans: The Homestead Act of 1862."

16 "Timber Culture Act," Wikipedia, https://en.wikipedia.org/wiki/Timber_Culture_Act#, accessed April 20, 2023.

17 Pacific Railway Act (1862), Milestone Documents, National Archives, https://www.archives.gov/milestone-documents/pacific-railway-act.

18 Morrill Act (1862), Milestone Documents, National Archives, https://www.archives.gov/milestone-documents/morrill-act.

19 Joseph W. Snell and Don D. Wilson, "The Birth of the Atchison, Topeka and Santa Fe Railroad," *Kansas Historical Quarterly* 34, no. 2 (Summer 1968): 113–42, https://www.kshs.org/p/the-birth-of-the-atchison-topeka-and-santa-fe-1/13184, accessed April 20, 2023.

20 "Topeka & Emporia Railroad," *Kanzas* [sic] (Kans.) *News*, February 12, 1859.

21 "The A., T. & S. F. Road—A Scrap of History," *Emporia* (Kans.) *News*, September 23, 1870.

22 "The A., T. & S. F. Road—A Scrap of History." *See also* "Topeka & Santa Fe Railroad and Hon. E. G. Ross," *Emporia* (Kans.) *News*, November 13, 1868; Snell and Wilson, "The Birth of the Atchison, Topeka and Santa Fe Railroad"; "Atchison, Topeka and Santa Fe Railway," Wikipedia, https://en.wikipedia.org/wiki/Atchison,_Topeka_and_Santa_Fe_Railway, accessed April 20, 2023.

23 Kansas Historical Society, "Finney County, Kansas," *Kansapedia*, https://www.kshs.org/kansapedia/finney-county-kansas/15283, accessed April 20, 2023.

24 "Garden City, Kan.," *Dodge City* (Kans.) *Times*, November 9, 1878.

25 "Garden City, Kansas," Wikipedia, https://en.wikipedia.org/wiki/Garden_City,_Kansas#19th_century, accessed April 20, 2023.

26 "Irrigation at Garden City," *Dodge City* (Kans.) *Times*, October 5, 1882.

27 Untitled article, *Dodge City* (Kans.) *Times*, December 17, 1885; "Garden City, Kansas," Wikipedia, https://en.wikipedia.org/wiki/Garden_City,_Kansas#19th_century.

28 "Garden City, Kansas," Wikipedia, https://en.wikipedia.org/wiki/Garden_City,_Kansas#19th_century.

29 Finney County Directory, 1886–87 (Garden City, Kans.: Finney County Historical Society reprint, n.d.); David D. Morgan to author, July 13, 2022.

30 David D. Morgan to author, November 18, 21, 2021.

31 Edward Everett Dale, *The Range Cattle Industry: Ranching on the Great Plains from 1865 to 1925* (Norman: University of Oklahoma Press, 1960), 91–93.

32 Jimmy M. Skaggs, "Cattle Trails in Oklahoma," in *Ranch and Range in Oklahoma*, ed. Jimmy M. Skaggs, (Oklahoma City: Oklahoma Historical Society, 1978), 17; untitled article, *Indian Chieftain*, August 27, 1885.

33 "Cattle-Growers Convention," *Indian Chieftain*, November 20, 1884; "St. Louis Convention," *Barber County* (Kans.) *Index*, December 4, 1885.

34 David D. Morgan to author, November 18, 21, 2021; Henry D. McCallum and Frances T. McCallum, *The Wire that Fenced the West* (Norman: University of Oklahoma Press, 1965), 128–39. Ranch foreman quoted in McCallum and McCallum, *The Wire that Fenced the West*, 133. *See also* Lynda Beck Fenwick, *Prairie Bachelor: The Story of a Kansas Homesteader and the Populist Movement* (Lawrence: University Press of Kansas, 2020), 24–26; Hightower, *1889*, 127.

35 David D. Morgan to author, December 26, 2023.

36 Alvin O. Turner, "Cherokee Outlet Opening," The Encyclopedia of Oklahoma History and Culture, Oklahoma Historical Society, https://www.okhistory.org/publications/enc/entry?entry=CH021, accessed April 20, 2023; Hightower, *Banking in Oklahoma before Statehood*, 108–09.

37 Bob L. Blackburn, "Unassigned Lands," The Encyclopedia of Oklahoma History and Culture, Oklahoma Historical Society, https://www.okhistory.org/publications/enc/entry?entry=UN001, accessed April 20, 2023; Rushes to Statehood: The Oklahoma Land Runs, National Cowboy and Western Heritage Center, https://nationalcowboymuseum.org/explore/rushes-statehood-oklahoma-land-runs/, accessed April 20, 2023.

38 For a thorough account of Guthrie's early days, *see* Gerald Forbes, *Guthrie: Oklahoma's First Capital* (Norman: University of Oklahoma Press, 1938). *See* also Hightower, *1889*, 130-35.

39 Hightower, *1889*, 130-35.

40 David D. Morgan to author, November 18, 21, 2021.

41 Untitled article, "Oklahoma," *Butler Weekly Times*, April 17, 1889.

42 Untitled article, *Barber County* (Kans.) *Index*, January 23, 1889.

43 "Wild with Joy," *Wichita Eagle*, March 7, 1889; "Washington Notes," *Iola* (Kans.) *Register*, March 15, 1889.

44 *Rushes to Statehood: The Oklahoma Land Runs*; Hightower, *1889*, 151–55; Fred L. Wenner, *The Story of Oklahoma and the Eighty-Niners, Retold on the Golden Anniversary* (Guthrie, Okla.: Co-operative Publishing Company, 1939), 12; Dan W. Peery, "The First Two Years, Part 1," *The Chronicles of Oklahoma* 7, no. 3 (September 1929): 283–84. For an introduction to Peery's three-part account of Oklahoma City's beginnings, *see* Dan W. Peery, "Introduction: The First Two Years," *The Chronicles of Oklahoma* 7, no. 3 (September 1929): 278–80.

45 Letter to Porter H. Morgan from Dick T. Morgan on March 21, 1889, DTMDC-CACRSC, https://dicktmorgan.omeka.net/items/show/1670, accessed July 11, 2022.

46 Letter to Ora and Porter Heath Morgan from Dick T. Morgan on March 28, 1889, DTMDC-CACRSC, https://dicktmorgan.omeka.net/items/show/1680, accessed July 8, 2022.

47 Letter to Ora and Porter Heath Morgan from Dick T. Morgan on March 29, 1889, DTMDC-CACRSC, https://dicktmorgan.omeka.net/items/show/1679, accessed July 8, 2022.

48 "Hon. Dick T. Morgan." William H. English Collection, IHS.

49 David D. Morgan to author, December 25, 2023.

50 "Resolutions Passed by the Christian Church and Sunday School," *Garden City* (Kans.) *Weekly Sentinel*, April 20, 1889; David D. Morgan to author, November 19, 21, 27, 29, December 3, 2021.

CHAPTER FOUR

1 David D. Morgan to author, November 18, 21, 24, December 3, 2021; "Hon. Dick T. Morgan," *Noble County* (Okla.) *Sentinel*, December 23, 1897.

2 Hamilton S. Wicks, "The Opening of Oklahoma," *Cosmopolitan* 7, no. 5 (September 1889): 460–61.

3 Wicks, "The Opening of Oklahoma," 464. *See also* "The Boomers Take Up their Assault from Arkansas City," *Chicago Tribune*, April 19, 1889.

4 Wicks, "Opening of Oklahoma," 464–65.

5 Marion Tuttle Rock, *Illustrated History of Oklahoma, Its Occupation by Spain*

and France–Its Sale to the United States–Its Opening to Settlement in 1889–and the Meeting of the First Territorial Legislature (Topeka, Kans.: O. B. Hamilton & Son, 1890), 20–22.

6 David D. Morgan to author, November 24, 26, 2021; Guthrie walkabout, September 13, 2022. *Kansas City Gazette* quoted in U.S. Government Land Office Street Signage, Guthrie, Oklahoma. Oklahoma Station was not officially rebranded as Oklahoma City until many years after the opening. For simplicity, the fledgling town will be referred to hereafter as Oklahoma City.

7 Linda D. Wilson, "Sturm's Oklahoma Magazine," The Encyclopedia of Oklahoma History and Culture, Oklahoma Historical Society, https://www.okhistory.org/publications/enc/entry?entry=ST058, accessed April 23, 2023.

8 James L. Brown, "Early and Important Litigations," *Sturm's Oklahoma Magazine* 8, no. 2 (April 1909): 26–30. According to Brown, a U.S. Land Office did not open in Oklahoma City until June 6, 1890. For more specific information on the presentation of appeals in land disputes, *see* Henry N. Copp, "Section X – Homesteading, Guide to," *The American Settler's Guide: A Popular Exposition of the Public Land System of the United States of America*, 12th ed. (Washington, D.C.: Published by the Editor, 1887), OHS Vertical Files. As David Morgan noted, sooner was a term that originated as an insult in the territorial period and was gaining respectability by the time of statehood in 1907. In the span of a generation, the meaning of "sooner" evolved from swindler and cheater into a moniker representing an energetic, can-do spirit.

9 David D. Morgan to author, December 3, 2021.

10 "Hon. Dick Morgan Oklahoma's Giant," *Tulsa Daily World*, October 22, 1917.

11 David D. Morgan to author, November 19, 24, 29, 2021.

12 "A History of Two Weeks," *Oklahoma Times*, May 9, 1889; Hightower, *1889*, 185–88.

13 Forbes, *Guthrie*, 8–10.

14 Dorman, "Dick T. Morgan, Republican from Oklahoma: Prelude to Congress, 1853–1907," 266–67.

15 Letter to Ora and Porter Heath Morgan from Dick T. Morgan on May 31, 1889, DTMDC-CACRSC, https://dicktmorgan.omeka.net/items/show/1678, accessed July 8, 2022.

16 Letter to Ora and Porter Heath Morgan from Dick T. Morgan on June 2, 1889, DTMDC-CACRSC, https://dicktmorgan.omeka.net/items/show/1677, accessed July 8, 2022.

17 Dan W. Peery, "The First Two Years, Part 1," *The Chronicles of Oklahoma* 7, no. 3 (September 1929): 306–7; Angelo C. Scott, *Story of Oklahoma City* (Oklahoma City: Times-Journal Publishing Co., 1939), 48; Irving Geffs (aka Bunky), *The First Eight Months of Oklahoma City* (Oklahoma City: McMasters Printing Co., 1890), 27–32.

18 "Speed for Governor," *Indianapolis News*, September 7, 1889.

19 "Horace Speed," Wikipedia, https://en.wikipedia.org/wiki/Horace_Speed#, accessed April 23, 2023.

20 "Speed for Governor."

21 "Speed for Governor."

22 "Speed for Governor." The Missouri Compromise of 1820 addressed growing sectional tensions over slavery. Signed by President James Monroe, the law admitted Missouri to the Union as a slave state and Maine as a free state. It also banned slavery from the remaining Louisiana Purchase lands north of Missouri's southern border. Jefferson famously dubbed the Missouri Compromise "a fire bell in the night" for failing to resolve the issue of slavery and putting off the day of reckoning.

23 "Frisco Convention," *Oklahoma City Daily Times*, September 11, 1889.

24 "Welcome to Oklahoma City," *Oklahoma City Daily Times*, September 17, 1889.

25 For an account of the congressional delegation's visit to Oklahoma City and their attendance at an equally elegant reception, *see* Hightower, *1889*, 211–14. *See also* Lloyd H. McGuire Jr., *Birth of Guthrie: Oklahoma's Run of 1889 and Life in Guthrie in 1889 and the 1890s* (San Diego: Lloyd H. McGuire Jr., 1998), 207.

26 "The Dick Morgan Banner," *Blackwell Times-Record*, August 5, 1920.

27 Letter to Ora and Porter Heath Morgan from Dick T. Morgan on April 13, 1890, DTMDC-CACRSC, https://dicktmorgan.omeka.net/items/show/1682, accessed March 24, 2022; David D. Morgan to author, November 19, 21, 2021; February 21, 2022.

28 McGuire, *Birth of Guthrie*, 208.

29 William Cronon, George Miles, and Jay Gitlin, "Becoming West: Toward a New Meaning for Western History," in *Under an Open Sky: Rethinking America's Western Past*, ed. William Cronon, George Miles, and Jay Gitlin (New York: W.W. Norton, 1992), 17; Edwin C. McReynolds, *Oklahoma: A History of the Sooner State* (Norman: University of Oklahoma Press, 1954), 292n28.

30 "Jubilation in Oklahoma," (Washington, D.C.) *Evening Star*, May 3, 1890.

31 "Gov. Steele: Pomp, Ceremony Welcome First Governor," *Guthrie Daily Leader*, April 18, 1976, folder 10, box 6, Orben Casey Collection, Research Division, Oklahoma Historical Society, Oklahoma City.

32 "Oklahoma Officials," *Indianapolis Journal*, May 9, 1890.

33 "New Appointees," (Washington, D.C.) *National Tribune*, May 15, 1890; Scott, *Story of Oklahoma City*, 109–11; LeRoy H. Fischer, "Oklahoma Territory, 1890–1907," *The Chronicles of Oklahoma* 53, no. 1 (Spring 1975): 4; "Gov. Steele: Pomp, Ceremony Welcome First Governor."

34 Dan W. Peery, "The First Two Years." Pt. 2., *The Chronicles of Oklahoma* 7, no. 4 (December 1929): 426.

35 Scott, *Story of Oklahoma City*, 109–14; Fischer, "Oklahoma Territory, 1890–1907," 3–8; McReynolds, *Oklahoma: A History*, 292–97. For an account of Old Greer County's anomalous status until the U.S. Supreme Court placed it in Oklahoma Territory in 1896, *see* Michael J. Hightower, "The Businessman's Frontier: C. C. Hightower, Commerce, and Old Greer County, 1891–1903," *The Chronicles of Oklahoma* 86, no. 1 (Spring 2008): 4–31.

36 Fischer, "Oklahoma Territory, 1890–1907," 4–5. For a thorough account of the Organic Act of May 2, 1890, *see* Hightower, *1889*, 228–33.

37 Kenneth R. Turner, "The Creation of No Man's Land," No Man's Land Historical Society, brochure series 1, June 1994, No Man's Land Collection, No Man's Land Museum, Goodwell, Oklahoma.

38 McReynolds, *Oklahoma: A History*, 292; V. Pauline Hodges, Harold Kachel, and Joe Lansden, *Images of America: Beaver County* (Charleston, S. C.: Arcadia Publishing, 2011), 45, 111.

CHAPTER FIVE

1 Forbes, *Guthrie*, 10.

2 David D. Morgan to author, November 30, 2021.

3 McGuire, *Birth of Guthrie*, 205–10.

4 Forbes, *Guthrie*, 10–11.

5 "George W. Steele," *Guthrie Daily News*, October 14, 1890; "Gov. Steele: Pomp, Ceremony Welcome First Governor."

6 "Vetoed," *Guthrie Daily News*, October 14, 1890.

7 Forbes, *Guthrie*, 14–15; "Delegate Election," *Oklahoma Daily Journal*, October 16, 1890.

8 Forbes, *Guthrie*, 16–17.

9 Peery, Dan W. "The First Two Years." Pt. 3. *The Chronicles of Oklahoma* 8, no. 3 (March 1930): 102–4.

10 David D. Morgan to author, February 14, June 26, 2023.

11 "Vetoed."

12 Rushes to Statehood: The Oklahoma Land Runs.

13 David D. Morgan to author, November 26, 2021, February 14, 2023; Dorman, "Dick T. Morgan, Republican from Oklahoma: Prelude to Congress, 1853–1907," 264.

14 C. J. Phillips, "Hon. Dick T. Morgan," *Osage Magazine* (September 1910): 18–21; David D. Morgan to author, November 24, 29, 2021.

15 Copp, *American Settler's Guide*.

16 Dick T. Morgan, *Dick T. Morgan's Manual of the United States Homestead, Townsite and Mining Laws*. Kansas City: Hudson-Kimberly Publishing Company, 1900. Dick T. Morgan, *Morgan's Manual of the United States, Homestead, Townsite, and Mining Laws*, DTMDC-CACRSC, https://dicktmorgan.omeka.net/items/show/1112, accessed July 9, 2022. For a copy of the 1900 edition, *see* Dick T. Morgan, *Morgan's Manual of the United States Homestead, Townsite and Mining Laws*, 5th ed. (Guthrie, Okla.: State Capital Printing Company, 1900), "Morgan, Dick T. *(Morgan's Manual) Homestead and Townsite Laws*," folder 6, box 19, Frederick Samuel Barde Collection, 1890–1916, Research Division, Oklahoma Historical Society, Oklahoma City (hereafter cited as Barde Collection). For a reprint of the 1893 edition, *see* Dick T. Morgan, *Morgan's Manual of the U.S. Homestead and Townsite Laws* (Making of the Modern Law Print Editions, Legal Treatises, 1800–1926). Reproduction from Harvard Law School Library, collection ID ocm25295751. *See also* Fitchett, *History of Noble County*, 227.

17 Stephen J. England, *Oklahoma Christians: A History of Christian Churches and the Start of the Christian Church (Disciples of Christ) in Oklahoma* (Bloomington, Minn.: Bethany Press, 1975), 79, 95.

18 England, *Oklahoma Christians*, 86, 97–98; Porter H. Morgan to Rev. Carl Covey, February 11, 1950, Morgan Family Collection.

19 David D. Morgan to author, November 19, 21, 24, 2021; Dorman, "Dick T. Morgan, Republican from Oklahoma: Prelude to Congress, 1853–1907," 271.

20 Hightower, *Banking in Oklahoma before Statehood*, 182; Forbes, *Guthrie*, 18.

21 Rushes to Statehood: The Oklahoma Land Runs; Hightower, *Banking in Oklahoma before Statehood*, 108-09; Turner, "Cherokee Outlet Opening"; David D. Morgan to author, February 14, 2023.

22 David D. Morgan to author, November 18, 21, 26, 2021; January 3, 2022.

23 Advertisement for Morgan & Pancoast, *Perry Daily Times*, November 21, 1893; Dick T. Morgan, 1893–1902, Morgan Family Collection.

24 "Free! Free!" *Perry Daily Times*, November 29, 1893.

25 "Early Perry Proves Mecca for Lawyers," unsourced newspaper article, n.d., Morgan Family Collection.

26 Porter H. Morgan to Rev. Carl Covey.

27 Porter H. Morgan to Rev. Carl Covey.

28 England, *Oklahoma Christians*, 83–84.

29 Lift Up Your Eyes Unto The Hills, First Christian Church, Perry, Oklahoma, 1949; Year Book 1958–1959—Our Year to Remember, Read and Unite, First Christian Church, Perry, Oklahoma; First Christian Church, Perry, Oklahoma, 1973; Christian Church Yearbook 1976, Perry, Oklahoma; "First Christians Observe 90th Anniversary," unsourced newspaper article, dated by hand October 27, 1983; "First Christian Church, Perry, 101 Years," *Oklahoma Christian*, November–December 1994; Mildred Highfill, "Dick T. Morgan," unsourced section of county history, n.d., all in Morgan Family Collection *See also* "Young People's Society of Christian Endeavor," Wikipedia, https://en.wikipedia.org/wiki/Young_People%27s_Society_of_Christian_Endeavour, accessed April 23, 2023; David D. Morgan to author, November 21, 2021.

30 David D. Morgan to author, December 7, 11, 2023. This story comes from a presentation given at the church's hundredth anniversary celebration. David Morgan later heard the story from relatives in attendance.

31 "A Letter from Dick T. Morgan," *Perry Daily Times*, September 29, 1894.

32 Untitled article, *Guthrie Daily Leader*, September 30, 1894.

33 Untitled article, *Perry Daily Times*, October 3, 1894.

34 Dorman, "Dick T. Morgan, Republican from Oklahoma: Prelude to Congress, 1853–1907," 271.

35 "Hon. Dick Morgan Oklahoma's Giant."

36 Untitled article, *Noble County Sentinel*, October 17, 1895; "At the Christian Church," *Perry Daily Enterprise*, November 4, 1895; Dick T. Morgan, 1893–1902, Morgan Family Collection.

37 "The Territorial Sunday School Convention," *Perry Daily Enterprise*, November 9, 1895; Dick T. Morgan, 1893–1902, Morgan Family Collection.

38 "Parents' Day," *Perry Enterprise*, November 22, 1895.

39 David D. Morgan to author, June 26, August 16, 17, 2023; Porter to Dear Papa, April 25, 1897, Morgan Family Collection.

40 "Cantata," *Perry Daily Enterprise-Times*, November 29, 1895.

41 "Christian," *Perry Daily Enterprise-Times*, December 26, 1895.

CHAPTER SIX

1 David D. Morgan, phone interview by author, March 8, 2022.

2 David D. Morgan to author, November 24, 2021.

3 Vernon S. Braswell, "The Oklahoma Free Homes Bill, 1892–1900," *The Chronicles of Oklahoma* 44, no. 4 (Winter 1966–67): 380–82; Mary Ann Blochowiak, "Justice Is Our Battle Cry: The Territorial Free Home League," *The Chronicles of Oklahoma* 62, no. 1 (Spring 1984): 38; Mary Ann Blochowiak, "Free Home League," The Encyclopedia of Oklahoma History and Culture, Oklahoma Historical Society, https://www.okhistory.org/publications/enc/entry.php?entry=FR014, accessed April 23, 2023.

4 David D. Morgan to author, November 18, 21, 2021.

5 George O. Carney, "Flynn, Dennis Thomas," The Encyclopedia of Oklahoma History and Culture, Oklahoma Historical Society, https://www.okhistory.org/publications/enc/entry?entry=FL006, accessed April 23, 2023.

6 "A Great Record," *Perry Daily Times*, October 29, 1894. Italics in original.

7 "A Great Record."

8 Braswell, "The Oklahoma Free Homes Bill, 1892-1900," 382; Blochowiak, "Justice Is Our Battle Cry," 39–41.

9 "City Schools," *Perry Enterprise-Times*, January 10, 1896.

10 "Rousing Meeting," *Perry Daily Enterprise-Times*, March 12, 1896.

11 "The Grand Concert," *Perry Daily Enterprise-Times*, May 2, 1896.

12 Untitled article, *Perry Enterprise-Times*, May 25, 1896. *See also* "Clara Cleghorn Hoffman," Wikipedia, https://en.wikipedia.org/wiki/Clara Cleghorn_Hoffman, accessed April 23, 2023; "Woman's Christian Temperance Union," Wikipedia, https://en.wikipedia.org/wiki/woman%27s_Christian_Temperance_Union, accessed April 23, 2023.

13 Oklahoma to Denver, flyer, June/July 1902, "Correspondence," folder 6, box 5; "Oklahoma Day," announcement, Oklahoma Sunday School Association, November 1902, "Correspondence," folder 6, box 5; Israel P. Black to Mrs. Ora H. Morgan, November 1, 1902, "Correspondence," folder 6, box 5; L. Haynes Buxton to Mrs. Ora H. Morgan, February 20, 1903, "Correspondence," folder 7, box 5; Report of the Superintendent of the Primary Department, "Correspondence," folder 7, box 5, all in DTMC-CACRSC.

14 "Sunday School Association," *Noble County Sentinel*, May 28, 1896.

15 "Sunday School Convention," *Noble County Sentinel*, August 20, 1896.

16 "Township Conventions," *Noble County Sentinel*, March 18, 1897.

17 "Bible Society," *Perry Enterprise-Times*, July 14, 1896.

18 David D. Morgan to author, November 25, 2021; Dick T. Morgan, *Morgan's Digest of Oklahoma Statutes and Supreme Court Decisions* (Perry, Okla. Terr.: Dick T. Morgan, 1897), Morgan Family Collection.

19 "Hon. Dick T. Morgan," *Noble County Sentinel*, December 23, 1897.

20 Memorial to the Congress of The United States, Oklahoma Territorial Free Home League, in Convention Assembled at El Reno, January 10, 1896, "Homesteads–Oklahoma," OHS Vertical Files.

21 "Good," *Perry Enterprise-Times*, January 16, 1896.

22 Free Homes in Oklahoma. Speech of Hon. Dennis T. Flynn, of Oklahoma, in the House of Representatives, Monday, March 16, 1896, "Homesteads–Oklahoma," OHS Vertical Files.

23 "Machine-Made Delegates," *Guthrie Daily Leader*, March 29, 1896.

24 "Machine-Made Delegates."

25 "Republican Convention of Noble County Met at the Opera House Today," *Perry Enterprise -Times*, August 29, 1896.

26 "Big Time at Pawnee, Dick Morgan Makes a Speech to a Large Audience," *Daily Oklahoma State Capital*, October 26, 1896.

27 "Bryan on Record," *Noble County Sentinel*, November 25, 1897.

28 "Endorsed by Dick T. Morgan," *Noble County Sentinel*, September 3, 1896.

29 David D. Morgan to author, November 21, 2021.

30 The *Perry Enterprise-Times*'s support for Morgan's candidacy cited in untitled article, *Noble County Sentinel*, April 21, 1898.

31 *The Edmond Republican*'s support for Morgan's candidacy cited in untitled article, *Perry Enterprise-Times*, April 28, 1898.

32 *The Woodward News*'s support for Morgan's candidacy cited in untitled article, *Perry Enterprise-Times*, April 28, 1898. Even though he had never served in the military, Morgan was often referred to as a colonel.

33 "Delegate Dick," *Perry Enterprise-Times*, August 18, 1898.

34 "Saturday's Convention," *Perry Enterprise-Times*, August 15, 1898; Dick T. Morgan, 1893–1902, Morgan Family Collection.

35 Untitled articles, *Perry Enterprise-Times*, August 25, 1898; "Morgan Delegates," *Perry Enterprise-Times*, August 25, 1898.

36 "The El Reno Delegation," *Perry Enterprise-Times*, August 25, 1898.

37 "Hon. Dennis T. Flynn," *Perry Enterprise-Times*, August 25, 1898.

38 "Convention Echoes," *Guthrie Daily Leader*, August 26, 1898.

39 "Dick T. Morgan," *Perry Enterprise-Times*, November 3, 1898.

40 Porter Morgan to Papa, August 27, 1898, series 1, folder 1, box 1, DTMC-CACRSC. As reported in the *Perry Enterprise-Times*, Orietta and Porter had taken the northbound train to Terre Haute in early August, leaving Dick to "work his way into the national house of representatives." *See* untitled article, *Perry Enterprise-Times*, August 4, 1898.

41 Letter to Ora Morgan from Dick T. Morgan on September 1, 1898, DTMDC-CACRSC, https://dicktmorgan.omeka.net/items/show/1681, accessed August 12, 2022.

42 Untitled article, *Perry Enterprise-Times*, March 2, 1899.

43 Blochowiak, "Justice Is Our Battle Cry," 45–46; Blochowiak, "Free Home League." The Colored Men's Protective League of Oklahoma convened in Perry in August 1897 and adopted resolutions, including resolution #7: "Resolved, That we endorse the free homestead policy of the republican party, and we urge the passage by congress of the satisfactory free homestead measure which has already passed the senate and is now pending before the house." *See* "League Resolutions," *Daily Oklahoma State Capital*, August 20, 1897.

44 Braswell, "The Oklahoma Free Homes Bill," 390; AZ Quotes, https://www.azquotes.com/quote/1378405, accessed April 23, 2023.

45 David D. Morgan, "Oklahoma Territory Celebrates the Passage of the Free Homes Act," *Alva Review Courier*, May 16, 2021.
46 Free Home Address of Hon. Dick T. Morgan of Perry, O.T. Address at El Reno, Oklahoma, February 16, 1900, "Speeches," folder 12, box 3, DTMC-CACRSC; "Morgan's Eloquence," Oklahoma State Capital, February 17, 1900.
47 DuBois and Mathews, *Galusha A. Grow*, 281–82.
48 Blochowiak, "Justice Is Our Battle Cry," 51–52. For an estimate of aggregate savings to homesteaders in today's dollars, *see* CPI Inflation Calculator, https://www.in2013dollars.com/us/inflation/1900?amount=15000000, accessed April 23, 2023; David D. Morgan to author, April 3, 2023.
49 "Celebration," *Oklahoma State Capital*, June 22, 1900.
50 Morgan, "Oklahoma Territory Celebrates the Passage of the Free Homes Act"; "Alva's Big Celebration," *Guthrie Daily Leader*, May 26, 1900.
51 "Free Homes!" *Blackwell Times-Record*, May 17, 1900; "Free Homes Ratification," *Perry Daily Journal*, May 25, 1900.
52 David D. Morgan to author, August 17, 2023.
53 Perry walkabout, September 16, 2022. Coincidentally, the Morgan brothers and I toured Perry on the 129th anniversary of the Cherokee Outlet run of September 16, 1893. As always, Perry was gearing up to celebrate its foundation story with a parade, rodeo, and reunions for its proud sons and daughters.

CHAPTER SEVEN

1 "Hoosiers," *Guthrie Daily Leader*, February 23, 1900.
2 Hoosier in Oklahoma – Speech by Dick T. Morgan. DTMDC-CACRSC, https://dicktmorgan.omeka.net/items/show/1154, accessed February 23, 2022. After his return to Indiana, former governor George W. Steele was elected to Congress. *See* untitled article, *Clay City* (Ky.) *Chronicle*, October 30, 1891. For Fred R. Morgan's announcement of his candidacy for probate judge of Logan County, *see* "For Probate Judge," *Oklahoma State Capital*, July 1, 4, 5, 7, 8, 1900.
3 Copp, *American Settler's Guide*.
4 Morgan, *Morgan's Manual* (1900), 33–34.
5 "Hon. Dick T. Morgan," (Kay County) *Republican News Journal*, March 23, 1900.
6 In July 1900, Morgan withdrew from the race for Congress. *See* "Hon. Dick T. Morgan Withdraws," *Oklahoma State Capital*, July 26, 1900; Aldrich, *Okie Jesus Congressman*, 106.
7 "Oklahoma Paragraphs," *Oklahoma State Capital*, June 2, 1900.
8 Untitled article, *Noble County Sentinel*, August 23, 1900. See also *Kiowa Chief*, February 1901, July 1901, Morgan Family Collection.
9 "Oklahoma Press Association," *Noble County Sentinel*, May 30, 1901.
10 "Kiowa and Comanche Opening," *Noble County Sentinel*, August 23, 1900.
11 "Kiowa-Comanche," *Noble County Sentinel*, September 27, 1900.
12 Oklahoma Offers Free Homes to 75,000 People!!, Dick T. Morgan sales and

marketing flyer, December 1900, Morgan Family Collection *See also* "Ho! For Oklahoma!" *Noble County Sentinel*, May 30, 1901.

13 "How to Get Free Homes," *Oklahoma State Capital*, July 15, 17, 31, 1900.

14 Rushes to Statehood: The Oklahoma Land Runs; David D. Morgan to author, November 18, 21, 24, 26, 28, 2021.

15 El Reno walkabout, September 15, 2022.

16 David D. Morgan to author, November 18, 21, 24, 26, 28, 2021.

17 First Christian Church, El Reno, Oklahoma, Seventy-fifth Anniversary Observance, March 28, 1965, First Christian Church of El Reno Collection. According to David Morgan, his great-grandfather held that position until 1907.

18 Dick T. Morgan to Mr. Harry Lee Fogg, November 16, 1901, Morgan Family Collection; Fogg Law Firm Collection, El Reno, Oklahoma.

19 Dick T. Morgan letterhead, Morgan Family Collection; Lynda Fogg to author, September 26, 2022.

20 "Statehood for Oklahoma and Indian Territory," *Oklahoma State Capital*, January 31, 1901.

21 "Statehood for Oklahoma and Indian Territory."

22 David D. Morgan to author, November 18, 19, 21, 24, 29, December 3, 2021; February 17, 2022.

23 "Statehood for Oklahoma and Indian Territory."

24 "Statehood for Oklahoma and Indian Territory."

25 "Morgan to Washington," *Weekly Oklahoma State Capital*, February 15, 1902.

26 "Dick Morgan for Congress," *Oklahoma State Capital*, March 18, 1902.

27 Advertisement, *Noble County Sentinel*, September 18, 1902.

28 *Norman Transcript* cited in untitled article, *Noble County Sentinel*, January 16, 1902.

29 Kosmerick, "Morgan, Dick Thompson."

30 "Hon. B. S. McGuire Chosen for Congress," *Oklahoma State Capital*, June 26, 1902.

31 "It Was Pleasing and Harmonious," *Oklahoma State Capital*, June 26, 1902; David D. Morgan to author, August 17, 2023.

32 "Issues in Oklahoma," (Washington, D.C.) *Evening Star*, October 22, 1902.

33 "Morgan on Statehood," *Oklahoma State Capital*, October 26, 1902.

34 "Morgan Well Pleased," *Woodward Dispatch*, May 1, 1903. For D. T. Flynn's explanation of his position on statehood, *see* "Issues in Oklahoma."

35 David D. Morgan to author, November 24, 2021.

36 "Fight for Statehood," (Washington, D.C.) *Evening Star*, November 18, 1902.

37 "Statehood Bill Goes Over Until Monday," *Oklahoma State Capital*, December 12, 1902.

38 Charles Wayne Ellinger, "The Drive for Statehood in Oklahoma, 1889–1906," *The Chronicles of Oklahoma* 41, no. 1 (Spring 1963): 15–37. Ferguson quoted p. 31.

39 David D. Morgan to author, November 19, 21, 24, 29, December 3, 2021; February 17, 2022. *See also* Dick Thompson Morgan, brief bio prepared for The Verdict, n.d., Morgan Family Collection.

40 United States Congress. House. Committee on the Territories, and United States Congress. House. *Statehood for Oklahoma: Hearing before the Committee on the Territories of the House of Representatives*, February 19, 1904. Washington: Gov't. print. off, 1904, 79–95, https://www.loc.gov/item/06001131/, accessed April 24, 2023.

CHAPTER EIGHT

1 David D. Morgan to author, November 19, 24, December 23, 2021.

2 "Territory Topics," *Woodward Dispatch*, December 9, 1904.

3 David D. Morgan, "Tales of a 'Land-Run' Lawyer," *Yankton* (S. Dak.) *Daily Press & Dakotan*, July 2, 2021; David D. Morgan to author, October 18, 2022; David D. Morgan FaceTime with author, October 24, November 7, 2022; Dick T. Morgan to Ora Morgan, June 29, 1904, Morgan Family Collection. For Morgan's appointment as register of the U.S. Land Office in Woodward, *see* Senate, *Congressional Record*, 58th Congress, 3rd session, December 14, 1904, 276, https://www.congress.gov/bound-congressional-record/1904/12/14/senate-section, accessed April 24, 2023.

4 Letter to Ora Morgan from Dick T. Morgan on December 7, 1904, DTMDC-CACRSC, https://dicktmorgan.omeka.net/items/show/1825, accessed March 18, 2022.

5 Letter to Ora Morgan from Dick T. Morgan on December 8, 1904. Morgan Family Collection.

6 Robin D. Hohweiler, interview by author, February 22, 2023; Woodward walkabout, February 22, 2023; Deena K. Fisher and Robin D. Hohweiler, *Woodward Past & Present* (Charleston, S. C.: Arcadia Publishing, 2021).

7 Letter to Ora Morgan from Dick T. Morgan on December 9, 1904, DTMDC-CACRSC, https://dicktmorgan.omeka.net/items/show/1824, accessed March 18, 2022; Letter to Ora Morgan from Dick T. Morgan on December 11, 1904, DTMDC-CACRSC, https://dicktmorgan.omeka.net/items/show/1823, accessed March 18, 2022.

8 David D. Morgan to author, November 18, 21, 24, 26, 2021, January 9, 2022; Louise B. James, *Below Devil's Gap: The Story of Woodward County* (Perkins, Okla.: Evans Publications, 1984), 152–54; Hohweiler interview. On the upside, Bolton was a town booster who complemented his journalism with founding the Oklahoma Livestock Association. As Hohweiler explained, "He was really the key guy in turning this place into a hub for the cattle industry."

9 Pyramid of P's for our Potent Pedagogues, DTMDC-CACRSC, https://dicktmorgan.omeka.net/items/show/951, accessed May 29, 2023; untitled article, *Woodward Dispatch*, July 21, 1905.

10 Henry George, *Progress and Poverty: An Inquiry into the Cause of Industrial Progress and Depressions and of Increase of Want with Increase of Wealth* (New York: Walter J. Black, 1942).

11 George quoted in George O. Carney, "Oklahoma's United States House Delegation and Progressives, 1901–1917" (PhD diss., Oklahoma State University, 1972), 2–3. For George's lifeboat analogy, *see* Henry George, *Progress and Poverty: Why There Are Recessions Amid Poverty and Plenty–and What to Do*

About It!, edited and abridged for modern readers by Bob Drake (New York: Robert Schalkenbach Foundation, 2010), 276.

12 Herbert Croly, *The Promise of American Life* (Cambridge, MA: The Belknap Press of Harvard University Press, 1965), 3.

13 Croly, *Promise of American Life*, 23, 45, 106.

14 "Who is a Progressive?" by Theodore Roosevelt, an Address at Louisville, Kentucky, April 3. Published in The Outlook (April 13, 1912): 809–13, The Unz Review: An Alternative Media Selection, https://www.unz.com/print/Outlook-1912apr13-00809, accessed April 24, 2023; Carney, "Oklahoma's United States House Delegation and Progressives, 1901–1917."

15 Richard Mize, "Sequoyah Convention," The Encyclopedia of Oklahoma History and Culture, Oklahoma Historical Society, https://www.okhistory.org/publications/enc/entry.php?entry=SE021, accessed April 24, 2023.

16 David D. Morgan to author, February 14, 2023.

17 Keith L. Bryant Jr., "Murray, William Henry David," The Encyclopedia of Oklahoma History and Culture, Oklahoma Historical Society, https://www.okhistory.org/publications/enc/entry.php?entry=MU014, accessed April 24, 2023; Robert L. Dorman, *Alfalfa Bill: A Life in Politics* (Norman: University of Oklahoma Press, 2018).

18 William H. Murray, "The Constitutional Convention," *The Chronicles of Oklahoma* 9, no. 2 (June 1931): 130.

19 Robert Henry and Bob Burke, *Gore and Owen: Oklahoma's First Two U.S. Senators* (Oklahoma City: Oklahoma Hall of Fame Publishing, 2022), 183–98.

20 Henry and Burke, *Gore and Owen*, 199–215.

21 Henry and Burke, *Gore and Owen*, 199–215; Murray, "Constitutional Convention," 130. *See also* Danney Goble, *Progressive Oklahoma* (Norman: University of Oklahoma Press, 1980), 193.

22 Murray, "Constitutional Convention," 133.

23 Mize, "Sequoyah Convention."

24 Charles Wayne Ellinger, "Congressional Viewpoint toward the Admission of Oklahoma as a State: 1902–1906," *The Chronicles of Oklahoma* 58, no. 3 (Fall 1980): 294; Charles Wayne Ellinger, "The Drive for Statehood in Oklahoma, 1889–1906," *The Chronicles of Oklahoma* 41, no. 1 (Spring 1963): 15–37.

25 Aldrich, *Okie Jesus Congressman*, 83–85.

26 "New State Negro Question," Address by Hon. E. J. Giddings, Oklahoma City, O.T., September 22, 1906, folder 30, box 19, Barde Collection. For Giddings's trip to the 1912 Democratic Convention in Baltimore, *see* PoliticalGraveyard.com, Speakers and Entertainers at the 1912 National Democratic Convention, https://politicalgraveyard.com/parties/D/1912/speakers.html, accessed April 24, 2023.

27 Giddings, "New State Negro Question."

28 Murray, "Constitutional Convention," 135; Danny M. Adkison, "Constitutional Convention," The Encyclopedia of Oklahoma History and Culture, Oklahoma Historical Society, https://www.okhistory.org/publications/enc/entry.php?entry=CO047, accessed April 24, 2023.

29 David D. Morgan to author, August 18, 2023.

30 Murray quoted in Victor Luckerson, "The Promise of Oklahoma," *Smithsonian* (April 2021), https://www. Smithsonianmag.com/history/unrealized-promise-oklahoma-180977174/, accessed April 24, 2023.
31 Rushes to Statehood: The Oklahoma Land Runs; Richard Mize, "Big Pasture," The Encyclopedia of Oklahoma History and Culture, Oklahoma Historical Society, https://www.okhistory.org/publications/enc/entry.php?entry=BI003, accessed April 24, 2023.
32 Adkison, "Constitutional Convention"; Luckerson, "Promise of Oklahoma."
33 Porter Morgan to Mama and Papa, June 10, 1907, Morgan Family Collection; Porter Morgan to Mama and Papa, August 20, 1907, series 1, folder 33, box 1, DTMC-CACRSC; David D. Morgan to author, October 24, November 7, 2022; December 11, 2023.
34 Our Country—What Made It Great by Dick T. Morgan, DTMDC-CACRSC, https://dicktmorgan.omeka.net/items/show/1147, accessed February 23, 2022; Republican Campaign Speech notes by Dick T. Morgan, DTMDC-CACRSC, https://dicktmorgan.omeka.net/items/show/1159, accessed March 17, 2022.
35 David D. Morgan to author, December 3, 2021, August 4, 2023.
36 Our Country—What Made It Great; Platform of Two great Political Parties 1856–1916 Inclusive, DTMDC-CACRSC, https://dicktmorgan.omeka.net/items/show/1003, accessed March 18, 2022.
37 Republican Campaign Speech notes by Dick T. Morgan, 1907, DTMDC-CACRSC, https://dicktmorgan.omeka.net/files/show/663, accessed April 24, 2023; David D. Morgan to author, November 28, 2021.
38 David D. Morgan to author, November 18, 21, 24, 2021.
39 Dick to "Ode," August 11, 1907, series 1, folder 33, box 1, DTMC-CACRSC. Underscore in original.
40 Adkison, "Constitutional Convention."
41 Aldrich, *Okie Jesus Congressman*, 91.

CHAPTER NINE

1 "Suffrage League Convention," *Muskogee Cimeter*, October 4, 1907; Luckerson, "Promise of Oklahoma."
2 "May Yet Beat Statehood," *Muskogee Cimeter*, October 4, 1907; David D. Morgan to author, February 14, 2023. On the eve of Oklahoma statehood, President Roosevelt appointed Bonaparte to investigate land fraud in Indian Territory. He was a grandson of Jerome Bonaparte, ruler of Westphalia at the behest of his brother, Napoleon I. As a sixty-something bachelor, he was the end of the line for America's connection to a man whose battle cry—*l'audace, l'audace, toujours l'audace!*—once thundered across Europe and struck fear into the hearts of kings. *See* Hightower, *Banking in Oklahoma before Statehood*, 312.
3 "Oklahoma A State," *Beaver Herald*, November 21, 1907; Hightower, *Banking in Oklahoma before Statehood*, 316-21; Michael J. Hightower, *Banking in Oklahoma, 1907–2000* (Norman: University of Oklahoma Press, 2014), 5–6.

4 "Oklahoma Settled in Union," *Guthrie Daily Leader*, November 18, 1907; Muriel H. Wright, "The Wedding of Oklahoma and Miss Indian Territory," *The Chronicles of Oklahoma* 35, no. 3 (Fall 1957): 255–59; Irvin Hurst, *The 46th Star: A History of Oklahoma's Constitutional Convention and Early Statehood* (Oklahoma City: Western Heritage Books, Inc., 1980), 32.

5 Nathan Turner to author, October 24, 2022.

6 Oscar Ameringer, *If You Don't Weaken*, foreword by Carl Sandburg (New York: Henry Holt and Company, 1940), 228. When it was published in 1940, *If You Don't Weaken* was compared favorably in the national press to such iconic memoirs as *The Education of Henry Adams* and *The Autobiography of Lincoln Steffens*.

7 James R. Scales and Danney Goble, *Oklahoma Politics: A History* (Norman: University of Oklahoma Press, 1982), 66; John Thompson, *Closing the Frontier: Radical Response in Oklahoma, 1889–1923* (Norman: University of Oklahoma Press, 1986), 100.

8 James M. Smallwood, "Partners in Progress: Banking and Agribusiness in Oklahoma," in *Banking in the West*, edited by Larry Schweikart, xx. (Manhattan, KS: Sunflower University Press, 1984), 13.

9 "The Landless Man and the Tenant Farmer," *Harlow's Weekly*, January 15, 1919.

10 Hightower, *Banking in Oklahoma, 1907–2000*, 43–49. *See also* Thompson, *Closing the Frontier*, 61; James R. Green, *Grass-Roots Socialism: Radical Movements in the Southwest, 1895–1943* (Baton Rouge: Louisiana State University Press, 1978), 5–7; Michael Kazin, *American Dreamers: How the Left Changed a Nation* (New York: Vintage Books, 2012); H. L. Meredith, "Oscar Ameringer and the Concept of Agrarian Socialism," *The Chronicles of Oklahoma* 45, no. 1 (Spring 1967): 77–83; Gilbert C. Fite, "Farmers' Alliance," The Encyclopedia of Oklahoma History and Culture, Oklahoma Historical Society, https://www.okhistory.org/publications/enc/entry?entry=FA017, accessed April 24, 2023; John Thompson, "Ameringer, Oscar (1870–1943)," The Encyclopedia of Oklahoma History and Culture, Oklahoma Historical Society, https://www.okhistory.org/publications/enc/entry?entry=AM014, accessed April 24, 2023.

11 Garin Burbank, *When Farmers Voted Red: The Gospel of Socialism in the Oklahoma Countryside, 1910–1924* (Westport, Conn.: Greenwood Press, 1976), 56–57.

12 Thompson, "Ameringer, Oscar"; Howard Zinn, *The Twentieth Century* (New York: HarperPerennial, 2003), 55; Hightower, *Banking in Oklahoma, 1907–2000*, 45.

13 Scales and Goble, *Oklahoma Politics*, 64; Green, *Grass-Roots Socialism*, 124.

14 Green, *Grass-Roots Socialism*, 39–40; Zinn, *The Twentieth Century*, 55.

15 Meagan Day, "When Oklahoma Was the Heartland of American Socialism," *Jacobin Magazine*, August 15, 2021, https://jacobinmag.com/2021/08/oklahoma-green-corn-rebellion-washington-wwi-tenant-farmer-poverty-socialist-party-renters-union-working-class-union-wcu, accessed April 25, 2023.

16 "'Jim Crow' Bills Are In," unsourced newspaper article, December 3, 1907, Scrapbook, July 8, 1907–May 16, 1908, box 43, vol. 19, 112-15, Barde Collection; Hurst, *The 46th Star*, 52; Hightower, *Banking in Oklahoma, 1907-2000*, 15, 409n55.

17 David D. Morgan to author, November 21, 2021, January 2, 2022; C. J. Phillips, "Hon. Dick T. Morgan: An Appreciation by C. J. Phillips," *Osage Magazine*.

18 Resolutions, Republicans of the Second Congressional District, February 26, 1908, "Morgan, Dick T. (politics)," folder 7, box 19, Barde Collection; Resolutions and Thanks of Members of the Woodward Commercial Club, and Citizens of Woodward, Oklahoma, to the Honorable Dick T. Morgan, March 1908, "Miscellaneous," folder 10, box 9, DTMC-CACRSC.

19 Document beginning with, "A very enthusiastic Republican meeting...," May 14, 1908, "Morgan, Dick T. (politics)," folder 7, box 19, Barde Collection.

20 "The Dick Morgan Banner."

21 David D. Morgan to author, January 2, 2022, February 14, 2023; "Prospective Congressmen Are Eyeing Redistricting," unsourced newspaper article, October 15, 1910, "Morgan, Dick T. (politics)," folder 7, box 19, Barde Collection; Jim Bissett, "Socialist Party," The Encyclopedia of Oklahoma History and Culture, Oklahoma Historical Society, https://www.okhistory.org/publications/enc/entry.php?entry=SO001, accessed April 25, 2023.

22 David D. Morgan to author, November 24, 2021, February 14, 2023. For more on Barritt Galloway as he approached his hundredth birthday in July 1989, *see* "Teacher of Immigrants Nearing Century Mark," *Oklahoma City Times*, July 24, 1989.

23 Julien C. Monnet, "The Latest Phase of Negro Disfranchisement," *Harvard Law Review* 26, no. 1 (November 1912): 42–63, https://doi.org/10.2307/1324271, accessed April 25, 2023; Dick T. Morgan, "A Partisan Measure," undated speech likely given in 1909, Morgan Family Collection; David D. Morgan to author, August 18, 2023. Oklahoma's amendment reads as follows: "No person shall be registered as an elector of this state or be allowed to vote in any election herein unless he be able to read and write any section of the Constitution of the State of Oklahoma; but no person, who was, on January 1, 1866, or at any time prior thereto entitled to vote under any form of government, or who, at that time, resided in some foreign nation, and no lineal descendant of such person shall be denied the right to register and vote because of his inability to so read and write sections of such Constitution. Precinct election inspectors having in charge the registration of electors shall enforce the provisions of this section at the time of registration, provided registration be required. Should registration be dispensed with, the provisions of this section shall be enforced by the precinct election officers, when electors apply for ballots to vote."

24 Monnet, "The Latest Phase of Negro Disfranchisement," 43.

25 Monnet, "The Latest Phase of Negro Disfranchisement," 61–62.

26 Dick Thompson Morgan, brief bio prepared for The Verdict, n.d., Morgan Family Collection; David D. Morgan to author, November 24, 2021, December 26, 2023. Morgan's campaign manager from 1910, Homer Boardmen, was the U.S. Attorney who prosecuted county election officials for enforcing the grandfather clause. He was fired shortly after Woodrow Wilson was elected President in 1916. David D. Morgan to author, February 14, 2023. *See also* Alfred L. Brophy, "*Guinn v. United States* (1915)," The Encyclopedia of Oklahoma History and Culture, Oklahoma Historical Society, https://www.okhistory.org/publications/enc/entry?entry=GU001, accessed April 26, 2023; "Guinn v. United States," Wikipedia, https://en.wikipedia.org/wiki/

Guinn_v._United_States#, accessed April 26, 2023; Edward Douglass White and Supreme Court of the United States, *U.S. Reports: Guinn v. United States, 238 U.S. 347*, 1915, Periodical, https://www.loc.gov/item/usrep238347/, accessed April 26, 2023.

27 *Congressional Record*, vol. 44, 4–8, cited in Dick T. Morgan's Official Record: How He Voted When in Congress, Taken from the Congressional Record (Oklahoma City: Warden Printing Co., n.d.), "Morgan, Dick Thompson," OHS Vertical Files; Carney, "Oklahoma's United States House Delegation and Progressives, 1901-1917," 89–91; "The Tariff on Gypsum," *Oklahoma State Capital*, April 6, 1909; "Payne-Aldrich Tariff Act," Wikipedia, https://en.wikipedia.org/wiki/Payne–Aldrich_Tariff_Act, accessed April 25, 2023; David D. Morgan to author, September 8, 9, 2021.

28 Carney, "Oklahoma's United States House Delegation and Progressives, 1901–1917," 98–104; Letter from Porter H. Morgan to 'Papa' on December 17, 1909—Personal letter, DTMDC-CACRSC, https://dicktmorgan.omeka.net/items/show/444, accessed March 23, 2023.

29 Carney, "Oklahoma's United States House Delegation and Progressives, 1901–1917," 98–104; "Payne-Aldrich Tariff Act," Wikipedia.

30 Carney, "Oklahoma's United States House Delegation and Progressives, 1901–1917," 89.

31 *Congressional Record*, vol. 44, 4758, vol. 44, 5143. Cited in Morgan's Official Record.

32 Down the Mississippi River: St. Louis to the Gulf, pamphlet, St. Louis Business Men's Down the Mississippi, League and the Lakes-to-Gulf Deep Waterway Assn., October 25, 1909, series 8, folder 2, box 8, DTMC-CACRSC; Letter from Dick T. Morgan to 'Son' on January 15, 1910—Personal letter, DTMDC-CACRSC, https://dicktmorgan.omeka.net/files/show/396, accessed March 23, 2023.

33 Democratic Congressional Committee, Second Congressional District, Morgan's Official Record, "Morgan, Dick Thompson," OHS Vertical Files; Carney, "Oklahoma's United States House Delegation and Progressives, 1901–1917," 118–19.

34 David D. Morgan to author, November 16, 2022; Carney, "Oklahoma's United States House Delegation and Progressives, 1901–1917," 119.

35 *Wichita Eagle* cited in "Morgan Always Present," unsourced newspaper article, dated by hand July 12, 1910, "Morgan, Dick T. (politics)," folder 7, box 19, Barde Collection; C. J. Phillips, "Hon. Dick T. Morgan: An Appreciation by C. J. Phillips," *Osage Magazine*.

36 "Former Indiana Man Tells about Oklahoma," *Indianapolis News*, July 1, 1910.

CHAPTER TEN

1 Aldrich, *Okie Jesus Congressman*, 91.

2 "Party O.K. for Taft and Tariff," unsourced newspaper article, dated by hand August 7, 1910, "County Attorney Resigns," unsourced newspaper article, September 22, 1910, "Morgan Here after Custer County Tour," unsourced newspaper article, October 1, 1910, all in "Morgan, Dick T. (politics)," folder 7, box 19, Barde Collection.

3 "Good Roads as the Hope of the Nation," *Baltimore News*, May 20, 1909, OS box 1; National Good Roads Congress, "Oklahoma," folder 6, box 4, both in DTMC-CACRSC.

4 "Fulton Clashes with this Rival," unsourced newspaper article, October 15, 1910, "Morgan, Dick T. (politics)," folder 7, box 19, Barde Collection.

5 "Prospective Congressmen Are Eyeing Redistricting," unsourced newspaper article, October 15, 1910, "Morgan, Dick T. (politics)," folder 7, box 19, Barde Collection.

6 Carney, "Oklahoma's United States House Delegation and Progressives, 1901–1917," 122–24.

7 Untitled article, *Oklahoma Farmer and Laborer*, September 30, 1910.

8 "Compare their Records," *Daily Oklahoman*, October 5, 1910.

9 "Labors of a Statesman," *Daily Oklahoman*, October 14, 1910; "The System Republicans," *Daily Oklahoman*, October 26, 1910.

10 "An Upright and Fearless Public Servant," unsourced campaign brochure, dated by hand 1910, "Morgan, Dick Thompson." OHS Vertical Files.

11 Carney, "Oklahoma's United States House Delegation and Progressives, 1901–1917," 137–40.

12 Statement of suit to Dick T. Morgan by Elmer Fulton, DTMDC-CACRSC, https://dicktmorgan.omeka.net/items/show/861, accessed March 27, 2023; "Fulton Will Contest Dick Morgan's Seat," *El Reno Daily American*, December 19, 1910.

13 Western Union Telegram from Dick T. Morgan to Porter Morgan on January 14, 1911, DTMDC-CACRSC, https://dicktmorgan.omeka.net/items/show/876, accessed March 27, 2023. The president of American National Bank, Frank P. Johnson, was the author's great-grandfather. *See also* Michener & Pence to Mr. Morgan, January 21, 1911, series 3, folder 25, box 2, DTMC-CACRSC.

14 Aldrich, *Okie Jesus Congressman*, 92; Carney, "Oklahoma's United States House Delegation and Progressives, 1901–1917," 139–40; Kosmerick, "Morgan, Dick Thompson"; Robert L. Dorman, "Dick T. Morgan, Republican from Oklahoma: The Congressional Years, 1908–20," *The Chronicles of Oklahoma* 100, no. 3 (Fall 2022): 267.

15 David D. Morgan to author, November 24, 25, 2021; Thoburn, *Standard History*, vol. 4, 1674.

16 "Sherman Antitrust Act," Wikipedia, https://en.wikipedia.org/wiki/Sherman_Antitrust_Act, accessed April 25, 2023.

17 David D. Morgan to author, November 25, 28, 2021.

18 "Speech – Control of Corporations: Control Must Begin When Competition Ceases," DTMDC-CACRSC, https://dicktmorgan.omeka.net/items/show/895, accessed February 23, 2022.

19 "Control of Corporations." In Greek mythology, nine muses, all daughters of Zeus, guided and inspired artists. Clio was the muse of history.

20 "Control of Corporations."

21 Carney, "Oklahoma's United States House Delegation and Progressives, 1901–1917," 198–201.

22 David D. Morgan to author, January 8, 2022.
23 "Morgan Wore Roosevelt Pin at Convention," *Guthrie Daily Star*, March 17, 1912.
24 H. G. Eastman to Hon. Wm. B. McKinley, March 8, 1912, series 2, folder 14, box 2, DTMC-CACRSC.
25 Dick T. Morgan to Porter H. Morgan, February 27, 1912, series 2, box 2, folder 14, DTMC-CACRSC.
26 Dick T. Morgan to Mr. Porter H. Morgan, May 2, 1912, series 2, folder 14, box 2, DTMC-CACRSC.
27 House. *Congressional Record* 48, part 9, 62nd Congress, 2nd session, July 9, 1912, 8800.
28 "Morgan Meeting," *Daily Oklahoman*, July 25, 1912.
29 Speech - Wealth: Its Conservation, Taxation, Control, Distribution, and Production, DTMDC-CACRSC, https://dicktmorgan.omeka.net/items/show/890, accessed May 30, 2023.
30 "Progressives Quit Reactionary Candidates," *Harlow's Weekly*, October 19, 1912.
31 "Tearing Off the Mask," *Daily Oklahoman*, October 14, 1912.
32 "Carney Will Guard People's Interests," *Daily Oklahoman*, November 3, 1912.
33 Letter from Dick T. Morgan to Ora on November 9, 1912, DTMDC-CACREC, https://dicktmorgan.omeka.net/items/show/1048, accessed April 3, 2023.
34 David D. Morgan to author, January 2, 2022; Carney, "Oklahoma's United States House Delegation and Progressives, 1901–1917," 207, 213; Aldrich, *Okie Jesus Congressman*, 92. For more on Socialism's appeal both nationally and in Oklahoma, *see* Adam Hochschild, *American Midnight: The Great War, A Violent Peace and Democracy's Forgotten Crisis* (New York and Boston: Mariner Books, 2022), 181–82. Roosevelt, quoted in Hochschild, *American Midnight*, 182.
35 David D. Morgan to author, January 2, 2022.
36 Dorman, "Dick T. Morgan from Oklahoma: The Congressional Years," 268.
37 David D. Morgan to author, December 3, 2021; Dorman, "Dick T. Morgan, Republican from Oklahoma: The Congressional Years," 269; John J. Carney, Dick T. Morgan, Mary S. Stotler, *Contested Election Case of John J. Carney v. Dick T. Morgan from the Second Congressional District of Oklahoma* (Leopold Classic Library, 2021), 3–7, 11–20. For Porter H. Morgan's brief on behalf of his father, *see* Contested Election Case: John J. Carney, Contestant, vs. Dick T. Morgan, Contestee, "Committee Reports," folder 14, box 4, DTMC-CACRSC. For Morgan's lobbying effort on behalf of Boardman's appointment as U.S. Attorney, *see* Letter from Dick Morgan to H. N. Boardman on May 23, 1912, DTMDC-CACRSC, https://dicktmorgan.omeka.net/items/show/669, accessed April 3, 2023.
38 "Inaugural Address of Gov. Woodrow Wilson," *Oklahoma State Capital*, January 18, 1911.
39 Carney, "Oklahoma's United States House Delegation and Progressives, 1901–1917," 189–90.
40 The Progressive (Bull Moose) Party went into rapid decline in elections up to 1918 and had disappeared altogether by 1920.

41 Woodrow Wilson, *The New Freedom: A Call for the Emancipation of the Generous Energies of a People* (New York: Doubleday, Page & Company, 1913); "The New Freedom: A Call for the Emancipation of the Generous Energies of a People," Wikipedia, https://en.wikisource.org/wiki/The_New_Freedom:_A_Call_for_the_Emancipation_of_the_Generous_Energies_of_a_People, 3–4, accessed April 25, 2023.

42 Wilson, *The New Freedom*, 5–6.

43 Wilson, *The New Freedom*, 20–21.

44 Wilson, *The New Freedom*, 36–40.

45 Thoburn, *Standard History*, vol. 4, 1674; David D. Morgan to author, November 24, 25, 2021.

46 Interstate Trade Commission Hearings before the Committee on Interstate and Foreign Commerce, House of Representatives, 63rd Congress, 2nd session, January 30 to February 16, 1914 (Washington: Government Printing Office, 1914), 162–94; Statement of Hon. Dick T. Morgan, A Representative in Congress from the State of Oklahoma, Saturday, February 7, 1914, 162, https://play.google.com/store/books/details/Interstate_Trade_Commission_Hearings_Sixty_third_C?id=vg09AAAAYAAJ&gl=US&pli=1, accessed April 25, 2023.

47 Interstate Trade Commission Hearings, 162–63; Platforms of the Two Great Political Parties, July 1912, "Platforms," folder 4, box 5, DTMC-CACRSC.

48 Interstate Trade Commission Hearings, 163–71.

49 Interstate Trade Commission Hearings, 180.

50 Interstate Trade Commission Hearings, 186.

51 Interstate Trade Commission Hearings, 191.

52 "Federal Trade Commission," Federal Trade Commission, https://www.ftc.gov/about-ftc/our-history, accessed April 25, 2023; "Federal Trade Commission," Wikipedia, https://en.wikipedia.org/wiki/Federal_Trade_Commission, accessed April 25, 2023; "Federal Trade Commission," Wikipedia, https://www.ftc.gov/about-ftc/our-history/our-seal, accessed April 25, 2023.

53 David D. Morgan to author, November 25, 28, 2021.

54 Cummins quoted in William E. Kovacic, "The Federal Trade Commission and Congressional Oversight of Antitrust Enforcement," *Tulsa Law Review* 17, no. 4 (Summer 1982): 592, https://digitalcommons.law.utulsa.edu/tlr/vol17/iss4/1/, accessed April 25, 2023.

55 Kovacic, "The Federal Trade Commission."

56 "Federal Trade Commission," Wikipedia, https://en.m.wikipedia.org/wiki/Federal_Trade_Commission, accessed July 16, 2023. Morgan delivered his "Control of Corporations" speech on February 20, 1912.

57 Andrew Glasser, "Woodrow Wilson Creates Federal Trade Commission, Sept. 26, 1914," *Politico*, September 26, 2012, https://www.politico.com/story/2012/09/this-day-in-politics-081672.

58 "Dick Thompson Morgan: 'Father of the FTC'," *Terre Haute Tribune Star*, April 22, 2018.

59 David D. Morgan to author, August 18, 2023.

60 David D. Morgan to author, February 14, 2023.

61 "Feds Open Probe on ChatGPT," *Charlottesville Daily Progress*, July 15, 2023.

62 David D. Morgan to author, July 14, 2023.

63 House. *Congressional Record* 51, part 15, 63rd Congress, 2nd session, September 10, 1914, 14941–14943.

CHAPTER ELEVEN

1 "Oscar Underwood," Wikipedia, https://en.wikipedia.org/wiki/Oscar_Underwood, accessed April 25, 2023; Carney, "Oklahoma's United States House Delegation and Progressives, 1901–1917," 222–23.

2 Carney, "Oklahoma's United States House Delegation and Progressives, 1901–1917," 223–29.

3 House. *Congressional Record* 50, part 6, 63rd Congress, 1st session, September 30, 1913, 5262–5265; Carney, "Oklahoma's United States House Delegation and Progressives, 1901–1917," 232.

4 House. *Congressional Record* 50, part 3, 63rd Congress, 1st session, July 5, 1913. 2324–26; Carney, "Oklahoma's United States House Delegation and Progressives, 1901–1917," 229–31. Wilson quoted p. 229.

5 O. M. W. Sprague, "The American Crisis of 1907," *Economic Journal* 18 (September 1908): 354–55; Robert F. Bruner and Sean D. Carr, *The Panic of 1907: Lessons Learned from the Market's Perfect Storm* (Hoboken, N.J.: John Wiley and Sons, Inc., 2007), 7.

6 Arthur M. Schlesinger Jr., ed., *The Almanac of American History* (New York: Putnam, 1983), 412–13; Alfred D. Chandler, "The Beginnings of 'Big Business' in American Industry," *Business History Review* 33, no. 1 (Spring 1959): 20; Bruner and Carr, *Panic of 1907*, 38–41; Sprague, "American Crisis," 357–60; Charles P. Kindleberger and Robert Z. Aliber, Manias, *Panics and Crashes: A History of Financial Crises* (Basingstoke, UK: Palgrave MacMillan, 2005), 28; Alexander D. Noyes, "A Year after the Panic of 1907," *Quarterly Journal of Economics* 23 (February 1909): 188; Liaquat Ahamed, *Lords of Finance: The Bankers Who Broke the World* (New York: Penguin, 2009), 53–54; Ron Chernow, *The Death of the Banker: The Decline and Fall of the Great Financial Dynasties and the Triumph of the Small Investor* (New York: Vintage Books, 1997), 105; Hightower, *Banking in Oklahoma, 1907–2000*, 6–8.

7 Bruner and Carr, *Panic of 1907*, 145.

8 "Aldrich Presents Plan of New Finance System," *Oklahoma State Capital*, January 18, 1911.

9 Carolyn G. Hanneman, "Weaver, Claude (1867–1954)," The Encyclopedia of Oklahoma History and Culture, Oklahoma Historical Society, https://www.okhistory.org/publications/enc/entry?entry=WE003, accessed April 26, 2023; Kenny L. Brown, "Owen, Robert Latham (1856–1947)," The Encyclopedia of Oklahoma History and Culture, Oklahoma Historical Society, https://www.okhistory.org/publications/enc/entry?entry=OW003, accessed April 26, 2023.

10 Henry and Burke, *Gore and Owen*, 211–14.

11 Henry and Burke, *Gore and Owen*, 218–28, 241–43.

12 House. *Congressional Record* 51, part 2, 63rd Congress, 1st session,

December 22, 1913, 1456–1459; Dick to Ode, September 13, 1913, series 1, box 1, folder 57, DTMC-CACRSC.

13 House. *Congressional Record* 51, part 2, 63rd Congress, 1st session, December 22, 1913, 1456–1459; David D. Morgan to author, November 25, 30, 2021; "National Bank Deposits to be Guaranteed," *Perry Daily Enterprise-Times*, December 4, 1913.

14 Modern History Project, The Federal Reserve Act, https://modernhistoryproject.org/mhp?Article=FedReserve&C=3.0#Act, accessed April 26, 2023; David D. Morgan to author, November 25, 30, 2021, May 24, 2023.

15 Brands, *American Colossus*, 618–19.

16 David D. Morgan to author, November 25, 30, 2021, May 24, 2023.

17 Carney, "Oklahoma's United States House Delegation and Progressives, 1901–1917," 33–34, 47–49; Dorman, "Dick T. Morgan from Oklahoma: The Congressional Years," 270.

18 David D. Morgan to author, February 14, 2023.

19 House. *Congressional Record* 51, part 10, 63rd Congress, 2nd session, June 1, 1914, 9564.

20 Aldrich, *Okie Jesus Congressman*, 92–93; David D. Morgan to author, February 14, 2023.

21 House. *Congressional Record* 51, part 4, 63rd Congress, 2nd session, February 19, 1914, 3658–3692.

22 Writings by Dick T. Morgan about the subject of Mother, Mother's Day, DTMDC-CACRSC, https://dicktmorgan.omeka.net/items/show/1132, accessed May 15, 2023.

23 David D. Morgan to author, November 26, 2021; Thoburn, *Standard History*, vol. 4, 1674–75.

24 Dick T. Morgan, *Land Credits: A Plea for the American Farmer* (New York: Thomas Y. Crowell Company, 1915), xii–xiii. *See also* "Published Book – Land Credits A Plea for The American Farmer by Dick T. Morgan," DTMDC-CACRSC, https://dicktmorgan.omeka.net/items/show/1051, accessed February 23, 2022.

25 *Report of the Country Life Commission: special message from the President of the United States transmitting the report of the Country Life Commission* (Washington: Government Printing Office, 1909). *See* "Liberty Hyde Bailey: A Man for All Seasons," Cornell University Library, https://rmc.library.cornell.edu/bailey/commission/commission_5.html, accessed April 26, 2023; "Country Life Movement," Wikipedia, https://en.wikipedia.org/wiki/Country_life_movement, accessed April 26, 2023.

26 Joanne Dearcopp and Christine Hill Smith, eds. Foreword by David M. Wrobel. *Unknown No More: Recovering Senora Babb* (Norman: University of Oklahoma Press, 2021), 112–15.

27 Morgan, *Land Credits*, 4.

28 Morgan, *Land Credits*, 77–78.

29 Morgan, *Land Credits*, 12–14.

30 Morgan, *Land Credits*, 213–14.

31 Morgan, *Land Credits*, 55.

32 Morgan, *Land Credits*, 49–50.

33 Morgan, *Land Credits*, 80–81.

34 Morgan, *Land Credits*, 119.

35 Morgan, *Land Credits*, 86.

36 Morgan, *Land Credits*, 106-7.

37 Morgan, *Land Credits*, 230.

38 "The Business of Farming," *The Nation*, February 17, 1916, OS box 1, DTMC-CACRSC.

39 Thoburn, *Standard History*, vol. 4, 1675.

40 Dick T. Morgan, "Government Aid: Rural Credits Division in Congress—How to Secure Unity and Harmony," *Farmers' Open Forum* 1, no. 4 (December 1915): 1, 13.

41 "Congressman Morgan at Lincoln Club," *Portland Sunday Press and Times*, February 13, 1916; "Nearly 300 Republicans Honor Memory of Lincoln, Big Banquet at Lafayette," *Portland Sunday Press and Times*, February 17, 1916, both in OS box 3, DTMC-CACRSC.

42 "Urgent Action on Rural Credits Bill," *Washington* (D.C.) *Times*, March 30, 1916.

43 House. *Congressional Record* 53, part 8, 64th Congress, 1st session, May 9, 1916, 7740–7741.

44 President Woodrow Wilson's secretary to Hon. Dick T. Morgan, July 12, 1916, Morgan Family Collection; David D. Morgan to author, December 4, 2021, July 14, 2023.

45 "Federal Farm Loan Act," Wikipedia, https://en.wikipedia.org/wiki/Federal_Farm_Loan_Act, accessed April 26, 2023; The Federal Farm Loan Act, approved July 17, 1916, "Bills," folder 12, box 4, DTMC-CACRSC.

46 Kent Crain and Felix Hensley, interview by author, March 16, 2011, Ponca City, Oklahoma, Michael J. Hightower Collection, Research Division, Oklahoma Historical Society, Oklahoma City, and follow-up correspondence, July 15, 2013, August 26, 2013, via phone and email; American AgCredit, http://www.agloan.com/, accessed April 26, 2023. *See also* Hightower, *Banking in Oklahoma, 1907–2000*, 294–95.

CHAPTER TWELVE

1 Aldrich, *Okie Jesus Congressman*, 93; Dick to Ode, September 13, 1916, series 1, folder 71, box 1, DTMC-CACRSC; "Charles W. Fairbanks," Wikipedia, https://en.wikipedia.org/wiki/Charles_W._Fairbanks; David D. Morgan, phone interview by author, April 12, 2023, Charlottesville and Oklahoma City. Had Republicans returned to the White House in 1916, Fairbanks would have been only the third (and only non-consecutive) vice president to serve under multiple presidents, after George Clinton and John C. Calhoun.

2 "Incidents of the Election," *Cimarron* (Boise City, Okla.) *News*, November 9, 1916.

3 "Hughes Is Elected," *Guymon Herald*, November 9, 1916.

4 Federal Farm Loan Bonds Supply Funds to Finance Farmers, *The First Year's Work*, advertisement, n.d., Morgan Family Collection.

5 Dick to Ode, April 2, 1917, "Correspondence," folder 1, box 2, DTMC-CACRSC.

6 David D. Morgan to author, January 2, 2022, March 14, 2023.

7 "Hon. Dick Morgan Oklahoma's Giant."

8 Letter from Dick T. Morgan to Friend on October 12, 1918, DTMDC-CACRSC, https://dicktmorgan.omeka.net/items/show/730, accessed April 3, 2023.

9 David D. Morgan to author, October 27, 2021, January 2, 2022.

10 Hochschild, *American Midnight*, 85–94.

11 Entered the War Reluctantly, speech by Dick T. Morgan, DTMDC-CACRSC, https://dicktmorgan.omeka.net/items/show/978, accessed July 10, 2023.

12 Day, "When Oklahoma Was the Heartland of American Socialism."

13 Dick to Ode, May 30, 1917, series 1, folder 2, box 2, DTMC-CACRSC.

14 House. *Congressional Record* 55, part 2, 65th Congress, 1st session, May 2, 1917, 1693–1725.

15 Hon. Dick T. Morgan, For His Personal Information and Use, Statement for May 1917, 1st Session, 65th Congress, DTMDC-CACRSC.

16 "Sedition Act of 1918," Wikipedia, https://en.wikipedia.org/wiki/Sedition_Act_of_1918#cite_ref-12; Hochschild, *American Midnight*, 60–61.

17 Day, "When Oklahoma Was the Heartland of American Socialism"; Scales and Goble, *Oklahoma Politics*, 88–89; Hightower, *Banking in Oklahoma, 1907–2000*, 48–49, 123.

18 "Daylight Attack Will Be Made on Defiant Draft Resisters," *Tulsa Daily World*, August 4, 1917.

19 Hochschild, *American Midnight*, 185–86.

20 "Uprising of the Clans," *Ada Star-Democrat*, August 10, 1917; "Arrest Socialists on Conspiracy Charge," *Ada Star-Democrat*, August 3, 1917. *See also* "Espionage Act of 1917," Wikipedia, https://en.wikipedia.org/wiki/Espionage_Act_of_1917.

21 David D. Morgan to author, October 27, 2021, January 2, 2022.

22 Speech – The President and Congress in War Times, DTMDC-CACRSC, https://dicktmorgan.omeka.net/items/show/915, accessed January 31, 2023.

23 "Departmental Reorganization Act," Wikipedia, https://en.wikipedia.org/wiki/Departmental_Reorganization_Act, accessed April 26, 2023; "Lee Slater Overman," Wikipedia, https://en.wikipedia.org/wiki/Lee_Slater_Overman, accessed April 26, 2023.

24 "Duty of the Hour," *Cimarron* (Boise City, Okla.) *News*, June 20, 1918, Personal Newspaper Clippings, DTMDC- CACRSC, https://dicktmorgan.omeka.net/items/show/1106, accessed March 3, 2022. For other references in Oklahoma newspapers, *see* "Duty of the Hour," *Helena Star*, June 20, 1918; *Cleo Chieftain*, June 21, 1918; *Enid Events*, June 20, 1918; *Morrison, Noble County, Transcript*, June 20, 1918; *Tyrone Observer*, June 20, 1918; *Wakita Herald*, June 19, 1918; *State Valley Star*, June 20, 1918; "Straight Talk," *Manchester Journal*, June 21, 1918; *Kremlin Journal*, June 20, 1918; *Medford Patriot Star*, June 20, 1918; *Fairview Enterprise*, June 21, 1918; *Buffalo Republican*, June 20, 1918; *Woodward News Bulletin*, June 21, 1918; *Rosston News*, June 20, 1918; *Pond*

Creek Vidette News, June 20, 1918; *Texhoma Times*, June 21, 1918; (Kay County) *Newkirk Republican News Journal*, June 21, 1918; *Avard Tribune*, June 21, 1918; *Beaver Herald*, June 20, 1918; *Fairview Republican*, June 21, 1918.

25 "Congressman Dick T. Morgan," *Alva Review Courier*, June 27, 1918.

26 "None Oppose Morgan for Congress in Primary," *Carmen Headlight*, June 21, 1918. *See also* "Dick T. Announces," *Curtis Courier*, June 20, 1918; "Dick Morgan Announces," *Perry Republican*, June 20, 1918; "For Congress," *Blackwell Times Record*, June 20, 1918.

27 Praise for Morgan and his support for Wilson's war policies can be found in "Congressman," *Ames Review*, June 21, 1918; "Morgan for Congress" *Enid Events*, June 20, 1918; "A Good Endorsement," *Morrison, Noble County, Transcript*, June 20, 1918; "Morgan for Congress," *Ponca City Daily Courier*, June 18, 1918; "Morgan for Congress," *State Valley Star*, June 20, 1918; "Morgan for Congress," *Red Rock Record*, June 20, 1918; "Morgan for Congress," *Supply Republican*, June 20, 1918; "Morgan for Congress," *Fairview Enterprise*, June 21, 1918; "Morgan for Congress," *Speermore Advocate*, June 21, 1918; "Morgan for Congress," *Woodward Democrat*, June 21, 1918; "Morgan for Congress," *Rosston News*, June 20, 1918; "Morgan for Congress," *Pond Creek Vidette News*, June 20, 1918; "Morgan Announces for Congress," *Texhoma Times*, June 21, 1918.

28 "Morgan for Congress," *Fairview Republican*, June 21, 1918; "Morgan for Congress," *Cherokee Republican*, June 21, 1918; Untitled article, *Covington Record*, July 4, 1918; "We're All for Morgan," *Buffalo Republican*, June 20, 1918.

29 "Dick T. Morgan for Congress," "A Good Endorsement," *Morrison, Noble County, Transcript*, June 20, 1918.

30 David D. Morgan to author, December 4, 2021.

31 "President Wilson Dragged into Mire," *Guymon Herald*, October 31, 1918.

32 "Make-Up of House," *Oklahoma City Times*, November 6, 1918; "How Votes for Congress Stand," *Washington* (D.C.) *Times*, November 6, 1918.

33 "Republicans Win General Victory," *Guymon Herald*, November 7, 1918;

David D. Morgan to author, July 9, 2023.

34 "Congress Probably Republican," *Beaver Herald*, November 7, 1918.

35 "Morgan Waits and Gets High Republican Place," *Oklahoma State Register*, March 13, 1919.

36 Dick to Ode, June 3, 1919, "Correspondence," folder 7, box 2, DTMC-CACRSC.

37 House. *Congressional Record* 58, part 1, 66th Congress, 1st session, May 30, 1919, 437.

38 Letter and full speech from Dick T. Morgan supporting the Homes for Soldiers Bill, financing information and biography. DTMDC-CACRSC, https://dicktmorgan.omeka.net/items/show/860, accessed January 15, 2023. For Morgan's comments on the homes for soldiers bill on the House floor, *see* House. *Congressional Record* 58, part 2, 66th Congress, 1st session, June 16, 1919, 1193–1198.

39 "The American Legion," *Harlow's Weekly*, October 1, 1919. On September 26, 1919, the State Executive Committee agreed to publish its articles in *Harlow's Weekly* as the official medium of the American Legion of Oklahoma.

See also "Morgan Is Active," *Harlow's Weekly*, December 10, 1919.

40 Letter and full speech from Dick T. Morgan supporting the Homes for Soldiers Bill, financing information and biography.

41 "About the Zinc Tariff," *Harlow's Weekly*, September 24, 1919.

42 Letter from W. R. Samuel to Dick T. Morgan, DTMDC-CACRSC, https://dicktmorgan.omeka.net/items/show/856, accessed January 15, 2023; Hon. Dick T. Morgan, "Financial Legislation from Next Congress to Meet Exigencies of Reconstruction," *State Banker* (August 1919), 9–10, 16–19, OS box 1, DTMC-CACRSC; Full speech "Homes for Soldiers" by Dick T. Morgan, DTMDC-CACRSC, https://dicktmorgan.omeka.net/items/show/857, accessed January 15, 2023.

43 Dick Thompson Morgan, brief bio prepared for The Verdict, n.d., Morgan Family Collection; "The Soldier and his Bonus," *Saturday Evening Post*, May 15, 1920, OS box 1, DTMC-CACRSC.

44 "Dyer Anti-Lynching Bill," Wikipedia, https://en.wikipedia.org/wiki/Dyer_Anti-Lynching_Bill, accessed April 26, 2023.

45 David D. Morgan to author, November 24, 2021.

46 "Dick Morgan Writes," (Oklahoma City) *Black Dispatch*, September 27, 1918. The Knights of Pythias is a fraternal organization and secret society founded in Washington, D.C., in 1864. Inspired by the legend of Damon and Pythias, members extolled the virtues of loyalty, honor, and friendship. At the peak of fraternal organizations' golden age, in the early 1920s, the Knights of Pythias boasted almost a million members. *See* "Knights of Pythias," Wikipedia, https://en.wikipedia.org/wiki/Knights_of_Pythias#, accessed April 26, 2023.

47 "Dick Morgan Writes Negro Veterans of American Wars," (Oklahoma City) *Black Dispatch*, October 31, 1919.

48 David D. Morgan to author, November 19, 2021, December 26, 2023.

49 "Patrick J. Kiger, "Why World War I Ended with an Armistice Instead of a Surrender," History, https://www.history.com/news/world-war-i-armistice-germany-allies, accessed April 26, 2023; "Armistice of November 11, 1918," Wikipedia, https://en.wikipedia.org/wiki/Armistice_of_11_November_1918, accessed April 26, 2023.

50 Bound Book, The League of Nations Report on the Plan for the League of Nations – Made by the President of the United States on Behalf of the Commission Constituted by the Preliminary Peace Conference in Session at Versailles, France, also the Address of The President in Relation Thereto, DTMDC-CACRSC, https://dicktmorgan.omeka.net/items/show/1127, accessed February 28, 2022.

51 Dick T. Morgan's handwritten position paper, untitled, n.d., "League of Nations," folder 1, box 4, DTMC-CACRSC.

52 Official Program, Tenth Annual Convention, Southern Commercial Congress, Baltimore, Maryland, December 8–15, 1918, series 6, folder 3, box 5, DTMC-CACRSC.

53 Speech – National Prohibition, DTMDC-CACRSC, https://dicktmorgan.omeka.net/items/show/901, accessed May 4, 2023.

54 "Volstead Act," Wikipedia, https://en.wikipedia.org/wiki/Volstead_Act, accessed April 26, 2023.

55 Morgan quoted in Dorman, "Dick T. Morgan from Oklahoma: The Congressional Years," 275; "Morgan on Dry Conference Committee," *Harlow's Weekly*, September 17, 1919.

56 Speech – House 46, DTMDC-CACRSC, https://dicktmorgan.omeka.net/items/show/919, accessed May 4, 2023.

57 Dorman, "Dick T. Morgan from Oklahoma: The Congressional Years," 275.

58 *Ponca City News* article reprinted in "News Supports Morgan," *Harlow's Weekly*, June 11, 1920.

59 "Presence Health has Rich History in Illinois," *Danville* (Ill.) *Commercial-News*, October 25, 2015; "Dick J. [sic] Morgan Dies in Illinois," (Washington, D.C.) *Evening Star*, July 6, 1920; Kosmerick, "Morgan, Dick Thompson"; David D. Morgan to author, November 22, December 4, 2021; February 24, 2022.

60 "Honorable Dick T. Morgan: Representative 8th Congressional District of Oklahoma the Last Roll Call at Danville, Illinois, July 5, 1920," *Woodward Democrat*, July 9, 1920; David D. Morgan to author, November 18, 21, 2021, May 25, 2023. The House Judiciary Committee has long been considered one of the most important committees in Congress. Representative Tom D. McKeown of Ada was among those who speculated on Morgan's likely assumption of the chairmanship, assuming Republicans retained control of the House. *See* "Hundreds View Body of Morgan," "Morgan Might Have Headed Judiciary Committee," *Daily Oklahoman*, July 9, 1920, OS box 3, DTMC-CACRSC.

61 "Congressman Morgan Dies," (Oklahoma City) *Black Dispatch*, July 9, 1920; Dick Thompson Morgan, brief bio prepared for The Verdict, n.d., Morgan Family Collection; David D. Morgan to author, November 23, 29, August 12, 2021.

EPILOGUE

1 "The Dick Morgan Banner." William P. Campbell of Kingfisher, acknowledged as the founder of the Oklahoma Historical Society in 1893, began his career as an unsalaried "historical custodian." *See* Bob L. Blackburn, "Oklahoma Historical Society," The Encyclopedia of Oklahoma History and Culture, Oklahoma Historical Society, https://www.okhistory.org/publications/enc/entry?entry=OK057, accessed June 2, 2023.

2 Dick T. Morgan (Late a Representative from Oklahoma). Memorial Addresses Delivered in the House of Representatives of the United States, Sixty-Sixth Congress, Third Session, February 27, 1921. Prepared under the Direction of the Joint Committee on Printing, Washington, 1922, 5–8, Morgan Family Collection; David D. Morgan to author, March 31, 2022. *See also* "Charles D. Carter," Wikipedia, https://en.wikipedia.org/wiki/Charles_D._Carter; "Frank Wheeler Mondell," Wikipedia, https://en.wikipedia.org/wiki/Frank_Wheeler_Mondell, both accessed June 2, 2023.

3 Memorial Addresses, 11–12; "The Dick Morgan Banner." William P. Campbell of Kingfisher, acknowledged as the founder of the Oklahoma Historical Society in 1893, began his career as an unsalaried "historical custodian." *See* Bob L. Blackburn, "Oklahoma Historical Society," The Encyclopedia of Oklahoma History and Culture, Oklahoma Historical Society,

https://www.okhistory.org/publications/enc/entry?entry=OK057, accessed June 2, 2023; "Everette B. Howard," Wikipedia, https://en.wikipedia.org/wiki/Everette_B._Howard, accessed June 2, 2023.

4 Memorial Addresses, 13–14; "William Wirt Hastings," Wikipedia, https://en.wikipedia.org/wiki/William_Wirt_Hastings, accessed June 2, 2023.

5 Memorial Addresses, 19–21; Todd J. Kosmerick, "Ferris, Scott," The Encyclopedia of Oklahoma History and Culture, Oklahoma Historical Society, https://www.okhistory.org/publications/enc/entry.php?entry=FE015, accessed June 2, 2023.

6 Memorial Addresses, 22–25; Todd J. Kosmerick, "Harreld, John William," The Encyclopedia of Oklahoma History and Culture, Oklahoma Historical Society, https://www.okhistory.org/publications/enc/entry.php?entry=HA031, accessed June 3, 2023.

7 Memorial Addresses, 28–30; Carolyn G. Hanneman, "McKeown, Thomas Deitz," The Encyclopedia of Oklahoma History and Culture, Oklahoma Historical Society, https://www.okhistory.org/publications/enc/entry.php?entry=MC032, accessed June 3, 2023.

8 Memorial Addresses, 33–34; Carolyn G. Hanneman, "McClintic, James Vernon," The Encyclopedia of Oklahoma History and Culture, Oklahoma Historical Society, https://www.okhistory.org/publications/enc/entry.php?entry=MC010, accessed June 3, 2023.

9 Memorial Addresses, 39–41; Carolyn G. Hanneman, "Swindall, Charles," The Encyclopedia of Oklahoma History and Culture, Oklahoma Historical Society, https://www.okhistory.org/publications/enc/entry.php?entry=SW005, accessed June 3, 2023. Swindall was quoting from the sixth stanza of Henry Wadsworth Longfellow's nine-stanza poem, "The Builders." *See* Henry Wadsworth Longfellow, "The Builders," Art of Manliness,www.artofmanliness.com/builders-henry-wadsworth-longfellow/.

10 Aldrich, *Okie Jesus Congressman*, 233–68; Carolyn G. Hanneman, "Herrick, Manuel," The Encyclopedia of Oklahoma History and Culture, Oklahoma Historical Society, https://www.okhistory.org/publications/enc/entry?entry=HE018, accessed January 18, 2024.

11 David and Kenyon Morgan interview, February 17, 2023; David Morgan interview, April 21, 2023. Porter and Clemmer's four children were Dick Deupree (born February 24, 1908), Martha Merle (born October 16, 1910), William Maxwell (born June 20, 1915), and Porter Harlan (born October 1, 1917). David D. Morgan to author, November 21, 23, 24, December 1, 2021.

12 David D. Morgan to author, January 1, 2024.

13 Mrs. Dick T. Morgan to Mrs. Tucker, August 5, 1902, folder 4, box 1, DTMC-CACRSC.

14 David Morgan interview, April 12, July 10, 2023.

15 Porter to Papa, May 31, 1920, "Correspondence," folder 8, box 2, DTMC-CACRSC.

16 Porter to Mama, June 22, 1921, Morgan Family Collection.

17 David D. Morgan to author, July 10, August 19, 2023.

18 "A Message from Jim Hepburn," unsourced newspaper article, circa June 7, 1922, Morgan Family Collection.

19 David Morgan interviews, April 5, 12, 2023; "Ulysses S. Stone," Wikipedia, https://en.wikipedia.org/wiki/Ulysses_S._Stone, accessed June 2, 2023. For Porter H. Morgan's selection as chairman of Oklahoma County's G.O.P., *see* Hon. Porter H. Morgan to Chairman, March 31, 1914; "Porter Morgan Heads Okla. County G.O.P.," unsourced newspaper article, n.d.; "P. H. Morgan Head of County G.O.P.," unsourced newspaper article, n.d.; all in "Committee Reports," folder 14, box 4, DTMC-CACRSC.

20 David and Kenyon Morgan interview, February 17, 2023; David Morgan interview, April 12, 21, July 10, 2023; Gilbert C. Fite to Mr. Porter Morgan, September 15, 1949, DTMC-CACRSC.

21 David Morgan's 2017 brief bio of Dick Thompson Morgan, prepared for Bob Blackburn, Morgan Family Collection; David D. Morgan, phone interviews by author, April 5, 12, 18, 21, 2023, Charlottesville and Oklahoma City; David D. Morgan to author, August 19, 2023.

22 Memorial Addresses, 32.

23 David D. Morgan interview, April 21, 2023.

24 Speech or Address by Dick T. Morgan, Fifty Years of Material and Religious Progress, DTMDC-CACRSC, https://dicktmorgan.omeka.net/items/show/1137, accessed May 4, 2023.

25 Morgan's commencement speech at Union Christian College was printed in the appendix to the *Congressional Record*. *See* House. *Congressional Record* 55, appendix, 65th Congress, 1st session, June 15, 1917, 334–36.

BIBLIOGRAPHY

ARCHIVAL, CORPORATE, PERSONAL, VERTICAL FILE COLLECTIONS

A. J. Barash Collection. Research Division, Oklahoma Historical Society. Oklahoma City, Oklahoma.

Brevier Legislative Reports, Indiana General Assembly. Indiana University, Maurer School of Law. Bloomington, Indiana.

Cherokee Strip Museum Collection. Perry, Oklahoma.

Congressional Record. Government Printing Office, Washington, D.C.

Dick T. Morgan Collection (DTMC). Carl Albert Congressional Research and Studies Center. Norman, Oklahoma.

Dick T. Morgan Digital Collection (DTMDC). Carl Albert Congressional Research and Studies Center. Norman, Oklahoma.

First Christian Church of El Reno Collection. El Reno, Oklahoma.

Fogg Law Firm Collection. El Reno, Oklahoma.

Frederick Samuel Barde Collection, 1890–1916. Research Division, Oklahoma Historical Society. Oklahoma City, Oklahoma.

HathiTrust Research Center, HathiTrust Digital Library (HTDL). Indiana University and the University of Illinois at Urbana-Champaign.

John Dunning Political Collection. Research Division, Oklahoma Historical Society. Oklahoma City, Oklahoma.

John E. Shanafelt Collection. Research Division, Oklahoma Historical Society. Oklahoma City, Oklahoma.

Joseph Thoburn Collection. Research Division, Oklahoma Historical Society. Oklahoma City, Oklahoma.

Mead Museum Collection. Yankton, South Dakota.

Michael J. Hightower Collection. Research Division, Oklahoma Historical Society. Oklahoma City, Oklahoma.

Morgan Family Collection. Oklahoma City, Oklahoma.

National Photo Company Collection Library of Congress. Washington, D.C.

No Man's Land Museum Collection. Goodwell, Oklahoma.

Oklahoma Historical Society Photo Archives. Research Division, Oklahoma Historical Society. Oklahoma City, Oklahoma.

Oklahoma Historical Society Vertical Files. Research Division, Oklahoma Historical Society, Oklahoma City, Oklahoma.

Oklahoma Territorial Museum Collection. Guthrie, Oklahoma.

Orben Casey Collection. Research Division, Oklahoma Historical Society. Oklahoma City, Oklahoma.

Plains Indians and Pioneers Museum Collection. Woodward, Oklahoma.

Prints and Photographs Division. Library of Congress. Washington, D.C.

Sidney Clarke Collection. Research Division, Oklahoma Historical Society. Oklahoma City, Oklahoma.

Virginia Sutton Collection. Research Division, Oklahoma Historical Society. Oklahoma City, Oklahoma.

William H. English Collection. Indiana Historical Society. Indianapolis, Indiana.

BOOKS, THESES, DISSERTATIONS

Ahamed, Liaquat. *Lords of Finance: The Bankers Who Broke the World*. New York: Penguin, 2009.

Aldrich, Gene. *The Okie Jesus Congressman: The Life of Manuel Herrick*. Oklahoma City, Okla.: Times-Journal Publishing Company, 1974.

Ameringer, Oscar. *If You Don't Weaken*. Foreword by Carl Sandburg. New York: Henry Holt and Company, 1940.

Argersinger, Peter H. *Representation and Inequality in Late Nineteenth-Century America: The Politics of Apportionment*. Cambridge: Cambridge University Press, 2012.

Bell, William A., ed. *Indiana School Journal* 22, no. 12. Indianapolis: Indiana State Teachers Association, 1877.

Brands, H. W. *American Colossus: The Triumph of Capitalism, 1865–1900*. New York: Anchor Books, 2010.

Bruner, Robert F., and Sean D. Carr. *The Panic of 1907: Lessons Learned from the Market's Perfect Storm*. Hoboken, N.J.: John Wiley and Sons, Inc., 2007.

Burbank, Garin. *When Farmers Voted Red: The Gospel of Socialism in the Oklahoma Countryside, 1910–1924*. Westport, Conn.: Greenwood Press, 1976.

Carney, George O. "Oklahoma's United States House Delegation and Progressives, 1901-1917." PhD diss., Oklahoma State University, 1972.

Carney, John J., Dick T. Morgan, and Mary S. Stotler. *Contested Election Case of John J. Carney v. Dick T. Morgan from the Second Congressional District of Oklahoma*. Leopold Classic Library, 2021. Originally published in 1913 by Thomas Jefferson University, Washington, D.C.

Chernow, Ron. *The Death of the Banker: The Decline and Fall of the Great Financial Dynasties and the Triumph of the Small Investor*. New York: Vintage Books, 1997.

Croly, Herbert. *The Promise of American Life*. Cambridge, MA: The Belknap Press of Harvard University Press, 1965.

Dale, Edward Everett. *The Range Cattle Industry: Ranching on the Great Plains from 1865 to 1925*. Norman: University of Oklahoma Press, 1960.

Dearcopp, Joanne, and Christine Hill Smith, eds. Foreword by David M. Wrobel. *Unknown No More: Recovering Senora Babb*. Norman: University of Oklahoma Press, 2021.

Dorman, Robert L. *Alfalfa Bill: A Life in Politics*. Norman: University of Oklahoma Press, 2018.

DuBois, James T., and Gertrude S. Mathews. *Galusha A. Grow: Father of the Homestead Law*. Boston: Houghton Mifflin, 1917.

England, Stephen J. *Oklahoma Christians: A History of Christian Churches and the Start of the Christian Church (Disciples of Christ) in Oklahoma*. Bethany, Okla.: Bethany Press, 1975.

Fenwick, Lynda Beck. *Prairie Bachelor: The Story of a Kansas Homesteader and the Populist Movement.* Lawrence: University Press of Kansas, 2020.

Finney County Directory, 1886–87. Garden City, Kans.: Finney County Historical Society reprint, n.d.

Fisher, Deena K., and Robin D. Hohweiler. *Woodward Past and Present.* Charleston, S. C.: Arcadia Publishing, 2021.

Fitchett, Allen D. “History of Noble County, Oklahoma.” Master’s thesis, Colorado State College of Education, 1938.

Forbes, Gerald. *Guthrie: Oklahoma’s First Capital.* Norman: University of Oklahoma Press, 1938.

Geffs, Irving (a.k.a. Bunky). *The First Eight Months of Oklahoma City.* Oklahoma City, Okla.: McMasters Printing Co., 1890.

George, Henry. *Progress and Poverty: An Inquiry into the Cause of Industrial Depressions and of Increase of Want with Increase of Wealth.* New York: Walter J. Black, 1942.

____________. *Progress and Poverty: Why There Are Recessions Amid Poverty and Plenty–and What to Do About It!* Edited and abridged for modern readers by Bob Drake. New York: Robert Schalkenbach Foundation, 2010.

Goble, Danney. *Progressive Oklahoma.* Norman: University of Oklahoma Press, 1980.

Goodyear, C. W. *President Garfield: From Radical to Unifier.* New York: Simon and Schuster, 2023.

Green, James R. *Grass-Roots Socialism: Radical Movements in the Southwest, 1895–1943.* Baton Rouge: Louisiana State University Press, 1978.

Henry, Robert, and Bob Burke. *Gore and Owen: Oklahoma’s First Two U.S. Senators.* Oklahoma City, Okla.: Oklahoma Hall of Fame Publishing, 2022.

Hightower, Michael J. *1889: The Boomer Movement, the Land Run, and Early Oklahoma City.* Norman: University of Oklahoma Press, 2018.

______________. *Banking in Oklahoma, 1907–2000.* Norman: University of Oklahoma Press, 2014.

______________. *Banking in Oklahoma before Statehood.* Norman: University of Oklahoma Press, 2013.

_________________. *Inventing Tradition: Cowboy Sports in a Postmodern Age.* Saarbrücken, Germany: VDM, 2008.

Hochschild, Adam. *American Midnight: The Great War, A Violent Peace, and Democracy’s Forgotten Crisis.* New York: Mariner Books, 2022.

Hodges, V. Pauline, Harold Kachel, and Joe Lansden. *Images of America: Beaver County.* Charleston, S. C.: Arcadia Publishing, 2011.

Hoig, Stan. *Came Men on Horses: The Conquistador Expeditions of Francisco Vázquez de Coronado and Don Juan de Oñate.* Boulder: University Press of Colorado, 2013.

Hurst, Irvin. *The 46th Star: A History of Oklahoma’s Constitutional Convention and Early Statehood.* Oklahoma City, Okla.: Western Heritage Books, Inc., 1980.

Ilisevich, Robert D. *Galusha A. Grow: The People’s Candidate.* Pittsburgh: University of Pittsburgh Press, 1988.

James, Louise B. *Below Devil’s Gap: The Story of Woodward County.* Perkins, Okla.: Evans Publications, 1984.

Kazin, Michael. *American Dreamers: How the Left Changed a Nation*. New York: Vintage Books, 2012.

Kindleberger, Charles P., and Robert Z. Aliber. *Manias, Panics and Crashes: A History of Financial Crises*. Basingstoke, UK: Palgrave MacMillan, 2005.

McCallum, Henry D., and Frances T. McCallum. *The Wire that Fenced the West*. Norman: University of Oklahoma Press, 1965.

McGuire, Lloyd H. Jr. *Birth of Guthrie: Oklahoma's Run of 1889 and Life in Guthrie in 1889 and the 1890s*. San Diego: Lloyd H. McGuire Jr., 1998.

McReynolds, Edwin C. *Oklahoma: A History of the Sooner State*. Norman: University of Oklahoma Press, 1954.

Morgan, Dick T. *Land Credits: A Plea for the American Farmer*. New York: Thomas Y. Crowell Company, 1915.

___________. *Morgan's Digest of Oklahoma Statutes and Supreme Court Decisions*. Perry, Okla. Terr.: Dick T. Morgan, 1897.

___________. *Morgan's Manual of the United States Homestead, Townsite and Mining Laws*. Kansas City: Hudson-Kimberly Publishing Company, 1900.

Osnos, Evan. *Wildland: The Making of America's Fury*. New York: Farrar Straus and Giroux, 2021.

Phillips, Clifton J. *Indiana in Transition: The Emergence of an Industrial Commonwealth*. Indianapolis: Indiana Historical Bureau and Indiana Historical Society, 1968.

Rock, Marion Tuttle. *Illustrated History of Oklahoma, Its Occupation by Spain and France–Its Sale to the United States–Its Opening to Settlement in 1889–and the Meeting of the First Territorial Legislature*. Topeka, Kans.: O. B. Hamilton and Son, 1890.

Scales, James R., and Danney Goble. *Oklahoma Politics: A History*. Norman: University of Oklahoma Press, 1982.

Schlesinger, Arthur M. Jr., ed. *The Almanac of American History*. New York: Putnam, 1983.

Scott, Angelo C. *Story of Oklahoma City*. Oklahoma City: Times-Journal Publishing, 1939.

Thoburn, Joseph B. *A Standard History of Oklahoma*, vol. 4. Chicago: American Historical Society, 1916.

Thompson, John. *Closing the Frontier: Radical Response in Oklahoma, 1889–1923*. Norman: University of Oklahoma Press, 1986.

Turner, Frederick Jackson. *The Frontier in American History*. Franklin Center, Penn.: The Franklin Library, 1977.

Walker, Henry Pickering. *The Wagonmasters: High Plains Freighting from the Earliest Days of the Santa Fe Trail to 1880*. Norman: University of Oklahoma Press, 1966.

Wenner, Fred L. *The Story of Oklahoma and the Eighty-Niners, Retold on the Golden Anniversary*. Guthrie, Okla.: Co-operative Publishing, 1939.

Wilson, Woodrow. *The New Freedom: A Call for the Emancipation of the Generous Energies of a People*. New York: Doubleday, Page and Company, 1913.

Zinn, Howard. *The Twentieth Century*. New York: HarperPerennial, 2003.

ARTICLES, BOOK CHAPTERS, UNPUBLISHED REPORTS, WEBSITES

Adkison, Danny M. "Constitutional Convention." The Encyclopedia of Oklahoma History and Culture. Oklahoma Historical Society. https://www.okhistory.org/publications/enc/entry.php?entry=CO047.

American Presidency Project. James A. Garfield, 20th President of the United States, 1881–1881, Inaugural Address, https://www.presidency.ucsb.edu/documents/inaugural-address-39.

"Atchison, Topeka and Santa Fe Railway." Wikipedia. Accessed April 20, 2023. https://en.wikipedia.org/wiki/Atchison,_Topeka_and_Santa_Fe_Railway.

Barnhart, John D. Review of *Colonel Dick Thompson, the Persistent Whig*, by Charles Roll. *Indiana Magazine of History* 44, no. 2 (June 1948): 202–4.

Bielik-Robson, Agata. "Another Conversion. Stanisław Brzozowski's 'Diary' as an Early Instance of the Post-secular Turn to Religion." *Studies in East European Thought* 63, no. 4 (November 2011): 279–91. https://www.jstor.org/stable/41477738.

Bissett, Jim. "Socialist Party." The Encyclopedia of Oklahoma History and Culture. Oklahoma Historical Society. Accessed April 25, 2023. https://www.okhistory.org/publications/enc/entry.php?entry=SO001.

Blackburn, Bob L. "Oklahoma Historical Society." The Encyclopedia of Oklahoma History and Culture. Oklahoma Historical Society. Accessed June 2, 2023. https://www.okhistory.org/publications/enc/entry?entry=OK057.

__________________. "Unassigned Lands." The Encyclopedia of Oklahoma History and Culture. Oklahoma Historical Society. Accessed April 20, 2023. https://www.okhistory.org/publications/enc/entry?entry=UN001.

Blochowiak, Mary Ann. "Free Home League." The Encyclopedia of Oklahoma History and Culture. Oklahoma Historical Society. Accessed April 23, 2023. https://www.okhistory.org/publications/enc/entry.php?entry=FR014.

__________________. "Free Homes Act." The Encyclopedia of Oklahoma History and Culture. Oklahoma Historical Society. https://www.okhistory.org/publications/enc/entry.php?entry=FR013.

__________________. "Justice Is Our Battle Cry: The Territorial Free Home League." *The Chronicles of Oklahoma* 62, no. 1 (Spring 1984): 38–55.

Braswell, Vernon S. "The Oklahoma Free Homes Bill, 1892–1900." *The Chronicles of Oklahoma* 44, no. 4 (Winter 1966–67): 380–90.

Brophy, Alfred L. "*Guinn v. United States (1915)*." The Encyclopedia of Oklahoma History and Culture. Oklahoma Historical Society. Accessed April 26, 2023. https://www.okhistory.org/publications/enc/entry?entry=GU001.

Brown, James L. "Early and Important Litigations." *Sturm's Oklahoma* 8, no. 2 (April 1909): 26–30.

Brown, Kenny L. "Owen, Robert Latham (1856–1947)." The Encyclopedia of Oklahoma History and Culture. Oklahoma Historical Society. Accessed April 26, 2023. https://www.okhistory.org/publications/enc/entry?entry=OW003.

Bryant, Keith L. Jr. "Murray, William Henry David." The Encyclopedia of Oklahoma History and Culture. Oklahoma Historical Society. Accessed April 24, 2023. https://www.okhistory.org/publications/enc/entry.php?entry=MU014.

Carney, George O. "Flynn, Dennis Thomas." The Encyclopedia of Oklahoma History and Culture. Oklahoma Historical Society. Accessed April 23, 2023. https://www.okhistory.org/publications/enc/entry?entry=FL006.

Chandler, Alfred D. "The Beginnings of 'Big Business' in American Industry." *Business History Review* 33, no. 1 (Spring 1959): 1–31.

"Charles D. Carter." Wikipedia. Accessed June 2, 2023. https://en.wikipedia.org/wiki/Charles_D._Carter.

"Charles W. Fairbanks." Wikipedia. Accessed June 2, 2023. https://en.wikipedia.org/wiki/Charles_W._Fairbanks.

"Clara Cleghorn Hoffman." Wikipedia. Accessed April 23, 2023. https://en.wikipedia.org/wiki/Clara_Cleghorn_Hoffman.

"Country Life Movement." Wikipedia. Accessed April 26, 2023. https://en.wikipedia.org/wiki/Country_life_movement.

Crockett, Norman L. "The Opening of Oklahoma: A Businessman's Frontier." *The Chronicles of Oklahoma* 56, no. 1 (Spring 1978): 85–95.

Cronon, William, George Miles, and Jay Gitlin. "Becoming West: Toward a New Meaning for Western History." In *Under an Open Sky: Rethinking America's Western Past*, edited by William Cronon, George Miles, and Jay Gitlin, 3–27. New York: W. W. Norton, 1992.

"Daniel W. Voorhees." Wikipedia. Accessed April 20, 2023. https://en.wikipedia.org/wiki/Daniel_W._Voorhees#Senator.

Day, Meagan. "When Oklahoma Was the Heartland of American Socialism." *Jacobin Magazine*, August 15, 2021. https://jacobinmag.com/2021/08/oklahoma-green-corn-rebellion-washington-wwi-tenant-farmer-poverty-socialist-party-renters-union-working-class-union-wcu.

"Departmental Reorganization Act." Wikipedia. Accessed April 26, 2023. https://en.wikipedia.org/wiki/Departmental_Reorganization_Act.

Dorman, Robert L. "Dick T. Morgan, Republican from Oklahoma: The Congressional Years, 1908–20." *The Chronicles of Oklahoma* 100, no. 3 (Fall 2022): 260–81.

_______________. "Dick T. Morgan, Republican from Oklahoma: Prelude to Congress, 1853–1907." *The Chronicles of Oklahoma* 99, no. 3 (Fall 2021): 260–83.

"Dred Scott." Wikipedia. Accessed April 20, 2023. https://en.wikipedia.org/wiki/Dred_Scott#Dred_Scott_v._Sandford.

"Dyer Anti-Lynching Bill." Wikipedia. Accessed April 26, 2023. https://en.wikipedia.org/wiki/Dyer_Anti-Lynching_Bill.

Ellinger, Charles Wayne. "Congressional Viewpoint toward the Admission of Oklahoma as a State: 1902–1906." *The Chronicles of Oklahoma* 58, no. 3 (Fall 1980): 283–95.

____________________. "The Drive for Statehood in Oklahoma, 1889–1906." *The Chronicles of Oklahoma* 41, no. 1 (Spring 1963): 15–37.

"Espionage Act of 1917." Wikipedia. Accessed April 20, 2023. https://en.wikipedia.org/wiki/Espionage_Act_of_1917.

"Eugene V. Debs." Wikipedia. Accessed April 20, 2023. https://en.wikipedia.org/wiki/Eugene_V._Debs.

"Everette B. Howard." Wikipedia. Accessed June 3, 2023. https://en.wikipedia.org/wiki/Everette_B._Howard.

"Federal Farm Loan Act." Wikipedia. Accessed April 26, 2023. https://en.wikipedia.org/wiki/Federal_Farm_Loan_Act.

"Federal Trade Commission." Wikipedia. Accessed April 25, 2023. https://en.wikipedia.org/wiki/Federal_Trade_Commission.

"Federal Trade Commission." Federal Trade Commission. Accessed April 25, 2023. https://www.ftc.gov/about-ftc/our-history.

"Federal Trade Commission." Federal Trade Commission. Accessed April 25, 2023. https://www.ftc.gov/about-ftc/our-history/our-seal.

Fischer, LeRoy H. "Oklahoma Territory, 1890–1907." *The Chronicles of Oklahoma* 53, no. 1 (Spring 1975): 3–8.

Fite, Gilbert C. "Farmers' Alliance." The Encyclopedia of Oklahoma History and Culture. Oklahoma Historical Society. Accessed April 20, 2023. https://www.okhistory.org/publications/enc/entry?entry=FA017.

"Frank Wheeler Mondell." Wikipedia. Accessed June 2, 2023. https://en.wikipedia.org/wiki/Frank_Wheeler_Mondell.

Fuller, A. James. "The Great War Governor: Oliver P. Morton and the War of the Rebellion in Indiana." Indiana Historical Bureau. Accessed April 20, 2023. https://www.in.gov/history/4428.htm.

"Galusha A. Grow." Wikipedia. Accessed April 20, 2023. https://en.wikipedia.org/wiki/Galusha_A._Grow.

"Garden City, Kansas." Wikipedia. Accessed April 20, 2023. https://en.wikipedia.org/wiki/Garden_City,_Kansas#19th_century.

Glasser, Andrew. "Woodrow Wilson Creates Federal Trade Commission, Sept. 26, 1914." *Politico*, September 26, 2012. https://www.politico.com/story/2012/09/this-day-in-politics-081672.

"Guinn v. United States." Wikipedia. Accessed April 26, 2023. https://en.wikipedia.org/wiki/Guinn_v._United_States#.

Hanneman, Carolyn G. "Herrick, Manuel." The Encyclopedia of Oklahoma History and Culture. Oklahoma Historical Society. Accessed January 18, 2024. https://www.okhistory.org/publications/enc/entry?entry=HE018.

__________________. "McClintic, James Vernon." The Encyclopedia of Oklahoma History and Culture. Oklahoma Historical Society. Accessed June 3, 2023. https://www.okhistory.org/publications/enc/entry.php?entry=MC010.

__________________. "McKeown, Thomas Deitz." The Encyclopedia of Oklahoma History and Culture. Oklahoma Historical Society. Accessed June 3, 2023. https://www.okhistory.org/publications/enc/entry.php?entry=MC032.

__________________. "Swindall, Charles." The Encyclopedia of Oklahoma History and Culture. Oklahoma Historical Society. Accessed June 3, 2023. https://www.okhistory.org/publications/enc/entry.php?entry=SW005.

________________. "Weaver, Claude (1867–1954)." The Encyclopedia of Oklahoma History and Culture. Oklahoma Historical Society. Accessed April 26, 2023. https://www.okhistory.org/publications/enc/entry?entry=WE003.

Hightower, Michael J. "The Businessman's Frontier: C. C. Hightower, Commerce, and Old Greer County, 1891–1903." *The Chronicles of Oklahoma* 86, no. 1 (Spring 2008): 4–31.

Homestead Act. Avalon Project. Documents in Law, History and Diplomacy. Lillian Goldman Law Library. Yale Law School. May 20, 1862. http://avalon.law.yale.edu/19th_century/homestead_act.asp.

Homestead Act of 1862. Educator Resources. National Archives. https://www.archives.gov/education/lessons/homestead-act.

"Horace Speed." Wikipedia. Accessed April 23, 2023. https://en.wikipedia.org/wiki/Horace_Speed#.

House, Albert V. "The Democratic State Central Committee of Indiana in 1880: A Case Study in Party Tactics and Finance." *Indiana Magazine of History* 58, no. 3 (September 1962): 179–210.

"James Brown Ray." Indiana Governor History. Accessed April 20, 2023. https://www.in.gov/governorhistory/2374.htm.

Kansas Historical Society. "Finney County, Kansas." *Kansapedia*. Accessed April 20, 2023. https://www.kshs.org/kansapedia/finney-county-kansas/15283.

Kiger, Patrick J. "Why World War I Ended with an Armistice Instead of a Surrender." History. Accessed April 26, 2023. https://www.history.com/news/world-war-i-armistice-germany-allies.

"Knights of Pythias." Wikipedia. Accessed April 26, 2023. https://en.wikipedia.org/wiki/Knights_of_Pythias#.

Kosmerick, Todd J. "Ferris, Scott." The Encyclopedia of Oklahoma History and Culture. Oklahoma Historical Society. Accessed June 2, 2023. https://www.okhistory.org/publications/enc/entry.php?entry=FE015.

________________. "Harreld, John William." The Encyclopedia of Oklahoma History and Culture. Oklahoma Historical Society. Accessed June 3, 2023. https://www.okhistory.org/publications/enc/entry.php?entry=HA031.

________________. "Morgan, Dick Thompson." The Encyclopedia of Oklahoma History and Culture. Oklahoma Historical Society. Accessed April 20, 2023. https://www.okhistory.org/publications/enc/entry.php?entry=MO019.

Kovacic, William E. "The Federal Trade Commission and Congressional Oversight of Antitrust Enforcement." *Tulsa Law Review* 17, no. 4 (Summer 1982): 587–671. Accessed June 3, 2024. https://digitalcommons.law.utulsa.edu/tlr/vol17/iss4/1/.

"Lee Slater Overman." Wikipedia. Accessed April 26, 2023. https://en.wikipedia.org/wiki/Lee_Slater_Overman.

"Liberty Hyde Bailey: A Man for All Seasons." Cornell University Library. Accessed April 26, 2023. https://rmc.library.cornell.edu/bailey/commission/commission_5.html.

Longfellow, Henry Wadsworth. "The Builders." Art of Manliness. www.artofmanliness.com/builders-henry-wadsworth-longfellow/.

Luckerson, Victor. "The Promise of Oklahoma." *Smithsonian* (April 2021). Accessed April 24, 2023. https://www. Smithsonianmag.com/history/unrealized-promise-oklahoma-180977174/.

McCullough, David. *The Course of Human Events*. National Endowment for the Humanities. Jefferson Lecture in the Humanities 2003. *See* Brainy Quote, https://www.brainyquote.com/quotes/david_mccullough_381227.

Meredith, H. L. "Oscar Ameringer and the Concept of Agrarian Socialism." *The Chronicles of Oklahoma* 45, no. 1 (Spring 1967): 77–83.

Mize, Richard. "Big Pasture." The Encyclopedia of Oklahoma History and Culture. Oklahoma Historical Society. Accessed April 24, 2023. https://www.okhistory.org/publications/enc/entry.php?entry=BI003.

___________. "Sequoyah Convention." The Encyclopedia of Oklahoma History and Culture. Oklahoma Historical Society. Accessed April 24, 2023. https://www.okhistory.org/publications/enc/entry.php?entry=SE021.

Modern History Project. The Federal Reserve Act. Accessed April 26, 2023. https://modernhistoryproject.org/mhp?Article=FedReserve&C=3.0#Act.

Monnet, Julien C. "The Latest Phase of Negro Disfranchisement." *Harvard Law Review* 26, no. 1 (November 1912): 42–63. https://doi.org/10.2307/1324271.

Morgan, Dick T. "Government Aid: Rural Credits Division in Congress—How to Secure Unity and Harmony." *The Farmers' Open Forum* 1, no. 4 (December 1915): 1, 13.

Morrill Act (1862). Milestone Documents. National Archives. https://www.archives.gov/milestone-documents/morrill-act.

Murray, William H. "The Constitutional Convention." *The Chronicles of Oklahoma* 9, no. 2 (June 1931): 126–38.

Noyes, Alexander D. "A Year after the Panic of 1907." *Quarterly Journal of Economics* 23 (February 1909): 185–212.

"Oscar Underwood." Wikipedia. Accessed April 25, 2023. https://en.wikipedia.org/wiki/Oscar_Underwood.

Pacific Railway Act (1862). Milestone Documents. National Archives. https://www.archives.gov/milestone-documents/pacific-railway-act.

"Payne-Aldrich Tariff Act." Wikipedia. Accessed April 25, 2023. https://en.wikipedia.org/wiki/Payne–Aldrich_Tariff_Act.

Peery, Dan W. "The First Two Years," Introduction. *The Chronicles of Oklahoma* 7, no. 3 (September 1929): 278–80.

___________. "The First Two Years," Part 1. *The Chronicles of Oklahoma* 7, no. 3 (September 1929): 281–322.

___________. "The First Two Years," Part 2. *The Chronicles of Oklahoma* 7, no. 4 (December 1929): 419–57.

___________. "The First Two Years," Part 3. *The Chronicles of Oklahoma* 8, no. 3 (March 1930): 94–128.

Phillips, C. J. "Hon. Dick T. Morgan: An Appreciation by C. J. Phillips." *Osage Magazine* (September 1910): 18–21.

"Ralph W. Moss (politician)." Wikipedia. Accessed April 20, 2023. https://en.wikipedia.org/wiki/Ralph_W._Moss_(politician).

"Richard Wigginton Thompson." Indiana State Library. Accessed April 20, 2023. https://www.in.gov/library/collections-and-services/manuscripts/indiana-lawyers-and-judges/hoosier-legal-literaries/richard-wigginton-thompson/.

Riddleberger, Patrick W. "George W. Julian: Abolitionist Land Reformer." *Agricultural History* 29, no. 3 (July 1955): 108–10.

Roosevelt, Theodore. "Who is a Progressive?" Address at Louisville, Kentucky, April 3, 1912. *The Outlook* (April 13, 1912): 809–13. Reprinted at Unz Review: An Alternative Media Selection. Accessed April 24, 2023. https://www.unz.com/print/Outlook-1912apr13-00809.

Rushes to Statehood: The Oklahoma Land Runs, National Cowboy and Western Heritage Center. Accessed April 20, 2023. https://nationalcowboymuseum.org/explore/rushes-statehood-oklahoma-land-runs/.

Sandefur, Ray H. "The Ingalls-Voorhees Debate of 1888." *Kansas Historical Quarterly* 17, no. 3 (August 1949): 243–53.

"Sedition Act of 1918." Wikipedia. Accessed May 20, 2024. https://en.wikipedia.org/wiki/Sedition_Act_of_1918#cite_ref-12.

"Sherman Antitrust Act." Wikipedia. Accessed April 25, 2023. https://en.wikipedia.org/wiki/Sherman_Antitrust_Act.

Skaggs, Jimmy M. "Cattle Trails in Oklahoma." In *Ranch and Range in Oklahoma*, edited by Jimmy M. Skaggs, 7–17. Oklahoma City: Oklahoma Historical Society, 1978.

Smallwood, James M. "Partners in Progress: Banking and Agribusiness in Oklahoma." In *Banking in the West*, edited by Larry Schweikart, xx. Manhattan, KS: Sunflower University Press, 1984.

Snell, Joseph W., and Don D. Wilson. "The Birth of the Atchison, Topeka and Santa Fe Railroad." *Kansas Historical Quarterly* 34, no. 2 (Summer 1968): 113–42.

Sprague, O. M. W. "The American Crisis of 1907." *Economic Journal* 18 (September 1908): 353–72.

"Stanislaw Brzozowski (writer)." Wikipedia. Accessed May 20, 2024. https://en.wikipedia.org/wiki/Stanisław_Brzozowski_(writer).

Thompson, John. "Ameringer, Oscar (1870–1943)." The Encyclopedia of Oklahoma History and Culture. Oklahoma Historical Society. Accessed April 24, 2023. https://www.okhistory.org/publications/enc/entry?entry=AM014.

"Timber Culture Act." Wikipedia. Accessed April 20, 2023. https://en.wikipedia.org/wiki/Timber_Culture_Act#.

Turner, Alvin O. "Cherokee Outlet Opening." The Encyclopedia of Oklahoma History and Culture. Oklahoma Historical Society. Accessed April 20, 2023. https://www.okhistory.org/publications/enc/entry?entry=CH021.

"Ulysses S. Stone." Wikipedia. Accessed May 20, 2024. https://en.wikipedia.org/wiki/Ulysses_S._Stone.

Volstead Act. Wikipedia. Accessed April 26, 2023. https://en.wikipedia.org/wiki/Volstead_Act.

"Whig Party." History. Accesssed April 20, 2023. https://www.history.com/topics/19th-century/whig-party.

White, Edward Douglass, and Supreme Court of the United States. *U.S. Reports: Guinn v. United States, 238 U.S. 347*. 1915. https://www.loc.gov/item/usrep238347/.

Wicks, Hamilton S. "The Opening of Oklahoma." *Cosmopolitan* 7, no. 5 (September 1889): 460–70.

"Will H. Hays." Wikipedia. Accessed April 20, 2023. https://en.wikipedia.org/wiki/Will_H._Hays.

"William Wirt Hastings." Wikipedia. Accessed May 20, 2024. https://en.wikipedia.org/wiki/William_Wirt_Hastings.

Wilson, Linda D. "Sturm's Oklahoma Magazine." The Encyclopedia of Oklahoma History and Culture. Oklahoma Historical Society. Accessed April 23, 2023. https://www.okhistory.org/publications/enc/entry?entry=ST058.

"Woman's Christian Temperance Union." Wikipedia. Accessed April 23, 2023. https://en.wikipedia.org/wiki/Woman%27s_Christian_Temperance_Union.

Wright, Muriel H. "The Wedding of Oklahoma and Miss Indian Territory." *The Chronicles of Oklahoma* 35, no. 3 (Fall 1957): 255–64.

"Young People's Society of Christian Endeavor." Wikipedia. Accessed April 23, 2023. https://en.wikipedia.org/wiki/Young_People%27s_Society_of_Christian_Endeavour.

NEWSPAPERS AND MAGAZINES (UNLESS OTHERWISE NOTED, ALL NEWSPAPERS WERE PUBLISHED IN OKLAHOMA)

Alva Review Courier
Ames Review
Avard Tribune
Barber County (Kans.) *Index*
Beaver Herald
(Oklahoma City) *Black Dispatch*
Blackwell Times-Record
Buffalo Republican
Butler (Mo.) *Weekly Times*
Carmen Headlight
Charlottesville (Va.)*Daily Progress*
Cherokee Republican
Chicago (Ill.) *Tribune*
Cimarron News
Clay City (Ky.) *Chronicle*
Cleo Chieftain
Covington (Ind.) *Record*
Curtis Courier
Daily Oklahoma State Capital
Daily Oklahoman
Danville (Ill.) *Commercial-News*
Dodge City (Kans.) *Times*
Emporia (Kans.) *News*
Enid Events
(Washington, D.C.) *Evening Critic*
(Washington, D.C.) *Evening Star*
Fairview Enterprise
Fairview Republican
Garden City (Kans.) *Weekly Sentinel*
Guthrie Daily Leader
Guthrie Daily News
Guymon Herald
Hagerstown (Ind.) *Exponent*
Harlow's Weekly
Helena Star
Indian Chieftain

Indiana State Sentinel
Indianapolis (Ind.) *Leader*
Iola (Kans.) *Register*
Kiowa Chief
Manchester Journal
Morrison, Noble County, Transcript
(Washington, D.C) *National Tribune*
Noble County Journal
Oklahoma City Daily Times
Oklahoma Daily Journal
Oklahoma State Capital
Oklahoma Sunday School Worker
Osage Magazine
Perry Daily Enterprise-Times
Perry Daily Times
Perry Enterprise-Times
Ponca City Daily Courier
Red Rock Record
Rosston News
Speermore Advocate
Supply Republican
Texhoma Times
Tyrone Observer
Wakita Herald
Weekly Oklahoma State Capital
Woodward Dispatch
Yankton (S. Dak.) *Daily Press & Dakotan*
Indianapolis (Ind.) *Journal*
Indianapolis (Ind.) *News*
Kanzas [sic] (Kans.) News
Kremlin Journal
Medford Patriot Star
(Washington, D.C) *National Republican*
Newkirk Republican News Journal
Noble County Sentinel
Oklahoma City Times
Oklahoma Farmer and Laborer
Oklahoma State Register
Oklahoma Times
Perry Daily Enterprise
Perry Daily Journal
Perry Enterprise
Perry Republican
Pond Creek Vidette News
(Kay County) *Republican News Journal*
State Valley Star
Terre Haute (Ind.)*Tribune-Star*
Tulsa Daily World
Wabash (Ind.) *Express*
Washington (D.C.) *Times*
Woodward Democrat
Woodward News Bulletin

INTERVIEWS

Kent Crain and Felix Hensley, interview by author, March 16, 2011. Ponca City, Oklahoma.

Robin D. Hohweiler, interview by author, February 22, 2023. Woodward, Oklahoma.

David D. Morgan, phone interviews by author, April 5, 12, 18, 21, 2023. Charlottesville, Virginia, and Oklahoma City.

David and Kenyon Morgan, interview by author, February 17, 2023. Oklahoma City, Oklahoma.

INDEX

Unless otherwise specified, cities, counties, towns, and geographic features are in Oklahoma

A

Achstetten, Bavaria, 202
Adams, John, xi, 27
Adamson, William G., 241
Admire, J. V., 140-42
African Americans / Blacks, 11, 21, 24-25, 56, 91, 134, 182-89, 194, 197-99, 205, 208-11, 224, 236, 259, 282, 294-95
Aldrich: Nelson W., 212, 223, 234; Plan, 254-55
Aldrich-Vreeland Act (1908), 254
Alexander, Charles R., 260
Alfred P. Murrah Federal Bldg., Oklahoma City, 113, 136
Allen, George M., 37
Allen, John M., 78
Allen, Robert, 9
American: AgCredit, 273-74; Bible Society, 120-21; Christian Missionary Society (ACMS), 96-97; Country Life Assn., 264; Dream, xviii, 38, 202, 225; exceptionalism, 239, 316-17; Legion of Oklahoma, 292; National Bank Bldg., 225; Railway Union (ARU), 29; Revolution, 4
Ameringer, Oscar, *If You Don't Weaken*, 202-04, 280
Amherst College, 44
Annapolis, Md., 44
Antelope Hills, 42
Anti-Horse Thief Assn., 129
Apache tribe / res. *See* Kiowa, Comanche, and Apache tribes / res.
Appeal to Reason, 204, 280
Arkansas River, 50-51, 55, 259
Arthur, Chester A., 26
Articles of Confederation, 26
Ascension Academy, Ind., 15-16
Atchison, Topeka, and Santa Fe Railroad (AT&SF), x, xvi, 37, 51-52, 55-57, 60, 63, 72, 78, 87, 92

B

Babb, Senora, 264
Bailey, Liberty Hyde, 264
Baker, Charles S., 78
Bank of England, 253
Banking and currency reform, 254-59, 277
Bard, Richard, xxi
Barnes, Cassius M., 129, 133-34, 139, 142, 165
Battle of Yorktown, 26
Baum Bldg., Oklahoma City, 219
Benedict, Omar K., 70-71, 108
Bennett, Mrs. Leo (a.k.a. Miss Indian Territory), 199
Big Business, 181, 184, 195, 213, 225-28, 232-34, 239-40, 246, 251-52, 315
Big Pasture, 189
Bismark Fair, 51
Blackburn, Bob, viii, xx, 314-15
Bloomfield, Ia., 169
Boardman, Homer H., 219, 236
Boggess, Edgar Forrest, 96-97, 104-06, 155
Bolshevik Revolution, 284
Bolton, Billy, 177, 340n8
Bonaparte, Charles J., 198, 342n2
Boomers / boomer movement, 38, 56-58, 63, 74
Bootleggers / bootlegging, 176
Boudinot, Elias C., 55
Bourbon Co., Ky., 3
Branstetter, Otto, 202
Brower, John, 118
Brown, Charles, 260
Brown, James L., 68-70, 89
Bryan, Mittie, 108
Bryan, William Jennings, 125, 188
Bryant, H. I., 224
Brzozowski, Stanisław, ix

Buchanan, James, 45
Buff, N. G., 25, 38
Bull Moose Party, 233-34, 237, 264. *See also* Progressive movement / Party / progressive(s) / progressivism
Burford, John H., 140
Butler (Mo.) *Weekly Times*, 57
Butternuts (a.k.a. copperheads), 6-7
Buzzard (first name unknown), 106

C

Callahan, James Y., 125-26, 129-30, 133
Camp Thompson, 6
Campbell, William P., 305, 355n1n3
Canadian County Historical Museum, 150
Canadian River, 55, 74, 89, 283
Canisius College, Buffalo, N. York, 115
Cannon, Joe, 208-15, 222-23, 230, 234
Canton, Ohio, 284
Carl Albert Congressional Research and Studies Center (CACRSC), xiii, xvi, xx-xxi, 314-15
Carney, John J., 235-37
Carter, Charles D., 306
Carver, Charles D., 196
Cather, Willa, 264
Catlin, R. H., 29
Central Law School. *See* Indiana: School of Law
Central Pacific Railway, 48
Charlie (Morgan's horse), 59, 73
Charlottesville, Va., ix, xii, 200
ChatGPT, 245-46
Cherokee(s), 55, 99, 182-84, 199-200; Nation, 55, 99, 164, 186, 306; Outlet, xiii, 55, 64-65, 70, 98-102, 105, 115-17, 202, 288, 305, 338n53; Strip, 98; Strip Live Stock Assn., 54; Strip Museum, 136-37
Chester, E. M., 97
Cheyenne and Arapaho tribes / res., xiii, 55, 92, 115-17, 151, 216
Chicago Times, 55
Chicago, Ill., 50, 75, 118, 171, 191, 295
Chickasaw Nation, 55-57, 164, 183, 186
Choctaw Railway, 155
Choctaw(s), 200; Nation, 164, 186
Christian Church, x, 3-4, 8, 15, 20, 53, 57, 71-72, 80, 96-98, 108, 120, 309; of Guthrie, 77; of Woodward, 177. *See also* Disciples of Christ
Christian Endeavor, 106-10
Christian Standard, 96-97
Christianity, 4, 24, 120
Church Extension Board of the Christian Church, 71, 104-06
Cibola, 41-42
Cimarron River, 55, 68, 78-79
Cincinnati, Ohio, 3
City National Bank of Lawton, 152
Civil rights bill for soldiers and sailors, 277-78
Civil War, ix, 6, 13, 18, 23, 30-32, 47, 55, 82, 97, 171, 182, 249, 270, 317; battle of Chattanooga, 82; battle of Missionary Ridge, 82
Clark, John F., 82
Clark, William, 42. *See also* Journey of Discovery
Clarke, Sidney, 74, 152-55, 165
Classen High School, Oklahoma City, 310
Clayton Antitrust Act (1914), 301
Cleveland, Grover / Cleveland adm., 58-59, 78, 82, 116, 124
Colored Men's Protective League of Oklahoma, 129
Columbia University, New York, 169-71
Columbus, Christopher, 317
Comanche tribe / res. *See* Kiowa, Comanche, and Apache tribes / res.
Commission on Country Life, 264
Communists, 292
Confederacy / Confederate(s), 5-7, 21, 34, 55-56, 160, 191, 194, 200, 270
Confederation Congress, 81
Congressional delegation to Unassigned Lands, 78-79
Congressional districts (Oklahoma):

District One, 186, 206, 222, 235-36, 306; District Two, 186, 205-08, 215, 219, 222-23, 230, 235-36, 306; District Three, 186, 222; District Four, 186, 308; District Five, 186, 255, 259, 307; District Six, 307; District Seven, 309; District Eight, 259-60, 275, 287-88, 294, 302
Congressional Record, 173, 318
Conquistadores, 41-42
Constitutional Convention (1889), 74-78
Constitutional Convention (a.k.a. Con Con, 1906), 186-90, 195, 200
Contested elections, 312; of 1910, 224-25; of 1912, 236-37
Copp, Henry N., 93
Cornell University, Ithaca, N. York, 264
Coronado, Francisco Vázquez de, 41, 42
Cosmopolitan, 63-64
Cottonwood River, 73
Couch, William, 56
Council Bill No. 7 (a.k.a. "capital bill," "Daniels bill"), 89-92
Countries / empires / nation states (excluding U.S.): Australia, 266; Austria-Hungary, 296; Bulgaria, 296; Canada, xv, 302, 306-07; China, 292; England, 253, 317; Egypt, 47, 177, 266; France, 42, 47, 284, 295, 317; German / Germany, 3, 202, 266, 272, 277-87, 296, 317; Italy, 266; Japan, 266; Mexico, 18, 41; Norway, 266; Ottoman Empire, 296
Covey, Carl, 104-105
Crain, Kent, 273-74
Crawford, Lucretia, 3
Creager, C. E., 222-23
Creek Nation, 182, 185
Crespin, Michael, xx
Croly, Herbert, *The Promise of American Life*, 180-81.
Cross Timbers, 55
Cross, William, 159-60
Cummins, Albert B., 244

D

Dallas, Tex., 108
Daniels, Arthur N., 89-92
Darwin, Charles, 239
Davenport, James S., 196
Davis, Jefferson, 7
Davis, John J., 235-36
Davis, Louis, 125
Davis, Webster, 52
Debs, Eugene, 29-30, 235, 280, 284
Declaration of Independence, 26, 47, 192-94, 287
Deep Fork River, 55
DeJager, Cheryl, xx, 136
Delaney, J. C., 142
Democratic Party, 11-13, 27-29, 45, 124-25, 159, 188, 193, 199, 203, 228, 237, 240, 251, 313
Department Reorganization Act (1918), 287
Des Moines, Ia., 155, 169
Detroit, Mich., 29
Deupree, Clemmer. *See* Morgan (née Deupree), Clemmer
Deupree, Harlan, 190
Dew, Tara, 151
Dille, John I., 140-42
Dingley Act (1897), 212
Disciples of Christ, x, 3-4, 8-9, 97-98, 169, 261. *See also* Christian Church
Ditch Witch, Perry, xx
Dodson, W. H., 200
Donaldson, John, 28
Dooley, A. H., 37
Douglas, Stephen A., 13. *See also* Lincoln-Douglas debates
Drake University, Des Moines, Ia., 168-69
Dred Scott v. Sanford (1857), 11
Dunjee, Irving, 295
Dunjee, Roscoe, 294-95
Durant, William A., 200
Dyer Anti-Lynching Bill, 294
Dyer, D. B., 64
Dyer, Leonidas C., 294

E

Eastman, H. G., 230
Eighth Circuit Court of Appeals, 210
Eighth Indiana Infantry, 81-82
El Reno businesses and organizations: Bethel Methodist Temple Church, 152; Denver, El Reno, & New Orleans Railway, 162; Fogg Law Firm, xx, 151-52; Rock Island Depot, 150; Sid's Diner, 151
El Reno, vii, xiii, xvii, xx, 82-83, 122, 126-27, 130, 135, 139, 144, 150-56, 162, 169-75, 205, 216, 235, 311
Eldridge House, Lawrence, Kans., 49
Elliott, Byron K., 18
Emancipation Proclamation, 132, 191
Entente, 295-96
Espionage Act (1917), 281-85
Evansville & Terre Haute Railroad, 14

F

Fairbanks, Charles W., 275
Fares, Kristin Morgan, xviii
Farm / rural credit system(s), 257, 264-74
Farmers' Alliance, 203
Feagan, O. R., 140
Federal Farm Loan: Act (1916), 272, 274-75; Board, 272-73, 276, 287; bonds, 276-77; commissioner, 297; System, 276
Federal Reserve: Act (1913), 255, 258, 263, 267, 273; banks, 256-58; System (a.k.a. the Fed), 258, 265
Federal Trade: Commission (FTC), 240, 243-45, 286-87, 316, 319; Act (1914), 245; Building, 240, 243-45
Ferguson, Tom, 144, 157-58, 164-65, 205
Ferris, Scott, 196, 307-08
Filson, Charles H., 198-99
Finney, David Wesley, 50
First Christian Church: of El Reno, xiv, 151; of Garden City, Kans., 61; of Guthrie, 71, 87, 97, 106, 155; of Oklahoma City, 303, 313; of Perry, 97-98, 106-09, 118-19; of Stillwater, 107; of Woodward, xii. *See also* Christian Church, Disciples of Christ
First National Bank: of Guthrie, 157; of Muskogee, 184, 255
Fite, Gilbert C., 313
Five Tribes, 164, 183-84. *See also* Cherokee(s), Chickasaw(s), Choctaw(s), Creek(s), Seminole(s) / nations / tribes / res.
Fletcher, Duncan U., 268
Flynn, Dennis Thomas, 115-17, 122-30, 133-36, 144, 154-59, 162-65, 206
Foch, Ferdinand, 295
Fogg, Harry Lee, 151-52
Fogg, Lynda, xx, 151
Fogg, Richard M., xx, 151
Fogg, Richard, 152
Fogg, Rupert, 152
Fogg, William, 152
Forest of Compiègne, 297
Fort Worth, Tex., 183
Fort: Reno, 216; Sill, 150; Sumter, S. Caro., 6
Founding Fathers, 26-28, 114, 189, 194, 227, 317
Fourteen Points, 296
Frakes, Asa, 3
Franco-Prussian War, 202
Franklin, Benjamin, 3
Frederick the Great, 266-68
Free Homes: Act (1900), 133; Bill, 116, 122-25; movement, 118, 130
French Revolution, 228
Frontier democracy, 74, 81
Fulton, Elmer L., 196, 205, 208, 215, 221-25, 305
Fulton, James R., 50-51
Fulton, William D., 50-51

G

Galbraith, C. A., 140
Galloway, Barritt, 208-09
Galveston, Tex., 108
Garfield, Eliza, 261
Garfield, James Abram, 9, 19-20, 25-26, 160, 211, 261

Geary, Jim, 64
George, D., 141
George, Henry, *Progress and Poverty: An Inquiry into the Cause of Industrial Progress and Depressions and of Increase of Want with Increase of Wealth*, 179-81
Gerry, Elbridge, 32
Gerrymander / gerrymandering, 32-37, 186-87, 190, 193, 222, 259; of 1885, 34-37
Gerth, Nathan, xx
Gettysburg Address, 321
Giddings, E. J., 186-87
Gilded Age, xvi, 25, 30, 55-56, 92, 159, 178-80, 197, 203-04, 253, 277, 318
Gillette, Frank, 154-55
Glass, Carter, 254-55
Glasser, Andrew, 245
Glenn, Mrs. Will, 108
Gold standard, 98, 125-26
Good Roads, 221, 231, 277
Gore, Thomas P., 255, 301-02
Grand Army of the Republic, 129
Grandfather clause of Oklahoma Constitution, 209-11, 224, 236, 344-45n26
Grant, Ulysses S. / Grant adm., 18, 82
Great American Desert, 42-43
Great Plains, 37, 41-43, 48-49, 54-55
Greeley, Horace, 39-41, 47, 162
Green Corn Rebellion, 283-84, 292
Green, Edward B., 82
Green, G. M., 260
Grow, Galusha A., 43-46, 123, 129-33
Guinn v. United States, 210-11
Guthrie businesses and organizations: Arion Dancing Club, 87; Calumet Club, 87; Chamber of Commerce, 86; Commercial National Bank, 64; First Baptist Church, 200; Hotel Springer, 78-79; Knights of Pythias, 86; Ladies' Social and Literary Society, 87; Masonic Lodge, 86; McKennon Opera House, 87; Northside and Pioneer Euchre Clubs, 87; Oklahoma Territorial Museum and Carnegie Library, 198; Palace Hotel, 89; Santa Fe Depot, 81; Whistler Club, 87; Young Men's Christian Assn. (YMCA), 86
Guthrie newspapers: *Daily Leader*, 107, 123-24, 127-28, 139-42; *Daily News*, 76, 88-91; *Daily Star*, 230; *Leader*, 199; *Oklahoma Farmer and Laborer*, 222-23; *State Capital*, 107-08; *Weekly Oklahoma State Capital*, 155
Guthrie, John, 64

H

Hamilton, Edward L., 228
Hansen, Megan, xxi
Harding, Warren G., 16
Harreld, John W., 307-08
Harriott, George F., 141
Harris, Z. A., 275-76
Harrison, Benjamin, 22-23, 30, 34-35, 58-59, 67-69, 76, 79-82, 85-87, 139-41, 155, 305. *See also* Harrison's Horse Race (a.k.a. the Run of '89)
Harrison's Horse Race (a.k.a. the Run of '89), 23, 67
Harvard Law Review, 210
Haskell, Charles N., 183, 188, 192, 198-99
Hastings, William W., 306-07
Havens, H. E., 153
Hays, John T., 16
Hays, Will H., 16
Heath, A. R., 15
Heath, Evan W., 28
Heath, Mary (née Maxwell), 15
Heath, Orietta. *See* Morgan, Orietta
Heinze, Arthur, 253
Heinze, Fritz Augustus, 253
Heinze, Otto, 253
Hell's Half Acre, 68
Henry, Robert L., 251-52
Hensley, Felix, 273-74
Henson, G. M., 275-76
Hepburn, Jim, 313
Herrick, Manuel, 310

Hertz, Kelly, xxi
Hightower, Judy Walston, xxi
Hill, Sadie, 109-10
Hillsboro, Ohio, 119
Hinton Theater, Muskogee, 182
Hobart National Bank, 152
Hoffman, Clara C., 119
Hohweiler, Robin, xiv, xx-xxi, 175-76
Holliday, Cyrus K., 49-50
Holman, William, 45
Home guard companies, 7
Homes for Soldiers Bill, 290-95, 303
Homestead Act (1862), 43-48, 52-53, 58, 113-17, 123, 129-35, 191, 329n11
Hoosier Reunion, 139-42, 150
Hoosier(s), 10, 30-31, 38, 59, 75-76, 79, 90, 139-44, 150, 163, 245, 280
Houston, James J., 117, 122, 129
Howard, Everette B., 306
Humphrey, Evans W., 14

I

Indian Appropriation Act / bill(s), 58-59, 78, 116-17
Indian Territory, x, xiii, 2, 23, 31, 37-38, 52-59, 62, 70, 75, 83-84, 86, 153-55, 160-67, 182-90, 197-205, 342n2; Dick T. Morgan, interest in and relocation to, x, xiii, 2, 38, 59; Organic Act, effect on, 83-84; ranching in, 54; Sequoyah Convention held in, 182-85; socioeconomic condition of, 201-05; soonerism in, 70; union with Oklahoma Territory and related controversy, 153-55, 160-67, 185-89, 197-98; union with Oklahoma Territory, Native American objection to, 163-64; wedding to Oklahoma Territory, 198-201
Indiana cities / towns: Ashboro, 2; Cambridge City, 17; Covington, 302; Hagerstown, 16-18, 22; Indianapolis, 16-17, 22, 36, 76, 139; Merom, 14-25; Middletown / Prairie Creek, ix, xvi, 1, 6-9, 13-17, 262; New Albany, 76; Sullivan, 14-16; Terre Haute, xvi, xx, 1-3, 6, 14, 18, 25, 28-30, 38, 41, 76, 79, 92, 217, 235, 302; Vincennes, 14
Indiana counties / townships: Sullivan Co., 3, 10, 14-15; Vigo Co., 1-3, 6-7, 13, 20-23, 29, 38, 41, 178, 261; Riley Township, 3
Indiana: Constitution, 23-24; Eighth District Republican Nominating Convention, 28-29; General Assembly, ix-x, xvi, 2-3, 6, 12, 21-25, 28, 34-38, 59, 144; Historical Society (IHS), xxi; House of Representatives, 22-24, 29, 37; Liquor League, 24-26; Republican State Central Committee, 28; School of Law, 17; Senate, 28-31; Statehouse, 10; Young Men's Republican Clubs of, 28
Indianapolis newspapers: *Journal*, 23, 35-37, 81-82; *Leader*, 23, 38; *News*, 75, 217; *Sentinel*, 18
Industrial democracy, 203
Industrial Workers of the World (IWW), 279-80, 283
Ingalls, John J., 325n25
Ingalls-Voorhees debate. *See* Ingalls, John J.
Ingram, W. A., 17
Interstate Commerce Commission (ICC), 227-34, 240, 286-87
Iowa tribe / res., 55, 92, 115

J

Jackman, C. M., 163
Jackson, Andrew, 5
Jefferson, Thomas, xi, 27, 45-46, 203, 239, 333n22
Jenkins, William M., 133
Jerome Commission, 83
Jerome, David H. *See* Jerome Commission
Jim Crow (laws), 184-87, 194-97, 201, 210-11, 294
Johnson, Frank P., 346n13
Johnson, Jerre, 144-45
Johnson, Jim, 141
Johnston, Henry S., 259-60
Johnston, James T., 29

Jones, Charles G. "Gristmill" (a.k.a. Mr. Oklahoma Territory), 199-200
Jones, Charles J., 50-51
Journey of Discovery, 42
Julian, George W., 46-47, 329n13

K

Kansas cities / towns: Arkansas City, 57, 61; Atchison, 49; Caldwell, 58; Dodge City, 50-52; Emporia, 49; Garden City, x, xvi, 37-38, 41, 50-63, 71-73, 92, 104; Kiowa, 115; Lawrence, 49; Salina, 120; Topeka, 49-51; Winfield, 76
Kansas City Gazette, 67
Kansas City, Mo., 50, 82, 159, 202
Kansas counties: Barber, 57-58, 96; Crawford, 204; Finney (formerly, Sequoyah), 50-53
Kansas newspapers: *Atchison Globe*, 49; *Barber County Index*, 54, 57; *Dodge City Times*, 51-52; *Emporia News*, 49-50; *Garden City Weekly Sentinel*, 61; *Kiowa Herald*, 115
Kapp-Königsberg, Dr., 266
Kearns, Thomas, 15
Kenner & Morgan. *See* Kenner, J. B.
Kenner, J. B., 72
Kiowa tribe / res., 117. *See also* Kiowa, Comanche, and Apache tribes / res.
Kiowa, Comanche, and Apache tribes / res., 117, 143-45, 148-50, 153, 189
Kirkwood, James, 129-30
Knights of Pythias, 294, 354n46
Kovacic, William E., 244

L

Ladd, W. J., 76-77
Lakeview Hospital, Danville, Ill., 302
Landschaften, 266-68, 272
Lane, Franklin K., 292
Langston University, Langston, 91
League of Nations, 296-99
Lee-Huckins Hotel, Oklahoma City, 235
Lewis, Meriwether, 42. *See also* Journey of Discovery
Library of Congress, xv, 225
Lincoln Club, 270
Lincoln, Abraham / Lincoln adm. / party of Lincoln, vii, ix-x, 6-7, 10, 13, 18, 22, 45-49, 132, 182, 191, 194, 270, 287, 315, 320, 321. *See also* Emancipation Proclamation, Gettysburg Address, Homestead Act (1862), Lincoln Club, Lincoln-Douglas debates
Lincoln-Douglas debates, 13, 182
Little River, 55
Lloyd, James T., 166
Locke, John, 45-46
Lockwood, J. H., 120
Lodge, Henry Cabot, 297
Long, Stephen S., 42
Longfellow, Henry Wadsworth, 309-10
Louisiana Purchase, 42, 333n22
Louisville, Ky., 181
Lurty, Warren, 82
Lutz, Barbara, 3

M

Madison, James, 27, 315
Manifest Destiny, 43
Mann-Elkins Act (1910), 214, 233
Mansur, Charles H., 78
Martin, Robert, 82-83
Marxism, 203
McCabe, E. P., 91, 134
McClintic, James V., 309
McCormick, Mike, xx, 3, 245
McCubbin's grocery, Perry, 129
McCullough, David, xx
McCumber, Porter James, 185
McDonald, Alva L., 234
McDonald, Joseph E., 22
McGuire, Bird S., 156-59, 163-65, 196, 206, 222-23, 235-36, 250-51
McKenzie, P. D., 235
McKeown, Thomas D., 308
McKinley, William B., 230
McKinley, William, 82, 124-25, 133-35, 139, 143, 228
McKinney, Ed S., 177
McLain, C. R., 64

McNeal, J. W., 157
McVeigh, Timothy, 113-14, 136
Meeks, Jim, xxi
Memphis, Tenn., 14
Mercantile National Bank, New York, 253
Merom Bluff Academy. *See* Union Christian College
Merrick, J. J., 140
Methodist Episcopal Church, 97
Miami (Fla.) *Herald*, xxi
Middletown Temperance Society, 17
MidFirst Bank, Oklahoma City, xii, xvi, 151
Mill, John Stuart, 46
Minneapolis, Minn., 292
Mississippi River, 14, 214
Missouri Compromise, 77, 333n22
Missouri River, 42
Monnet, Julian C., 210, 344n23n24n25
Monroe, J. M., 73, 77, 97, 163
Moores, Merrill, 17
Morgan & Davis, Garden City, Kans., 52
Morgan & Morgan, Garden City, Kans., 52
Morgan (née Deupree), Clemmer, 169-72, 189, 302, 310-14, 356n11; Porter Heath Morgan, divorce from, 313; Porter Heath Morgan, marriage to, 169
Morgan Standard, 293
Morgan, C. H., 4
Morgan, D. J., xvi
Morgan, David, vii-ix, xii-xxi, 3, 6, 15, 19, 26, 30, 37-38, 52-54, 57, 60-63, 67, 71, 85, 92-93, 97, 102, 107-09, 114-15, 121, 126, 130, 134-37, 150-53, 158, 165, 169-76, 182-83, 188-91, 195, 198-200, 208-11, 215, 225-26, 230, 236, 243-46, 258-59, 263, 271, 277-78, 285, 288-89, 293-95, 310-16
Morgan, Dick Deupree, 311
Morgan, Dick Thompson, committee assignments / legislation: Committee of Committees, membership on, 290; Federal Farm Loan Act, signed into law, 272; Federal Trade Commission, signed into law, 243; House Judiciary Committee, membership on, xv, 240, 286, 290, 301-303, 355n60
Morgan, Dick Thompson, elections: Indiana House of Representatives, 1880, 18; U.S. House of Representatives, 1908, 208; 1910, 224; 1912, 235; 1914, 260; 1916, 276; 1918, 289
Morgan, Dick Thompson, policies: banking and currency reform, 255-59, 262-63, 270-74, 277; civil rights for Blacks, 25, 209-11, 236-37, 294-95; civil rights for Native Americans, 160, 182-83, 260-61; civil rights for soldiers, 277-78; control of corporations, 192-93, 225-29, 232-34, 240-47, 277; free homes for free men, 114-18, 122-25, 130-37; good roads, 221, 231, 277; homes for soldiers, 290-95, 303; income tax, 214, 231, 277; labor rights and higher wages, 206-07, 232, 277; popular election of senators, 277; postal savings banks, 214, 231; presidential powers during wartime, 281-82, 285-89; prohibition, 169, 195, 277, 298-300; rural credit, 257, 263-74, 307; statehood for Oklahoma Territory, 152-55, 159-67, 205; tariffs, 191, 212-16, 221-24, 231-32, 239, 250-51, 277; women's suffrage, 23-25, 76-77, 181, 277
Morgan, Dick Thompson, publications: *Land Credits: A Plea for the American Farmer*, 249, 262-71, 307-09; "Government Aid: Rural Credits Division in Congress—How to Secure Unity and Harmony," 269-70; *Morgan's Digest of Oklahoma Statutes and Supreme Court Decisions*, 121; *Morgan's Manual of the United States Homestead, Mining and Townsite Laws*, 93, 102, 121, 142-45, 149-50, 190, 306-08, 316
Morgan, Dick Thompson, relocations: Bonesteel and Yankton, S. Dak., xvi, 170-71; El Reno, xiii, 150-51; Garden City, Kans., x, xvi, 37-41; Guthrie, x,

xiii, 63; Perry, xiii, 99-102; Woodward, xiii-xiv, 173

Morgan, Dick Thompson, speeches: campaign speech for reelection to Indiana House of Representatives, 26-28; Commencement Address, Union Christian College, 317-21; Control of Corporations, 226-29, 233, 240-41, 246; Entered the War Reluctantly, 279; Fifty Years of Material and Religious Progress, 317; Free Home Address of Hon. Dick T. Morgan of Perry, O.T., 130-32; Mother's Day; Our Country—What Made It Great, 261-62; National Prohibition, 298-99; nominating speech to appoint Benjamin Harrison of Indiana to U.S. Senate, 22-23; Pyramid of P's for the Potent Pedagogue, 177-78; Short Term Farm Credits, 297; Soldier-Aid Legislation, 291-92; statehood for Oklahoma Territory, 159-61; The Hoosier in Oklahoma, 140-42; The President and Congress in War Times, 275, 285-87

Morgan, Dick Thompson: birth, 4; Central Law School, graduation, 17-18; church building activities, x-xii, 53, 61, 71-73, 87, 96-98, 104-09, 118-21, 137, 151, 155, 305; death, 302-03; eulogies on behalf of, delivered by congressmen, 306-10; Orietta Heath, marriage to, 16; Porter Heath, birth of, 18; Prairie Creek High School, graduation, 13; teaching career, Prairie Creek, 8, Hagerstown, 16-17; Union Christian College, graduation, 15

Morgan, Ellen Records, xvi, xx-xxi, 3, 171-72, 245

Morgan, Flora, 17

Morgan, Frances Ann, 1-5, 8-9, 13-14

Morgan, Fred, 37, 52, 171, 338n2

Morgan, H. L., 17

Morgan, J. P. (no relation to Dick T. Morgan), 253, 258, 283

Morgan, Kenyon, vii-viii, xii-xxi, 109, 135-37, 151, 198-200, 314-16

Morgan, Martha Merle, 311, 356n11

Morgan, Orietta (née Heath, a.k.a. Ora, Ode), xi, xv-xviii, 15-19, 37-38, 41, 56, 59-60, 72-73, 79-80, 87-88, 102, 108-09, 119, 128, 158, 169, 172-77, 195, 235, 258, 275-77, 280, 290, 300-02, 306-14; death, 313; Dick Thompson Morgan, marriage to, 16; Porter Heath, birth of, 18; Union Christian College, graduation, 16

Morgan, Porter Harlan, 311, 356n11

Morgan, Porter Heath, xviii, 19, 23, 41, 56, 59, 72-73, 79-80, 88, 104-05, 109-10, 128, 163, 168-72, 189-90, 205, 213, 225, 231, 275, 303, 306, 310-13, 337n40, 356n11, 357n19; birth, 18-20; Clemmer Deupree, divorce from, 313; Clemmer Deupree, marriage to, 169; death, 313-14; Faye Roblin, marriage to, 313; University of Chicago Law School, graduation, 189

Morgan, Valentine, 3-9, 13-14

Morgan, William Maxwell, 311, 356n11

Morrill Act (1862), 48

Morrill, John, 48

Morton, Oliver P., 6, 10-13, 17, 21-23, 31

Moss, Ralph W., 1-2

Mother's Day, 261-62

Murphy, Arthur Phillips, 185

Murray, William H. (a.k.a. Alfalfa Bill), 183-85, 188-89, 192-94, 230

N

National: Assn. of Manufacturers, 251; Bank of Anadarko, 152; Banking Act, 184; Democratic Convention, 186; Farm Loan Association (NFLA), 272-73, 276; Monetary Commission, 254-55; Prohibition Act (1919), 299; Register of Historic Places, xiv, 151; Reserve Bank, 254; War Labor Board, 287

Native Americans, 42-43, 56, 67-68, 199, 201, 260-61; Indian Territory statehood, opposition to, 153-55, 160, 182-85

Neff, Robert A., 155

Nelson, Crystal, xxi

Nelson, Thomas H., 13, 18, 38
Nester(s), 53
Neutral Strip. *See* Oklahoma: Panhandle
New Deal, 258-59
New England, 162
New Freedom, 238, 246
New Orleans, La., 14
New York Stock Exchange, 253
New York: *Times*, 293; *Tribune*, 39-41, 47
Niagara Falls, 302
Niblack, Leslie G., 199
No Man's Land. *See* Oklahoma: Panhandle
Noble Co.: Bible Society, 120; Sunday School Assn., 119-20
Noble Township Sunday School Assn., 120
Noble, John W., 93, 142
Norris, Frank, *The Octopus*, 264
Norris, George W., 297
North Canadian River, 55
Northwest Ordinance (1787), 81
Norton, James H., 219

O

Oak Grove school house, 120
Occidental Hotel, Garden City, Kans., 50-51
Ohio Constitutional Convention, 233
Ohio River, 14
Oklahoma cities / towns: Ada, 283, 308; Alva, 99, 133-35, 174, 207, 309; Anadarko, 106, 152, 216, 221; Apache, 152; Binger, 152; Blackwell, 145; Boise City, 84; Bridgeport, 152; Chandler, 235-36; Chickasha, 152; Clinton, 219-21, 230; Deer Creek (later, Guthrie), 57; Dewey, 294; East Guthrie, 73-76; El Reno, xiii, xvii, xx, 82-83, 122, 126-27, 130, 135, 139, 144, 150-56, 162-63, 169-75, 205, 216, 235, 311; Enid, 99, 157, 163, 275, 309; Eufaula, 164; Frisco, 74-75, 78, 89; Ft. Cobb, 152; Guthrie, x, xiii, xvii, 57, 61-92, 96-98, 102-06, 109, 115, 130, 139-43, 150-52, 155, 164, 173-74, 184-85, 195, 198-201, 217, 223, 305; Guymon, 84; Harrison, 152; Hobart, 106, 152; Kingfisher, 68, 87-89, 140-42; Langston, 91; Lawton, 106, 152, 188-89; Lone Dove, 283; Lone Wolf, 152; Muskogee, 182-83, 199, 294; Newkirk, 133, 141; Norman, xiii, xvi, xx, 83, 110, 314-15; Oklahoma City, xii-xvi, 57, 68, 72-74, 78-79, 83-92, 109, 113, 123-24, 137, 141-42, 152, 165, 185-86, 189, 197-99, 202-05, 208, 216-19, 224-25, 231, 235, 275, 294, 303-06, 310, 313-14, 332n6n8; Okmulgee, 295; Pawnee, 125, 275; Perry, xiii, xvii, xx, 97-99, 102-21, 124-25, 128, 135-37, 143-45, 150-51, 156, 169, 172-73, 275, 305, 310; Ponca City, 273; Pond Creek, 159-64; Sasakwa, 283; Sayre, 152; Sickles, 152; Stillwater, 83, 107; Tulsa, 275, 294, 306; Vinita, 208; Walnut Creek (later, Purcell), 57; West Guthrie, 73; Woodward, x-xiv, xvii, xx, 1, 99, 173-78, 196, 205-08, 216, 242, 246, 302-05, 309, 340n8
Oklahoma City newspapers: *Black Dispatch*, 294-95, 303; *Daily Oklahoman*, xvi, 213, 223, 234, 288; *Daily Times*, 78; *Harlow's Weekly*, 202, 234, 292-93, 353-54n39; *Real Estate Register*, 156
Oklahoma counties: Alfalfa, 99, 259; Beaver, 84, 88, 117, 186, 259; Blaine, 186, 219; Bryan, 200; Caddo, 150, 186; Canadian, 84, 150-51, 155, 158, 186; Cimarron, 84, 259, 276; Cleveland, 84, 186; Comanche, 150, 186, 189; Cotton, 189; Custer, 186, 219, 221; Ellis, 99; Garfield, 99, 186, 259; Grant, 99, 186, 259; Harper, 99, 259; Hughes, 283; Kay, 99, 117, 133, 143, 155, 186, 259; Kingfisher, 84, 155, 186; Logan, 84, 88, 186; Major, 99, 259; Noble, xx, 99, 108, 117-20, 124-27, 135-36, 156, 186, 259, 288; Oklahoma, 84, 90, 155, 186, 205, 259, 313; Okmulgee, 283, 313; Pawnee, 99, 117, 125, 186; Payne, 84, 186; Pontotoc, 283; Pottawatomie, 186, 283; Seminole, 282-83; Texas, 84, 259;

Tillman, 189; Woods, 99, 186, 259; Woodward, 99, 162, 186, 259
Oklahoma country. *See* Unassigned Lands
Oklahoma newspapers: *Ada Star-Democrat*, 284; *Alva Review Courier*, 130, 134, 288; *Beaver Herald*, 199; *Blackwell Times-Record*, 79; *Carmen Headlight*, 288; *Cimarron News*, 276; *Edmond Republican*, 126; *Fairview Republican*, 288; *Guymon Herald*, 276, 289; *Kiowa Chief*, 145, 149; *Kiowa Herald*, 115; *Morrison Transcript*, 288; *Muskogee Cimeter*, 197; *Noble County Sentinel*, 121, 145, 156-57; *Norman Transcript*, 156; *Oklahoma State Register*, 290; *Ponca City News*, 302; *Republican News Journal*, 143-44; *Tulsa Daily World*, 70, 108, 277-78, 283
Oklahoma State Banker, 293
Oklahoma Territory, x, xiii, 3-4, 31, 43, 70-71, 75, 80-84, 87-93, 97-98, 102-06, 111-12, 115-17, 121, 124-25, 130-34, 139-44, 152-67, 171-80, 189, 194, 198-202, 246; Hoosiers in positions of authority in, 139-42; union with Indian Territory and related controversy, 152-55, 159-67, 197-98; wedding to Indian Territory, 198-201. *See also* Oklahoma: Enabling Act (1906), Oklahoma: Organic Act (1890)
Oklahoma: Bank Guaranty Law (1908), 256; Christian Missionary Society (OCMS), 97, 104, 107, 151; City Golf and Country Club, xii-xiii; congressional districts (per Oklahoma Enabling Act, 1906), 185-86; Corporation Commission, 192-93; Enabling Act (1906), 185-88, 192-93; Historical Society, xx, 198, 273, 305, 314; History Center, xiii; National Guard, xi; Organic Act (1890); Panhandle, 83-84; Press Assn., 129, 145; State Bankers Assn., 293; Station (later, Oklahoma City), 57, 332n6; Territorial Free Home League, 113, 117, 122, 129, 133-39, 305
Old Greer County, 83, 333n35
Olds, Fred, 200
OpenAI, 245-46
Orner, Bert, 141
Osage Nation, 187
Ottawa, Canada, 302, 306-07
Otti, Joseph, 275
Otto C. Heinze and Co., 253
Overholser, Henry, 141
Overman, Lee S., 287
Overstreet, Samuel L., 140
Owen, Narcissa, 183
Owen, Robert L., 183-84, 255-56
Owen-Glass Federal Reserve Act (1913), 254-59

P

Pacific Ocean, 42, 46
Pacific Railway Act (1862), 48
Pancoast, J. L., 85, 93-96, 102, 129
Panic: of 1873, 179; of 1893, 98, 122-24; of 1907, 252-54
Partridge, George, W., 219
Pawnee tribe / res., 55
Payne, David L., 56
Payne, Sereno E., 211-12
Payne-Aldrich Tariff, 211-16, 219-23, 249
Peery, Dan, 89-90
Perkins, Bishop W., 78
Perry businesses and organizations: Carnegie Library, 102; Kumback Lunch, 136; Ladies Aid Society, 106; Perry Mining Co., 118
Perry newspapers: *Daily Enterprise*, 108; *Daily Enterprise-Times*, 110-11, 118-19; *Daily Times*, 85, 107-08, 116-17; *Weekly Times*, 102
Peters, Samuel R., 78
Phillips University, Enid, 163, 275, 303, 309
Phillips, C. J., 2
Picardy, France, 295
Piercy, J. Will, 75-77
Pieree, I. N., 17
Pioneer Women's Museum, Ponca City, 273

Pitzer, J. H., 140
Plumb, Preston B., 35, 49, 60
Politico, 245
Populist movement / Party / populist(s) / populism, 92, 125-28, 179, 184, 188, 199, 203, 235, 255
Porter, Albert Gallatin, 19-23, 38, 211
Portland, Me., 270
Pottawatomi tribe / res., 92, 115-17
Powers, Reverend (first name unknown), 106
Preemption Act (1841), 43-45, 52-53, 93, 122, 131
Preston, James H., 297
Princeton University, Princeton, N. Jer., 237
Progressive Era / movement / Party / progressive(s) / progressivism, x-xii, xx, 7, 24, 43, 50, 141-42, 179-82, 189-90, 194-97, 205-07, 210-16, 222-26, 230-40, 244-52, 260, 264, 274-77, 290, 315, 318-19
Prohibition, 169, 176, 189, 195, 277, 298-300; Party, 260
Promontory, Utah, 48
Provisional government(s), 68, 74, 79-81
Pryse, JA, xx
Public domain / land policy, x, 43-46, 122, 131, 143
Public Land Strip. *See* Oklahoma: Panhandle
Pullman Palace Car Co., 29; strike, 29
Putnam Heights Elementary School, Oklahoma City, 109

Q–R

Quapaw Agency, 37, 52
Quincy, Calif., 310
Ragsdale, J. M., 64
Range cattle industry, 53-54
Ray, James, 3
Ray, John, 3
Reapportionment, 32-34. *See also* Gerrymander(ing)
Reconstruction treaties of 1866, 55
Reconstruction, 12, 30-32, 210
Red River, 83, 189
Red Scare, 284
Republican: Central Committee, 164-65; Conventions, 107, 126, 190-91; Gerrymandering Board, 186-87; National Committee, 16; Party (GOP), x-xii, 6, 10-12, 23, 28, 45, 60, 92, 107, 124-26, 155-61, 165, 173, 187, 191, 195-97, 206-07, 228-29, 234, 240, 245, 270, 286-88, 313
Reserve Assn. of America, 254
Revenue Act (1913), 249
Riverside (Ia.) *Leader*, 115
Roberts, J. C., 142
Robertson, James, 290
Robinson, Mikel, xiv, xx, 176
Roblin, Faye, 313
Rock, Marion Tuttle, *Illustrated History of Oklahoma*, 63-65
Rocky Mountains, 42, 162
Roman Catholic Church, 97
Roosevelt, Theodore, x-xiv, 157-58, 164, 170, 173-75, 178-82, 189, 194, 197-98, 206, 223-37, 246, 264, 275, 279, 342n2
Rose Hill Cemetery, Oklahoma City, 303
Rosebud res., S. Dak., xvi, 170-72
Rosenthal, Cindy, xx
Rousseau, Jean-Jacques, 284
Run: of April 22, 1889 (a.k.a. Harrison's Horse Race), x, xiii, 23, 65-67, 80, 92, 96, 121, 137-39, 151, 189, 194, 206; of September 22, 1891, 92, 115, 131; of April 19, 1892, xiii, 151; of September 16, 1893, 103-04, 288, 305, 338n53

S

Sabbath School, 80, 120
Sac and Fox tribes / res., 55, 92, 115
Sacramento, Calif., 48
Salazar, Don Juan de Oñate y, 42
Samuel, W. R., 293
San Francisco earthquake, 252-53
Santa Fe Depot, Guthrie, 81
Santa Fe Trail, 42

Saturday Courier, 28
Saturday Evening Post, 293
Sawyer, G. W., 112, 152
Sayre, Warren G., 83
Schloss, Philip, 30
Scothorn, John W., 142
Scott, Angelo C., 72-74
Scott, Dred, 11. See also *Dred Scott v. Sanford* (1857)
Scott, Harriett, 11
Seay, Abraham J., 82, 155, 165
Second District: Democratic Congressional Committee, 215; Republican Congressional Committee, 219
Second National Good Roads Congress, 221
Sedition Act (1918), 282
Selective Service Act (1917), 280-81
Senate Bill No. 1, 205
Sequoyah Convention, 182-85, 188, 255
Shawnee tribe / res., 55, 92, 115
Sherman Antitrust Act (1890), 226-28, 233, 241-42, 301
Sherman, Joe, 216, 219
Sherman, John, 226
Sherman, William T., 82
Single statehood, 153, 158-67
Sioux Nation / res., 170
Siple, William B., 292
Slavery , 5, 11, 21, 24-25, 44-45, 191, 270, 329n13
Smith, Sherman M., 305
Smith-Lever Act (1914), 264
Socialist movement / Party / socialist(s) / socialism, 29, 202-04, 208, 224, 235-36, 239, 260, 275-76, 279-84
Solon (Athenian lawgiver), 130
Sooner(s) / soonerism, 58, 69, 85, 143, 332n8
South America, 266
South Canadian River, 283
South Dakota businesses and organizations: Bonesteel Supper Club, Bonesteel, 171; Mead Cultural Education Center, Yankton, xxi, 172; Pierce Hotel, Yankton, 172
South Dakota cities / towns: Bonesteel, xvi, 170-72; Chamberlain, 170; Fairfax, 170; Yankton, xvi, xxi, 170-72
South Dakota newspapers: *Bonesteel Enterprise*, xxi, 171; *Yankton Daily Press & Dakotan*, xxi, 172-73
Southern Commercial Congress, 297
Spanish flu, 302
Spanish-American War, 141, 171
Spears, John, 282
Speed, Horace, 76, 82, 139-40
Spitzenberger, Doug, xxi, 171
Springer Amendment, 58
Springer, William M., 58, 78
St. Louis Globe-Democrat, 269
St. Louis, Mo., 54, 123, 126, 214
Standpatter(s) / standpatterism, 212-14, 222-24, 234, 239, 245, 251-54
Stars and Stripes, 292
Staunton, Va., 239
Steele, George W., 81-83, 87-92, 139-41, 338n2
Steele, Meta, 91
Stevens, John A., 50
Stocksinger, D. M., 76-77
Stone, John F., 97, 141
Stone, Ulysses S., 313
Stowe, Harriett Beecher, *Uncle Tom's Cabin*, 186
Sturm's Oklahoma Magazine, 68, 332n8
Suffrage League, 197
Sunday School Assn., 97, 119-20, 131
Swindall, Charles, 309-10
System Republican(s), 223

T

Taft, William Howard, 212-15, 219, 224, 230-31, 234-37, 269, 289-90, 320
Tanner, George, 73
Taylor, William L., 17-18
Temperance movement, 24
Tenants / tenancy, 47, 202, 280, 283, 292
Terra Nueva, 41

Terre Haute, Ind. newspapers: *Daily Courier*, 28, 56, 103; *Daily Express*, 37; *Evening Courier*, 37; *Tribune-Star*, 245
Terrell (first name unknown), 77
Territorial: delegate to Congress, 89, 115-16, 126-28, 143-44, 157; Sunday School Assn., 119; Sunday School Convention, 109
Territories (excluding Indian, Oklahoma territories): Arizona, 116, 159, 163; New Mexico / Territory / Nuevo Mexico, 42, 53, 116, 159, 163, 205, 259; Utah, 116
Texas fever (a.k.a. Spanish fever), 53
Thanksgiving cantata, 110-11
The Christian Evangelist, xi, 4
The Farmer's Open Forum, 269-70
The Nation, 269
Thompson, David, 3, 14
Thompson, Rachel, 3
Thompson, Richard Wigginton, 6
Thompson's Ferry, 3, 14
Tiffany and Co., 243
Timber Culture Act (1873), 47-48, 52-53
Times Publishing Co., Perry, 103
Tincher, Jasper, 316
Tishomingo, Chickasaw Nation, 183
Toadsuck, Tex., 183
Trans-Mississippi Congress, 129
Trapp, Martin C., xi
Treaty of Versailles, 299
Tulsa Law Review, 244
Turner, Frederick Jackson, *Frontier thesis of American history*, xix
Turner, John Kenneth, 280
Turner, Nathan, 198-200
Twain, Mark, xvi, xix, 202
Twin Territories, 154, 160, 182, 185-88, 194, 201, 222. *See also* Indian Territory, Oklahoma Territory
Twine, W. H., 197

U

U.S. House of Representatives, xi, 29, 82, 116, 129, 144, 185, 212, 254, 297, 307, 320; Banking Committee, 254-55, 271-72; Committee of Committees, 290; Committee on Elections, 225; Committee on Public Information, 287; Committee on Public Lands, 232, 307; Committee on Territories, 161-63, 167, 201; Indian Affairs Committee, 307; Judiciary Committee, xv, 240, 286, 290, 299-303, 355n60; Republican Steering Committee, 291
U.S. Land Office(s), 114, 131, 141, 189; Alva, 207; El Reno, 150-51; Garden City, Kans., 52; Guthrie, 62, 67-68, 72, 87, 140-42, 305; Kingfisher, 140-43; Oklahoma City, 142, 332n8; Perry, xiii, 102-05, 113, 125; Woodward, x, xiii-xiv, 173-78, 196, 207, 246, 309
U.S. Senate, 12-13, 22-23, 31, 35, 45, 59, 124, 157-59, 164, 173, 206, 211-12, 243-44, 250-51, 255, 258, 264, 294, 297-99, 301-02, 307; Committee on Banking and Currency (a.k.a. Senate Banking Committee), 255, 270; Committee on Territories, 159-61
U.S.: Bureau of Engraving and Printing, 277; Bureau of Standards, 262; Constitution, 13, 24-25, 32-33, 77, 81, 189, 192, 210, 225-28, 281, 299; Constitution, Eighteenth Amendment to, 299; Constitution, Fifteenth Amendment to, 210; Constitution, Fourteenth Amendment to, 210; Dept. of Justice Antitrust Division, 243; District Court, Wichita, Kans., 70; Infantry, 81-82; Supreme Court, 11, 210-11, 225, 244; Treasury Dept., 267, 276
Unassigned Lands, xiii, 23, 54-60, 64-78, 81-84, 87, 91-92, 114, 117, 130-31, 140, 151
Underwood, Oscar Wilder, 249-52
Union Christian College (UCC), Merom, Ind., xvi, 14-17, 20, 317
Union: Army, 12, 22, 29, 82; Pacific Railway, 48; Train Station, Washington, D.C., xv
University: High School, Norman, 110;

of Chicago Law School, 169-70, 189; of Oklahoma, Norman, 110, 210, 313; of Oklahoma, College of Law, Norman, 210; of Texas Law School, Austin, Tex., xxi; of Virginia, Charlottesville, Va., xiii
Urgency Deficiency Appropriation Bill, 214

V

Vedra, Amy, xxi
Volstead Act. *See* National Prohibition Act (1919)
Volstead, Andrew, 299-300
Voorhees, Daniel W., 12-13, 18, 31, 76, 325n25
Voorhees-Nelson debates. *See* Voorhees, Daniel W., Nelson, Thomas H.
Voter Registration Act, 209
Vreeland, Edward B., 254

W

Wabash (Ind.) *Express*, 11
Wabash River, 3, 7, 14, 41
Walkabouts: Indiana, xvi, 3; Kansas, xvi; Oklahoma, xiii-xvii, xx, 67-68, 135-37, 150-52, 174-76, 198-201; South Dakota, xvi, 171-72; Washington, D.C., xiv-xvi
War: Finance Corporation, 287; Industries Board, 287; Powers Bill, 286
Washington and Lee University, Lexington, Va., 183
Washington, Booker T., 187
Washington, D.C. businesses and organizations: Christian Church, 80; Congress Hall Hotel, xv, 300; Dewey Hotel, 231; Ebbitt House, 59; General Land Office, 69; Longworth House Bldg., xv, 300; Michener & Pence, 225
Washington, D.C. newspapers: *Evening Critic*, 36; *Evening Star*, 81, 164; *National Republican*, 36; *Times*, 271
Washington, George, 320
Washington's Farewell Address, 27
Weaver, Claude, 255
Webster, Daniel, 27
Wells, H. G., 295
Western Investment Co., 156
Whig Party, 5-6
White House, Washington, D.C., xv, 19, 26, 30, 59, 124-25, 237, 254, 271
Wichita Mountains, 145
Wichita res., 117
Wickham, Charles B., 294
Wicks, Hamilton, 63-65
Wikipedia, 244
Wilder, Laura Ingalls, 264
Williams, Michael, 198
Williams, Robert L., 283
Williams, Virtes, 107
Wilson, Alfred M., 83
Wilson, Woodrow, 237-46, 249-51, 254, 261, 264, 271-72, 277-89, 296-97, 309; *The New Freedom: A Call for the Emancipation of the Generous Energies of a People*, 238-39
Wobblies, 279. *See also* Industrial Workers of the World (IWW)
Wolf, Joseph, 4
Wollman, Kelly, xx, 171
Women's Christian Temperance Union (WCTU), 77, 119
Women's suffrage, 24, 76-77, 119, 189, 277
Woodward businesses and organizations: Al's Steakhouse, 176; Central Hotel, 174-77; Dick T. Morgan Republican Club, 207-08, 305; McDonald Photography Studio, 175; Plains Indians and Pioneers Museum, xiv, xx, 174-76; Presbyterian Church, 177; Woodward Main Street, 175
Woodward newspapers: *Democrat*, 177, 302-03; *Dispatch*, 162, 173; *News*, 126
Working Class Union (WCU), 204-05, 279-80, 283
World War I, 47, 277- 87, 295-97, 311
World War II, 293, 311

X-Y-Z

York, Jill, 151
Youngdale, Beth, xxi